公式TOEIC®
Listening & Reading
問題集
10

IIBC

一般財団法人 国際ビジネスコミュニケーション協会

ETS, the ETS logo, PROPELL, TOEIC and TOEIC BRIDGE are registered trademarks of ETS, Princeton, New Jersey, USA, and used in Japan under license.
Portions are copyrighted by ETS and used with permission.

ETS TOEIC
OFFICIAL TEST
PREPARATION
AND LEARNING

ETS, the ETS logo, PROPELL, TOEIC and TOEIC BRIDGE are registered trademarks of
ETS, Princeton, New Jersey, USA, and used in Japan under license. Portions are copyrighted by ETS and used with permission.

はじめに

本書は『公式 TOEIC® Listening & Reading 問題集』シリーズの第10弾です。2016年5月実施の公開テストから加わった出題形式に対応し、実際と同じテスト形式で2回分の問題を掲載しています。TOEIC® Listening & Reading Test の受験準備にお使いください。

本シリーズの特長

- 問題は全て、ETSが実際のテストと同じプロセスで制作しています。
- サンプル問題とテスト2回分の問題(200問×2回、計400問)を掲載し、リスニングセクションはTOEIC®公式スピーカーによる音声が収録されています。
  - ＊実際のテストでは、担当スピーカーや発音の種類(どの国の発音か)の割合が変更される場合があります。
- 素点から参考スコア範囲が算出可能です。
- 正解を導くための詳しい解説の他、学習の助けとなる語注「Words & Phrases」(Part 3、4、6、7)や表現紹介のコーナー「Expressions」(Part 6、7)を掲載しています。

付属CD・特典の音声について

- CDは一般的なプレーヤーで再生できます。また、CDの音声をパソコンなどの機器に取り込んで再生することもできます。
- 特典として、TEST 1、2 のリーディングセクションの以下の音声をダウンロードすることができます。問題に解答した後の学習用教材としてご活用ください。
  - 正解が入った問題音声(Part 5、6)
  - 文書の音声(Part 7)

音声ダウンロードの手順： ＊株式会社 Globee が提供するサービス abceed への会員登録(無料)が必要です。

1. パソコン・スマートフォンで音声ダウンロード用のサイトにアクセスします。
   (右の QR コードまたはブラウザから https://app.abceed.com/audio/iibc-officialprep へ)
2. 表示されたページから、abceed の新規会員登録を行います。既に会員の場合は、ログイン情報を入力して上記 1. のサイトへアクセスします。
3. 上記 1. のサイトにアクセス後、本教材の画像をクリックします。クリックすると、教材詳細画面へ遷移します。
4. スマートフォンの場合は、アプリ「abceed」の案内が出ますので、アプリからご利用ください。パソコンの場合は、教材詳細画面の「音声」のアイコンからご利用ください。

   ＊音声は何度でもダウンロード・再生ができます。ダウンロードについてのお問い合わせは下記へ
   Eメール：support@globeejphelp.zendesk.com (お問い合わせ窓口の営業日：祝日を除く月〜金曜日)
   ＊特典音声は、必ず一度TEST 1、2 のリーディングセクションの問題に解答した後に、ご利用ください。詳しい使い方は、別冊『解答・解説』p.200 をご参照ください。

本書が、TOEIC® Listening & Reading Test の出題形式の理解と受験準備、そして皆さまの英語学習のお役に立つことを願っております。

2023 年 10 月
一般財団法人 国際ビジネスコミュニケーション協会

目　次

本誌

＊解答用紙は112ページの後ろに綴じ込まれています。

別冊 『解答・解説』

TOEIC® Listening & Reading Test について

TOEIC® Listening & Reading Test とは？

TOEIC® Listening & Reading Test（以下、TOEIC® L&R）は、TOEIC® Programのテストの一つで、英語における Listening（聞く）と Reading（読む）の力を測定します。結果は合格・不合格ではなく、リスニングセクション5〜495点、リーディングセクション5〜495点、トータル10〜990点のスコアで評価されます。スコアの基準は常に一定であり、英語能力に変化がない限りスコアも一定に保たれます。知識・教養としての英語ではなく、オフィスや日常生活における英語によるコミュニケーション能力を幅広く測定するテストです。特定の文化を知らないと理解できない表現を排除しているので、誰もが公平に受けることができる「グローバルスタンダード」として活用されています。

問題形式

● リスニングセクション（約45分間・100問）とリーディングセクション（75分間・100問）から成り、約2時間で200問に解答します。

● テストは英文のみで構成されており、英文和訳や和文英訳といった設問はありません。

● マークシート方式の一斉客観テストです。

● リスニングセクションにおける発音は、米国・英国・カナダ・オーストラリアが使われています。

＊テスト中、問題用紙への書き込みは一切禁じられています。

リスニングセクション（約45分間）

パート	Part Name	パート名	問題数
1	Photographs	写真描写問題	6
2	Question-Response	応答問題	25
3	Conversations	会話問題	39
4	Talks	説明文問題	30

リーディングセクション（75分間）

パート	Part Name	パート名	問題数
5	Incomplete Sentences	短文穴埋め問題	30
6	Text Completion	長文穴埋め問題	16
7	• Single passages • Multiple passages	1つの文書 複数の文書	29 25

開発・運営団体について

TOEIC® L&Rは、ETSによって開発・制作されています。ETSは、米国ニュージャージー州プリンストンに拠点を置き、TOEIC® ProgramやTOEFL、GRE（大学院入学共通試験）を含む約200のテストプログラムを開発している世界最大の非営利テスト開発機関です。

日本におけるTOEIC® L&Rを含むTOEIC® Programの実施・運営は、一般財団法人 国際ビジネスコミュニケーション協会（IIBC）が行っています。IIBCは、公式教材の出版やグローバル人材育成など、「人と企業の国際化」の推進に貢献するための活動を展開しています。

本書の構成と使い方

本書は、本誌と別冊に分かれています。それぞれの主な内容は以下の通りです。
- 本誌 …… 「サンプル問題」「TEST 1」「TEST 2」「解答用紙」
- 別冊『解答・解説』…… 「参考スコア範囲の算出方法」「正解一覧」「解答・解説」「CDトラック・特典音声ファイル 一覧表」「音声を使った学習例の紹介」

本誌

サンプル問題（29問）[本誌p.8-27] 全パートから合計29問を掲載しています。 **CD 1 02-10**

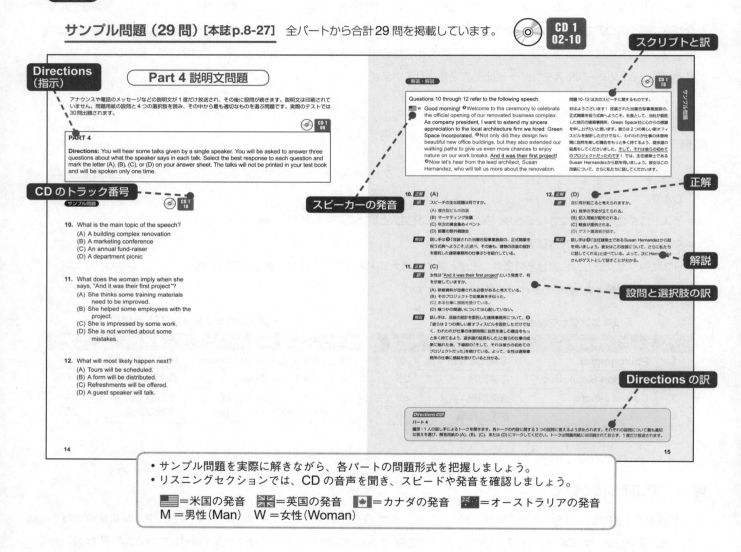

- サンプル問題を実際に解きながら、各パートの問題形式を把握しましょう。
- リスニングセクションでは、CDの音声を聞き、スピードや発音を確認しましょう。

🇺🇸 ＝米国の発音　🇬🇧 ＝英国の発音　🇨🇦 ＝カナダの発音　🇦🇺 ＝オーストラリアの発音
M＝男性（Man）　W＝女性（Woman）

TEST 1 [本誌p.29-70] **CD 1 11-92**　　**TEST 2 [本誌p.71-111]** **CD 2 01-82**

TEST 1、2ともに、実際のテストと同じ、合計200問で構成されています。

リスニングセクション 　　100問　　約45分間
リーディングセクション 　100問　　75分間

予行演習として時間を計って解答し、時間配分の参考にしたり、伸ばしたい分野や弱点を把握したり、使い方を工夫してみましょう。

別冊『解答・解説』

参考スコア範囲の算出方法 [別冊 p.4]

正解数を基に、参考スコア範囲を算出できます。

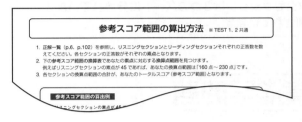

正解一覧 [TEST 1 ➡ 別冊 p.6　TEST 2 ➡ 別冊 p.102]

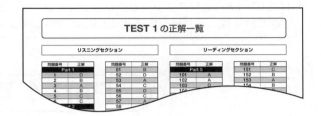

解答・解説 [TEST 1 ➡ 別冊 p.7-101　TEST 2 ➡ 別冊 p.103-197]

表記の説明は、別冊 p.2-3 をご覧ください。

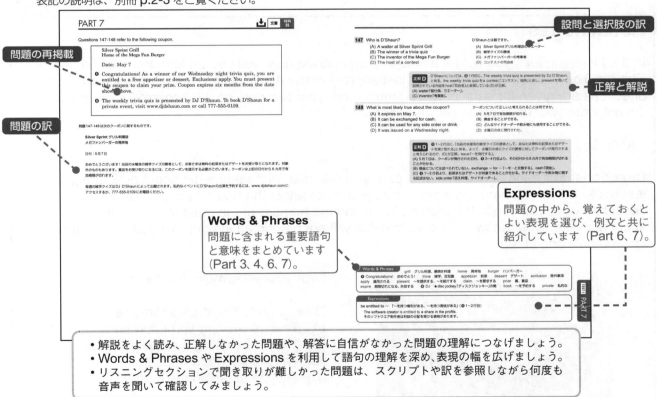

問題の再掲載

問題の訳

設問と選択肢の訳

正解と解説

Words & Phrases
問題に含まれる重要語句と意味をまとめています（Part 3、4、6、7）。

Expressions
問題の中から、覚えておくとよい表現を選び、例文と共に紹介しています（Part 6、7）。

- 解説をよく読み、正解しなかった問題や、解答に自信がなかった問題の理解につなげましょう。
- Words & Phrases や Expressions を利用して語句の理解を深め、表現の幅を広げましょう。
- リスニングセクションで聞き取りが難しかった問題は、スクリプトや訳を参照しながら何度も音声を聞いて確認してみましょう。

CD トラック・特典音声ファイル 一覧表
[別冊 p.198-199]

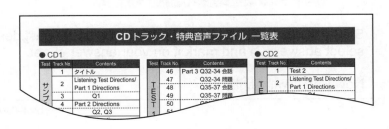

サンプル問題

TOEIC® Listening & Reading Test（以下、TOEIC® L&R）の問題形式を、サンプル問題を使ってご紹介します。サンプル問題は、全部で29問（リスニングセクション12問、リーディングセクション17問）です。問題の番号は連番になっており、実際のテストの問題番号とは異なります。

> TOEIC® L&Rのリスニングセクションは4つ、リーディングセクションは3つのパートに分かれています。
> 問題用紙には、各パートの最初にDirectionsが英文で印刷されています。

Part 1 写真描写問題

1枚の写真について4つの短い説明文が1度だけ放送されます。説明文は印刷されていません。4つのうち写真を最も適切に描写しているものを選ぶ問題です。実際のテストでは6問出題されます。

CD 1 02

LISTENING TEST

In the Listening test, you will be asked to demonstrate how well you understand spoken English. The entire Listening test will last approximately 45 minutes. There are four parts, and directions are given for each part. You must mark your answers on the separate answer sheet. Do not write your answers in your test book.

PART 1

Directions: For each question in this part, you will hear four statements about a picture in your test book. When you hear the statements, you must select the one statement that best describes what you see in the picture. Then find the number of the question on your answer sheet and mark your answer. The statements will not be printed in your test book and will be spoken only one time.

Look at the example item below.

Now listen to the four statements.
(A) They're moving some furniture.
(B) They're entering a meeting room.
(C) They're sitting at a table.
(D) They're cleaning the carpet.

Statement (C), "They're sitting at a table," is the best description of the picture, so you should select answer (C) and mark it on your answer sheet.

Now Part 1 will begin.

＊上記枠内の網掛けの部分は音声のみで、問題用紙には印刷されていません。

CD 1
03

サンプル問題

1.

解答・解説

1. Look at the picture marked number 1 in your test book.

🇦🇺 M (A) A truck is stopped at a stoplight.
(B) A man is using a gardening tool.
(C) Some people are sitting on the grass.
(D) Some workers are cutting down a tree.

正解 (B)

解説 gardeningは「造園、園芸」、toolは「用具、道具」という意味。

訳 問題用紙にある問題1の写真を見てください。

(A) トラックが停止信号で止まっている。
(B) 男性が造園用具を使っている。
(C) 何人かの人々が芝生の上に座っている。
(D) 何人かの作業員が木を切り倒している。

Directions の訳

リスニングテスト

リスニングテストでは、話されている英語をどのくらいよく理解しているかが問われます。リスニングテストは全体で約45分間です。4つのパートがあり、各パートにおいて指示が与えられます。答えは、別紙の解答用紙にマークしてください。問題用紙に答えを書き込んではいけません。

パート1

指示：このパートの各設問では、問題用紙にある写真について、4つの説明文を聞きます。説明文を聞いて、写真の内容を最も適切に描写しているものを選んでください。そして解答用紙の該当する問題番号にあなたの答えをマークしてください。説明文は問題用紙には印刷されておらず、1度だけ放送されます。

下の例題を見てください。

では4つの説明文を聞きましょう。
(A) 彼らは家具を動かしている。
(B) 彼らは会議室に入ろうとしている。
(C) 彼らはテーブルのところに座っている。
(D) 彼らはカーペットを掃除している。

(C)の文、"They're sitting at a table"（彼らはテーブルのところに座っている）がこの写真を最も適切に描写しているので、(C)を選び、解答用紙にマークします。

ではパート1が始まります。

Part 2 応答問題

1つの質問または発言と、3つの応答がそれぞれ1度だけ放送されます。質問も応答も印刷されていません。質問に対して最も適切な応答を選ぶ問題です。実際のテストでは25問出題されます。

PART 2

Directions: You will hear a question or statement and three responses spoken in English. They will not be printed in your test book and will be spoken only one time. Select the best response to the question or statement and mark the letter (A), (B), or (C) on your answer sheet.

Now let us begin with question number 2.

＊上記枠内の網掛けの部分は音声のみで、問題用紙には印刷されていません。

サンプル問題

2. Mark your answer on your answer sheet.
3. Mark your answer on your answer sheet.

解答・解説

2. W Are you taking an international or a domestic flight?

    M (A) I'd prefer a window seat.
       (B) He moved there last year.
       (C) I'm flying internationally.

正解 **(C)**

解説 A or B? の形で、国際線と国内線のどちらの便に乗るのかを尋ねているのに対し、「国際線の飛行機で行く」と答えている(C)が正解。

訳 あなたは国際線の便に乗りますか、それとも国内線の便ですか。

(A) 私は窓側の席を希望します。
(B) 彼は昨年、そこへ引っ越しました。
(C) 私は国際線の飛行機で行きます。

3. M Shouldn't we hire more salespeople?

    W (A) I'm glad they went.
       (B) A higher profit.
       (C) Let's look at the budget.

正解 **(C)**

解説 「もっと販売員を雇った方がいいのではないか」という男性の発言に対し、「予算を見てみよう」と雇用の検討を示唆している(C)が正解。

訳 私たちはもっと販売員を雇った方がいいのではありませんか。

(A) 私は、彼らが行ってうれしいです。
(B) より高い利益です。
(C) 予算を見てみましょう。

Directions の訳

パート2

指示： 英語による1つの質問または発言と、3つの応答を聞きます。それらは問題用紙には印刷されておらず、1度だけ放送されます。質問または発言に対して最も適切な応答を選び、解答用紙の (A)、(B)、または (C) にマークしてください。

では、問題2から始めましょう。

問題の訳

答えを解答用紙にマークしてください。

会話が1度だけ放送され、その後に設問が続きます。会話は印刷されていません。問題用紙の設問と4つの選択肢を読み、その中から最も適切なものを選ぶ問題です。実際のテストでは39問出題されます。

PART 3

Directions: You will hear some conversations between two or more people. You will be asked to answer three questions about what the speakers say in each conversation. Select the best response to each question and mark the letter (A), (B), (C), or (D) on your answer sheet. The conversations will not be printed in your test book and will be spoken only one time.

サンプル問題

5th Annual Agricultural Fair

Day 1—Vegetables
Day 2—Dairy
Day 3—Flowers
Day 4—Baked goods

4. Which department is the man most likely calling?

(A) Receiving
(B) Catering
(C) Security
(D) Finance

5. Why does the man apologize?

(A) He has forgotten his badge.
(B) His report will be late.
(C) A meeting location has to be changed.
(D) A shipment must be delivered after business hours.

6. What does the woman say she will do?

(A) Arrange additional workspace
(B) Publish some materials
(C) Issue a temporary pass
(D) Ask staff to work late

7. Why do the speakers want to attend the fair?

(A) To advertise a new business
(B) To find local food suppliers
(C) To sell some products
(D) To participate in a workshop

8. What does the man say he has downloaded?

(A) An electronic book
(B) A mobile phone application
(C) Some photographs
(D) Some tickets

9. Look at the graphic. Which day do the speakers decide to attend the fair?

(A) Day 1
(B) Day 2
(C) Day 3
(D) Day 4

Questions 4 through 6 refer to the following conversation.　問題4-6 は次の会話に関するものです。

🇦🇺 M Hello. ❶I'm expecting an extra-large load of clothing racks delivered to the store today, and they'll arrive after business hours. Are you the person I should inform about this?

もしもし。今日お店に、洋服ラックの特大の積み荷が配達される予定ですが、それらは営業時間の後に着きます。あなたがこの件についてお知らせすべき方でしょうか。

🇬🇧 W Yes, ❷I'm head of Receiving. But ❸you're supposed to have suppliers make deliveries during business hours.

はい、私が荷受け部門の責任者です。でも、供給業者には、営業時間中に配達してもらうことになっているはずですが。

🇦🇺 M ❹I'm sorry, but this is the only time the supplier can deliver them, and we need the racks for a fashion show we're having tomorrow.

申し訳ありません。しかし、これが、供給業者がそれらを配達できる唯一の時間帯で、私たちが明日開催するファッションショーには、そのラックが必要なんです。

🇬🇧 W I understand. ❺I'm not sure which of my staff members is working tonight, but I'll ask one of them to stay late to accept the delivery.

分かりました。今夜うちのスタッフの誰が勤務するのか定かではありませんが、配達物を受け取るために遅くまで残るよう、彼らのうちの1人に頼みます。

---

4. 正解 **(A)**

訳 男性はどの部署に電話をかけていると考えられますか。

(A) 荷受け
(B) ケータリング
(C) 警備
(D) 財務

解説 男性からの電話に応答した女性は❷「私が荷受け部門の責任者だ」と答え、その後も2人は配達物の受け取りについて話をしている。

5. 正解 **(D)**

訳 男性はなぜ謝罪していますか。

(A) 自分のバッジを忘れたから。
(B) 報告書が遅れるから。
(C) 会議の場所が変更されなければならないから。
(D) 荷物が営業時間の後に配達されざるを得ないから。

解説 ❶「積み荷が配達される予定だが、それらは営業時間の後に着く」という男性の報告に対し、女性が❸「供給業者には、営業時間中に配達してもらうことになっているはず」と指摘している。それに対して男性は❹で、「申し訳ない」と謝罪後「これが、供給業者がそれらを配達できる唯一の時間帯で、私たちが明日開催するファッションショーには、そのラックが必要だ」と事情を説明している。よって、正解は(D)。

6. 正解 **(D)**

訳 女性は何をすると言っていますか。

(A) 追加の作業スペースを手配する。
(B) 資料を公表する。
(C) 臨時の通行証を発行する。
(D) スタッフに遅くまで勤務するよう頼む。

解説 女性は❺「今夜うちのスタッフの誰が勤務するのか定かではないが、配達物を受け取るために遅くまで残るよう、彼らのうちの1人に頼む」と述べている。stay late を work late「遅くまで勤務する」と表した(D)が正解。

Directions の訳

パート3

指示：2人あるいはそれ以上の人々の会話を聞きます。各会話の内容に関する3つの設問に答えるよう求められます。それぞれの設問について最も適切な答えを選び、解答用紙の (A)、(B)、(C)、または (D) にマークしてください。会話は問題用紙には印刷されておらず、1度だけ放送されます。

Questions 7 through 9 refer to the following conversation and schedule.

W Pedro, ❶I know we're still looking for local fresh food suppliers for our new restaurant. We should check out the Agricultural Fair next month.

M That's a good idea. It's a major event, so many local farmers will be there. ❷I downloaded the fair's mobile phone application. The app has a lot of helpful information, including a schedule. Which day do you think we should go?

W Well, it looks like they'll have dairy vendors on the second day.

M Hmm, I just contacted a dairy company that might work for us. ❸We really need a vegetable supplier though…

W Oh, OK. ❹They have a day for showcasing vegetable farmers. Let's go then.

問題7-9 は次の会話と予定表に関するものです。

Pedro、私たちはまだ、うちの新しいレストランのために、地元の生鮮食品の供給業者を探しているわよね。来月の農業フェアを見てみるべきだわ。

それは良い考えだね。大きなイベントだから、多数の地元の農業経営者たちがそこにいるだろう。僕はフェアの携帯電話用アプリをダウンロードしたよ。このアプリには、予定表を含め、役立つ情報がたくさんあるんだ。僕たちはどの日に行くべきだと思う？

そうね、乳製品の販売業者は2日目にいるみたいね。

うーん、僕はうちに合いそうな乳製品会社に連絡を取ったばかりなんだ。僕たちには野菜の供給業者はぜひとも必要だけど…。

ああ、分かったわ。野菜農家の出展日があるわ。そのときに行きましょう。

---

7. 正解 **(B)**

訳 なぜ話し手たちはフェアに行きたいと思っていますか。

(A) 新しい店を宣伝するため。
(B) 地元の食品供給業者を見つけるため。
(C) 製品を販売するため。
(D) 講習会に参加するため。

解説 女性は❶「私たちはまだ、うちの新しいレストランのために、地元の生鮮食品の供給業者を探している。来月の農業フェアを見てみるべきだ」と提案し、男性もそれに同意している。よって、(B)が適切。

8. 正解 **(B)**

訳 男性は何をダウンロードしたと言っていますか。

(A) 電子書籍
(B) 携帯電話用アプリ
(C) 数枚の写真
(D) 数枚のチケット

解説 男性は❷「僕はフェアの携帯電話用アプリをダウンロードした」と述べている。

9. 正解 **(A)**

訳 図を見てください。話し手たちはどの日にフェアへ行くことに決めますか。

(A) 1日目
(B) 2日目
(C) 3日目
(D) 4日目

解説 ❸「僕たちには野菜の供給業者がぜひとも必要だ」という男性の発言に対し、女性は❹「野菜農家の出展日がある。そのときに行こう」と提案している。予定表から、野菜農家が集まる日は1日目だと分かる。予定表のbaked goodsはクッキーやパンなどのオーブンで焼いた食品を指す。

図の訳

第5回　年次農業フェア
1日目 ― 野菜
2日目 ― 乳製品
3日目 ― 花
4日目 ― パン・焼き菓子

Part 4 説明文問題

アナウンスや電話のメッセージなどの説明文が1度だけ放送され、その後に設問が続きます。説明文は印刷されていません。問題用紙の設問と4つの選択肢を読み、その中から最も適切なものを選ぶ問題です。実際のテストでは30問出題されます。

PART 4

Directions: You will hear some talks given by a single speaker. You will be asked to answer three questions about what the speaker says in each talk. Select the best response to each question and mark the letter (A), (B), (C), or (D) on your answer sheet. The talks will not be printed in your test book and will be spoken only one time.

サンプル問題

10. What is the main topic of the speech?

    (A) A building complex renovation
    (B) A marketing conference
    (C) An annual fund-raiser
    (D) A department picnic

11. What does the woman imply when she says, "And it was their first project"?

    (A) She thinks some training materials need to be improved.
    (B) She helped some employees with the project.
    (C) She is impressed by some work.
    (D) She is not worried about some mistakes.

12. What will most likely happen next?

    (A) Tours will be scheduled.
    (B) A form will be distributed.
    (C) Refreshments will be offered.
    (D) A guest speaker will talk.

Questions 10 through 12 refer to the following speech.

🇺🇸 W　Good morning! ❶Welcome to the ceremony to celebrate the official opening of our renovated business complex. As company president, I want to extend my sincere appreciation to the local architecture firm we hired: Green Space Incorporated. ❷Not only did they design two beautiful new office buildings, but they also extended our walking paths to give us even more chances to enjoy nature on our work breaks. <u>And it was their first project!</u> ❸Now let's hear from the lead architect, Susan Hernandez, who will tell us more about the renovation.

問題 10-12 は次のスピーチに関するものです。

おはようございます！ 改装された当複合型事業施設の、正式開業を祝う式典へようこそ。社長として、当社が委託した地元の建築事務所、Green Space 社に心からの感謝を申し上げたいと思います。彼らは 2 つの美しい新オフィスビルを設計しただけでなく、われわれが仕事の休憩時間に自然を楽しむ機会をもっと多く持てるよう、遊歩道の延長もしてくださいました。<u>そして、それは彼らの初めてのプロジェクト</u>だったのです！ では、主任建築士である Susan Hernandez から話を伺いましょう。彼女はこの改装について、さらに私たちに話してくださいます。

---

10. 正解 **(A)**

訳　スピーチの主な話題は何ですか。

(A) 複合型ビルの改装
(B) マーケティング会議
(C) 年次の資金集めイベント
(D) 部署の野外親睦会

解説　話し手は❶「改装された当複合型事業施設の、正式開業を祝う式典へようこそ」と述べ、その後も、建物の改装の設計を委託した建築事務所の仕事ぶりを紹介している。

11. 正解 **(C)**

訳　女性は "And it was their first project" という発言で、何を示唆していますか。

(A) 研修資料が改善される必要があると考えている。
(B) そのプロジェクトで従業員を手伝った。
(C) ある仕事に感銘を受けている。
(D) 幾つかの間違いについては心配していない。

解説　話し手は、改装の設計を委託した建築事務所について、❷「彼らは 2 つの美しい新オフィスビルを設計しただけでなく、われわれが仕事の休憩時間に自然を楽しむ機会をもっと多く持てるよう、遊歩道の延長もした」と彼らの仕事の成果に触れた後、下線部の「そして、それは彼らの初めてのプロジェクトだった」を続けている。よって、女性は建築事務所の仕事に感銘を受けていると分かる。

12. 正解 **(D)**

訳　次に何が起こると考えられますか。

(A) 見学の予定が立てられる。
(B) 記入用紙が配布される。
(C) 軽食が提供される。
(D) ゲスト講演者が話す。

解説　話し手は❸「主任建築士である Susan Hernandez から話を伺いましょう。彼女はこの改装について、さらに私たちに話してくれる」と述べている。よって、次に Hernandez さんがゲストとして話すことが分かる。

Directionsの訳

パート 4

指示：1 人の話し手によるトークを聞きます。各トークの内容に関する 3 つの設問に答えるよう求められます。それぞれの設問について最も適切な答えを選び、解答用紙の (A)、(B)、(C)、または (D) にマークしてください。トークは問題用紙には印刷されておらず、1 度だけ放送されます。

ここからはリーディングセクションです。
実際のテストでは、リスニングセクションの終わりに"This is the end of the Listening test. Turn to Part 5 in your test book."（これでリスニングテストは終了です。問題用紙のパート5に進んでください。）というアナウンスがありますので、それが聞こえたらリーディングセクションの解答を始めます。

Part 5 短文穴埋め問題

4つの選択肢の中から最も適切なものを選び、不完全な文を完成させる問題です。実際のテストでは30問出題されます。

READING TEST

In the Reading test, you will read a variety of texts and answer several different types of reading comprehension questions. The entire Reading test will last 75 minutes. There are three parts, and directions are given for each part. You are encouraged to answer as many questions as possible within the time allowed.

You must mark your answers on the separate answer sheet. Do not write your answers in your test book.

PART 5

Directions: A word or phrase is missing in each of the sentences below. Four answer choices are given below each sentence. Select the best answer to complete the sentence. Then mark the letter (A), (B), (C), or (D) on your answer sheet.

サンプル問題

13. Before ------- with the recruiter, applicants should sign in at the personnel department's reception desk.

(A) meets
(B) meeting
(C) to meet
(D) was met

14. Stefano Linen Company suggests requesting a small fabric ------- before placing your final order.

(A) bonus
(B) sample
(C) feature
(D) model

13. 正解 **(B)**

訳　採用担当者と会う前に、応募者の方々は人事部の受付で署名して到着を記録してください。

(A) 動詞の三人称単数現在形
(B) 動名詞
(C) to不定詞
(D) 受動態の過去形

解説　選択肢は全て動詞meet「会う」の変化した形。文頭からカンマまでの部分に主語と動詞がないため、Beforeは前置詞と考えられる。前置詞に続く空所には名詞の働きをする語句が入るので、動名詞の(B) meetingが適切である。sign in「署名して到着を記録する」。

14. 正解 **(B)**

訳　Stefanoリネン社は、お客さまが最終的な注文をなさる前に、小さな布地見本をご要望になることをお勧めしています。

(A) 特別手当
(B) 見本
(C) 特徴
(D) 模型

解説　選択肢は全て名詞。空所の後ろは「お客さまが最終的な注文をする前に」という意味。(B) sample「見本」を空所に入れるとsmall fabric sample「小さな布地見本」となり、注文前に要望するものとして適切で、意味が通る。

Directionsの訳

リーディングテスト

リーディングテストでは、さまざまな文章を読んで、読解力を測る何種類かの問題に答えます。リーディングテストは全体で75分間です。3つのパートがあり、各パートにおいて指示が与えられます。制限時間内に、できるだけ多くの設問に答えてください。

答えは、別紙の解答用紙にマークしてください。問題用紙に答えを書き込んではいけません。

パート5

指示：以下の各文において語や句が抜けています。各文の下には選択肢が4つ与えられています。文を完成させるのに最も適切な答えを選びます。そして解答用紙の (A)、(B)、(C)、または (D) にマークしてください。

Part 6 長文穴埋め問題

4つの選択肢の中から最も適切なものを選び、不完全な文書を完成させる問題です。実際のテストでは16問出題されます。

PART 6

Directions: Read the texts that follow. A word, phrase, or sentence is missing in parts of each text. Four answer choices for each question are given below the text. Select the best answer to complete the text. Then mark the letter (A), (B), (C), or (D) on your answer sheet.

サンプル問題

Questions 15-18 refer to the following article.

❶ SAN DIEGO (May 5)—Matino Industries has just bolstered its image with environmentally conscious customers thanks to its ------- to reduce its use of nonrenewable energy to less
15.
than 20 percent within five years. -------. Best practices guidelines are already being revised
16.
------- powering down and disconnecting equipment when not in use. In addition, solar-panel
17.
arrays are slated for installation on-site as early as next year. When weather ------- are clear,
18.
these panels will offset Matino's reliance on the power grid, as they already do for a growing list of companies.

＊❶は解説の中で説明している文書中の段落番号等を示しています。問題用紙には印刷されていません。

15. (A) product
 (B) commitment
 (C) contest
 (D) workforce

16. (A) Discounts on all its products have increased Matino's customer base.
 (B) Management predicts that the takeover will result in a net financial gain.
 (C) To achieve this goal, the company will begin by improving its energy efficiency.
 (D) The initial step will involve redesigning the company's logo and slogans.

17. (A) been encouraging
 (B) have encouraged
 (C) encourages
 (D) to encourage

18. (A) conditions
 (B) instructions
 (C) views
 (D) reports

問題 15-18 は次の記事に関するものです。

> サンディエゴ（5 月 5 日）──Matino 産業社は、同社の再生不能エネルギーの使用を 5 年以内に 20 パーセント未満に削減するという公約のおかげで、環境意識の高い顧客にとっての同社のイメージを強化したところである。*この目標を達成するために同社は、自社のエネルギー効率を改善することから始める予定だ。機器を使用していないときには電源を落として接続を切ることを推奨するために、最良実践ガイドラインがすでに改定されているところである。さらに、早くも来年には、ソーラーパネルの列が構内に設置される予定である。天候条件が晴れのときには、これらのパネルが、増え続ける多くの企業に対してすでにそうしているように、Matino 社の送電網依存を弱めることになる。

*問題 16 の挿入文の訳

15. 正解 **(B)**

訳
(A) 製品
(B) 公約
(C) 競争
(D) 全従業員

解説 ❶ の 1～3 行目は「Matino 産業社は、同社の-------のおかげで、同社のイメージを強化したところだ」というのが、文の中心の意味。空所の後ろの「同社の再生不能エネルギーの使用を 5 年以内に 20 パーセント未満に削減すること」は、空所に入る名詞の内容を示していると考えられるので、文意から (B) commitment「公約」が適切。

16. 正解 **(C)**

訳
(A) 全ての自社製品に対する割引が、Matino 社の顧客基盤を拡大してきた。
(B) 経営陣は、その企業買収は財務上の純利益をもたらすと予測している。
(C) この目標を達成するために同社は、自社のエネルギー効率を改善することから始める予定だ。
(D) 第 1 段階には、会社のロゴとスローガンを作り直すことが含まれる予定だ。

解説 空所の前の文では、Matino 産業社が同社の再生不能エネルギーの使用を 5 年以内に 20 パーセント未満に削減することが述べられている。この内容を this goal で受けて、目標達成のために同社がこれから取り組むことを挙げている (C) が流れとして適切。

17. 正解 **(D)**

訳
(A) 〈be 動詞の過去分詞＋現在分詞〉
(B) 現在完了形
(C) 動詞の三人称単数現在形
(D) to 不定詞

解説 選択肢は全て動詞 encourage「～を推奨する」が変化した形。空所の前に〈主語＋動詞〉の形があり、and や or などの接続詞もないことから、空所に動詞は入らない。空所には、to 不定詞の (D) to encourage が適切。

18. 正解 **(A)**

訳
(A) 条件
(B) 指示
(C) 見解
(D) 報道

解説 空所を含む文の、文頭からカンマまでは「天候-------が晴れのときには」という意味。these panels 以降では、その際にソーラーパネルがもたらす効果について述べられている。「天候条件が晴れのときには」とすると意味が通るため、(A) conditions「条件」が適切。

Directions の訳

パート 6

指示：以下の文書を読んでください。各文書の中で語や句、または文が部分的に抜けています。文書の下には各設問の選択肢が 4 つ与えられています。文書を完成させるのに最も適切な答えを選びます。そして解答用紙の (A)、(B)、(C)、または (D) にマークしてください。

Part 7 読解問題

いろいろな形式の、1つもしくは複数の文書に関する問題が出題されます。設問と4つの選択肢を読み、その中から最も適切なものを選ぶ問題です。実際のテストでは1つの文書に関する問題が29問、複数の文書に関する問題が25問出題されます。

PART 7

Directions: In this part you will read a selection of texts, such as magazine and newspaper articles, e-mails, and instant messages. Each text or set of texts is followed by several questions. Select the best answer for each question and mark the letter (A), (B), (C), or (D) on your answer sheet.

サンプル問題

Questions 19-20 refer to the following text-message chain.

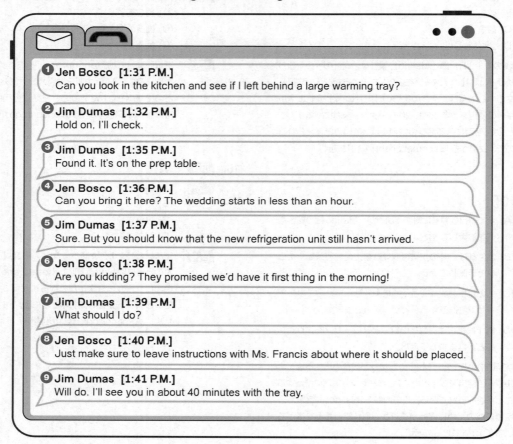

❶ Jen Bosco [1:31 P.M.]
Can you look in the kitchen and see if I left behind a large warming tray?

❷ Jim Dumas [1:32 P.M.]
Hold on, I'll check.

❸ Jim Dumas [1:35 P.M.]
Found it. It's on the prep table.

❹ Jen Bosco [1:36 P.M.]
Can you bring it here? The wedding starts in less than an hour.

❺ Jim Dumas [1:37 P.M.]
Sure. But you should know that the new refrigeration unit still hasn't arrived.

❻ Jen Bosco [1:38 P.M.]
Are you kidding? They promised we'd have it first thing in the morning!

❼ Jim Dumas [1:39 P.M.]
What should I do?

❽ Jen Bosco [1:40 P.M.]
Just make sure to leave instructions with Ms. Francis about where it should be placed.

❾ Jim Dumas [1:41 P.M.]
Will do. I'll see you in about 40 minutes with the tray.

---

19. For whom do the writers most likely work?

(A) A catering company
(B) A home-improvement store
(C) A kitchen-design company
(D) An appliance manufacturer

20. At 1:38 P.M., what does Ms. Bosco most likely mean when she writes, "Are you kidding"?

(A) She thinks Mr. Dumas is exaggerating.
(B) She knew she would have to wait a long time.
(C) She expects the refrigeration unit to arrive soon.
(D) She is upset that a delivery has not been made.

解答・解説

問題19-20は次のテキストメッセージのやり取りに関するものです。

Jen Bosco [午後1時31分]
調理場の中をのぞいて、私が大きな保温トレーを置き忘れたかどうかを確かめてくれるかしら。

Jim Dumas [午後1時32分]
待ってて、確認するよ。

Jim Dumas [午後1時35分]
見つけた。調理台の上にあるよ。

Jen Bosco [午後1時36分]
それをここに持ってきてくれる？ 結婚式が1時間足らずで始まるの。

Jim Dumas [午後1時37分]
もちろん。でも、新しい冷蔵装置がまだ届いていないことを知っておいた方がいいよ。

Jen Bosco [午後1時38分]
冗談でしょう？ 朝一番には私たちにそれを届けてくれると、彼らは約束したのよ。

Jim Dumas [午後1時39分]
僕はどうしたらいい？

Jen Bosco [午後1時40分]
とにかく、どこにそれを置けばいいか、Francisさんに必ず指示を残しておいて。

Jim Dumas [午後1時41分]
そうするよ。約40分後にトレーを持って君に会うね。

---

19. **正解** **(A)**

訳 書き手たちはどこに勤めていると考えられますか。

(A) ケータリング会社
(B) ホームセンター
(C) キッチン設計会社
(D) 電化製品メーカー

解説 ❶と❷のやり取りから、書き手たちの職場には調理場があることが分かる。また❹で、BoscoさんがDumasさんに保温トレーを結婚式の場に持ってくるよう伝えていることから、書き手たちは料理を作り配達を行っていると考えられる。よって、(A)が適切。

20. **正解** **(D)**

訳 午後1時38分にBoscoさんは、"Are you kidding"という発言で、何を意味していると考えられますか。

(A) Dumasさんが誇張していると思っている。
(B) 長い間待たなくてはならないことを知っていた。
(C) 冷蔵装置がもうすぐ届くだろうと見込んでいる。
(D) 配達が行われていないことに動揺している。

解説 Dumasさんが❺「新しい冷蔵装置がまだ届いていないことを知っておいた方がいい」と伝えたのに対して、Boscoさんは「冗談でしょう？」と驚きを示し、「朝一番には私たちにそれを届けてくれると、彼らは約束した」と続けている。つまり、Boscoさんは配達が約束通りに行われていないことに動揺していると考えられる。

Directions の訳

パート7

指示：このパートでは、雑誌や新聞の記事、Eメールやインスタントメッセージなどのさまざまな文書を読みます。1つの文書または複数の文書のセットにはそれぞれ、幾つかの設問が続いています。各設問について最も適切な答えを選び、解答用紙の(A)、(B)、(C)、または(D)にマークしてください。

Questions 21-24 refer to the following Web page.

---

http://straubuniversityschoolofmedicine.edu/vendors/rfp0023

❶ Straub University School of Medicine is currently seeking a vendor to provide surgical gloves, laboratory coats, and protective goggles. The university requires high-quality, hospital-grade equipment for its students and faculty and is especially interested in providers who currently work with local hospitals and clinics.

❷ You can download the complete Request for Proposal (RFP) instructions from our Web site. Below is a summary of the proposal requirements. — [1] —.

- A standard proposal form, which can be downloaded from our Web site
- A general description of the provider and its experience in the industry
- Product descriptions with a complete list of specifications and prices
- Contact information of three current or recent clients who are able to speak to the quality of the provider's products or services

❸ If you have any questions about the RFP, please submit them in writing to queries@straub.edu by July 20. — [2] —. Responses to questions will be posted publicly on the Straub University School of Medicine's Web page on August 4.

❹ Proposals must be received no later than August 15. — [3] —. All submissions will be thoroughly reviewed, and the winning proposal will be announced on September 10. A contract will be finalized with the strongest candidate that same month, and the agreement will take effect starting October 1. — [4] —.

---

21. Who are the instructions intended for?

(A) Sellers of medical supplies
(B) Applicants for hospital jobs
(C) Hospital administrators
(D) Medical students

22. What are candidates required to submit?

(A) Questions about the proposal
(B) Professional references
(C) An application fee
(D) Product samples

23. When will candidates learn if they have been selected?

(A) In July
(B) In August
(C) In September
(D) In October

24. In which of the positions marked [1], [2], [3], and [4] does the following sentence best belong?

"All documentation must arrive by this date in a sealed envelope addressed to the School of Medicine's Purchasing Department."

(A) [1]
(B) [2]
(C) [3]
(D) [4]

解答・解説

問題 21-24 は次のウェブページに関するものです。

http://straubuniversityschoolofmedicine.edu/vendors/rfp0023

Straub 大学医学部は現在、手術用手袋、白衣、保護用ゴーグルを供給してくれる業者を求めています。本学は、学生と教授陣向けの、高品質で病院仕様の備品を必要としており、特に、地元の病院や診療所と現在取引をしている販売会社に関心があります。

本学のウェブサイトから、提案依頼書（RFP）の指示一式をダウンロードすることができます。以下は提案要件の概略です。

・定型の提案書式。本学のウェブサイトからダウンロード可能
・販売会社の概要および業界における同社の経験
・仕様および価格の全一覧を付した、製品の説明
・販売会社の製品あるいはサービスの質について述べることのできる、現在もしくは最近の顧客 3 社の連絡先

RFP について何かご質問がございましたら、それらを文書で 7 月 20 日までに queries@straub.edu 宛てにご提出ください。ご質問に対する回答は、8 月 4 日に Straub 大学医学部のウェブページ上で公開されます。

提案書は 8 月 15 日必着です。*全ての書類は、封書でこの日付までに医学部の購買部宛てに到着しなければなりません。全ての提出物は入念に検討され、採用された提案書は 9 月 10 日に発表されます。契約書は最有力候補業者とその同月に最終的な形にされ、契約は 10 月 1 日より発効します。

*問題 24 の挿入文の訳

---

21. 【正解】 **(A)**

【訳】 この指示は誰に向けられていますか。

(A) 医療用品の販売会社
(B) 病院の職への応募者
(C) 病院の管理者
(D) 医学生

【解説】 ❶ 1～2 行目に「Straub 大学医学部は現在、手術用手袋、白衣、保護用ゴーグルを供給する業者を求めている」とあり、❷ では提案要件の概略について、❹ では提出期日や選考過程などについて説明されている。よって、この指示は医療用品の販売会社に向けたものだと分かる。

22. 【正解】 **(B)**

【訳】 候補者は何を提出することを求められていますか。

(A) 提案書に関する質問
(B) 取引上の照会先
(C) 申込金
(D) 製品の見本

【解説】 ❷ で提案要件の概略として挙げられている箇条書きの 4 点目に、「販売会社の製品あるいはサービスの質について述べることのできる、現在もしくは最近の顧客 3 社の連絡先」とある。

23. 【正解】 **(C)**

【訳】 候補者はいつ、自分が選出されたかどうかを知りますか。

(A) 7 月
(B) 8 月
(C) 9 月
(D) 10 月

【解説】 ❹ 2 行目に、the winning proposal will be announced on September 10「採用された提案書は 9 月 10 日に発表される」とある。

24. 【正解】 **(C)**

【訳】 [1]、[2]、[3]、[4]と記載された箇所のうち、次の文が入るのに最もふさわしいのはどれですか。

「全ての書類は、封書でこの日付までに医学部の購買部宛てに到着しなければなりません」

(A) [1]
(B) [2]
(C) [3]
(D) [4]

【解説】 挿入文は書類の提出方法と宛先を伝えている。(C) [3]に入れると、挿入文中の this date「この日付」が ❹ 1 行目の August 15 を指し、提案書の提出期日に続けて提出方法と宛先を伝える自然な流れとなる。

Questions 25-29 refer to the following article, e-mail, and Web page.

❶ (November 6)—The Rudi's store at 47 Kask Highway in Glencoe Park will shut its doors next Saturday, adding another empty building to the local landscape. The shutdown is one of a rash of store closings in the greater Billington area and is a result of two major forces. First, Rudi's has changed its business plan, relying increasingly on online sales. Second, much of the traffic on Kask Highway has been rerouted to the recently completed bypass, resulting in fewer potential customers passing through Billington.

❷ Other Rudi's closings over the past two years include the store at 38 Quail Hill Road, the store at 21 Lowell Boulevard, and the downtown megastore at 59 Claremont Street on the banks of the Corks River. A Rudi's spokesperson stated that no further closures are expected.

To:	nathanpaugh@ioscodesign.com
From:	ccovey@tedesintl.com
Subject:	Tedes Building
Date:	January 25

Dear Mr. Paugh,

❶ The preliminary drawings you sent are right on target. I think your proposal to demolish most of the east wall and install floor-to-ceiling windows is terrific. If we were to leave everything as it now is, we would end up with a rather somber interior.

❷ Let's keep the current stairway where it is so that people can walk straight through the entrance and up to the second floor meeting rooms. We can configure the remaining area in the center of the first floor as open work space, with the executive offices off to the left side against the west wall. Including a large picture window at the entrance to the fitness center in the back of the first floor space is also a good idea.

❸ Please move forward with drawing up draft plans for our board's approval.

Thank you,

Cynthia Covey

http://www.buildingmonthly.com/readersreviews

| HOME | LATEST ISSUE | **READERS' REVIEWS** | ADVERTISERS |

The new Tedes corporate building
Posted by Monty K.

❶ Tedes International has opened its corporate headquarters in a former Rudi's megastore building. In an area with many vacated retail buildings, one is now a workplace for over 400 Tedes employees. Corporations looking for prime real estate should take notice.

❷ The interior design of the Tedes Building is notable for its mixed use of open and closed space. The entrance is open and inviting and leads to a wide staircase up to the second floor, which houses offices for upper management. Large windows installed as one of the exterior walls create a bright atmosphere in the open work space and nearby meeting rooms, while boats glide by on the river right in front of them. On my visit, several employees were exercising on fitness bikes in full view at the rear of the first-floor space.

25. What is the purpose of the article?

(A) To notify readers of recent job openings
(B) To publicize an online sale
(C) To report on a store closing
(D) To alert motorists to changing traffic patterns

26. Who most likely is Mr. Paugh?

(A) An artist
(B) An architect
(C) A real estate agent
(D) A reporter

27. Which former Rudi's location did Tedes International choose for its headquarters?

(A) 47 Kask Highway
(B) 38 Quail Hill Road
(C) 21 Lowell Boulevard
(D) 59 Claremont Street

28. What aspect of the design suggested by Ms. Covey was ultimately rejected?

(A) The replacement of a wall with windows
(B) The layout of the entrance
(C) The inclusion of a fitness center
(D) The location of the offices

29. What is implied by the reviewer?

(A) Tedes International is planning to expand.
(B) Tedes International wants to sell its property.
(C) Vacant buildings have great potential.
(D) Local businesses may experience reduced profits.

問題25-29は次の記事、Eメール、ウェブページに関するものです。

1. 記事

（11月6日）──グレンコーパークのカスク街道47番地にあるRudi's社の店舗は、次の土曜日に扉を閉ざし、その地域の風景にもう1棟空きビルを加えることになる。この閉店は、ビリントン広域圏で頻発する店舗の閉鎖の1つであり、2つの大きな影響力によるものである。第1に、Rudi's社が事業計画を変更し、オンライン販売に一層依存するようになったこと。第2に、カスク街道の交通の大部分が、最近完成した迂回路の方へ流れ、ビリントンを通る潜在顧客が減少する結果となったことだ。

過去2年間のRudi's社の他の閉店には、クウェイルヒル通り38番地の店舗、ローウェル大通り21番地の店舗、そしてコークス川岸のクレアモント通り59番地にあった中心街の超大型店舗が含まれる。Rudi's社の広報担当者は、これ以上の閉店は一切予定されていないと明言した。

2. Eメール

受信者：nathanpaugh@ioscodesign.com
送信者：ccovey@tedesintl.com
件名：Tedes ビル
日付：1月25日

Paugh様

お送りくださった仮の図面は、まさに期待通りのものです。東側の壁の大半を取り壊し、床から天井までの窓を設置するという貴殿のご提案は素晴らしいと思います。もし何もかも現状のままにしておいたとしたら、最終的にかなり陰気な内装になってしまうでしょう。

今の階段は、そのままの場所で残しましょう。そうすれば人々が入り口をまっすぐ通り抜け、2階の会議室に歩いて上がっていけます。1階の中央にある残りの区域は開放的な作業スペースとし、重役の執務室を左側へ、西の壁際に配置することができます。1階スペースの奥にあるフィットネスセンターへの入り口に大きな一枚ガラスの窓を入れることも良いアイデアです。

当社役員会の承認に向けて、設計図の草案の作成を進めてください。

よろしくお願いいたします。

Cynthia Covey

3. ウェブページ

http://www.buildingmonthly.com/readersreviews

| ホーム | 最新号 | 読者レビュー | 広告主 |

Tedes 社の新しいビル
Monty K. 投稿

Tedesインターナショナル社は、かつてRudi's社の超大型店舗だった建物に本社を開設した。空き家となった小売店のビルが多数ある地域において、1棟は今や400名超のTedes社の従業員の職場である。優良な不動産を求めている企業は注目すべきである。

Tedesビルの内部設計は、開放的スペースと閉鎖的スペースを取り混ぜて使用していることで注目に値する。入り口は広々として、いざなうようであり、2階に至る広い階段に通じている。2階には、経営上層部のための執務室が入っている。外壁の一部として設置された大型の窓は、開放的な作業スペースと近くの会議室に明るい雰囲気を作り出し、他方で、すぐ目の前にある川をボートが滑るように進む。私の訪問時には、数名の従業員が1階スペースの奥で、よく見える所でフィットネスバイクで運動をしていた。

25. 正解 (C)

訳 記事の目的は何ですか。

(A) 読者に最近の求人を知らせること。
(B) オンラインのセールを宣伝すること。
(C) 店舗の閉鎖を報道すること。
(D) 車を運転する人に、交通パターンの変化について注意を喚起すること。

解説 **1**の記事の**❶**1〜3行目に、「グレンコーパークのカスク街道47番地にあるRudi's社の店舗は、次の土曜日に扉を閉ざす」とあり、その後も閉店の要因などが述べられている。よって、記事の目的はRudi's社の店舗の閉鎖を報道することだと分かる。

26. 正解 (B)

訳 Paughさんとは誰だと考えられますか。

(A) 芸術家
(B) 建築家
(C) 不動産仲介人
(D) 記者

解説 Paughさんは**2**のEメールの受信者。Eメールの本文では、**❶**1行目で「お送りくださった仮の図面は、まさに期待通りのものだ」と伝えられ、建物の設計についての話が続いている。さらに、**❸**で「設計図の草案の作成を進めてほしい」と依頼を受けていることから、Paughさんは建築家と考えられる。

27. 正解 (D)

訳 Tedesインターナショナル社は、かつてのRudi's社のどの場所を本社に選びましたか。

(A) カスク街道47番地
(B) クウェイルヒル通り38番地
(C) ローウェル大通り21番地
(D) クレアモント通り59番地

解説 **3**のウェブページの**❶**1〜2行目に、「Tedesインターナショナル社は、かつてRudi's社の超大型店舗だった建物に本社を開設した」とある。**1**の記事の**❷**3〜5行目に、閉店したRudi's社の店舗の1つとして、「コークス川岸のクレアモント通り59番地にあった中心街の超大型店舗」が挙げられているので、(D)が正解。

28. 正解 (D)

訳 Coveyさんによって示された設計のどの点が、最終的に不採用とされましたか。

(A) 壁を窓で置き換えること
(B) 入り口の配置
(C) フィットネスセンターを含めること
(D) 執務室の位置

解説 Coveyさんは**2**のEメールの送信者。仮の図面を作ったPaughさんに対して、**❷**2〜4行目で「1階の中央にある残りの区域は開放的な作業スペースとし、重役の執務室を左側へ、西の壁際に配置することができる」と述べている。一方、完成したビルの読者レビューを載せた**3**のウェブページには、**❷**2〜3行目に「入り口は広々として、いざなうようであり、2階に至る広い階段に通じている。2階には、経営上層部のための執務室が入っている」とあることから、重役の執務室はCoveyさんが提案した1階ではなく、2階に配置されたと分かる。

29. 正解 (C)

訳 レビュー投稿者によって何が示唆されていますか。

(A) Tedesインターナショナル社は拡大する予定である。
(B) Tedesインターナショナル社は同社の不動産を売却したいと思っている。
(C) 空きビルは大きな可能性を持っている。
(D) 地元の企業は減益を経験するかもしれない。

解説 **3**のウェブページの読者レビューの**❶**1〜3行目で、Tedesインターナショナル社がかつてRudi's社の超大型店舗だった建物に本社を開設したことで、空きビル1棟が今や多数の従業員の職場へと変化したことが述べられている。続けて「優良な不動産を求めている企業は注目すべきだ」とあることから、レビュー投稿者は空きビルに大きな可能性があることを示唆していると考えられる。

採点・結果について

TOEIC® Listening & Reading Test のテスト結果は合格・不合格ではなく、リスニングセクション 5～495 点、リーディングセクション 5～495 点、トータル 10～990 点のスコアで、5 点刻みで表示されます。このスコアは、常に評価基準を一定に保つために統計処理が行われ、英語能力に変化がない限りスコアも一定に保たれる点が大きな特長です。

テスト結果は以下の方法でお知らせいたします。
※スケジュールは、日米の祝日の影響により、遅れる場合がございます。

- **● 試験日から 17 日後：インターネットでスコア表示**
  表示開始後、ご登録 E メールアドレスへご案内のメールを送信いたしますので、TOEIC 申込サイトからログインしてご覧ください。

- **● 試験日から 19 日後：デジタル公式認定証を発行**
  スコア表示日の 2 日後を目途に、同じページで確認できます。TOEIC 申込サイトからログインしてご覧ください。

- **● 試験日から 30 日以内：公式認定証を発送**
  お申し込み時のご住所に発送いたします。

Official Score Certificate（公式認定証）のサンプル

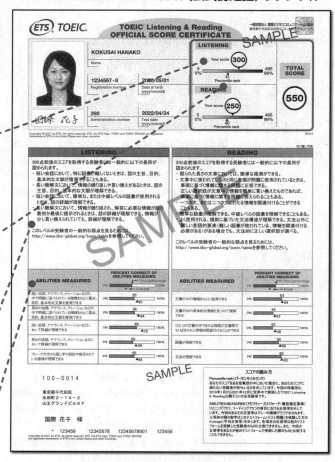

Your Score（スコア）：
今回取得したリスニング、リーディングの各セクションスコアです。右側にトータルスコアが記載されます。

Percentile Rank（パーセンタイルランク）：
あなたが取得したスコアに満たない受験者が全体でどのくらいを占めているかをパーセンテージで示しています。
例えば、リスニングでスコア 300 点、パーセンタイルランクが 41%という場合には、リスニングスコア 300 点未満の受験者が全体の 41%いることを示します。つまり、リスニングスコア 300 点を取得した受験者は上位 59%に位置することになります。

Score Descriptors（スコアディスクリプターズ）：
レベル別評価です。今回取得したスコアをもとに、あなたの英語運用能力上の長所が書かれています。

Abilities Measured（アビリティーズメジャード）：
項目別正答率です。リスニング、リーディングの 5 つの項目における正答率を示しています。

TOEIC® Listening & Reading 公開テストのお申し込み

IIBC公式サイト https://www.iibc-global.org にてテスト日程、申込方法、注意事項をご確認の上、申込受付期間内にお申し込みください。試験の実施方法などに変更があった場合には IIBC 公式サイト等でご案内いたします。

お問い合わせ

一般財団法人 国際ビジネスコミュニケーション協会　IIBC 試験運営センター
〒 100-0014　東京都千代田区永田町 2-14-2　山王グランドビル
TEL：03-5521-6033（土・日・祝日・年末年始を除く 10:00 ～ 17:00）

TEST 1

＊解答用紙は本誌 p.112 の後ろに綴じ込まれています。

実際のテストでは問題用紙の裏側に、以下のようなテスト全体についての指示が印刷されています。この指示を念頭においてテストに取り組みましょう（和訳は別冊 p.5 に掲載されています）。

General Directions

This test is designed to measure your English language ability. The test is divided into two sections: Listening and Reading.

You must mark all of your answers on the separate answer sheet. For each question, you should select the best answer from the answer choices given. Then, on your answer sheet, you should find the number of the question and fill in the space that corresponds to the letter of the answer that you have selected. If you decide to change an answer, completely erase your old answer and then mark your new answer.

LISTENING TEST

In the Listening test, you will be asked to demonstrate how well you understand spoken English. The entire Listening test will last approximately 45 minutes. There are four parts, and directions are given for each part. You must mark your answers on the separate answer sheet. Do not write your answers in your test book.

PART 1

Directions: For each question in this part, you will hear four statements about a picture in your test book. When you hear the statements, you must select the one statement that best describes what you see in the picture. Then find the number of the question on your answer sheet and mark your answer. The statements will not be printed in your test book and will be spoken only one time.

Statement (C), "They're sitting at a table," is the best description of the picture, so you should select answer (C) and mark it on your answer sheet.

1.

2.

GO ON TO THE NEXT PAGE

3.

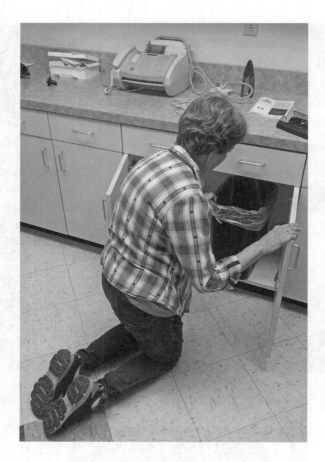

4.

5.

6.

GO ON TO THE NEXT PAGE →

PART 2

Directions: You will hear a question or statement and three responses spoken in English. They will not be printed in your test book and will be spoken only one time. Select the best response to the question or statement and mark the letter (A), (B), or (C) on your answer sheet.

7. Mark your answer on your answer sheet.

8. Mark your answer on your answer sheet.

9. Mark your answer on your answer sheet.

10. Mark your answer on your answer sheet.

11. Mark your answer on your answer sheet.

12. Mark your answer on your answer sheet.

13. Mark your answer on your answer sheet.

14. Mark your answer on your answer sheet.

15. Mark your answer on your answer sheet.

16. Mark your answer on your answer sheet.

17. Mark your answer on your answer sheet.

18. Mark your answer on your answer sheet.

19. Mark your answer on your answer sheet.

20. Mark your answer on your answer sheet.

21. Mark your answer on your answer sheet.

22. Mark your answer on your answer sheet.

23. Mark your answer on your answer sheet.

24. Mark your answer on your answer sheet.

25. Mark your answer on your answer sheet.

26. Mark your answer on your answer sheet.

27. Mark your answer on your answer sheet.

28. Mark your answer on your answer sheet.

29. Mark your answer on your answer sheet.

30. Mark your answer on your answer sheet.

31. Mark your answer on your answer sheet.

PART 3

Directions: You will hear some conversations between two or more people. You will be asked to answer three questions about what the speakers say in each conversation. Select the best response to each question and mark the letter (A), (B), (C), or (D) on your answer sheet. The conversations will not be printed in your test book and will be spoken only one time.

32. What does the woman ask about?
    (A) A parking spot
    (B) A site map
    (C) A training schedule
    (D) A catering order

33. What does the woman imply when she says, "I'm getting concerned"?
    (A) Some items are unavailable.
    (B) A delivery could be late.
    (C) A weather forecast is poor.
    (D) A schedule has been updated.

34. What event is being held?
    (A) A dance recital
    (B) A graduation rehearsal
    (C) An award ceremony
    (D) A technology exhibit

35. Why is the man calling?
    (A) He would like to place an order.
    (B) He needs to set up an account.
    (C) He needs help with a technical problem.
    (D) He would like to make an appointment.

36. What is the man's job?
    (A) Marketing associate
    (B) Fitness trainer
    (C) Data scientist
    (D) Product manager

37. Who will join the conversation?
    (A) A manager
    (B) A specialist
    (C) A salesperson
    (D) A contractor

38. What does the woman ask the man to do?
    (A) Take a photograph
    (B) Write a note
    (C) Test some software
    (D) Look at a revision

39. What type of product is mentioned?
    (A) Furniture
    (B) Mobile phones
    (C) Clothing
    (D) Headsets

40. What is causing a problem for the speakers?
    (A) A supply issue
    (B) A piece of software
    (C) A material in a product
    (D) An audio file

41. Where does the woman work?
    (A) At a pet store
    (B) At a restaurant
    (C) At a catering company
    (D) At an accounting firm

42. Why does the woman call the man?
    (A) To complain about a delay
    (B) To update an order
    (C) To acknowledge receipt of an item
    (D) To explain a delivery method

43. What does the woman say she will do?
    (A) Review a bill
    (B) Contact another employee
    (C) Help load a truck
    (D) Send a payment

GO ON TO THE NEXT PAGE

44. What event is being discussed?

(A) A training session
(B) A trade fair
(C) A job interview
(D) An investors' meeting

45. Who most likely is the man?

(A) A salesperson
(B) A teacher
(C) A computer programmer
(D) A warehouse manager

46. What does the man agree to do?

(A) Make an apology
(B) Share some suggestions
(C) Modify a meeting time
(D) Postpone a trip

47. Where most likely are the speakers?

(A) In a publisher's office
(B) In a public library
(C) In a bookstore
(D) In a classroom

48. Why does the woman say, "I usually don't like science fiction"?

(A) To decline an offer
(B) To give advice
(C) To change the subject
(D) To accept a compliment

49. What information does the man ask for?

(A) A name
(B) A phone number
(C) A due date
(D) An e-mail address

50. What are the speakers discussing?

(A) Hiring new employees
(B) Merging two companies
(C) Investing money in a company
(D) Changing an employment contract

51. Who are the women?

(A) Lawyers
(B) Doctors
(C) Investors
(D) Receptionists

52. What do the women express concern about?

(A) Agency fees
(B) Insurance costs
(C) A filing system
(D) Work experience

53. Why does the man call the woman?

(A) To change a reservation
(B) To extend a registration time
(C) To inquire about meal options
(D) To sign up for a special promotion

54. What allows the man to avoid paying a fee?

(A) A coupon
(B) A computer error
(C) A membership program
(D) An early purchase date

55. What will the man receive after the telephone call?

(A) A free sample
(B) A customer survey
(C) An updated invoice
(D) A confirmation e-mail

56. What are the speakers discussing?

(A) A news article
(B) A fund-raiser
(C) A loan application
(D) A job interview

57. What problem does the man mention?

(A) A missing document
(B) A property dispute
(C) A project delay
(D) An accounting error

58. When will the man contact Ms. Ross?

(A) Later today
(B) Tomorrow
(C) Next week
(D) Next month

59. Where does the conversation most likely take place?

(A) At a law office
(B) At a retail store
(C) At an advertising agency
(D) At a graphic design company

60. Why does the woman request a signature?

(A) To finalize a contract
(B) To obtain an employee badge
(C) To grant a parking permit
(D) To process a payment

61. What does Hiroki say he is going to do next?

(A) Greet a new client
(B) Prepare a work space
(C) Introduce staff members
(D) Review some policy changes

Blue Brook Outdoor Supplies

Receipt	July 10
Binoculars	$30
Batteries	$ 7
Utensils	$20
Hiking poles	$65
Total	$122

62. Look at the graphic. What is the price of the item the speakers are mainly discussing?

(A) $30
(B) $7
(C) $20
(D) $65

63. What does the man ask the woman for?

(A) An e-mail address
(B) A water bottle
(C) A bag
(D) A document

64. What will the woman most likely do next?

(A) Look up some information online
(B) Shop for some items
(C) Go to a different store
(D) Call her husband

GO ON TO THE NEXT PAGE

Greenview Garden Center

Garden center classes	Saturdays 10 A.M.–Noon
Soil preparation	April 2
Planning your garden	April 9
Building a frame	April 16
Dealing with pests	April 23

🚄 **Departures**

Time	Destination	Track
10:00 A.M.	Branburg	1
11:20 A.M.	Middletown	2
12:10 P.M.	Pleasantville	3
1:00 P.M.	Cashmere	4

65. Why does the man suggest attending gardening classes?

(A) He wants to start a gardening business.
(B) The speakers will be working in a garden.
(C) The classes were recommended to him.
(D) The classes are taught by his friend.

66. Look at the graphic. Which class does the woman say she can attend?

(A) Soil preparation
(B) Planning your garden
(C) Building a frame
(D) Dealing with pests

67. What does the woman say she will do next?

(A) Contact a colleague
(B) Register online
(C) Buy equipment
(D) Research local suppliers

68. Look at the graphic. What track will the speakers' train leave from?

(A) Track 1
(B) Track 2
(C) Track 3
(D) Track 4

69. What delayed the woman?

(A) Car problems
(B) A blocked railroad crossing
(C) A work emergency
(D) Bridge construction

70. What does the woman offer to do?

(A) Purchase a beverage
(B) Exchange a ticket
(C) Reserve a rental car
(D) Buy a newspaper

PART 4

Directions: You will hear some talks given by a single speaker. You will be asked to answer three questions about what the speaker says in each talk. Select the best response to each question and mark the letter (A), (B), (C), or (D) on your answer sheet. The talks will not be printed in your test book and will be spoken only one time.

71. Where is the announcement taking place?
    (A) At a music festival
    (B) At a car show
    (C) At a sports arena
    (D) At a farmers market

72. What problem does the speaker mention?
    (A) A pathway needs repairs.
    (B) A thunderstorm is predicted.
    (C) A vehicle is blocking an entryway.
    (D) A product is out of stock.

73. What are some of the listeners reminded to do?
    (A) Pick up a flyer
    (B) Enter a drawing
    (C) Bring reusable bags
    (D) Listen to a local performer

74. Where does the speaker work?
    (A) At an investment firm
    (B) At a furniture store
    (C) At an accounting office
    (D) At a manufacturing plant

75. What requirement does the listener have?
    (A) Low costs
    (B) Quick delivery
    (C) High quality
    (D) Reliable customer service

76. What financial option does the speaker mention?
    (A) A free trial
    (B) A low-interest loan
    (C) Renting to buy
    (D) Paying each month

77. According to the speaker, what has recently happened?
    (A) A building's lease has expired.
    (B) A competing theater opened.
    (C) Ticket sales have dropped.
    (D) Loan payments have been late.

78. What does the speaker want the listeners to do?
    (A) Select a new food vendor
    (B) Brainstorm alternative hiring practices
    (C) Test new theater seating
    (D) Discuss strategies to attract customers

79. What will the speaker do next?
    (A) Present an annual report
    (B) Evaluate a film contract
    (C) Introduce a guest speaker
    (D) Review recycling policies

80. Who most likely is the speaker?
    (A) An art collector
    (B) An advertising agent
    (C) A librarian
    (D) A filmmaker

81. What is the purpose of the message?
    (A) To confirm a project schedule
    (B) To discuss a new art exhibit
    (C) To request access to a collection
    (D) To organize a youth-outreach program

82. What does the speaker offer to provide?
    (A) A list of items
    (B) A signed contract
    (C) Professional certification
    (D) Examples of past work

GO ON TO THE NEXT PAGE

83. What is the speaker explaining?

    (A) How to open a craft store
    (B) How to make a display for a trade show
    (C) How to prepare for extra business
    (D) How to create new advertising

84. According to the speaker, why will a new payment option be introduced?

    (A) To reduce some costs
    (B) To speed up customer service
    (C) To meet a loan requirement
    (D) To accept online purchases

85. Why does the speaker say, "There will be training for all staff"?

    (A) To provide information about new products
    (B) To reassure workers about a new process
    (C) To remind staff of an upcoming holiday
    (D) To apply for a booth at the craft fair

86. According to the speaker, what has recently happened?

    (A) A restaurant hired a new chef.
    (B) A business received an award.
    (C) A competitor announced a new project.
    (D) An event schedule was updated.

87. Who most likely is the listener?

    (A) A professor
    (B) A photographer
    (C) A software developer
    (D) A journalist

88. What does the speaker imply when he says, "be sure to mention the *Margate Guide*"?

    (A) Mr. Fantini was given some incorrect information previously.
    (B) Mr. Fantini should subscribe to a local publication.
    (C) Mr. Fantini will be more likely to agree to an interview.
    (D) Mr. Fantini will appreciate some advice.

89. What problem does the speaker mention?

    (A) His company lost a business opportunity.
    (B) A worker is leaving the business.
    (C) The cost of materials is rising.
    (D) A business trip was canceled.

90. What type of work do the listeners most likely do?

    (A) Landscaping
    (B) Building construction
    (C) Music production
    (D) Web development

91. What does the speaker say he will know in a couple of weeks?

    (A) Whether more workers will be hired
    (B) Whether a payment was correct
    (C) Whether the city council will hold an event
    (D) Whether his business will do certain work

92. Where does the speaker work?

    (A) In a veterinary office
    (B) In a pharmacy
    (C) In a recording studio
    (D) In an accounting office

93. What does the speaker say is problematic?

    (A) A company policy
    (B) A business expansion plan
    (C) Press coverage of a recent event
    (D) Competitors' market strategies

94. Why does the speaker say, "Formal clothes can be very expensive"?

    (A) To indicate surprise at a recent trend
    (B) To provide support for a request
    (C) To correct an employee's mistake
    (D) To acknowledge a change in price

Current Discounts	
Résumé support	10%
Cover letter editing	20%
Designing business cards	30%
Interview practice	50%

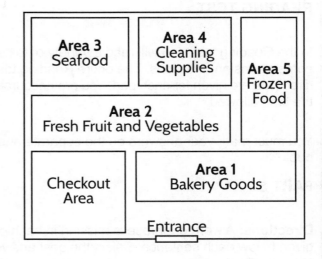

95. What is the advertisement mainly about?

(A) Providing job training
(B) Starting a new business
(C) Finding the right job
(D) Understanding customer needs

96. According to the speaker, which job has the most listings?

(A) Salesperson
(B) Editor
(C) Graphic designer
(D) IT specialist

97. Look at the graphic. Which service is mentioned in the advertisement?

(A) Résumé support
(B) Cover letter editing
(C) Designing business cards
(D) Interview practice

98. What is the purpose of the cooking demonstrations?

(A) To teach about healthy food choices
(B) To try out new cooking equipment
(C) To train some new staff
(D) To promote new store products

99. Look at the graphic. Where will a cooking demonstration be held this month?

(A) In Area 1
(B) In Area 2
(C) In Area 3
(D) In Area 4

100. What does the speaker invite the listeners to do?

(A) Suggest some recipes
(B) Change a work shift
(C) Obtain an employee discount
(D) Use a break room

This is the end of the Listening test. Turn to Part 5 in your test book.

GO ON TO THE NEXT PAGE

READING TEST

In the Reading test, you will read a variety of texts and answer several different types of reading comprehension questions. The entire Reading test will last 75 minutes. There are three parts, and directions are given for each part. You are encouraged to answer as many questions as possible within the time allowed.

You must mark your answers on the separate answer sheet. Do not write your answers in your test book.

PART 5

Directions: A word or phrase is missing in each of the sentences below. Four answer choices are given below each sentence. Select the best answer to complete the sentence. Then mark the letter (A), (B), (C), or (D) on your answer sheet.

101. Makiro Furniture customers can easily ------- the shelving units using only simple tools.
  (A) assemble
  (B) assembled
  (C) assembling
  (D) assembles

102. Mr. Zhao will ------- work on international accounts while Ms. Gutierrez is on leave.
  (A) temporarily
  (B) comparatively
  (C) nearly
  (D) highly

103. According to the builder, the ------- of the main entrance will be completed in three weeks.
  (A) renovate
  (B) renovates
  (C) renovated
  (D) renovation

104. The park will remain open ------- the weather changes dramatically.
  (A) by
  (B) unless
  (C) common
  (D) fast

105. Ms. Ansah's ------- report was excellent and needed no further revisions.
  (A) initial
  (B) initially
  (C) initiate
  (D) initiates

106. Parkfield Fruit Bars have been made ------- added sugar since 1950.
  (A) between
  (B) over
  (C) without
  (D) against

107. The sales team has provided an ------- of customer preferences.
  (A) analyze
  (B) analytical
  (C) analysis
  (D) analytically

108. Ms. Sato is considered to be ------- talented for such a young painter.
  (A) indirectly
  (B) rapidly
  (C) carefully
  (D) exceptionally

109. Next month's town festival will feature a ------- author.
  (A) celebrate
  (B) celebrates
  (C) celebrated
  (D) to celebrate

110. Car travel ------- the northern part of Willingboro will be difficult until the road repair projects are completed.

(A) through
(B) under
(C) among
(D) upon

111. Tonight's substitute ------- are listed on a separate piece of paper inserted in the theater program.

(A) perform
(B) performers
(C) performing
(D) performance

112. All cakes were ------- to customers as expected on Saturday morning.

(A) trusted
(B) delivered
(C) responded
(D) prevented

113. Beginning on August 1, the ------- Sunday lunch menu will be offered on Saturdays as well.

(A) popularity
(B) popularize
(C) popularly
(D) popular

114. Please let Ms. Choi know which staff members we will be sending as ------- to the engineering trade show.

(A) techniques
(B) pieces
(C) debtors
(D) representatives

115. New patients are advised to arrive fifteen minutes ------- their appointment time in order to complete the required paperwork.

(A) into
(B) before
(C) beside
(D) within

116. During his training period, Mr. Yun became ------- better at addressing the needs of customers.

(A) progress
(B) progressed
(C) progressive
(D) progressively

117. The flower-arranging workshop will be held in the large meeting room ------- over 30 people register by the May 1 deadline.

(A) at
(B) if
(C) even
(D) instead

118. Food display cases must be maintained at a ------- temperature to keep products fresh.

(A) steady
(B) mature
(C) punctual
(D) curious

119. The staff does not know ------- mobile phone was left behind in the conference room.

(A) neither
(B) whose
(C) nobody
(D) whoever

120. The first ------- of the Wilson Motors advertising campaign is to increase consumer awareness of the product.

(A) plant
(B) sound
(C) goal
(D) room

121. The final cost ------- only slightly from the estimate we had received earlier in the year.

(A) variety
(B) varied
(C) various
(D) variation

GO ON TO THE NEXT PAGE

122. Since Mr. Park has worked in ------- accounting and marketing, he will bring much-needed experience to Mr. Lee's team.

(A) both
(B) either
(C) whether
(D) although

123. The visitor center at Wengle corporate headquarters is located ------- across from the main entrance to the complex.

(A) direct
(B) direction
(C) directly
(D) directed

124. Washly Architects submitted a particularly ------- bid to design the new city office building.

(A) imminent
(B) competitive
(C) abandoned
(D) heavier

125. Farrier Auto Repair, ------- recently changed ownership, will expand its facilities considerably.

(A) about
(B) which
(C) so that
(D) not only

126. Our customized training sessions will show you how to make your business extremely -------.

(A) alternate
(B) existent
(C) negotiated
(D) profitable

127. Hotel guests who would like to ------- tomorrow's hike should contact the concierge, Ms. Jeong.

(A) play with
(B) look through
(C) participate in
(D) adapt to

128. Here at the Jeju Financial Group, we pride ------- on offering personalized guidance to satisfy clients' needs.

(A) us
(B) our
(C) ourselves
(D) ours

129. ------- Ms. Lim finishes filing the receipts, she can start processing the new orders.

(A) Further
(B) Also
(C) Once
(D) Rather

130. The conference center has recently become ------- with several local businesses.

(A) affiliated
(B) crafted
(C) given
(D) shown

PART 6

Directions: Read the texts that follow. A word, phrase, or sentence is missing in parts of each text. Four answer choices for each question are given below the text. Select the best answer to complete the text. Then mark the letter (A), (B), (C), or (D) on your answer sheet.

Questions 131-134 refer to the following recipe.

How to Make Dried Orange Peel

Many delicious recipes contain dried orange peel. Those cooking at home, though, will discover that dried orange peel can be difficult to find in grocery stores. Luckily, it is simple to make at home. ------- . After washing and drying the fruit, use a sharp paring knife or peeler and remove
131.
only the bright orange peel. ------- , arrange the peels on a dish in a sunny place for 2–3 days until
132.
dried and crispy. There is also a ------- way to make them. Some cooks ------- the peels in a
133.   **134.**
low-heat oven for a few hours instead.

131. (A) Dried lemon peel is also an excellent addition to many meals.
     (B) You can purchase dried orange peels on our Web site.
     (C) Start by using fresh oranges that are not bruised or soft.
     (D) Check them every fifteen minutes to be sure they do not turn brown.

132. (A) Nevertheless
     (B) Besides
     (C) Overall
     (D) Next

133. (A) cheaper
     (B) quicker
     (C) taller
     (D) earlier

134. (A) place
     (B) places
     (C) to place
     (D) had placed

GO ON TO THE NEXT PAGE

July 7

Camila and Rafael Martin
58 Hotspur Lane
Springfield, MO 63015

Dear Camila and Rafael,

Everyone at Palmyra Realty hopes you are settling into your new home. In addition to getting to know both of you, I enjoyed meeting your children when we took our last look at the property. ------- . As a token of our thanks, we will be sending you a gift certificate from Imagi Designs. I
135.
hope ------- will help you put the finishing touches on your home.
136.

Also, I have a small favor to ask of you. Palmyra Realty has been nominated for the Franklin County People's Choice Award for the best real estate agency. We love working with clients to find their ideal homes. We would certainly ------- your vote!
137.

I am always ------- for questions. And please consider Palmyra for any future transactions.
138.

All the best,

Elisa Lee
Real Estate Agent
Palmyra Realty

135. (A) There are several design experts in your neighborhood.
(B) Palmyra Realty is sincerely grateful for your business.
(C) Renting apartments has become competitive in Franklin County.
(D) I have worked in real estate for twenty years.

136. (A) he
(B) enough
(C) each
(D) it

137. (A) respond to
(B) consider
(C) appreciate
(D) understand

138. (A) avails
(B) availing
(C) available
(D) availability

Questions 139-142 refer to the following excerpt from a guidebook.

Coming into the city of Dahlberg, you will see that the skyline is dominated by a tall, pyramid-shaped ------- . This unusual building was designed by Finnish architect Erno Tuokkola.
139.
Although he is best known for designing private residences, Mr. Tuokkola also designed several public buildings in Dahlberg. ------- . Five stories tall and ------- in 2003, it contains nearly a
140. **141.**
million books. It is hard to believe that the building received ------- reviews when it was first built.
142.
Architects now rightly praise the building, and it has since become one of the city's best-loved landmarks.

139. (A) statue
(B) structure
(C) sign
(D) hill

140. (A) The Pink Pyramid, as it is often called, is home to the city's Central Library.
(B) His custom-designed homes can be seen throughout Finland.
(C) Dahlberg is located on a thin strip of land between two lakes.
(D) Mr. Tuokkola never achieved the fame of some other Finnish architects.

141. (A) completing
(B) completely
(C) completed
(D) completeness

142. (A) important
(B) independent
(C) numerous
(D) critical

GO ON TO THE NEXT PAGE

Questions 143-146 refer to the following article.

SEOUL (May 2)—Experienced local business leader Ms. Binna Hyeon will ------- Chin-Hae
                                                         143.

Communications in the role of chief operations officer. Ms. Hyeon began her career at Chin-Hae

Communications. Five years ago, she left the company to serve ------- an area manager for
                                                              144.

Bishop Technology's North American division. ------- .
                                         145.

"I'm pleased to welcome Ms. Hyeon back to Chin-Hae Communications to lead operations," said
Geon Kim, president and CEO of Chin-Hae. "Based on her record at Bishop Technology, I
believe Ms. Hyeon will be instrumental in helping Chin-Hae Communications achieve its goal of
becoming the communications leader in Asia."

Chin-Hae Communications is a major ------- of IT services for businesses in South Korea.
                                                     146.

---

143. (A) rejoin
    (B) affect
    (C) recommend
    (D) visit

144. (A) of
    (B) in
    (C) as
    (D) to

145. (A) Bishop Technology plans to close
         several facilities worldwide.
    (B) Ms. Hyeon greatly expanded Bishop
         Technology's market share in her
         area.
    (C) Bishop Technology plans to interview
         Ms. Hyeon.
    (D) The two companies once considered
         forming a partnership.

146. (A) provide
    (B) provided
    (C) providing
    (D) provider

PART 7

Directions: In this part you will read a selection of texts, such as magazine and newspaper articles, e-mails, and instant messages. Each text or set of texts is followed by several questions. Select the best answer for each question and mark the letter (A), (B), (C), or (D) on your answer sheet.

Questions 147-148 refer to the following coupon.

> Silver Sprint Grill
> Home of the Mega Fun Burger
>
> Date: May 7
>
> Congratulations! As a winner of our Wednesday night trivia quiz, you are entitled to a free appetizer or dessert. Exclusions apply. You must present this coupon to claim your prize. Coupon expires six months from the date shown above.
>
> The weekly trivia quiz is presented by DJ D'Shaun. To book D'Shaun for a private event, visit www.djdshaun.com or call 777-555-0109.

147. Who is D'Shaun?
    (A) A waiter at Silver Sprint Grill
    (B) The winner of a trivia quiz
    (C) The inventor of the Mega Fun Burger
    (D) The host of a contest

148. What is most likely true about the coupon?
    (A) It expires on May 7.
    (B) It can be exchanged for cash.
    (C) It can be used for any side order or drink.
    (D) It was issued on a Wednesday night.

GO ON TO THE NEXT PAGE

MEMO

To: All Staff
From: Maintenance
Date: Monday, March 9

Because of a delay in the delivery of some materials, repairs to the roof will not be made today. The work has been postponed until Thursday, March 12.

As previously noted, the building will remain fully accessible while the repairs are being made. However, you may experience some distractions from the sound of power tools and maintenance workers overhead. Because we are in a slow period in our production cycle, we expect the impact to be minimal.

Thank you for your cooperation as we ensure that our building is a safe and comfortable place to work. Please contact the maintenance department directly with any questions.

149. What is the purpose of the memo?

(A) To announce a schedule change
(B) To warn about hazardous conditions
(C) To seek input about needed repairs
(D) To offer a reminder about workplace safety

150. How is the work expected to affect employees?

(A) It will cause part of the building to be closed.
(B) It will create some loud noise.
(C) It will lead to some power outages.
(D) It will disrupt package deliveries.

Questions 151-152 refer to the following text-message chain.

Sarah Fuller (8:48 A.M.)
Are you going to be in the office this afternoon?

Jack Bennett (8:49 A.M.)
I am. What's going on?

Sarah Fuller (8:50 A.M.)
I just got a call that the new furniture for the lobby can be delivered early if someone is there to sign for it. I'm working from home today because my car is in the repair shop. I can't be there to sign for the furniture and show them where to put it.

Jack Bennett (8:53 A.M.)
Do you know what time it would be delivered? I was planning to leave at 4 this afternoon.

Sarah Fuller (8:55 A.M.)
Let me check.

Sarah Fuller (9:13 A.M.)
The delivery company says between 1 and 2 p.m.

Jack Bennett (9:15 A.M.)
That works for me.

Sarah Fuller (9:16 A.M.)
Thank you so much. I'll e-mail you the layout, so you can tell them where to place the furniture. It will be nice to finally get some new furniture. The lobby has looked so empty since we removed the old furniture.

151. What is indicated about Ms. Fuller?

(A) She works for a furniture delivery company.
(B) She has to leave work at 4:00 P.M.
(C) She is unable to come to the office today.
(D) She has not yet removed the old furniture.

152. At 9:15 A.M., what does Mr. Bennett most likely mean when he writes, "That works for me"?

(A) He plans to work late today.
(B) He will accept a furniture shipment.
(C) He can drive Ms. Fuller to the office.
(D) He likes the style of the new furniture.

GO ON TO THE NEXT PAGE

Questions 153-155 refer to the following Web page.

https://www.dublinwaxzoo.ie

| Home | About Us | Tickets | Contact |

The Dublin Wax Zoo is the world's first museum zoo. Visitors can see life-size wax replicas of all their favourite animals. Both children and adults are amazed when they compare their own size to the enormous replicas of the blue whale and the African elephant. The wax zoo's newest additions are now open as well: the wax primate house and the African safari trolley ride.

Tickets are €20 for adults, €14 for youths aged 12–18, and €10 for children under 12. See the Web site's ticket page to order.

And remember, parking is always free at the Dublin Wax Zoo!

153. What is suggested about the replica of the blue whale?

(A) It is the same size as a real blue whale.
(B) It has been copied for display in another wax zoo.
(C) It is exhibited outdoors.
(D) Viewing it requires an additional fee.

154. What is indicated about the wax zoo?

(A) It includes replicas of famous people.
(B) There are two new areas.
(C) The safari trolley ride has live animals.
(D) The parking garage will open soon.

155. How much is a ticket for someone who is 12 years old?

(A) €10
(B) €14
(C) €16
(D) €20

Questions 156-157 refer to the following form.

Joyous Mode Fashions
Job Application

Name: Regina Riyad
E-mail address: reginariyad@myemail.com

Question: Explain in detail why you would be a good manager at Joyous Mode Fashions. Describe relevant experience and anything else that qualifies you for the position.

Applicant Answer: I understand how challenging it can be to find clothing that is both fashionable and affordable. As a salesperson at Boutique Cecilia, where I worked for three years, I specialized in helping customers find flattering clothing within their price range. Although I was not in management, with the owner's permission I launched a text-messaging program. I notified customers of the arrival of new merchandise that I thought would suit them. In this way, I built a loyal base of repeat customers, increasing store profits by almost 20 percent per month.

I believe my retail background and the initiative I have shown make me a good choice for the manager role at Joyous Mode Fashions.

---

156. What is true of Ms. Riyad?

(A) She is applying for a bookkeeping position.
(B) She previously worked at Joyous Mode Fashions.
(C) She has several years of experience working in retail.
(D) She specializes in designing clothing.

157. Why did Ms. Riyad text customers at her previous job?

(A) To alert them to new items they might like
(B) To notify them that payments were due
(C) To offer them discounts on merchandise
(D) To notify them that their orders were ready

GO ON TO THE NEXT PAGE

To:	Seema Singh <ssingh@jademail.com>
From:	Jenny Paek <jpaek@kotarusengineering.com>
Date:	28 October
Subject:	Invoice 58202

Dear Ms. Singh,

— [1] —. On behalf of the Kotarus Engineering Company, I want to thank you for the work you did performing some much-needed data entry. Without contributions from freelance workers such as yourself, our project managers would not be able to check easily on the progress of projects or plan their schedules. We were very impressed with how quickly and accurately you were able to complete your assignments. — [2] —.

I have received and approved your invoice. It is being processed, and payment will be mailed to you within 30 days. — [3] —. If you would prefer to receive future payments by direct deposit, contact our accounts payable department. — [4] —.

Please let me know at your earliest convenience when you are available to take on additional work for Kotarus Engineering. I look forward to working with you again.

Sincerely,

Jenny Paek

158. What is a purpose of the e-mail?

(A) To process a request for direct deposit
(B) To acknowledge receipt of an invoice
(C) To invite a vendor to bid on a job
(D) To negotiate a payment amount

159. What is indicated about Ms. Singh?

(A) She works in the accounts payable department.
(B) She is a project manager.
(C) She inputs data.
(D) She travels frequently.

160. In which of the positions marked [1], [2], [3], and [4] does the following sentence best belong?

"In fact, you are among the finest consultants we have worked with."

(A) [1]
(B) [2]
(C) [3]
(D) [4]

About the Eierdorff Bio Company

Do you have a plastic product you want to bring to market? Let Eierdorff Bio help you! Whether you are searching for a new manufacturer of plastic materials or looking to switch to a more Earth-friendly option, we can help. Eierdorff Bio is one of the world's most trusted manufacturers of compostable plastic. We have worked with companies around the globe to produce everything from disposable cutlery to cell phone cases and more.

We can work with you at any stage of your business process, including designing and drafting. At our central facility in Denmark, we can meet multiple manufacturing needs, including polymer casting, 3-D printing, and injection molding. Contact one of our certified technicians today to begin bringing your product to reality!

Visit our Web site at productintros@eierdorffbio.dk for more information.

TEST 1

161. What service does Eierdorff Bio offer?

(A) Overseas moving and storage
(B) Waste management consultation
(C) Electronics repair
(D) Plastics manufacturing

162. Who most likely is the intended audience for the advertisement?

(A) Business owners
(B) Chemical engineers
(C) Environmental activists
(D) Phone technicians

163. The word "meet" in paragraph 2, line 2, is closest in meaning to

(A) encounter
(B) satisfy
(C) connect
(D) present

GO ON TO THE NEXT PAGE

```
┌─────────────────────────────────────────────────────────────────────┐
│ ▌▌▌▌▌▌▌▌▌▌▌▌▌▌▌▌▌▌▌▌        *E-mail*        ▌▌▌▌▌▌▌▌▌▌▌▌▌▌▌▌▌▌▌▌ │
├─────────────────────────────────────────────────────────────────────┤
```

To:	gmccafferty@greyharbor.ca
From:	mtoskala@norston.ca
Date:	2 June
Subject:	News from Norston

Dear Mr. McCafferty,

Thank you for being a loyal customer for the past three years. As the premier business-to-business provider of office supplies for North America, we at Norston are constantly renewing our stock. Although our annual catalogue shipped out two months ago, we wanted to alert you to some product updates that have occurred since then.

• Our Eikennen office chair is now priced at $149 instead of $179.

• The Votna desk now comes in mahogany and oak in addition to cedar.

• The Bygden filing cabinet is available in white and grey in addition to black.

• Our Glamnor videoconference camera now includes a built-in microphone.

We also want to announce the long-awaited launch of our new Web site: www.norston.ca. There you can sign up for our weekly newsletter, which is full of updates and great deals. The first 50 subscribers are eligible to win a new Tyrgo laser printer worth $350!

Sincerely,

Mia Toskala
Norston

---

164. What is the main purpose of the e-mail?

(A) To thank a customer for a recent purchase
(B) To announce some inventory changes
(C) To request a contract renewal
(D) To apologize for a delayed release

165. What is indicated about Norston?

(A) It manages many retail outlets.
(B) It mails catalogs every two months.
(C) It sells primarily to other companies.
(D) It sells office furniture exclusively.

166. What is indicated about the Eikennen chair?

(A) Its price was lowered.
(B) Its materials were changed.
(C) Its color options were increased.
(D) Its design became sturdier.

167. How can Norston customers potentially receive a free promotional item?

(A) By placing an order from the catalog
(B) By subscribing to a newsletter
(C) By giving feedback on a new Web site
(D) By purchasing three or more products

NORTH CITY NEWS

Local shoe store thrives in digital age

NORTH CITY (October 18)—It is uncommon for independent retailers to stay viable long enough to celebrate their sixtieth anniversary. One of these rare businesses is Morro's Shoe Store, a popular athletic footwear seller on Twelfth Avenue owned by resident Stan Morro. It has even thrived amid competition from online retailers. — [1] —. Mr. Morro's father, Patrick, established the store after he moved from Detmar Valley to North City. The elder Morro had learned about the shoe industry from working in several shoe stores in Detmar Valley. After moving, he opened his store in North City on Fortieth Avenue. When the younger Morro took over the business, he moved the shop to its current location on Twelfth Avenue.

Stan Morro received a stroke of luck when North University built a new regional campus in the city. "Thanks to the university's sports programs, demand for athletic shoes really took off," he said. "We also expanded our selection of merchandise to offer shoes in all sizes and styles." — [2] —. To keep up with business trends, he launched an online shop a few years ago. However, he noted that most of his regular customers prefer to visit the store and try on shoes for themselves. He explained that online shoppers get "satisfactory" results when they order shoes made by the same brand as the worn-out shoes they are replacing. — [3] —.

Earlier in the month, *Shoe Retailing Horizons*, an industry trade magazine, named Morro's Shoe Store the third-best retailer in the region. — [4] —. Mr. Morro said that "attentive customer service" is the key to his store's success.

168. What is mentioned about Patrick Morro?

(A) He designed a line of sports shoes.
(B) He opened a store after relocating.
(C) He designed a store's Web site.
(D) He was hired to work in his son's store.

169. According to the article, what is true about North City?

(A) It has two stadiums for sporting events.
(B) It has a factory that manufactures athletic footwear.
(C) It hosts conventions for the athletic apparel industry.
(D) It is the site of a university campus.

170. What is indicated about Morro's Shoe Store?

(A) It will soon return to its original location.
(B) It is currently hiring new staff members.
(C) It has recently been recognized in another publication.
(D) It will expand in the upcoming year.

171. In which of the positions marked [1], [2], [3], and [4] does the following sentence best belong?

"Even so, many customers come to the store to exchange shoes they purchased online."

(A) [1]
(B) [2]
(C) [3]
(D) [4]

GO ON TO THE NEXT PAGE

Questions 172-175 refer to the following online chat discussion.

Sharon Li [10:55 A.M.]
Have you both entered your department's July data in the monthly sales spreadsheet yet?

Juan Ayers [10:58 A.M.]
I have not entered it yet for the mobile phone department. Why?

Sharon Li [10:59 A.M.]
Each department is supposed to enter its data by tomorrow, and I can only find the spreadsheet from the last fiscal year. Where can I find the current one? I need to enter the data for the kitchen appliance department.

Linda Davies [11:00 A.M.]
I just entered the data for the camera department. The new spreadsheet is on the company shared drive. Do you want me to send you the link?

Sharon Li [11:02 A.M.]
No—I can find it. I just didn't think to look there. Thanks so much!

Linda Davies [11:12 A.M.]
My pleasure.

172. What type of business do the writers most likely work for?

- (A) An electronics store
- (B) A sporting goods store
- (C) A clothing shop
- (D) An auto repair shop

173. What does Mr. Ayers need to do soon?

- (A) Write a sales report
- (B) Update a document
- (C) Send Ms. Li a link to the shared drive
- (D) Open a new desktop calendar

174. What does Ms. Li want to know about a new spreadsheet?

- (A) Its password
- (B) Its length
- (C) Its location
- (D) Its owner

175. At 11:12 A.M., what does Ms. Davies most likely mean when she writes, "My pleasure"?

- (A) She is pleased that a company initiative was successful.
- (B) She is happy to train some new colleagues.
- (C) She feels relieved that a workday is ending.
- (D) She is happy to help Ms. Li with her request.

GO ON TO THE NEXT PAGE

News Team Continues to Grow

PORTLAND (January 25)—Beginning next month, Chelsea Lee will join *Quetic News*. Ms. Lee spent the past ten years of her career at the *Singleton Times*. While there, she developed its podcast platform, both producing and hosting some of the most widely streamed news podcasts in the country. The podcast she hosted, *News Now*, focused on detailing each day's top stories.

Her experience with digital media was one reason that *Quetic News* wanted to bring Ms. Lee on board. Last year, it announced that it would be branching out into video and audio in addition to its print news. While Ms. Lee is among a number of journalists new to the network, she is perhaps the most well-known. She already has a large and loyal following. "We are thrilled that Ms. Lee will be joining *Quetic News*. Her extensive experience, creativity, and ability to connect with listeners will make her a valued part of our team," said Daniel Koblin, editor in chief.

Ms. Lee is developing a weekly podcast, yet to be named. Unlike her daily podcast, this show will take an in-depth look into one news story at a time. The premiere episode is scheduled for April 20.

E-Mail Message

To: Chelsea Lee <chelsea.lee@opalmail.com>
From: Michael Tan <m.tan@mailhost.com>
Subject: Best of luck!
Date: January 29

Hi, Chelsea,

I wanted to wish you good luck with your new job! Sadly, I can't make it to your going-away party next Sunday. I will be away on assignment in Detroit reporting on a car show. While I'm there, I'll be exploring a story about new technology for fuel efficiency developed by Petman Motors.

But I did want to say it's been a pleasure and privilege working with you these last few years, and I will certainly be tuning in to your new podcast.

All the best,

Michael

176. What is the purpose of the article?

(A) To announce a new employee at *Quetic News*
(B) To advertise a new service at the *Singleton Times*
(C) To detail a famous musician's career
(D) To discuss the trend of podcasting

177. What is mentioned about *Quetic News*?

(A) It was founded ten years ago.
(B) It has a fellowship program for emerging journalists.
(C) It is expanding its digital media platforms.
(D) It hosts a popular daily podcast.

178. What is mentioned in the article about a new podcast?

(A) It will be titled *News Now*.
(B) It will be aired every day of the week.
(C) Each episode will focus on one topic.
(D) Some episodes will have a guest host.

179. According to the e-mail, what will Ms. Lee most likely do next Sunday?

(A) Travel to Detroit
(B) Report on new technology
(C) Go to a car show
(D) Attend a party

180. What is likely true about Michael Tan?

(A) He is a reporter at *Quetic News*.
(B) He is Ms. Lee's new boss.
(C) He will host a television news show premiering in April.
(D) He works at the *Singleton Times*.

GO ON TO THE NEXT PAGE

More Coffee Please
Online Store Checkout

Name: James Faure
Mailing address: 3450 Pollard St., Conway, NH 03813
Order date: September 3

Order:

Code	Product	Description	Price
W025	Dancing beans mug	Ceramic coffee mug	$11.00
J999	Decca coffee grinder	Electric, 7 grind settings	$28.99
P838	Whole coffee beans, regular	5 pounds Captain dark roast	$38.99
A636	Whole coffee beans, decaffeinated	5 pounds Colombia decaffeinated	$42.99
		Shipping	$0.00
		Total	$121.97

All items are shipped from our California facility.
We offer free shipping to addresses in the United States with orders over $100.
Our products are also available in our seventeen stores throughout the United States.

Review: More Coffee Please
Reviewer: James Faure
October 8
Rating: ★★★★★

More Coffee Please opened only a few years ago, and their business has grown quickly. It is easy to see why. Their Decca coffee grinder is the best ever. I am very particular about my coffee and have used electric coffee grinders that were more expensive than this one. With the Decca grinder, whatever setting I use, the grinds are perfectly consistent. Also, their decaffeinated coffee is rich and flavorful. On top of that, their dancing beans mug looks great. Many at my office admire it. Everything they sell is worth a try.

181. What is indicated on the order form?

(A) Mr. Faure ordered both tea and coffee.
(B) Mr. Faure did not pay for shipping.
(C) Mr. Faure visited a store in California.
(D) Mr. Faure used a coupon with his order.

182. Why did Mr. Faure write a review?

(A) To describe a More Coffee Please store
(B) To complain about an order he made
(C) To recommend More Coffee Please products
(D) To advise people to drink only decaffeinated coffee

183. What does Mr. Faure indicate about the Decca product?

(A) It arrived quickly.
(B) It runs quietly.
(C) It has a low price.
(D) It grinds beans evenly.

184. What does Mr. Faure say about the decaffeinated coffee?

(A) It has a light color.
(B) It is delicious.
(C) It was sent by mistake.
(D) It was too expensive.

185. How much did Mr. Faure pay for the product that his coworkers like?

(A) $11.00
(B) $28.99
(C) $38.99
(D) $42.99

GO ON TO THE NEXT PAGE

TEST 1

Questions 186-190 refer to the following form, e-mail, and flyer.

The Black Hinge—Booking Form

Name of Main Act	*The Rick Candies*
Musical Genre	*Rhythm and Blues*
Date(s) of Performance(s)	*April 29*
Contact Name	*Santiago Martinez*
Contact E-mail	*smartinez@rapidonet.com*
Main acts must arrange their own opening acts. Who will your opening act be?	*DJ Cosmic Center, techno music*
Questions or special requests?	*Do you offer any services or amenities? We would like dressing rooms for both the main act and the opening act.*

To:	Santiago Martinez <smartinez@rapidonet.com>
From:	Yuko Miura <ymiura@theblackhinge.com>
Subject:	Booking your performance
Date:	January 17

Dear Santiago,

We've received your booking form and are delighted to welcome The Rick Candies to The Black Hinge on April 29! Regarding your special request, we can only accommodate the main act.

Here are some show details to note:

• Performance time at The Black Hinge is 7–11 P.M.

• The desired stage-time split is up to the main and opening acts, but typically the opening act plays 7–8 P.M. and the main act plays 8:30–11 P.M.

• Regarding payment, you may choose one of the following two options:

1. A $300 flat payment to be divided among the two musical acts as they see fit.

2. The proceeds of a $10-per-guest cover charge. Acts may keep the money collected at the door minus a 10% fee, which will be paid to the person who collects the cover charge from guests. This person will be provided by The Black Hinge.

• We can provide a table for you to sell your band's merchandise, but no staff from The Black Hinge will be available to supervise the table.

Sincerely,

Yuko Miura

THE RICK CANDIES
featuring special guest DJ Cosmic Center

April 29 @ The Black Hinge, Chicago
Cover Charge: $10
7–8 P.M.: DJ Cosmic Center
8:30–11 P.M.: The Rick Candies

Join us for an unforgettable night with The Rick Candies, four soulful rhythm and blues performers from Peoria. The quartet takes its inspiration from the legends who pioneered the music we love. Come early to hear DJ Cosmic Center kick things off with an eclectic techno music set. Merchandise will be available for sale after the show.

186. In the e-mail, what is indicated about selling merchandise?

(A) The Black Hinge prohibits sales of merchandise inside the venue.
(B) The Black Hinge takes a percentage of sales.
(C) The band can sell T-shirts through The Black Hinge's Web site.
(D) The band must provide its own staff to sell any merchandise.

187. What amenity will the main act receive?

(A) Snacks
(B) Beverages
(C) A dressing room
(D) Transportation to and from the venue

188. Who most likely is Ms. Miura?

(A) A cook at The Black Hinge
(B) A social media consultant
(C) A security officer
(D) A booking manager

189. What decision did The Rick Candies make about the performance?

(A) To replace the opening act
(B) To include dancers in the performance
(C) To take payment from a cover charge
(D) To have a different time split than Ms. Miura recommended

190. What does the flyer indicate about The Rick Candies?

(A) The group consists of four performers.
(B) The group's members are from Chicago.
(C) The group plays techno music.
(D) The group's members are performing together for the first time.

GO ON TO THE NEXT PAGE

Breeman's Bakery

We bake with the freshest fruits! No artificial flavoring or preservatives!

Muffins—We offer bran, blueberry, and banana nut. Buy ten and get one for free!

Cakes—Try our chocolate, vanilla, and lemon flavors with your choice of icing and fruit filling. All cakes are made to order. Please allow two days for orders to be filled.

Cookies—We only make chocolate chip, but they are the best!

Pies—Choose from five fruit fillings. Pies are available both fresh and frozen.

A full product list is available at www.breemansbakery.com. Order online or call (208) 555-0112.

Early Winter Storm

IDAHO FALLS (November 14)—The area's first winter storm arrived early today, Thursday morning, leaving significant snowfall. Many highways and local roads will be closed throughout Thursday. By Friday morning, most major roads should be open again. The cold spell will not last long, as the forecast for Friday, Saturday, and Sunday is for temperatures slightly above freezing.

On a positive note, winter sports enthusiasts can prepare to enjoy themselves earlier than usual this year. According to meteorologist Elizabeth Merkot, residents can expect heavy snows to occur early this winter. "Last year, the region's winter sports facilities did not open until the middle of December, but this year they plan to open at the end of November. Get your gear ready and make your reservations!"

```
┌─────────────────────────────────────────────────────────────────┐
│                          *E-mail*                                 │
├─────────────────────────────────────────────────────────────────┤
│  To:        Dennis Hattori <dhattori86@jackanddennisgrocery.com>  │
│  From:      Laura Breeman <lbreeman@breemansbakery.com>           │
│  Date:      November 14                                           │
│  Re:        Today's snowstorm                                     │
├─────────────────────────────────────────────────────────────────┤
```

Dear Mr. Hattori,

This message is about two issues with your Breeman's Bakery orders. First, because of the unexpected storm, our drivers will not be going out today. Will it be acceptable if we deliver your fresh items tomorrow?

The second issue is regarding your order for December. I need to let you know about a change we make to our order form every winter. Starting in December, when supplies of fresh fruit are harder to get, we bake a smaller assortment of products. When I took your December order over the phone, I forgot to take this into consideration. Please visit our updated Web site to resubmit your December order.

Thank you for your flexibility.

Sincerely,

Laura Breeman
Owner, Breeman's Bakery

191. According to the flyer, how do the pies differ from other Breeman's Bakery items?

(A) They must be ordered two days in advance.
(B) The minimum order for them is ten.
(C) They are sold in various sizes.
(D) They are available frozen as well as fresh.

192. What does the article recommend that local residents do?

(A) Participate in outdoor activities
(B) Go to a movie theater
(C) Learn to bake at home
(D) Visit Idaho Falls on Thursday

193. According to the e-mail, why does Breeman's Bakery change its order form every winter?

(A) Its drivers need more time to make deliveries.
(B) It begins selling special holiday items.
(C) It is unable to obtain a wide variety of fresh fruits.
(D) It increases the assortment of items for sale.

194. What products are NOT affected by the change in the order form?

(A) Muffins
(B) Cakes
(C) Cookies
(D) Pies

195. According to Ms. Breeman, when can the driver deliver Mr. Hattori's order?

(A) On Thursday
(B) On Friday
(C) On Saturday
(D) On Sunday

GO ON TO THE NEXT PAGE →

Free Roofing Estimates from Ellwood Roofs!

The roof on this building was recently repaired by Ellwood Roofs. Does your roof need work? We can help you with the following.

- Damage from hail or falling tree branches

- Leaks from age and normal wear

- Problems arising from poorly installed roofing

When you contact us for an appointment, mention the address where you saw this sign and get a 10 percent discount!

Contact Ellwood Roofs at 202-555-0116 or info@ellwoodroofs.com.

To:	Information <info@ellwoodroofs.com>
From:	Ned Kuan <nkuan@porterwillcondominiums.com>
Date:	September 19
Subject:	Roof work

To Whom It May Concern:

I manage Porterwill Condominiums, and we have had some damage from the recent storms. I saw your sign at 124 Sagamore Drive in Carnville.

I was wondering what kind of a price you could offer me for repairing the roofs of six buildings. All the roofs have the same dimensions, and they all have asphalt shingles. However, in cases where the damage is serious, I would consider replacing those roofs with metal, wooden, or composite shingles.

Please let me know when we can meet to discuss this.

Thanks,

Ned Kuan, Porterwill Condominiums

E-mail

To:	Ned Kuan <nkuan@porterwillcondominiums.com>
From:	Guillermo Ellwood <gellwood@ellwoodroofs.com>
Date:	September 20
Subject:	RE: Roof work

Dear Ned,

Thanks for getting in touch. We offer additional discounts when we undertake larger projects such as the one you are describing. So I'm sure we can arrive at a pricing arrangement we will both be happy with.

Let me see the kind of damage you are describing. If we can preserve most of the original roof, then sticking with the original material will save you a great deal of money. I can come by next Monday to see things for myself.

Thanks,

Guillermo Ellwood, Owner, Ellwood Roofs

---

196. Where is the sign for Ellwood Roofs most likely located?

(A) On a highway billboard
(B) In a bus station
(C) In a hotel lobby
(D) In front of a building

197. According to the first e-mail, how were the condominium roofs damaged?

(A) By animals
(B) By storms
(C) By age
(D) By inexperienced workers

198. Why most likely did Mr. Kuan mention where he had seen the sign?

(A) To get a 10 percent discount
(B) To provide a reason for moving the sign
(C) To show where his condominiums are located
(D) To specify the type of roof he would like

199. Why does Mr. Ellwood express certainty about an arrangement?

(A) Because Mr. Kuan needs to have his roofs repaired immediately
(B) Because he and Mr. Kuan have already settled on a material
(C) Because Ellwood Roofs offers discounts on large projects
(D) Because he and Mr. Kuan have already spent a lot of time negotiating

200. What shingle material would enable Mr. Kuan to save the most money?

(A) Asphalt
(B) Wood
(C) Metal
(D) Composite

Stop! This is the end of the test. If you finish before time is called, you may go back to Parts 5, 6, and 7 and check your work.

NO TEST MATERIAL ON THIS PAGE

TEST 2

CD 2
01-82

＊解答用紙は本誌 p.112 の後ろに綴じ込まれています。

実際のテストでは問題用紙の裏側に、以下のようなテスト全体についての指示が印刷されています。
この指示を念頭においてテストに取り組みましょう（和訳は別冊 p.5 に掲載されています）。

General Directions

This test is designed to measure your English language ability. The test is divided into two sections: Listening and Reading.

You must mark all of your answers on the separate answer sheet. For each question, you should select the best answer from the answer choices given. Then, on your answer sheet, you should find the number of the question and fill in the space that corresponds to the letter of the answer that you have selected. If you decide to change an answer, completely erase your old answer and then mark your new answer.

LISTENING TEST

In the Listening test, you will be asked to demonstrate how well you understand spoken English. The entire Listening test will last approximately 45 minutes. There are four parts, and directions are given for each part. You must mark your answers on the separate answer sheet. Do not write your answers in your test book.

PART 1

Directions: For each question in this part, you will hear four statements about a picture in your test book. When you hear the statements, you must select the one statement that best describes what you see in the picture. Then find the number of the question on your answer sheet and mark your answer. The statements will not be printed in your test book and will be spoken only one time.

Statement (C), "They're sitting at a table," is the best description of the picture, so you should select answer (C) and mark it on your answer sheet.

1.

2.

GO ON TO THE NEXT PAGE

3.

4.

5.

6.

GO ON TO THE NEXT PAGE

PART 2

Directions: You will hear a question or statement and three responses spoken in English. They will not be printed in your test book and will be spoken only one time. Select the best response to the question or statement and mark the letter (A), (B), or (C) on your answer sheet.

7. Mark your answer on your answer sheet.

8. Mark your answer on your answer sheet.

9. Mark your answer on your answer sheet.

10. Mark your answer on your answer sheet.

11. Mark your answer on your answer sheet.

12. Mark your answer on your answer sheet.

13. Mark your answer on your answer sheet.

14. Mark your answer on your answer sheet.

15. Mark your answer on your answer sheet.

16. Mark your answer on your answer sheet.

17. Mark your answer on your answer sheet.

18. Mark your answer on your answer sheet.

19. Mark your answer on your answer sheet.

20. Mark your answer on your answer sheet.

21. Mark your answer on your answer sheet.

22. Mark your answer on your answer sheet.

23. Mark your answer on your answer sheet.

24. Mark your answer on your answer sheet.

25. Mark your answer on your answer sheet.

26. Mark your answer on your answer sheet.

27. Mark your answer on your answer sheet.

28. Mark your answer on your answer sheet.

29. Mark your answer on your answer sheet.

30. Mark your answer on your answer sheet.

31. Mark your answer on your answer sheet.

PART 3

Directions: You will hear some conversations between two or more people. You will be asked to answer three questions about what the speakers say in each conversation. Select the best response to each question and mark the letter (A), (B), (C), or (D) on your answer sheet. The conversations will not be printed in your test book and will be spoken only one time.

32. Where does the woman work?
    (A) At a museum
    (B) At a corporate headquarters
    (C) At a health clinic
    (D) At a television studio

33. Why is the man calling?
    (A) To confirm a business trip
    (B) To cancel an interview
    (C) To discuss some test results
    (D) To reschedule an appointment

34. What will the man do next?
    (A) Download some files
    (B) Provide an identification number
    (C) Check a calendar
    (D) Complete a payment

35. What are the speakers mainly discussing?
    (A) A staff training initiative
    (B) A sales call
    (C) A funding increase
    (D) A business trip

36. What is the man looking forward to?
    (A) A signing ceremony
    (B) A quarterly meeting
    (C) Interviewing job applicants
    (D) Conducting market research

37. What does the woman say about a budget committee?
    (A) She is not happy with the committee's decision.
    (B) She will not head the committee next year.
    (C) The committee has hired new staff.
    (D) The committee should meet more often.

38. Where most likely do the speakers work?
    (A) At a restaurant
    (B) At a grocery store
    (C) At a factory
    (D) At a shipping company

39. What problem does the man discuss?
    (A) Some product information is incorrect.
    (B) Some items arrived broken.
    (C) Some expenses have increased.
    (D) Some equipment is not working.

40. What does the man suggest that the woman do?
    (A) Conduct an interview
    (B) Update a payment method
    (C) Contact a supplier
    (D) Update some staff members

41. What is the man planning to do?
    (A) Renovate a home
    (B) Attend a concert
    (C) Purchase a building
    (D) Hold a training seminar

42. Why does the woman say, "We're having new flooring installed"?
    (A) To reject a suggestion
    (B) To explain a benefit
    (C) To make a request
    (D) To provide directions

43. What will the woman do next?
    (A) Write a letter
    (B) Clean a patio
    (C) Check a booking schedule
    (D) Cancel a reservation

GO ON TO THE NEXT PAGE

TEST 2

44. Where is the conversation taking place?

(A) At a train station
(B) In a restaurant
(C) In a conference room
(D) At a shopping center

45. Why does the man request a change?

(A) An event was moved.
(B) A product was not delivered.
(C) A meeting was postponed.
(D) A service was canceled.

46. What does Sara suggest?

(A) Visiting a tourist attraction
(B) Making a dinner reservation
(C) Rescheduling a meeting
(D) Working on a presentation

47. Where does the conversation take place?

(A) In a florist shop
(B) In an assembly room
(C) In an electronics store
(D) In a restaurant

48. What problem does the man mention?

(A) A poor sound system
(B) Bad lighting
(C) Not enough seats
(D) A late delivery

49. Why will the woman talk to Ms. Sasaki?

(A) To help prepare a speech
(B) To reserve a meeting room
(C) To check on a florist-shop order
(D) To get help with some equipment

50. What does the man want to know?

(A) Whether an applicant was hired
(B) Whether a deadline was extended
(C) Whether an announcement was made
(D) Whether a research project has begun

51. What does the woman imply when she says, "The meeting isn't over yet"?

(A) A suggestion will be used.
(B) A technical problem has been resolved.
(C) A security office has not been contacted.
(D) A decision has not been revealed.

52. What does the woman suggest about the battery project?

(A) It was originally her idea.
(B) It may not make money at first.
(C) It is nearly completed.
(D) It will be sold to another company.

53. Where does the conversation most likely take place?

(A) In a classroom
(B) In an automobile dealership
(C) In an electronics store
(D) In a newspaper office

54. Why does the man get the manager?

(A) To address a complaint
(B) To report some damage
(C) To unlock a display case
(D) To show a sample product

55. What will happen after Sunday?

(A) A new shipment will arrive.
(B) A discount will no longer be in effect.
(C) A repair will be completed.
(D) A new employee will start work.

56. What part of the company do the speakers work in?

(A) Finance
(B) Product development
(C) Information technology
(D) Sales

57. What does the man say about a company dinner?

(A) He will meet a new client there.
(B) He is helping with preparations for it.
(C) He may not be able to attend.
(D) He would like to bring a guest.

58. What does the woman say she will check?

(A) Some meeting notes
(B) A guest list
(C) Some company policies
(D) A corporate calendar

59. What are the speakers mainly discussing?

(A) Media coverage of their company's products
(B) Advertising options for new products
(C) Additional employees for a product launch
(D) Testing of a new product line

60. What are the speakers impressed with?

(A) The durability of a product
(B) Cost-saving measures
(C) The visual appeal of a product
(D) The positive reputation of a company

61. What does the woman offer to do?

(A) Organize a meeting
(B) Take some pictures
(C) Conduct some interviews
(D) Send some results

Downtown Office	
Role	**Main Contact**
Technology support	Emily Kalkhof
Case-intake lead	Lucas Betz
Office manager	Eun-Young Jun
Paralegal manager	Joyce Reno

62. What is the woman calling about?

(A) A shipment
(B) A job listing
(C) A product review
(D) A schedule change

63. What problem does the woman mention?

(A) A flaw in a product
(B) Difficulty finding a building
(C) A long commute
(D) A Web site error

64. Look at the graphic. Who will the woman speak with next?

(A) Emily Kalkhof
(B) Lucas Betz
(C) Eun-Young Jun
(D) Joyce Reno

TEST 2

GO ON TO THE NEXT PAGE

Directory

Department	Floor
Accounting	2
Printing	3
Newsroom	4
Editorial Services	5

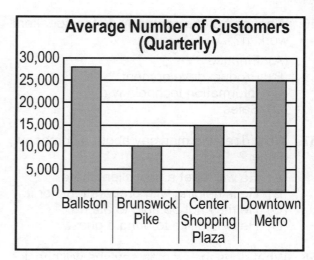

65. Look at the graphic. Where is the woman's appointment?

(A) On floor 2
(B) On floor 3
(C) On floor 4
(D) On floor 5

66. What does the man warn the woman about?

(A) A broken air conditioner
(B) A canceled delivery
(C) Employee absences
(D) Crowds in the building

67. What does the man ask the woman to do?

(A) Submit a payment
(B) Fill out a form
(C) Book an appointment
(D) Call a coworker

68. Look at the graphic. Which store did the woman visit today?

(A) Ballston
(B) Brunswick Pike
(C) Center Shopping Plaza
(D) Downtown Metro

69. Why is the woman concerned?

(A) A facility failed a test.
(B) A store closed early.
(C) More staff may be needed.
(D) New designs are not approved.

70. What does the man suggest?

(A) Visiting more stores
(B) Creating some advertisements
(C) Launching an online survey
(D) Purchasing more inventory

PART 4

Directions: You will hear some talks given by a single speaker. You will be asked to answer three questions about what the speaker says in each talk. Select the best response to each question and mark the letter (A), (B), (C), or (D) on your answer sheet. The talks will not be printed in your test book and will be spoken only one time.

71. What information does the speaker give the listener?

(A) A policy has changed.
(B) A construction plan is being reviewed.
(C) An advertising campaign has started.
(D) A permit request was approved.

72. What does the speaker say the listener should do next?

(A) Submit a traffic-control plan
(B) Write a summary of the film's story
(C) Confirm a project schedule
(D) Attend an information session

73. What can the listener do to make the process happen more quickly?

(A) Pay an additional fee
(B) Use an online portal
(C) Make an in-person delivery
(D) Provide an e-mail address

74. Why does the speaker thank the listeners?

(A) For participating in a survey
(B) For carpooling to work
(C) For taking an additional shift
(D) For attracting new customers

75. What will the listeners do first?

(A) Load some trucks
(B) Paint an office
(C) Complete a sale
(D) Design a new product

76. Why should the listeners speak to Mary?

(A) To sign in
(B) To request an identification card
(C) To arrange payment details
(D) To give a lunch order

77. Where does the speaker work?

(A) At a restaurant
(B) At a shopping mall
(C) At a concert hall
(D) At a museum

78. What does the speaker recommend?

(A) Reading a biography
(B) Taking a break
(C) Watching a film
(D) Purchasing souvenirs

79. What does the speaker tell the listeners to do?

(A) Remain silent
(B) Take some notes
(C) Scan their tickets
(D) Open some books

80. What does the speaker want to discuss?

(A) A television program
(B) A product demonstration
(C) A hiring event
(D) A store opening

81. What does the speaker imply when she says, "The phone has easily passed all internal testing"?

(A) She thinks sales targets will be met.
(B) She hopes to receive good reviews.
(C) She believes a program needs changes.
(D) She agrees with a staff suggestion.

82. What does the speaker ask the listeners to do?

(A) Send a list of preferences
(B) Attend a training
(C) View a presentation
(D) Test a product

TEST 2

83. What will the speaker most likely attend?

(A) A museum opening
(B) A concert
(C) An awards ceremony
(D) A sports event

84. Why does the speaker say, "We plan to take public transportation"?

(A) To suggest that there will be good weather
(B) To show that a distance is very short
(C) To explain a request
(D) To indicate that some traffic is expected

85. What does the speaker mention about an e-mail?

(A) Some documents were not included.
(B) Some links to certain Web sites did not work.
(C) It should be forwarded to others.
(D) It contained clear instructions for a task.

86. What does the factory produce?

(A) Furniture
(B) Automobiles
(C) Clothing
(D) Appliances

87. What does the speaker say about a machine?

(A) It is new.
(B) It has been ordered.
(C) It is malfunctioning.
(D) It requires special training.

88. According to the speaker, what might human resources do next?

(A) Arrange for promotions
(B) Hire some additional workers
(C) Allow staff to work overtime
(D) Provide additional health benefits

89. What type of event is being held?

(A) A running race
(B) A holiday parade
(C) A speech
(D) A seasonal sale

90. According to the speaker, why is the event special?

(A) More people are expected to participate than in the past.
(B) It features local products.
(C) It has happened for 50 years.
(D) Admission is free.

91. What does the speaker recommend some of the listeners do?

(A) Try some new equipment
(B) Select seats online
(C) Bring a friend
(D) Arrive early

92. What is the topic of the broadcast?

(A) International sports
(B) Classical music
(C) Community news
(D) Home-improvement advice

93. According to the speaker, what should the listeners do on a Web site?

(A) Submit reviews
(B) View interviews with visitors
(C) Download information about the museum
(D) Read about local art classes

94. Why does the speaker say, "You could be next"?

(A) To suggest that the listeners enter a contest
(B) To encourage the listeners to call in
(C) To recommend a local restaurant
(D) To promote a job fair

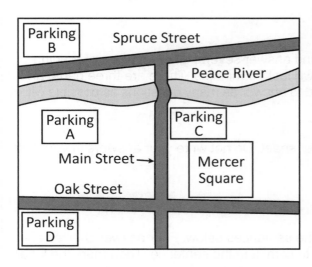

Advertisement Stage	Advertisement Type
1	TV
2	Radio
3	Internet
4	Newspaper

95. What kind of event is the speaker discussing?

(A) A local festival
(B) An art exhibition
(C) An automobile show
(D) A bicycle race

96. What kind of company do the listeners work for?

(A) A catering company
(B) A cookware retailer
(C) An art supply store
(D) A parking facility

97. Look at the graphic. Where are the listeners told to park?

(A) Parking A
(B) Parking B
(C) Parking C
(D) Parking D

98. What product category is being discussed?

(A) Vehicles
(B) Electronics
(C) Appliances
(D) Clothes

99. Look at the graphic. Which stage is the group in?

(A) Stage 1
(B) Stage 2
(C) Stage 3
(D) Stage 4

100. What does the speaker ask the listeners to do?

(A) Interview a colleague about their work experience
(B) Evaluate some advertising submissions from a vendor
(C) Test a product
(D) Produce some work samples

This is the end of the Listening test. Turn to Part 5 in your test book.

GO ON TO THE NEXT PAGE

READING TEST

In the Reading test, you will read a variety of texts and answer several different types of reading comprehension questions. The entire Reading test will last 75 minutes. There are three parts, and directions are given for each part. You are encouraged to answer as many questions as possible within the time allowed.

You must mark your answers on the separate answer sheet. Do not write your answers in your test book.

PART 5

Directions: A word or phrase is missing in each of the sentences below. Four answer choices are given below each sentence. Select the best answer to complete the sentence. Then mark the letter (A), (B), (C), or (D) on your answer sheet.

101. Ms. Choi will explain some of the ------- features of the new marketing software.

(A) excite
(B) exciting
(C) excitedly
(D) excitement

102. The admission ------- at the Altkirch Museum is €13 for nonmembers.

(A) fee
(B) view
(C) curve
(D) doorway

103. Topscore Auto Parts uses modern inventory systems to replenish its stock -------.

(A) continue
(B) continually
(C) continuation
(D) continual

104. A new market will be located ------- Mason's Automobile Dealership and the Grace Theater.

(A) down
(B) along
(C) across
(D) between

105. Marketing has not yet decided ------- sandals to feature during Folberg Shoes' spring sale.

(A) which
(B) that
(C) this
(D) those

106. The principal of Wilson Oak Primary School ------- students as they arrived for their first day.

(A) depended
(B) planned
(C) greeted
(D) wondered

107. Zelwick Fashions will open its outlet in the suburbs ------- in the center of the city.

(A) out of
(B) by far
(C) rather than
(D) less than

108. Although some water from the storm entered the shop's basement, there was no -------.

(A) recount
(B) damage
(C) caution
(D) bargain

109. Irons and ironing boards are available to Stennett Hotel guests upon -------.

(A) request
(B) to request
(C) requested
(D) requester

110. The finance department ------- reviews its quarterly statements carefully before they are released.

(A) always
(B) ahead
(C) somewhat
(D) almost

111. Though Bylertech's new video game is still being developed, some of its features have already been -------.

(A) reveal
(B) revealed
(C) revealingly
(D) to reveal

112. Ms. Takahashi's business trip will begin next Monday, ------- she leaves for Paris.

(A) when
(B) despite
(C) such as
(D) as well as

113. Because Mr. Lau has shown great ------- to his team, he was promoted to senior manager.

(A) dedicate
(B) dedicated
(C) dedicating
(D) dedication

114. Employees named to the innovations team should decide ------- themselves how to divide the work.

(A) under
(B) among
(C) about
(D) from

115. Leeds Accounting Group is seeking an administrative assistant ------- a variety of office tasks.

(A) performs
(B) performed
(C) is performing
(D) to perform

116. At Thimbleweeds, the prices of carpets are fixed, so customers do not have to worry about ------- costs.

(A) recruitment
(B) added
(C) observed
(D) accommodation

117. Based on her ------- approach to land-use management, Ms. Yoon was appointed to the Fairview Development Committee.

(A) thinks
(B) thinker
(C) thoughtful
(D) thoughtfulness

118. Westville Research employees have the leadership skills needed to ------- one or more assigned projects.

(A) disturb
(B) involve
(C) reduce
(D) oversee

119. Almost all of Samsoline's new fitness centers became ------- within the first year of business.

(A) profit
(B) profited
(C) profitably
(D) profitable

120. The ------- of sweet chocolate and salty toppings has made Kimmy's Coated Pretzels a sales success.

(A) maintenance
(B) resistance
(C) understanding
(D) combination

GO ON TO THE NEXT PAGE ▶

121. Northland Spices ------- large amounts of paperwork when its new tracking software becomes operational.

(A) will eliminate
(B) eliminating
(C) to eliminate
(D) has eliminated

122. Springfield has completed renovations on the town hall to make it more ------- to all visitors.

(A) accessible
(B) eager
(C) tactful
(D) abrupt

123. Anberg Telecommunications sends customers monthly ------- of upcoming payment deadlines.

(A) reminded
(B) reminds
(C) reminders
(D) to remind

124. The city has ------- increased the budget to better support community programs.

(A) substantially
(B) nearly
(C) accidentally
(D) tightly

125. New patients should arrive early ------- that they have time to fill out the required paperwork.

(A) so
(B) because
(C) for
(D) even

126. BD's Car Services may have to ------- its hiring policy in light of the worker shortage.

(A) filter
(B) locate
(C) reconsider
(D) see

127. ------- volunteers to organize the retirement party for Ms. Chung will need to invite her family.

(A) Whom
(B) When
(C) Whose
(D) Whoever

128. The marine-biology building will be named after Dr. Mellisa Vasquez, who has conducted ------- research on dolphins.

(A) sociable
(B) groundbreaking
(C) amused
(D) cluttered

129. To meet increased customer demand just before the holiday, salesclerks had to work ------- more hours than usual.

(A) signify
(B) signified
(C) significant
(D) significantly

130. Highlake Toys sends a confirmation message to customers ------- they place an order online.

(A) during
(B) in particular
(C) along with
(D) as soon as

PART 6

Directions: Read the texts that follow. A word, phrase, or sentence is missing in parts of each text. Four answer choices for each question are given below the text. Select the best answer to complete the text. Then mark the letter (A), (B), (C), or (D) on your answer sheet.

Questions 131-134 refer to the following article.

Construction of Research Facility to Begin

KANSAS CITY (February 10)—Next month, construction will begin on a new research facility on Glenmore University's campus. The project ------- in collaboration with Lansing Pharmaceuticals.
131.
The facility will be a cutting-edge research center featuring state-of-the-art equipment.
------- , it will offer expanded opportunities for faculty and students in the university's
132.
world-renowned biomedical engineering programs.

Glenmore University has long been an important part of Kansas City's ------- . Once finished, the
133.
new research facility will bring hundreds of additional jobs to the community. ------- .
134.

131. (A) to finance
    (B) will finance
    (C) is being financed
    (D) to be financed

132. (A) Additionally
    (B) Although
    (C) For instance
    (D) As long as

133. (A) protocol
    (B) economy
    (C) routine
    (D) training

134. (A) Cooperation between universities and corporations has increased.
    (B) Glenmore University offers 105 graduate programs.
    (C) Lansing Pharmaceuticals was founded in 1956.
    (D) The project is expected to be completed in three years.

GO ON TO THE NEXT PAGE

Village Brook Hotel and Conference Center: Guest Review

I recently coordinated a conference at Village Brook and had a very positive experience. Though large, the hotel is well laid out and thus easy ------- . The hotel staff were all extremely
135.
knowledgeable and supportive. ------- . They made my job quite easy.
136.

The conference center and hotel are connected. Therefore, the facilities were ------- for the
137.
attendees who stayed overnight.

The hotel rooms themselves were a bit small, but they were comfortable and clean. Some attendees with street-facing rooms said traffic could be loud at night. So, if ------- is a concern,
138.
request rooms facing the courtyard instead of facing the street.

–S. Bak

---

135. (A) to navigate
(B) navigation
(C) navigator
(D) to have navigated

136. (A) Village Brook consistently earns high customer ratings.
(B) We got a reduced rate on rooms because we booked as a group.
(C) They even helped me plan a special dinner at a restaurant in town.
(D) I was expecting the rooms to be larger.

137. (A) optional
(B) convenient
(C) understandable
(D) important

138. (A) choice
(B) space
(C) usage
(D) noise

From: Kyung-Sook Gwan <ksookgwan@towen.ca>
To: Nancy Davis <ndavis75@mailcrate.com>
Date: 2 December
Subject: Cowriting opportunities

Dear Ms. Davis,

Let me begin by introducing myself. I am Kyung-Sook Gwan, and I ------- Towen Ltd., a leading
                                                                      139.
publisher based in Vancouver. I was referred to you by Dr. James Wilen, ------- said you were
                                                                         140.
invaluable as a cowriter for the Brinwald Life Science Series.

I would like to speak with you about several writing opportunities. Towen Ltd. is working with a
number of ------- physicians. In fact, they are widely recognized experts in their fields.
          141.
Nevertheless, they need assistance from experienced cowriters such as you with developing
their manuscripts.

I believe we have some opportunities you would enjoy. ------- .
                                                       142.

Sincerely,

Kyung-Sook Gwan

TEST 2

139. (A) represent
     (B) represents
     (C) representing
     (D) representative

140. (A) which
     (B) what
     (C) when
     (D) who

141. (A) extensive
     (B) standard
     (C) prominent
     (D) thankful

142. (A) Your book was published three weeks
         ago.
     (B) We are pleased to offer you a full-time
         teaching position.
     (C) I am very sorry for any issues this has
         caused.
     (D) Please contact me whenever you are
         able.

GO ON TO THE NEXT PAGE

Questions 143-146 refer to the following notice.

Cromley City Recycling Guidance

Recycling Center – 11 North Water Street   *Web site – www.cromleyrecycle.com*

------- . **143.** Residents who miss their recycling collection day are encouraged to drop off their recyclable items at the Cromley City Recycling Center. The center is open 24 hours a day, seven days a week, and we have clearly marked bins ------- **144.** acceptable recycling materials. If you are uncertain about ------- **145.** your items can be recycled, visit our Web site and go to the "Recycling Inquiry" section.

Computers and other types of electronic waste are accepted only during regular business hours, from 8:00 A.M. to 4:00 P.M., when employees are on duty. The center is not ------- **146.** outside business hours, and residents are prohibited from leaving electronics without checking in first.

---

143. (A) The recycling department invites the public to attend all its board meetings.
(B) Recyclables are picked up every other Thursday from all properties in the city.
(C) Once sorted, recyclables are sent on to be used for manufacturing new items.
(D) Changes to the recycling regulations are approved by the sanitation department.

144. (A) in
(B) up
(C) for
(D) than

145. (A) still
(B) another
(C) whether
(D) while

146. (A) staffed
(B) reflected
(C) capable
(D) dependable

PART 7

Directions: In this part you will read a selection of texts, such as magazine and newspaper articles, e-mails, and instant messages. Each text or set of texts is followed by several questions. Select the best answer for each question and mark the letter (A), (B), (C), or (D) on your answer sheet.

Questions 147-148 refer to the following memo.

MEMO

From: Takori Apartment Management
To: All Residents
Re: Car park
Date: 15 October

Sections 1 through 4 of the car park at the apartment complex will be closed for repair on a rotating basis in November. Please move your car to the guest parking area near the clubhouse during work on your section. Depending on what each section needs, there may be asphalt paving, seal coating, pothole repair, painting, or some combination of these four task types.

Work will begin on section 1 in early November. We will work on the sections in numerical order, and we expect that each section will take one week to complete. We apologize for any inconvenience, but as you know, this work is essential.

Thank you.

147. What is the purpose of the memo?
(A) To introduce residents to a new facility
(B) To encourage residents to attend an event
(C) To inform residents about a likely inconvenience
(D) To explain a change in plans to residents

148. According to the memo, about how long will it take for the entire project to be completed?
(A) One week
(B) Two weeks
(C) Three weeks
(D) Four weeks

GO ON TO THE NEXT PAGE

https://www.oberlanderdestinations.com/employment

Thank you for your interest in Oberlander Destinations, the world's fastest-growing resort chain. Before submitting your materials, please be sure you have done the following.

1. Completed all mandatory fields (marked with *)

2. Attached a résumé (and, optionally, a cover letter)

3. Accurately inputted your passport information (which will be encrypted for security)

4. Agreed to the Terms and Conditions

5. Checked the "Agree to Use of Electronic Signature" box and typed your full name

149. Who most likely would view the Web page?

(A) A resort guest
(B) An online shopper
(C) A customs official
(D) A job seeker

150. What is NOT a submission requirement?

(A) A résumé
(B) Passport data
(C) A cover letter
(D) An electronic signature

Elwidge Lavender Festival

A major part of every Elwidge summer for over 100 years, the Elwidge Lavender Festival attracts thousands of visitors from the region and around the world. But how did it get started? — [1] —.

In the early twentieth century, lavender was widely farmed in the areas surrounding Elwidge for use in perfumes and other toiletries. — [2] —. One year, after a dispute with an Elwidge soap maker, a group of area farmers found themselves with a surplus of lavender. To get rid of the flowers, the farmers set up stands in the center of town to sell them to the residents. — [3] —.

Today, the lavender festival features vendors selling not only lavender flowers but an extraordinary assortment of handmade goods from around the region. — [4] —. Visitors young and old can also enjoy a funfair with a variety of carnival rides and activities along with dozens of food vendors selling a wide selection of foods.

151. What is probably true about the lavender festival?

(A) It is best suited for older people.
(B) It is well-known in many countries.
(C) It is unpopular with locals.
(D) It is attractive to people who enjoy cold-weather activities.

152. What are NOT mentioned in the article as part of the lavender festival?

(A) Musical performances
(B) Products for sale
(C) Carnival rides
(D) Different kinds of foods

153. In which of the positions marked [1], [2], [3], and [4] does the following sentence best belong?

"Thus, the lavender festival was created."

(A) [1]
(B) [2]
(C) [3]
(D) [4]

TEST 2

GO ON TO THE NEXT PAGE

Questions 154-155 refer to the following text-message chain.

Ravi Carelli (11:05 A.M.)
I think we need to do another test run of our marketing strategy presentation before we go to Sarsoni Luggage tomorrow. What do you think?

Jeanine Ika (11:07 A.M.)
It is a little complicated in places, isn't it?

Ravi Carelli (11:09 A.M.)
Exactly. We want to be as clear and smooth as possible in our delivery. How about this afternoon?

Jeanine Ika (11:12 A.M.)
Is 3 P.M. a good time for you?

Ravi Carelli (11:15 A.M.)
That works. I'll come to your office.

154. At 11:07 A.M., what does Ms. Ika most likely mean when she writes, "It is a little complicated in places, isn't it"?

(A) She does not understand some directions.
(B) She agrees with a suggestion.
(C) She worked very hard on a task.
(D) She believes some luggage is difficult to use.

155. What is most likely true about Mr. Carelli?

(A) He is Ms. Ika's client.
(B) He is dissatisfied with Ms. Ika's work.
(C) He is an employee of Sarsoni Luggage.
(D) He is a colleague of Ms. Ika's.

Please describe the employee's achievements and note any areas for improvement.

Ms. Diamos is a valuable member of the accounting team I oversee. She transitioned to her current position as manager of accounts receivable only six months ago. Since that time, she has automated the billing process, drawing on her broad knowledge of accounting software. Additionally, she cleaned up the accounts-receivable database and developed a plan to recover overdue amounts.

Ms. Diamos is always ready to help a colleague and quickly absorbs all the instruction I give her. In terms of development, I'd like to see her gain experience in preparing and presenting reports to top-level management.

---

156. Who most likely wrote the review?

(A) An administrative assistant
(B) A client
(C) A supervisor
(D) A technology-support staff member

157. What part of Ms. Diamos' job does the review mention?

(A) Paying invoices
(B) Improving billing procedures
(C) Managing the technology team
(D) Keeping the office clean

TEST 2

GO ON TO THE NEXT PAGE

News from Drakely Storage

Let's admit it: the storage business has never been regarded as being particularly dynamic or innovative. Think about the storage facilities you've seen—they've probably been rows of dull, nondescript steel buildings. — [1] —. But recently, the industry has been undergoing some exciting changes. Here's a quick overview of a recent cutting-edge development in the world of self-storage.

As storage companies open more new facilities, they are placing more focus on amenities to bring in tenants. Many new facilities provide attractive features such as staffed offices, keypad entry, and climate-controlled storage units. In urban areas, multistory facilities may exhibit visually appealing architectural features to blend in with their surroundings. — [2] —.

Increasingly, the ground floor of storage properties is being used for offices and shops. An example of this can be seen in one of Drakely Storage's own facilities, located on Seventh Avenue in a thriving arts district in Vancouver, British Columbia. — [3] —. Haubert Ltd., the facility's newest tenant, has established a retail outlet on the storage facility's first floor. This fast-growing clothing company offers stylish clothing, which customers can see and try on in person at the outlet.

This is only one example of new ideas in the modern self-storage industry. It seems likely that the industry will continue to make exciting advances in the coming years. — [4] —.

158. What is the purpose of the article?

(A) To highlight the need for more storage facilities

(B) To describe a trend in the storage industry

(C) To compare storage facilities in different regions

(D) To explain the process of renting a storage unit

159. What does the article indicate about the Drakely Storage facility in Vancouver?

(A) It houses the company's marketing department.

(B) It was decorated by neighborhood artists.

(C) It includes retail space for an apparel maker.

(D) It currently has no vacant storage space.

160. In which of the positions marked [1], [2], [3], and [4] does the following sentence best belong?

"With their fine exterior detail, some of these structures can even be mistaken for charming historic buildings."

(A) [1]

(B) [2]

(C) [3]

(D) [4]

Questions 161-164 refer to the following e-mail.

To:	Veronica Maybank <vmaybank@wbc.org.nz>
From:	Nicholas Teakel <nteakel@zipmail.co.nz>
Date:	11 October
Subject:	Book Club Talk

Dear Ms. Maybank,

Thank you for inviting me to speak at a future meeting of the Wellington Book Club. I understand you meet on the first Friday of every month at Hilldale Hall at 8:00 P.M. and expect presentations to last about one hour, after which the floor will be open for questions and comments from members of the club.

I would be honoured to address the club. My latest travel memoir has just been published, and I would be delighted to speak about it to your group. It is a detailed account of my travels to Kyoto and my meeting with one of Japan's foremost experts on cherry trees. My schedule is clear for the next two months. Please note that after that time I will go on a book tour.

Please let me know as soon as possible what date you have in mind. I will bring a computer with presentation software, but it would be helpful if you could provide a screen so that I may include photographs of Kyoto and the trees.

Best regards,

Nicholas Teakel

TEST 2

161. What most likely is Mr. Teakel's profession?

(A) Author
(B) Travel agent
(C) Computer technician
(D) Gardener

162. What typically happens at the book club meetings at about 9:00 P.M.?

(A) Itineraries and schedules are distributed.
(B) Documentary films from Asia are shown.
(C) Tea and snacks are served.
(D) A speaker and audience members have a conversation.

163. The word "clear" in paragraph 2, line 4, is closest in meaning to

(A) open
(B) plain
(C) bright
(D) direct

164. What does Mr. Teakel require Ms. Maybank's assistance with?

(A) Purchasing plane tickets
(B) Displaying photographs
(C) Repairing a computer
(D) Translating a lecture

GO ON TO THE NEXT PAGE

Questions 165-168 refer to the following discussion-board chain.

Marlene Hesbeth [2:15 P.M.] Does anyone have any suggestions for a small printer?

Horace Vicarro [2:29 P.M.] Do you need it for home or office use?

Marlene Hesbeth [2:45 P.M.] I have a small business in my home, so I'd like an attractive one that's fast and efficient. Oh, and without much maintenance. It's got to be easy to use and reasonably priced.

Jack Tigret [2:59 P.M.] I work for Gansen Computers. We are having a big sale on printers. I can help you select the model based on your needs. If you have time, take a look at our Web site: www.gansencomputers.com.

Horace Vicarro [3:02 P.M.] I have a small home-based business too. I had lots of bad experiences with printers, but now I have a Portell 500 that has scanning, faxing, color printing, and two-sided printing. Plus, it practically runs itself!

Marlene Hesbeth [3:05 P.M.] Impressive! Only, how much does it cost?

Jareem Mullica [3:10 P.M.] Based on my experience, I would go for the DVQ brand. Their printers can be expensive, but they make models that fit into extremely tight spaces. I can't say how much this has helped me!

Horace Vicarro [3:13 P.M.] I got the Portell 500 on sale, but I don't think they are very costly at full price. Let me find my receipt.

---

165. What is the main purpose of the discussion board?

(A) For consumers to sell their used electronics

(B) For the public to share questions and information

(C) For manufacturers to educate consumers about products

(D) For salespeople to advertise merchandise

166. What is indicated about Gansen Computers?

(A) It is offering a discount on printers.

(B) It is having a sale on desktop computers.

(C) It offers free printer-repair services.

(D) It specializes in corporate sales.

167. At 3:05 P.M., what does Ms. Hesbeth imply when she writes, "Impressive"?

(A) She likes a recommended Web site.

(B) She trusts Mr. Tigret's judgment.

(C) She admires Mr. Vicarro's home business.

(D) She likes the features of a product.

168. What can be concluded about Mr. Mullica?

(A) He is a friend of Ms. Hesbeth's.

(B) He lacks experience with printers.

(C) His work area has limited room for equipment.

(D) He once owned a Portell 500 printer.

Avyjet 938 Launch

MADRID (12 April)—Production on the long-awaited Avyjet 938 aircraft has come to a halt because of an issue with parts for the entertainment system.

Avyjet, which is based in Spain, is having components for the entertainment system shipped from its partner factories in France and Germany. Unfortunately, those factories are waiting on materials needed to finish producing their respective parts.

According to Avyjet's chief production officer, Guillermo Garcia, it may seem simple but it is not a quick fix. "The planes were designed to use components that were specifically manufactured by our partners in France and Germany," Mr. Garcia said to aviation journalists at a press conference.

The Avyjet 938 has been promoted as being the most comfortable passenger aircraft ever made. Sandrikha Airlines has expressed interest in purchasing several planes from Avyjet to increase the size of its fleet and expand the number of routes it flies. Avyjet says it has several other large contracts it is currently negotiating.

TEST 2

169. The word "issue" in paragraph 1, line 3, is closest in meaning to

(A) problem
(B) edition
(C) distribution
(D) result

170. What does the article mention about Avyjet?

(A) It is considering some new routes.
(B) Its planes are designed to haul cargo.
(C) It obtains parts from multiple production sites.
(D) Its leadership structure recently changed.

171. What is suggested about Sandrikha Airlines?

(A) It wants to grow its business.
(B) It flies mostly in European countries.
(C) It is considered the most comfortable airline.
(D) It is negotiating to have new entertainment systems installed.

GO ON TO THE NEXT PAGE

Job Opening at Genevierne Hospital

Position: Licensed electrician

Anticipated Start Date: 14 January

Location: All fifteen structures on the hospital system complex and surrounding grounds

Reports to: The head of maintenance

Major Duties:

1. Installs and maintains motors, coils, transformers, generators, pumps, substations, and all related control equipment.

2. Complies with all regulations, including general safety policies and procedures. Inspects and maintains equipment and tools to ensure their proper operation. Stays up-to-date on the techniques of electrical work.

3. Performs and documents preventive maintenance for electrical equipment and machinery.

4. Designs custom functional electric circuitry for electrical systems as needed.

Application review begins 3 December.

To apply: Send résumé and cover letter to Jonas Lewing, director of human resources, at jlewing@ghs.org.

---

172. What is included in the job listing?

(A) The name of the job's supervisor
(B) The salary range
(C) The date that the listing was posted
(D) The name of the employer

173. What does the listing indicate about the hospital?

(A) It includes multiple buildings.
(B) It is still under construction.
(C) It has a new air-conditioning system.
(D) It is operated by a nonprofit corporation.

174. What is a stated requirement of the job?

(A) To stay informed of practices in the field
(B) To complete daily task lists by the end of each day
(C) To file monthly electrical inspection reports
(D) To perform landscaping work on hospital grounds

175. According to the job listing, what will happen on December 3?

(A) Applications will start to be accepted.
(B) Human resources will begin evaluating job candidates.
(C) The candidate selected for the position will be announced.
(D) The successful candidate will start the job.

GO ON TO THE NEXT PAGE

Lewisport Ferry Service

Customer: Juanita Harris
Order date: September 5
Confirmation number: 3442
Round-trip reservation for October 14
Departing Lewisport at 8:30 A.M.
Departing Jonas Island at 4:30 P.M.

2 adult tickets	$24.00
1 vehicle	$31.00
Order total	$55.00

Departure: To board the ferry, your vehicle must be in line 30 minutes in advance of the departure time. Failure to meet this requirement will result in the loss of your reservation.

Rescheduling: Reservations can be rescheduled by calling the ticket office at least one day before a scheduled departure.

Refunds: The Lewisport Ferry Service does not issue refunds.

Vehicle regulations: In accordance with government regulations, your vehicle's engine must be off while the ferry is under way.

Arrival time: The trip between Lewisport and Jonas Island takes about 45–60 minutes. Arrival times vary depending on weather conditions.

From:	June Washburn <jwashburn@jonasislandproperties.com>
To:	Juanita Harris <jharris@renovationsright.com>
Sent:	September 12
Subject:	Planning meeting

Hello, Ms. Harris,

I am sorry to inform you that we need to find a different date for the planning meeting to discuss the Jonas Island Hotel renovations.

Unfortunately, our director of operations will not be available on October 14. He will be away on other business from October 11 until October 20. Since he is the project leader, his presence at the meeting is essential. He asked me to try to reschedule our meeting for October 25.

Kindly let me know if you and Mr. Kokura are available on that day. We apologize for the inconvenience.

June Washburn, Administrative Assistant
Jonas Island Properties

176. What information is NOT included in the reservation?

(A) A confirmation number
(B) The refund policy
(C) Exact arrival times
(D) Rescheduling directions

177. What government regulation is mentioned in the reservation?

(A) Automobiles must be turned off when the ferry is moving.
(B) Passengers must present photo identification.
(C) A confirmation number must be displayed in the automobile.
(D) Only one passenger is allowed per vehicle.

178. What is the purpose of the e-mail?

(A) To propose a different location
(B) To postpone a scheduled meeting
(C) To welcome Ms. Harris to Jonas Island
(D) To share architectural plans for a project

179. What can be concluded about Ms. Harris?

(A) She had expected Ms. Washburn to meet her at the ferry.
(B) She had planned to leave her car in Lewisport.
(C) She had expected to spend two days on Jonas Island.
(D) She had planned to travel together with Mr. Kokura.

180. What will Ms. Harris most likely do?

(A) Call the ferry ticket office by October 13
(B) Arrive at the ferry by 8:30 A.M. on October 14
(C) Rent a car for Mr. Kokura
(D) Find another location for the meeting

GO ON TO THE NEXT PAGE

News Editor Promoted

KEENE (December 1)—Jay Diaz, the current news editor for the Keene *Daily Arrival* newspaper, will soon become the executive editor. Mr. Diaz is a seasoned journalist who started at the *Daily Arrival* almost ten years ago. He has worked for local papers around the state, writing about local education issues for many years before moving into high school and college sports.

Mr. Diaz takes over for Sandra Hoyer, who has held the position at the *Daily Arrival* for twenty years. She also wrote for various newspapers here in California as well as in her hometown of Miami, Florida, for a brief period. Ms. Hoyer is best known for her award-winning series on regional culinary traditions.

E-Mail Message

To:	Maria Jackson <mjackson@ardinmail.com>
From:	Sandra Hoyer <shoyer@mailcrate.com>
Date:	December 1
Subject:	Retirement news

Dear Maria,

I'm writing to let you know about my retirement in a few weeks. The last time we talked, I mentioned that I was thinking about retiring, but now I'm really doing it!

You are one of the first people I wanted to tell personally about this, given how important you have been in my career. If you had not taken a chance and hired me as a local restaurant reviewer all those years ago in San Diego, I may never have become a journalist. It's been a very rewarding career, and I owe much of it to you! But now, I am looking forward to returning to my hometown to spend more time with my family.

Thanks again for being such a wonderful mentor to me all those years ago. I hope all is well with you in Austin.

Best,

Sandra

181. What does the article indicate about the *Daily Arrival*?

(A) It is currently hiring reporters.
(B) It has a new online edition.
(C) It is published in California.
(D) It is celebrating its twentieth anniversary.

182. What topic is Ms. Hoyer most known for writing about?

(A) Cooking
(B) Fashion
(C) Sports
(D) Education

183. What is one purpose of the e-mail?

(A) To reveal a significant decision
(B) To suggest a restaurant for a celebration
(C) To offer someone a job
(D) To ask for a letter of recommendation

184. According to the e-mail, what position did Ms. Jackson most likely hold?

(A) Travel agent
(B) Journalism professor
(C) Fashion designer
(D) Newspaper editor

185. Where will Ms. Hoyer most likely live once she retires?

(A) Keene
(B) Miami
(C) San Diego
(D) Austin

GO ON TO THE NEXT PAGE

Questions 186-190 refer to the following Web site, e-mail, and map.

https://www.menloartscentre.ie/submissions

| Home | About | Events | **Submissions** |

The Menlo Arts Centre will once again hold its celebrated Spring Art Show. The show attracts many art lovers eager to appreciate new works and potentially take home a one-of-a-kind art piece. Both professional and amateur visual artists are invited to submit their work. A panel of area art experts will judge submissions. Accepted art will be displayed in the Willowbrook Gallery of the Menlo Arts Centre from 1 April to 15 April.

Artists can submit up to twelve pieces. The categories for submission are watercolour, oil painting, drawing, collage, graphic art, printmaking, sculpture, and photography. Applications are due by 5 January, and applicants will be notified by 15 February if any of their pieces have been accepted. Artists must live within 100 kilometres of Menlo, be over the age of 18, and not be related to a panel member.

If accepted, artists set the prices for their artwork and are responsible for framing and transporting their pieces.

	E-mail
To:	Leandra Hislop <lhislop@amail.ie>
From:	Hina Kaji <hkaji@menloartscentre.ie>
Subject:	Menlo Arts Centre submission results
Date:	15 February
Attachment:	🖇 contract

Dear Ms. Hislop,

We are excited to let you know that the Menlo Arts Centre panel has reviewed your submission and would like to include all twelve of your pieces in the Spring Art Show. Yours were standout submissions among a record number of applications. The panel was impressed by the vivid images of life in Menlo in your series of photographs.

Please sign and return the attached contract if you would still like to participate. Once we have your contract, our show manager will reach out to you with further details.

Sincerely,

Hina Kaji, Spring Art Show Chair

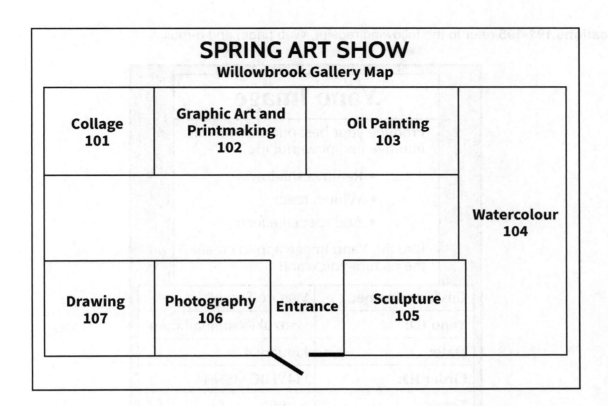

SPRING ART SHOW
Willowbrook Gallery Map

Collage 101	Graphic Art and Printmaking 102	Oil Painting 103	Watercolour 104
Drawing 107	Photography 106	Entrance	Sculpture 105

186. What is true about the Spring Art Show?

(A) Its theme will be *Spring in Menlo*.
(B) It will feature only professional artists.
(C) It will take place over one week.
(D) It will feature artwork for sale.

187. According to the Web site, what will happen on April 1?

(A) Applications will be due for the Spring Art Show.
(B) The judges will send letters to applicants.
(C) The Spring Art Show will begin.
(D) Winning artists will receive awards.

188. According to the Web site, what are accepted artists responsible for?

(A) Paying an entrance fee
(B) Hanging their artwork
(C) Bringing their artwork to the gallery
(D) Writing an artist biography

189. What can be concluded about Ms. Hislop?

(A) She grew up in the town of Menlo.
(B) She submitted the maximum number of pieces.
(C) She is well-known for her artwork.
(D) She submitted work in multiple categories.

190. In what room will Ms. Hislop's work most likely be displayed?

(A) 103
(B) 104
(C) 105
(D) 106

GO ON TO THE NEXT PAGE

TEST 2

Yano Image

Produce your best photos with this intuitive and powerful tool.

- Remove shadows
- Whiten teeth
- Add special effects

Use the Yano Image app to create the picture you want!

Customer name:	Wataru Suzuki
Yano ID:	wsuzuki@sunmail.com
Date:	January 4
Order ID:	H4YHJGMSSM
Total:	$3.99

---

https://www.yano.com

Yano Image	Yano Music	**Customer Service**	Account Sign In

Request a Refund for Yano Apps Purchases

All purchases from Yano Image and Yano Music are eligible for a full refund when requests are made within 24 hours of purchase. You may request a refund online by following these steps.

1. Sign in to your Yano account at yano.com.

2. Go to the drop-down menu titled "What Is the Issue?" and select "Refunds."

3. Choose the app or subscription for which you desire a refund.

4. Describe the reason you are requesting a refund.

Refund requests take up to 48 hours to process. Please note that once your refund request is processed, you will lose access to the app or subscription immediately.

To:	Wataru Suzuki <wsuzuki@sunmail.com>
From:	Customer Support <customersupport@yano.com>
Date:	January 6
Subject:	Refund request
Attachment:	🔗 Yano document R34

Dear Mr. Suzuki,

This e-mail confirms receipt of your refund request. The purchase price has been credited to your account. You may view the details in the "Claims Status" section of your Yano account.

I appreciate your continued support as a loyal customer. Remember that your account has a full list of your current app subscriptions along with renewal dates.

To help us serve you better, please take a few minutes to complete the attached survey to let us know your opinion about the Yano Image app.

Best regards,

Vincent Pham, Customer Service Manager

191. According to the receipt, what can Yano Image do?

(A) Recommend beauty products
(B) Edit photographs
(C) Create photo albums
(D) Identify fashion trends

192. What does the Web page indicate about refund requests?

(A) They require a customer signature.
(B) They are processed within 48 hours.
(C) They can be made by calling the customer service department.
(D) They require a manager's approval.

193. What is most likely true about Mr. Suzuki regarding his request?

(A) He will be refunded $3.99.
(B) He should expect another e-mail in two days.
(C) He needs to open a new customer account.
(D) He must fill out a survey to finalize the process.

194. What can be concluded about Mr. Suzuki?

(A) He recently signed in to his Yano store account.
(B) He used the Yano Image app for one week.
(C) He did not intend to purchase the Yano Image app.
(D) He wants to make a purchase at Yano Books.

195. What is indicated about Mr. Suzuki in the e-mail?

(A) He is having trouble opening an account.
(B) He wants to renew a membership.
(C) He is a Yano employee.
(D) He has purchased products from Yano before.

GO ON TO THE NEXT PAGE

Biography About Chef Tops Nonfiction Bestseller List

TORONTO (January 8)—*Rochelau's Savory Dreams*, Brandon Dawsly's new biography of pioneering chef Christiane Rochelau, has just reached the top spot in this week's nonfiction bestseller list.

Dawsly, whose previous biographies of football stars and celebrities have also made the list, has confirmed his status as a titan in the genre.

Delmina Trevisano, editor in chief at Fisley Books, which published the Rochelau biography, had high praise for the book.

"Rochelau was a pioneering figure in Canadian cuisine," said Trevisano, "and Dawsly beautifully captures both the trials and successes in her life."

Trevisano is reportedly in talks with Greenlight Group about a possible cinematic adaptation of *Rochelau's Savory Dreams*. If it materializes, the film would be the latest in a series of documentaries about innovative chefs.

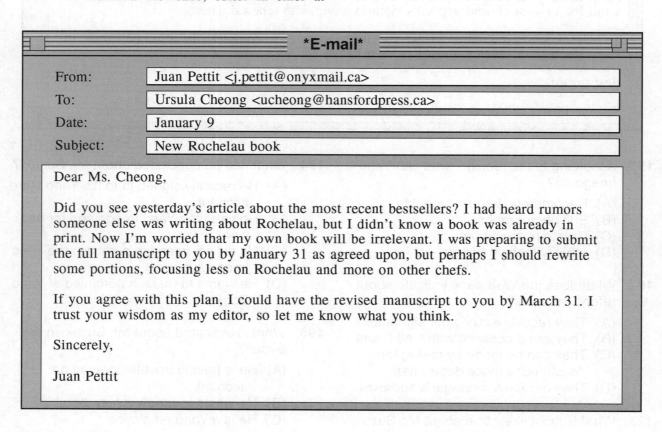

E-mail

From:	Juan Pettit <j.pettit@onyxmail.ca>
To:	Ursula Cheong <ucheong@hansfordpress.ca>
Date:	January 9
Subject:	New Rochelau book

Dear Ms. Cheong,

Did you see yesterday's article about the most recent bestsellers? I had heard rumors someone else was writing about Rochelau, but I didn't know a book was already in print. Now I'm worried that my own book will be irrelevant. I was preparing to submit the full manuscript to you by January 31 as agreed upon, but perhaps I should rewrite some portions, focusing less on Rochelau and more on other chefs.

If you agree with this plan, I could have the revised manuscript to you by March 31. I trust your wisdom as my editor, so let me know what you think.

Sincerely,

Juan Pettit

From:	Ursula Cheong <ucheong@hansfordpress.ca>
To:	Juan Pettit <j.pettit@onyxmail.ca>
Date:	January 9
Subject:	RE: New Rochelau book

Dear Mr. Pettit,

Please don't worry! I spoke to Fisley's top editor on the phone on January 3 when I saw they had a Rochelau book on the shelves. From what I can tell, Dawsly's book focuses on Rochelau's early life and her personal relationships, whereas your book is more about the restaurant scene in Canada. We may only need to change your title or tailor the marketing blurbs to emphasize your differences. Let's stick to the original schedule as planned, and after I read your manuscript we can decide if any big changes are necessary. In any case, your book wouldn't hit the stands until June 1 at the earliest, and by then people will have largely forgotten about the Dawsly biography. I have faith in your work, so just keep writing!

Sincerely,

Ursula Cheong

196. What is indicated in the article about Mr. Dawsly?

(A) His book has been the top seller for five weeks.
(B) He has written multiple best-selling books.
(C) He often plays football with celebrities.
(D) He has lived in Canada for most of his life.

197. According to the article, what kind of company is Greenlight Group?

(A) An automobile manufacturer
(B) A restaurant chain
(C) A book publisher
(D) A film studio

198. According to the first e-mail, why is Mr. Pettit concerned?

(A) Another writer has published a book similar to his.
(B) He heard rumors that his editor was switching firms.
(C) He was not able to finish his book manuscript on time.
(D) His recent book dropped off the bestseller list.

199. Who did Ms. Cheong most likely speak to?

(A) Brandon Dawsly
(B) Christiane Rochelau
(C) Delmina Trevisano
(D) Juan Pettit

200. By when should Mr. Pettit send a manuscript?

(A) January 9
(B) January 31
(C) March 31
(D) June 1

Stop! This is the end of the test. If you finish before time is called, you may go back to Parts 5, 6, and 7 and check your work.

公式 TOEIC® Listening & Reading 問題集 10 （音声 CD 2 枚付）

2023 年 10 月 19 日　第 1 版 第 1 刷発行

著者	ETS
編集協力	株式会社 カルチャー・プロ
	株式会社 WIT HOUSE
発行元	一般財団法人 国際ビジネスコミュニケーション協会
	〒 100-0014
	東京都千代田区永田町 2-14-2
	山王グランドビル
	電話 (03) 5521-5935
印刷	大日本印刷株式会社

乱丁本・落丁本・不良本はお取り換えします。許可なしに転載、複製することを禁じます。
ETS, the ETS logo, PROPELL, TOEIC and TOEIC BRIDGE are registered trademarks of
ETS, Princeton, New Jersey, USA, and used in Japan under license.
Portions are copyrighted by ETS and used with permission.
Printed in Japan
ISBN 978-4-906033-71-3

TEST 1

解答用紙

REGISTRATION No.
受験番号

フリガナ
NAME
氏名

LISTENING SECTION

Part 1

No.	ANSWER A B C D
1	A B C D
2	A B C D
3	A B C D
4	A B C D
5	A B C D
6	A B C D
7	A B C D
8	A B C D
9	A B C D
10	A B C D

Part 2

No.	ANSWER A B C
11	A B C
12	A B C
13	A B C
14	A B C
15	A B C
16	A B C
17	A B C
18	A B C
19	A B C
20	A B C

No.	ANSWER A B C
21	A B C
22	A B C
23	A B C
24	A B C
25	A B C
26	A B C
27	A B C
28	A B C
29	A B C
30	A B C

Part 3

No.	ANSWER A B C D
31	A B C D
32	A B C D
33	A B C D
34	A B C D
35	A B C D
36	A B C D
37	A B C D
38	A B C D
39	A B C D
40	A B C D

No.	ANSWER A B C D
41	A B C D
42	A B C D
43	A B C D
44	A B C D
45	A B C D
46	A B C D
47	A B C D
48	A B C D
49	A B C D
50	A B C D

No.	ANSWER A B C D
51	A B C D
52	A B C D
53	A B C D
54	A B C D
55	A B C D
56	A B C D
57	A B C D
58	A B C D
59	A B C D
60	A B C D

No.	ANSWER A B C D
61	A B C D
62	A B C D
63	A B C D
64	A B C D
65	A B C D
66	A B C D
67	A B C D
68	A B C D
69	A B C D
70	A B C D

Part 4

No.	ANSWER A B C D
71	A B C D
72	A B C D
73	A B C D
74	A B C D
75	A B C D
76	A B C D
77	A B C D
78	A B C D
79	A B C D
80	A B C D

No.	ANSWER A B C D
81	A B C D
82	A B C D
83	A B C D
84	A B C D
85	A B C D
86	A B C D
87	A B C D
88	A B C D
89	A B C D
90	A B C D

No.	ANSWER A B C D
91	A B C D
92	A B C D
93	A B C D
94	A B C D
95	A B C D
96	A B C D
97	A B C D
98	A B C D
99	A B C D
100	A B C D

READING SECTION

Part 5

No.	ANSWER A B C D
101	A B C D
102	A B C D
103	A B C D
104	A B C D
105	A B C D
106	A B C D
107	A B C D
108	A B C D
109	A B C D
110	A B C D

No.	ANSWER A B C D
111	A B C D
112	A B C D
113	A B C D
114	A B C D
115	A B C D
116	A B C D
117	A B C D
118	A B C D
119	A B C D
120	A B C D

Part 6

No.	ANSWER A B C D
121	A B C D
122	A B C D
123	A B C D
124	A B C D
125	A B C D
126	A B C D
127	A B C D
128	A B C D
129	A B C D
130	A B C D

No.	ANSWER A B C D
131	A B C D
132	A B C D
133	A B C D
134	A B C D
135	A B C D
136	A B C D
137	A B C D
138	A B C D
139	A B C D
140	A B C D

Part 7

No.	ANSWER A B C D
141	A B C D
142	A B C D
143	A B C D
144	A B C D
145	A B C D
146	A B C D
147	A B C D
148	A B C D
149	A B C D
150	A B C D

No.	ANSWER A B C D
151	A B C D
152	A B C D
153	A B C D
154	A B C D
155	A B C D
156	A B C D
157	A B C D
158	A B C D
159	A B C D
160	A B C D

No.	ANSWER A B C D
161	A B C D
162	A B C D
163	A B C D
164	A B C D
165	A B C D
166	A B C D
167	A B C D
168	A B C D
169	A B C D
170	A B C D

No.	ANSWER A B C D
171	A B C D
172	A B C D
173	A B C D
174	A B C D
175	A B C D
176	A B C D
177	A B C D
178	A B C D
179	A B C D
180	A B C D

No.	ANSWER A B C D
181	A B C D
182	A B C D
183	A B C D
184	A B C D
185	A B C D
186	A B C D
187	A B C D
188	A B C D
189	A B C D
190	A B C D

No.	ANSWER A B C D
191	A B C D
192	A B C D
193	A B C D
194	A B C D
195	A B C D
196	A B C D
197	A B C D
198	A B C D
199	A B C D
200	A B C D

TEST 2

解答用紙

REGISTRATION No.
受験番号

フリガナ
N A M E
氏名

LISTENING SECTION

Part 1

No.	ANSWER A B C D
1	A B C D
2	A B C D
3	A B C D
4	A B C D
5	A B C D
6	A B C D
7	A B C D
8	A B C D
9	A B C D
10	A B C D

Part 2

No.	ANSWER A B C
11	A B C
12	A B C
13	A B C
14	A B C
15	A B C
16	A B C
17	A B C
18	A B C
19	A B C
20	A B C
21	A B C
22	A B C
23	A B C
24	A B C
25	A B C
26	A B C
27	A B C
28	A B C
29	A B C
30	A B C

Part 3

No.	ANSWER A B C D
31	A B C
32	A B C D
33	A B C D
34	A B C D
35	A B C D
36	A B C D
37	A B C D
38	A B C D
39	A B C D
40	A B C D
41	A B C D
42	A B C D
43	A B C D
44	A B C D
45	A B C D
46	A B C D
47	A B C D
48	A B C D
49	A B C D
50	A B C D
51	A B C D
52	A B C D
53	A B C D
54	A B C D
55	A B C D
56	A B C D
57	A B C D
58	A B C D
59	A B C D
60	A B C D

Part 4

No.	ANSWER A B C D
61	A B C D
62	A B C D
63	A B C D
64	A B C D
65	A B C D
66	A B C D
67	A B C D
68	A B C D
69	A B C D
70	A B C D
71	A B C D
72	A B C D
73	A B C D
74	A B C D
75	A B C D
76	A B C D
77	A B C D
78	A B C D
79	A B C D
80	A B C D
81	A B C D
82	A B C D
83	A B C D
84	A B C D
85	A B C D
86	A B C D
87	A B C D
88	A B C D
89	A B C D
90	A B C D
91	A B C D
92	A B C D
93	A B C D
94	A B C D
95	A B C D
96	A B C D
97	A B C D
98	A B C D
99	A B C D
100	A B C D

READING SECTION

Part 5

No.	ANSWER A B C D
101	A B C D
102	A B C D
103	A B C D
104	A B C D
105	A B C D
106	A B C D
107	A B C D
108	A B C D
109	A B C D
110	A B C D
111	A B C D
112	A B C D
113	A B C D
114	A B C D
115	A B C D
116	A B C D
117	A B C D
118	A B C D
119	A B C D
120	A B C D
121	A B C D
122	A B C D
123	A B C D
124	A B C D
125	A B C D
126	A B C D
127	A B C D
128	A B C D
129	A B C D
130	A B C D

Part 6

No.	ANSWER A B C D
131	A B C D
132	A B C D
133	A B C D
134	A B C D
135	A B C D
136	A B C D
137	A B C D
138	A B C D
139	A B C D
140	A B C D

Part 7

No.	ANSWER A B C D
141	A B C D
142	A B C D
143	A B C D
144	A B C D
145	A B C D
146	A B C D
147	A B C D
148	A B C D
149	A B C D
150	A B C D
151	A B C D
152	A B C D
153	A B C D
154	A B C D
155	A B C D
156	A B C D
157	A B C D
158	A B C D
159	A B C D
160	A B C D
161	A B C D
162	A B C D
163	A B C D
164	A B C D
165	A B C D
166	A B C D
167	A B C D
168	A B C D
169	A B C D
170	A B C D
171	A B C D
172	A B C D
173	A B C D
174	A B C D
175	A B C D
176	A B C D
177	A B C D
178	A B C D
179	A B C D
180	A B C D
181	A B C D
182	A B C D
183	A B C D
184	A B C D
185	A B C D
186	A B C D
187	A B C D
188	A B C D
189	A B C D
190	A B C D
191	A B C D
192	A B C D
193	A B C D
194	A B C D
195	A B C D
196	A B C D
197	A B C D
198	A B C D
199	A B C D
200	A B C D

公式 TOEIC®
Listening & Reading
問題集
10

別冊 『解答・解説』

一般財団法人 国際ビジネスコミュニケーション協会

ETS, the ETS logo, PROPELL, TOEIC and TOEIC BRIDGE are registered trademarks of
ETS, Princeton, New Jersey, USA, and used in Japan under license.
Portions are copyrighted by ETS and used with permission.

ETS TOEIC®

OFFICIAL TEST
PREPARATION
AND LEARNING

目　次

解答・解説で使われている表記の説明

● **CDのトラック番号（Part 1 〜 4）**

会話の音声が **CD 1** のトラック番号 **46** に、
問題の音声が **CD 1** のトラック番号 **47** に入っていることを示しています。

● **スクリプトの前の記号（Part 1 〜 4）**

🇺🇸 ＝ 米国の発音
🇬🇧 ＝ 英国の発音
🇨🇦 ＝ カナダの発音
🇦🇺 ＝ オーストラリアの発音

M ＝ 男性（Man）
W ＝ 女性（Woman）

● **スクリプト中の ❶ ❷ 等の番号（Part 3、4）**

解説の中で説明している箇所を示しています。

PART 3

💿 | 会話 CD 1 46 | 問題 CD 1 47 |

Questions 32 through 34 refer to the following conversation.

🇺🇸 W Hello, Martin. Thank you for helping set up this event here at the convention center with your staff. ❶Have you heard from the caterers today?

🇨🇦 M ❷Nothing yet, surprisingly.

🇺🇸 W I'm getting concerned.

🇨🇦 M ❸I agree. Let's give them a call. Maybe there's been some miscommunication or some other type of mistake.

🇺🇸 W Yes. ❹I hope they have the correct date for this event. ❺The award ceremony is starting in just a few hours.

問題32-34は次の会話に関するものです。

こんにちは、Martin。このコンベンションセンターでの本イベントの設営をあなたのところのスタッフと一緒に手伝ってくれて、ありがとうございます。今日、ケータリング業者から連絡はありましたか。

驚いたことに、まだ何もありません。

私は心配になってきています。

同感です。先方に電話しましょう。何か伝達の不備やその他の種類のミスがあったのかもしれません。

そうですね。先方がこのイベントの正確な日程を把握しているとよいのですが。表彰式はほんの数時間後に始まるのですから。

32 What does the woman ask about?

(A) A parking spot
(B) A site map
(C) A training schedule
(D) A catering order

女性は何について尋ねていますか。

(A) 駐車場所
(B) 会場の地図
(C) 研修の予定
(D) ケータリングの注文

| 正解 D | 女性は、イベントの準備の手伝いに対するお礼を述べた後、❶「今日、ケータリング業者から連絡はあったか」と尋ねている。よって、(D)が正解。catering「仕出し、ケータリング」、order「注文」。
(A) parking spot「駐車場所」。
(B) site「場所、敷地」。
(C) training「研修」、schedule「予定(表)」。 |

33 What does the woman imply when she says, "I'm getting concerned"?

(A) Some items are unavailable.

| 正解 B | ❶で、ケータリング業者から連絡があったかと尋ねる女性に対し、男性は❷「驚いたことに、まだ何もない」と答えている。これ |

● **色の区別**

青字：正答に関する解説や語句の意味
黒字：誤答に関する解説や語句の意味

●特典音声ファイルの番号（Part 5 〜 7）

「45-46」は特典音声のファイル番号を示しています。ダウンロード音声ファイルのタイトル名に、「特典 45」、「特典 46」と表示されています。

●文書中の ❶❷ 等の番号（Part 6、7）

解説の中で説明している文書中の段落番号等を示しています。解説文中の段落番号に続く行数は、英文中の各段落の何行目かを表しています。

●文書を示す **1** **2** 等の番号（Part 7 複数の文書）

解説の中で説明している文書を示しています。

●Words & Phrases（Part 3、4、6、7）

会話やトーク、文書などに含まれる重要な語句と意味を紹介しています。Part 6、7 では、上記に示した **1** **2** や ❶❷ の番号により、本文で使われている場所が参照できます。

●Expressions（Part 6、7）

文書の中から、知っておくと便利な表現を例文とともに紹介しています。覚えて使えるようになると、大変便利です。

> **Expressions**
> **make it to 〜**　「〜に都合がつく、〜に参加できる」（**2**の❶ 1〜2行目）
> I hope you can make it to the reception on Friday.
> あなたが金曜日のレセプションに出られるとよいのですが。

＊『公式 TOEIC® Listening & Reading 問題集 10』の特典として、ダウンロード音声の中には、TEST 1、2 のリーディングセクションの以下の音声が入っています。音声ダウンロードの手順は本誌 p. 3 をご参照ください。
- ・正解が入った問題音声（Part 5、6）
- ・文書の音声（Part 7）

参考スコア範囲の算出方法 ※ TEST 1、2 共通

1. 正解一覧（p.6、p.102）を参照し、リスニングセクションとリーディングセクションそれぞれの正答数を数えてください。各セクションの正答数がそれぞれの素点となります。
2. 下の参考スコア範囲の換算表であなたの素点に対応する換算点範囲を見つけます。
   例えばリスニングセクションの素点が 45 であれば、あなたの換算点範囲は「160 点〜230 点」です。
3. 各セクションの換算点範囲の合計が、あなたのトータルスコア（参考スコア範囲）となります。

参考スコア範囲の算出例

リスニングセクションの素点が **45** で、リーディングセクションの素点が **64** だった場合、トータルスコアは ① と ② の合計である ③ 415—570 の間ということになります。

	素点	換算点範囲	
リスニングセクション	45	160 — 230	①
リーディングセクション	64	255 — 340	②
トータルスコア（参考スコア範囲）		415 — 570	③（①＋②）

参考スコア範囲の換算表

リスニングセクション		リーディングセクション	
素点	換算点範囲	素点	換算点範囲
96 — 100	475 — 495	96 — 100	460 — 495
91 — 95	435 — 495	91 — 95	425 — 490
86 — 90	405 — 470	86 — 90	400 — 465
81 — 85	370 — 450	81 — 85	375 — 440
76 — 80	345 — 420	76 — 80	340 — 415
71 — 75	320 — 390	71 — 75	310 — 390
66 — 70	290 — 360	66 — 70	285 — 370
61 — 65	265 — 335	61 — 65	255 — 340
56 — 60	240 — 310	56 — 60	230 — 310
51 — 55	215 — 280	51 — 55	200 — 275
46 — 50	190 — 255	46 — 50	170 — 245
41 — 45	160 — 230	41 — 45	140 — 215
36 — 40	130 — 205	36 — 40	115 — 180
31 — 35	105 — 175	31 — 35	95 — 150
26 — 30	85 — 145	26 — 30	75 — 120
21 — 25	60 — 115	21 — 25	60 — 95
16 — 20	30 — 90	16 — 20	45 — 75
11 — 15	5 — 70	11 — 15	30 — 55
6 — 10	5 — 60	6 — 10	10 — 40
1 — 5	5 — 50	1 — 5	5 — 30
0	5 — 35	0	5 — 15

実際のテストでは問題用紙の裏側に、以下のようなテスト全体についての指示が印刷されています。この指示を念頭においてテストに取り組みましょう。

General Directions

This test is designed to measure your English language ability. The test is divided into two sections: Listening and Reading.

You must mark all of your answers on the separate answer sheet. For each question, you should select the best answer from the answer choices given. Then, on your answer sheet, you should find the number of the question and fill in the space that corresponds to the letter of the answer that you have selected. If you decide to change an answer, completely erase your old answer and then mark your new answer.

全体についての指示

このテストはあなたの英語言語能力を測定するよう設計されています。テストはリスニングとリーディングという 2 つのセクションに分けられています。

答えは全て別紙の解答用紙にマークしてください。それぞれの設問について、与えられた選択肢から最も適切な答えを選びます。そして解答用紙の該当する問題番号に、選択した答えを塗りつぶしてください。答えを修正する場合は、元の答えを完全に消してから新しい答えをマークしてください。

TEST 1 の正解一覧

リスニングセクション

問題番号	正解
Part 1	
1	D
2	B
3	A
4	B
5	C
6	C
Part 2	
7	C
8	A
9	B
10	C
11	A
12	C
13	B
14	C
15	B
16	B
17	C
18	A
19	B
20	A
21	C
22	B
23	A
24	C
25	B
26	C
27	A
28	B
29	B
30	C
31	A
Part 3	
32	D
33	B
34	C
35	C
36	D
37	B
38	D
39	B
40	C
41	A
42	B
43	D
44	A
45	A
46	B
47	C
48	A
49	A
50	A

問題番号	正解
51	B
52	D
53	A
54	C
55	D
56	C
57	A
58	B
59	A
60	B
61	C
62	A
63	D
64	B
65	B
66	C
67	A
68	B
69	D
70	A
Part 4	
71	D
72	C
73	B
74	B
75	A
76	C
77	C
78	D
79	A
80	D
81	C
82	A
83	C
84	B
85	B
86	A
87	D
88	C
89	A
90	A
91	D
92	A
93	A
94	B
95	C
96	D
97	D
98	D
99	A
100	B

リーディングセクション

問題番号	正解
Part 5	
101	A
102	A
103	D
104	B
105	A
106	C
107	C
108	D
109	C
110	A
111	B
112	B
113	D
114	D
115	B
116	D
117	B
118	A
119	B
120	C
121	B
122	A
123	C
124	B
125	B
126	D
127	C
128	C
129	C
130	A
Part 6	
131	C
132	D
133	B
134	A
135	B
136	D
137	C
138	C
139	B
140	A
141	C
142	D
143	A
144	C
145	B
146	D
Part 7	
147	D
148	D
149	A
150	B

問題番号	正解
151	C
152	B
153	A
154	B
155	B
156	C
157	A
158	B
159	C
160	B
161	D
162	A
163	B
164	B
165	C
166	A
167	B
168	B
169	D
170	C
171	C
172	A
173	B
174	C
175	D
176	A
177	C
178	C
179	D
180	D
181	B
182	C
183	D
184	B
185	A
186	D
187	C
188	D
189	C
190	A
191	D
192	A
193	C
194	C
195	B
196	D
197	B
198	A
199	C
200	A

PART 1

CD 1 13-15

TEST 1 PART 1

1

2

3

1 M

(A) He's washing a car.
(B) He's sweeping a driveway.
(C) He's carrying some tools.
(D) He's working on a wheel.

(A) 彼は車を洗っている。
(B) 彼は私道を掃いている。
(C) 彼は道具を運んでいる。
(D) 彼は車輪の作業をしている。

正解 D 男性は車のwheel「車輪」を両手で支えながら何らかの作業をしている。work on 〜「〜（修理などの作業）に取り組む」。
(A) 車は写っているが、男性は洗車をしているところではない。wash「〜を洗う」。
(B) 男性は道を掃いてはいない。sweep「〜を掃く、〜の掃き掃除をする」、driveway「（道路から家・車庫への）私有車道」。
(C) 男性はtool「道具」を運んではいない。carry「〜を運ぶ」。

2 W

(A) The woman is typing on a computer keyboard.
(B) The man is holding a telephone handset.
(C) They're shaking hands with each other.
(D) They're putting away some files.

(A) 女性はコンピューターのキーボードでタイプしている。
(B) 男性は電話の受話器を握っている。
(C) 彼らは互いに握手している。
(D) 彼らはファイルを片付けている。

正解 B 男性はtelephone handset「電話の受話器」を手に持っている。
(A) 女性はキーボードに触れてはいない。type「（キーボードなどで）打つ、タイプする」。
(C) 2人は握手を交わしてはいない。shake hands with 〜「〜と握手する」、each other「互い（に）」。
(D) 2人はファイルを片付けているところではない。put away 〜「〜を片付ける」。

3 W

(A) She's kneeling on the floor.
(B) She's wiping a countertop.
(C) She's installing handles on a cabinet.
(D) She's plugging in an electronic device.

(A) 彼女は床に膝をついている。
(B) 彼女は調理台を拭いている。
(C) 彼女は戸棚に取っ手を取り付けている。
(D) 彼女は電子機器のプラグをコンセントに差し込んでいるところである。

正解 A 女性はfloor「床」に両膝をついている。kneel「膝をつく」。
(B) countertop「調理台、カウンター」は写っているが、女性はそれを拭いてはいない。wipe「〜を拭く」。
(C) 女性はcabinet「戸棚」の中を見ている様子で、それにhandle「取っ手」を取り付けているところではない。install「〜を取り付ける」。
(D) electronic device「電子機器」は写っているが、女性はそのプラグをコンセントに差し込んでいるところではない。plug in 〜「〜のプラグをコンセントに差し込む」。

7

4

5

6

---

4 🇦🇺 M

(A) He's repairing a windowpane.
(B) He's waiting at a counter.
(C) He's arranging rugs in a building lobby.
(D) He's reading a street sign.

(A) 彼は窓ガラスを修理している。
(B) 彼はカウンターで待っている。
(C) 彼は建物のロビーで敷物を配置している。
(D) 彼は道路標識を読んでいる。

| 正解 **B** | counter「カウンター」の前に男性が立っており、受付の担当者の応対を待っている。 |

(A) 男性はwindowpane「窓ガラス」を修理してはいない。repair「～を修理する」。
(C) 男性はrug「敷物」の上に立っているが、それを配置しているところではない。arrange「～を配置する」、building「建物」、lobby「ロビー」。
(D) 写真は屋内の様子を写しており、street sign「道路標識」は見当たらない。

---

5 🇨🇦 M

(A) People are riding bicycles down a busy road.
(B) People have lined up to buy camping equipment.
(C) Bags have been scattered on the ground.
(D) Bags are being loaded into a large vehicle.

(A) 人々が交通量の多い道路を自転車で走っている。
(B) 人々がキャンプ用品を買うために一列に並んでいる。
(C) バッグが地面のあちこちに置かれている。
(D) バッグが大型車両の中に積み込まれているところである。

| 正解 **C** | 多数のバッグがground「地面」のあちこちに置かれた状態である。〈have been＋過去分詞〉で「～された状態である」という意味。scatter「～を一面にばらまく、～をあちこちに置く」。 |

(A) ride「～に乗る、～に乗って行く」、bicycle「自転車」、down「～に沿って、～を通って」、busy「混雑した、交通量の多い」。
(B) 人々は一列に並んではいない。line up「一列に並ぶ」、camping「キャンプ」、equipment「備品、用具」。
(D) load「～を積む」、vehicle「車両」。

---

6 🇬🇧 W

(A) There are some posters displayed in front of a store.
(B) There are cans of food stacked on the floor.
(C) Empty shopping carts have been placed together.
(D) Customers are taking cards from some shelves.

(A) 幾つかのポスターが店の前に掲示されている。
(B) 食品の缶詰が床に積み重ねられている。
(C) 空のショッピングカートがまとめて置かれている。
(D) 客が棚からカードを取っている。

| 正解 **C** | ショッピングカートが1カ所にまとめて置かれている。empty「空の」、place「～を置く」、together「一緒に（して）」。 |

(A) 写っているのは店内であり、店の前ではない。また、ポスターも確認できない。display「～を掲示する」。
(B) 食品の缶詰は写っていない。can「缶詰（の缶）」、stack「～を積み重ねる」。
(D) カードのようなものが多数並んだ棚はあるが、customer「客」は見当たらない。shelvesはshelf「棚」の複数形。

PART 2

7 🇬🇧 W Which cubicle would you prefer?

🇦🇺 M (A) At the end of this month.
(B) A new consultant.
(C) The one near the window.

どの作業ブースをご希望ですか。

(A) 今月末に。
(B) 新任のコンサルタントです。
(C) 窓の近くのものです。

正解 C Which ～?でどの作業ブースを希望するかと尋ねているのに対し、「窓の近くのもの」と、特定のブースを指定している(C)が正解。oneは質問にあるcubicle「(仕切られた)小区画、(オフィスの個人用)作業ブース」を受けている。prefer「～をより好む」。
(A) 時期は尋ねられていない。
(B) consultant「顧問、コンサルタント」。

---

8 🇬🇧 W When is the new Web site going to be launched?

🇨🇦 M (A) After it gets a final review.
(B) Mr. Davies, I think.
(C) The shipment arrived on Saturday.

新しいウェブサイトはいつ運用開始される予定ですか。

(A) 最終的な見直しを受けた後です。
(B) Daviesさんだと思います。
(C) その荷物は土曜日に到着しました。

正解 A When ～?で新しいウェブサイトの運用開始時期を尋ねているのに対し、最終的な見直しを受けた後というタイミングを伝えている(A)が正解。itは質問にあるthe new Web siteを指す。launch「～を開始する、～を世に出す」。final「最終的な」、review「見直し、審査」。
(B) 人物は尋ねられていない。
(C) 時期に言及しているが、荷物の到着日を伝える発言は質問への応答にならない。shipment「出荷品」、arrive「到着する」。

---

9 🇨🇦 M Where is the accounting department?

🇺🇸 W (A) I'll wear a warm jacket.
(B) On the third floor.
(C) Probably at four o'clock.

経理部はどこですか。

(A) 私は暖かい上着を着用することにします。
(B) 3階です。
(C) おそらく4時に。

正解 B Where ～?で経理部がある場所を尋ねているのに対し、「3階だ」と特定のフロアを答えている(B)が正解。accounting「会計学、経理」、department「部署」。floor「階」。
(A) 質問にあるwhereと同じ音のwear「～を着用する」に注意。
(C) 時刻は尋ねられていない。

---

10 🇦🇺 M Why was the company picnic postponed?

🇬🇧 W (A) I ordered ten of them.
(B) On their social media account.
(C) Because it's supposed to rain.

会社の野外親睦会はなぜ延期されたのですか。

(A) 私はそれらを10個注文しました。
(B) 彼らのソーシャルメディアアカウントに。
(C) 雨が降る見込みだからです。

正解 C Why ～?で野外親睦会が延期された理由を尋ねているのに対し、Becauseを用いて「雨が降る見込みだから」と、当日の天候という理由を伝えている(C)が正解。company picnic「野外で行う会社の親睦会・パーティー」、postpone「～を延期する」。be supposed to do「～することになっている、～するはずである」。
(A) themが何を指すか不明。また、注文内容を伝える発言では応答にならない。order「～を注文する」。
(B) 媒体については尋ねられていない。

---

11 🇺🇸 W Do you want to attend that extra training session?

🇨🇦 M (A) Yes, I could use some more practice.
(B) I like the green ones better.
(C) I stayed there about three years ago.

その追加の研修会に出席したいですか。

(A) はい、もう少し練習できればありがたいです。
(B) 緑色のものの方がいいと思います。
(C) 私は約3年前にそこに滞在しました。

正解 A 追加の研修会に出席したいかと尋ねているのに対し、Yesと肯定し、「もう少し練習できればありがたい」と出席を希望する理由を伝えている(A)が正解。attend「～に出席する」、extra「追加の、臨時の」、training session「研修会」。could use ～「～が得られるとありがたい」。
(B) 代名詞のonesが何を表しているか不明。
(C) thereがどこを指すか不明。

12 🇺🇸 W Who's picking up the lunch order?

🇦🇺 M　(A) There is plenty of parking.
　　　(B) Yes, I told the waiter.
　　　(C) Marcela from the front desk.

誰が昼食の注文品を受け取ることになっていますか。
(A) 駐車場所はたくさんあります。
(B) はい、私は給仕係に伝えました。
(C) 受付のMarcelaです。

正解 **C**　Who ～?で昼食用に注文したものを受け取る予定の人物を尋ねているのに対し、「受付のMarcelaだ」と具体的に名前を挙げて答えている(C)が正解。Who'sはWho isの短縮形。pick up ～「～を受け取る」、order「注文(品)」。front desk「受付」。
(A) plenty of ～「たくさんの～」、parking「駐車場所」。
(B) 質問にあるlunch orderと関連するwaiter「給仕係」に注意。注文品を受け取る人物が尋ねられているので、Yes/Noでは応答にならない。

13 🇨🇦 M How much juice does the recipe call for?

🇬🇧 W　(A) With a lot of fruit.
　　　(B) About a liter.
　　　(C) They're very careful.

そのレシピにはどれくらいの量のジュースが必要ですか。
(A) たくさんの果物を使ってです。
(B) 1リットルくらいです。
(C) 彼らは非常に注意深いです。

正解 **B**　How much ～?でレシピに必要なジュースの量を尋ねているのに対し、「1リットルくらいだ」とおおよそその分量を答えている(B)が正解。call for ～「～を必要とする」。liter「リットル」。
(A) 質問にあるjuiceと関連し得るfruit「果物」が含まれるが、ジュースの量が尋ねられているので、材料を伝える発言は応答にならない。
(C) Theyが誰を指すか不明。careful「注意深い」。

14 🇺🇸 W Which package was delivered last night?

🇦🇺 M　(A) She lives in the city center.
　　　(B) With great care.
　　　(C) The box for Mr. Nakamura.

どの小包が昨夜配達されましたか。
(A) 彼女は市の中心部に住んでいます。
(B) 十分に注意してです。
(C) Nakamuraさん宛ての箱です。

正解 **C**　Which ～?で昨夜配達されたのはどの小包かと尋ねているのに対し、「Nakamuraさん宛ての箱だ」と具体的に答えている(C)が正解。package「小包」、deliver「～を配達する」。
(A) Sheが誰を指すか不明。center「中心部」。
(B) with care「注意して」には、配達物の注意書きなどで「取扱注意」の意味もあり、packageやdeliveredから連想され得るが、応答にならない。

15 🇨🇦 M Should we meet in my office or in the conference room?

🇺🇸 W　(A) We'll have a vegetarian meal, please.
　　　(B) I prefer the conference room.
　　　(C) A table and some chairs.

私の執務室で集まるのがいいですか、それとも会議室がいいですか。
(A) ベジタリアン向けの食事をお願いします。
(B) 会議室の方がいいです。
(C) テーブル1卓と椅子が数脚です。

正解 **B**　A or B?の形で、男性の執務室で集まるのがいいか、あるいは会議室がいいかと尋ねている。これに対し、「会議室の方がいい」と、希望の場所として後者を選択している(B)が正解。meet「会合する、集まる」、conference room「会議室」。prefer「～をより好む」。
(A) 質問にあるmeetと同音のmeat「肉」から連想され得るvegetarian「ベジタリアン(の)」やmeal「食事」に注意。
(C) 質問にあるofficeやconference roomと関連し得るtableやchairsを含むが、応答にならない。

16 🇬🇧 W I can look at your computer if you still need help.

🇨🇦 M　(A) I know you did.
　　　(B) That would be great, thanks.
　　　(C) A software application.

まだ手助けが必要でしたら、私があなたのコンピューターを見てあげますよ。
(A) あなたがしたということは知っています。
(B) そうしてもらえるとうれしいです、ありがとう。
(C) ソフトウエア・アプリケーションです。

正解 **B**　まだ手助けが必要なら自分がコンピューターを見てあげるという発言に対し、「そうしてもらえるとうれしい、ありがとう」と、申し出を受けた上で感謝の気持ちを伝えている(B)が正解。thatは、女性が男性のコンピューターを見ることを指している。look at ～「～を見る、～を調べる」。
(A) コンピューターを見てあげるという申し出に対し、過去のことを述べる発言は合わない。
(C) コンピューターに関連した発言だが応答になっていない。

TEST1 PART 2

17 🇦🇺 M What color should the dancers' costumes be?

🇬🇧 W (A) A low cost.
(B) If they fit well.
(C) Blue would work best.

ダンサーたちの衣装は何色がいいでしょうか。
(A) 安い費用です。
(B) それらがぴったり合うなら。
(C) 青色が最適でしょう。

正解 **C** What ～?で衣装を何色にすべきかと尋ねているのに対し、「青色が最適だろう」と具体的な色を答えている(C)が正解。costume「衣装」。work「うまくいく、都合がいい」。
(A) 質問にあるcostumesと似た音を含むcost「費用」に注意。費用は話題にされていない。
(B) theyがcostumesを指すとしても、衣装が合うかどうかに関する発言は応答にならない。fit「ぴったり合う」。

18 🇺🇸 W Would you like me to bring the flowers for Ms. Cho to her office?

🇦🇺 M (A) She's working at home today.
(B) A maintenance request.
(C) The apartment is quite large.

Choさんへの花を彼女の執務室に持って行きましょうか。
(A) 彼女は今日、在宅勤務をしています。
(B) 整備の依頼です。
(C) そのマンション住戸はかなり大きいです。

正解 **A** Would you like me to do ～?は直訳すると「あなたは私に～してほしいか」であり、「～しましょうか」と相手に申し出るニュアンスとなる。Choさんへの花を彼女の執務室に持って行こうかと申し出ているのに対し、Yes/Noでは答えずに彼女が在宅勤務だと伝えることで、Choさんが不在で花を渡せないことを示唆している(A)が正解。work at home「家で仕事をする、在宅勤務をする」。
(B) maintenance「整備」、request「依頼」。
(C) apartment「共同住宅の一戸分の区画」。

19 🇨🇦 M Do you have the latest issue of the magazine?

🇬🇧 W (A) Are those new jeans?
(B) No, not yet.
(C) A famous journalist.

その雑誌の最新号はありますか。
(A) それは新しいジーンズですか。
(B) いいえ、まだです。
(C) 有名なジャーナリストです。

正解 **B** 雑誌の最新号はあるかと尋ねているのに対し、Noと答え、not yet「まだだ」と、未入手であることを伝えている(B)が正解。latest「最新の」、issue「(雑誌などの)号」。
(A) 質問にあるmagazineと似た音を含むjeansに注意。
(C) 人物は尋ねられていない。journalist「報道記者、ジャーナリスト」。

20 🇦🇺 M How is this microwave oven different from others?

🇺🇸 W (A) It has a longer warranty.
(B) It's too hot in this room.
(C) We have several.

この電子レンジは他のものとどう違うのですか。
(A) より長期間の保証が付いています。
(B) この部屋の中は暑過ぎます。
(C) 私たちは幾つか持っています。

正解 **A** How ～?で、特定の電子レンジが他のものとどう違うのかを尋ねている。これに対し、保証期間がより長いという相違点を伝えている(A)が正解。Itは質問にあるthis microwave ovenを指す。microwave oven「電子レンジ」。warranty「保証(書)」。
(B) 質問にあるmicrowave ovenと関連するhotが含まれるが、部屋の暑さを伝える発言は応答にならない。
(C) several「幾つか」が、何を指すのか不明。

21 🇬🇧 W Who's assigned to check tickets for the concert tonight?

🇨🇦 M (A) The performance was wonderful.
(B) The printer is very fast.
(C) I haven't seen the work schedule yet.

誰が今夜のコンサートのチケット確認業務を割り当てられていますか。
(A) その公演は見事でした。
(B) そのプリンターはとても速いです。
(C) 私はまだ業務スケジュールを見ていません。

正解 **C** Who ～?で、チケット確認業務を割り当てられている人物を尋ねている。これに対し、業務スケジュールを未確認であることを述べて誰が担当者か知らないことを示唆している(C)が正解。Who'sはWho isの短縮形。assign ～ to do「～に…する業務を割り当てる」。
(A) 質問にあるconcertと関連するperformance「公演」を含むが、公演の感想は尋ねられていない。
(B) プリンターは話題にされていない。

22 🇬🇧 W Why hasn't Yuko sent the party invitations yet?

🇦🇺 M (A) The festival should be very exciting.
(B) Has the guest list been finalized?
(C) The paper is high quality.

Yukoはなぜ、パーティーの招待状をまだ送っていないのですか。
(A) その祭りはきっととても楽しいでしょうね。
(B) 招待客名簿は最終決定されたのですか。
(C) その用紙は高品質です。

正解 **B**　Why 〜?の否定疑問文で、Yukoがパーティーの招待状をまだ送っていない理由を尋ねているのに対し、「招待客名簿は最終決定されたのか」と聞き返し、招待状が発送できる段階にあるかどうかを確認している(B)が正解。invitation「招待状」。guest list「招待客名簿」、finalize「〜を最終的な形にする、〜を仕上げる」。
(A) festival「祭り、祝祭」、exciting「心躍るような」。
(C) 用紙やその品質は話題にされていない。high quality「高品質」。

---

23 🇨🇦 M Could you tell me where the notebooks are?

🇺🇸 W (A) Sure, I'll show you, actually.
(B) A seasonal sale.
(C) Thank you for the offer.

ノートがどこにあるか教えていただけますか。
(A) はい、私が実際にご案内しましょう。
(B) 季節限定のセールです。
(C) お申し出をありがとうございます。

正解 **A**　Could you 〜?でノートがある場所を教えてほしいと依頼しているのに対し、Sureと快諾し、「私が実際に案内する」と申し出ている(A)が正解。show「〜に見せる、〜に示す」、actually「実際に」。
(B) セールに関連することには言及されていない。seasonal「季節の」。
(C) 申し出に対しての謝意を伝える発言は、依頼に対する応答にならない。offer「申し出」。

---

24 🇦🇺 M When will the prototype of the game be ready?

🇺🇸 W (A) We won our match yesterday.
(B) The car will be here soon.
(C) By February first.

そのゲームの試作品はいつ準備ができますか。
(A) 私たちは昨日、試合に勝ちました。
(B) 車は間もなくここに到着します。
(C) 2月1日までに。

正解 **C**　When 〜?でゲームの試作品の準備ができる時期を尋ねている。これに対し、「2月1日までに」と具体的な期日を伝えている(C)が正解。prototype「試作品」。
(A) 質問にあるgameには「試合、競技」という意味もあるが、試合は話題にされていない。match「試合」。
(B) soonと時期に言及しているが、車の到着は話題にされていない。

---

25 🇺🇸 W This suitcase seems too small.

🇨🇦 M (A) Let's try another hotel.
(B) I've used it on trips before.
(C) The seat was comfortable.

このスーツケースは小さ過ぎるように思えます。
(A) 別のホテルに当たってみましょう。
(B) 私は以前、旅行でそれを使用したことがありますよ。
(C) その座席は快適でした。

正解 **B**　スーツケースが小さ過ぎるように思えるという発言に対し、以前旅行でそれを使用したという自分の経験を述べて、そのスーツケースで用が足りることを暗に伝えている(B)が正解。itは発言にあるthis suitcaseを指す。seem「〜のようだ、〜に思われる」。
(A) 発言にあるsuitcaseと関連し得るhotelが含まれるが、別のホテルに当たってみようという提案は発言とかみ合わない。try「〜を試す、〜に当たってみる」。
(C) seat「座席」の感想は尋ねられていない。comfortable「快適な」。

---

26 🇬🇧 W Where will we place the ads for the new phone?

🇦🇺 M (A) The staff is there now.
(B) I spoke with her yesterday.
(C) The design isn't even finished yet.

当社はどこに新しい電話機の広告を出す予定ですか。
(A) スタッフは今、そこにいます。
(B) 私は昨日、彼女と話をしました。
(C) まだデザインが仕上がってさえいませんよ。

正解 **C**　Where 〜?で広告をどこに出す予定かと尋ねているのに対し、デザインが仕上がってさえいないことを述べてまだ広告が出せる段階にはないことを暗に伝えている(C)が正解。place an ad「広告を出す（adはadvertisementの略）」。
(A) thereがどこを指すか不明。staffは集合名詞であり、「職員、スタッフ」の全体を指す。
(B) herが誰を指すか不明。

TEST1 PART 2

27 ［🇨🇦］M　Shouldn't the plumber be here by now?

［🇬🇧］W　(A) Traffic has been terrible today.
(B) People like the gym showers.
(C) Some home renovations.

配管工はもうここに来ていてもいいはずではありませんか。
(A) 今日は交通状況がひどいのです。
(B) 人々はそのジムのシャワーが気に入っています。
(C) 住宅の改修です。

正解 A	否定疑問文で、配管工がすでに到着しているはずではないのかと尋ねているのに対し、「今日は交通状況がひどい」と述べ、交通渋滞によって到着が遅れている可能性を示唆している (A)が正解。plumber「配管工」、by now「今ごろはもう、今ごろまでには」。traffic「交通(量)」、terrible「ひどい、ひどく悪い」。 (B) 質問にあるplumberと関連し得るshowersが含まれるが、応答になっていない。 (C) renovation「改修」。

28 ［🇺🇸］W　Why don't we take the train into the city instead?

［🇨🇦］M　(A) We enjoyed the museum.
(B) The bus is almost here.
(C) Near the countryside.

代わりに、市内まで電車に乗って行きませんか。
(A) 私たちは博物館を満喫しました。
(B) バスはもうすぐここに到着しますよ。
(C) 田舎の近くです。

正解 B	Why don't we ～?は「～しませんか」という提案の表現。代わりに電車に乗って市内へ行くという提案に対し、「バスはもうすぐここに到着する」と述べ、女性の提案に賛成ではないことを示唆した(B)が正解。instead「その代わりに」。almost「もう少しで」。 (A) 行動したことやその感想は尋ねられていない。 (C) 位置は尋ねられていない。countryside「田舎」。

29 ［🇦🇺］M　Do you want me to make an appointment with our lawyer?

［🇺🇸］W　(A) That hair salon is always booked.
(B) Is her office open on Saturdays?
(C) The building on Fourth Street.

当社の弁護士との面会の予約を取りましょうか。
(A) あの美容院は常に予約でいっぱいです。
(B) 彼女の事務所は土曜日に開いているのですか。
(C) 4番街に面している建物です。

正解 B	Do you want me to do?は「あなたは私に～してほしいか(＝私が～しようか)」と相手に申し出る表現。弁護士との面会の予約を取ろうかという申し出に対し、「彼女の事務所は土曜日に開いているのか」と聞き返し、予約を取れるのか確認している(B)が正解。herはour lawyer'sを表す。make an appointment「会う約束をする、面会の予約をする」、lawyer「弁護士」。 (A) 質問にあるappointmentと関連し得るbook「～を予約する」に注意。 (C) 場所は尋ねられていない。building「建物」。

30 ［🇬🇧］W　Will the snack vending machines be placed inside or outside the store?

［🇦🇺］M　(A) The car radio is not working.
(B) I saw them.
(C) The manager will tell us soon.

軽食の自動販売機は店内に設置されるのですか、それとも店外ですか。
(A) 車のラジオは故障しています。
(B) 私はそれらを目にしました。
(C) 店長がもうすぐ教えてくれるでしょう。

正解 C	A or B?の形で、自動販売機の設置予定場所は店内と店外のどちらかと尋ねている。これに対し、「店長がもうすぐ教えてくれるだろう」と、設置場所は間もなく知らされるという予測を伝えている(C)が正解。snack「軽食」、vending machine「自動販売機」、place「～を設置する」、inside「～の内側に」。manager「責任者、管理者」。 (A) workは「作動する」という意味で、not workingで「故障して」を表す。 (B) themがvending machinesを指すとしても、自販機の設置予定場所を問う質問への応答にならない。

31 ［🇨🇦］M　The welcome reception for new staff is Thursday evening, isn't it?

［🇺🇸］W　(A) The office will be closed then for cleaning.
(B) No, they look like a strong group.
(C) Her application is very good.

新しいスタッフの歓迎会は木曜日の晩ですよね?
(A) その時、オフィスは清掃のため閉まっています。
(B) いいえ、彼らは有能なグループに見えます。
(C) 彼女の応募書類は大変優れています。

正解 A	肯定文の文末に ～, isn't it?を付けて「～ですよね」と、新しいスタッフの歓迎会が木曜日の晩であることを確認している。これに対し、「その時、オフィスは清掃のため閉まっている」と述べ、木曜日の晩にオフィスで歓迎会が開かれることはなさそうだと暗に伝えている(A)が正解。thenはon Thursday eveningを表す。welcome reception「歓迎会」。 (C) application「応募(書類)」。

13

PART 3

会話 CD 1 46 | 問題 CD 1 47

Questions 32 through 34 refer to the following conversation.

問題32-34は次の会話に関するものです。

🇺🇸 W Hello, Martin. Thank you for helping set up this event here at the convention center with your staff. ❶Have you heard from the caterers today?

こんにちは、Martin。このコンベンションセンターでの本イベントの設営をあなたのところのスタッフと一緒に手伝ってくれて、ありがとうございます。今日、ケータリング業者から連絡はありましたか。

🇨🇦 M ❷Nothing yet, surprisingly.

驚いたことに、まだ何もありません。

🇺🇸 W I'm getting concerned.

私は心配になってきています。

🇨🇦 M ❸I agree. Let's give them a call. Maybe there's been some miscommunication or some other type of mistake.

同感です。先方に電話しましょう。何か伝達の不備やその他の種類のミスがあったのかもしれません。

🇺🇸 W Yes. ❹I hope they have the correct date for this event. ❺The award ceremony is starting in just a few hours.

そうですね。先方がこのイベントの正確な日程を把握しているとよいのですが。表彰式はほんの数時間後に始まるのですから。

---

32 What does the woman ask about?

(A) A parking spot
(B) A site map
(C) A training schedule
(D) A catering order

女性は何について尋ねていますか。

(A) 駐車場所
(B) 会場の地図
(C) 研修の予定
(D) ケータリングの注文

正解 D 女性は、イベントの準備の手伝いに対するお礼を述べた後、❶「今日、ケータリング業者から連絡はあったか」と尋ねている。よって、(D)が正解。catering「仕出し、ケータリング」、order「注文」。
(A) parking spot「駐車場所」。
(B) site「場所、敷地」。
(C) training「研修」、schedule「予定(表)」。

---

33 What does the woman imply when she says, "I'm getting concerned"?

(A) Some items are unavailable.
(B) A delivery could be late.
(C) A weather forecast is poor.
(D) A schedule has been updated.

"I'm getting concerned" という発言で、女性は何を示唆していますか。

(A) 幾つかの品物が入手できない。
(B) 配達が遅れるかもしれない。
(C) 天気予報が当てにならない。
(D) 予定表が更新された。

正解 B ❶で、ケータリング業者から連絡があったかと尋ねる女性に対し、男性は❷「驚いたことに、まだ何もない」と答えている。これに対して女性は、下線部の発言で心配になってきていると述べ、男性は❸で、女性に同意してから業者に電話することを提案している。その後、女性は❺で表彰式が間もなく始まることを気にしている。これらから、女性は下線部の発言で、ケータリング業者の配達が間に合わない可能性を示唆して心配していると考えられる。imply「〜を示唆する」。delivery「配達」。
(A) item「品物」、unavailable「入手不可能な」。
(C) weather forecast「天気予報」、poor「質の悪い」。
(D) update「〜を更新する」。

---

34 What event is being held?

(A) A dance recital
(B) A graduation rehearsal
(C) An award ceremony
(D) A technology exhibit

どんなイベントが開催されるところですか。

(A) ダンスの発表会
(B) 卒業式の予行演習
(C) 表彰式
(D) テクノロジー機器の展示会

正解 C 女性は❹で、ケータリング業者がイベントの正確な日程を把握しているとよいがと述べてから、❺「表彰式はほんの数時間後に始まる」と発言している。よって、(C)が正解。hold「〜を開催する」。
(A) recital「独演会、発表会」。
(B) graduation「卒業式」、rehearsal「予行演習」。
(D) technology「科学技術、テクノロジー(機器)」、exhibit「展示会」。

Words & Phrases

help *do* 〜するのを手伝う　set up 〜 〜を準備する
convention center コンベンションセンター ★会議や博覧会のための施設　hear from 〜 〜から連絡をもらう
caterer ケータリング業者、仕出し業者　surprisingly 驚いたことに　concerned 心配して　agree 同意する
miscommunication 伝達ミス　mistake 間違い　correct 正しい　award ceremony 表彰式　in 〜 〜後に

Questions 35 through 37 refer to the following conversation.

 M Hello, ❶I'm calling because I can't access my company's cloud database. ❷Would you be able to help me?

 W Sure thing. What company are you calling from?

 M Tuckahoe Insurance Group. We store everything online. This is a real problem for me. ❸I'm a product manager, and I can't access the files for any of our products.

 W I'm sorry to hear that. OK, I'm going to place you on hold for a moment. ❹I'm getting a specialist to join us on the line.

問題35-37は次の会話に関するものです。

もしもし、うちの会社のクラウドデータベースにアクセスできないのでお電話しています。助けていただくことはできますか。

もちろんです。どちらの会社からお電話されていますか。

Tuckahoe保険グループ社です。当社は全てのものをオンライン上に保存しています。これは私には一大事です。私は商品マネジャーなのですが、当社のどの商品のファイルにもアクセスすることができないのです。

それは申し訳ございません。承知しました、少しの間、お電話を保留にいたします。専門家に、この通話に加わってもらいますね。

35 Why is the man calling?

(A) He would like to place an order.
(B) He needs to set up an account.
(C) He needs help with a technical problem.
(D) He would like to make an appointment.

男性はなぜ電話をしているのですか。
(A) 彼は注文をしたいと思っている。
(B) 彼はアカウントを設定する必要がある。
(C) 彼は技術的な問題で助けを必要としている。
(D) 彼は予約を入れたいと思っている。

正解 C 男性は❶「自分の会社のクラウドデータベースにアクセスできないので電話している」と、電話した理由を伝え、続けて❷で助けを求めている。よって、❶で述べられたコンピューター上の問題をa technical problemと表している(C)が正解。technical「技術的な」。
(A) place an order「注文をする」。
(B) アカウントの設定は話題にされていない。accessやcloudなどの語から連想され得る点に注意。set up ~「~を設定する」。
(D) 予約については話題にされていない。make an appointment「予約を入れる、会う約束をする」。

36 What is the man's job?

(A) Marketing associate
(B) Fitness trainer
(C) Data scientist
(D) Product manager

男性の仕事は何ですか。
(A) マーケティング担当者
(B) フィットネスコーチ
(C) データ科学者
(D) 商品マネジャー

正解 D どの会社から電話しているかと尋ねられた男性は、社名と状況説明をして、❸「私は商品マネジャーだ」と自分の仕事に言及している。(D)が正解。
(A) associate「仕事仲間、提携者」。
(B) trainer「トレーナー、コーチ」。
(C) scientist「科学者」。

37 Who will join the conversation?

(A) A manager
(B) A specialist
(C) A salesperson
(D) A contractor

誰が会話に加わりますか。
(A) 管理者
(B) 専門家
(C) 販売員
(D) 請負業者

正解 B 男性から状況を聞いた女性は、電話を保留にすると伝えた後、❹「専門家に、この通話に加わってもらう」と述べている。よって、間もなく専門家を交えた電話での会話が行われると分かるので、(B)が正解。
(A) 男性が自分は商品マネジャーであると述べているだけ。manager「管理者」。
(C) salesperson「販売員」。
(D) contractor「(工事)請負業者」。

TEST1 PART 3

Words & Phrases

access ~にアクセスする
cloud クラウド ★cloud computingの略で、インターネット上でデータの保存・利用を行うシステムを指す
be able to do ~することができる Sure thing. もちろん。 ★返事で用いる insurance 保険 store ~を保存する
product 製品、商品 on hold (電話口で)保留にして for a moment 少しの間 get ~ to do ~に…してもらう
specialist 専門家 join ~に加わる on the line 電話に出て

Questions 38 through 40 refer to the following conversation.

問題38-40は次の会話に関するものです。

W Hi, Mark. ❶Would you be able to look over this design revision?

こんにちは、Mark。このデザインの修正版に目を通していただくことはできますか。

M ❷Is it for the prototype mobile phones we've been working on?

それは、当社がずっと取り組んでいる携帯電話の試作品用ですか。

W ❸Yes. It's the most important project for the product development team.

そうです。製品開発チームにとっての最重要プロジェクトです。

M OK. What would you like me to examine?

分かりました。私は何を吟味すればよいでしょうか。

W ❹The plastic shell covering the phone wasn't very durable and cracked easily. ❺We want to use a new material, but it requires us to change the design a little.

電話機を覆うプラスチック製カバーがあまり頑丈ではなく、簡単にひびが入ったのです。私たちは新しい素材を使用したいと思っているのですが、それにはデザインを少し変更する必要があります。

M OK, yes, ❻we can't have the plastic shell breaking. I'll take a look at your design revision.

なるほど、そうですね、プラスチック製カバーが割れるようではいけませんね。あなたのデザインの修正版を見てみます。

---

38 What does the woman ask the man to do?

(A) Take a photograph
(B) Write a note
(C) Test some software
(D) Look at a revision

女性は男性に何をするよう頼んでいますか。

(A) 写真を撮る
(B) メモを書き留める
(C) ソフトウエアのテストをする
(D) 修正版を見る

正解 D 女性は男性に声を掛け、❶「このデザインの修正版に目を通してもらうことはできるか」と頼んでいるので、(D)が正解。look at 〜「〜を見る、〜を調べる」。
(A) photograph「写真」。
(B) note「メモ」。
(C) test「〜のテストをする」。

---

39 What type of product is mentioned?

(A) Furniture
(B) Mobile phones
(C) Clothing
(D) Headsets

どんな種類の製品について述べられていますか。

(A) 家具
(B) 携帯電話
(C) 衣料品
(D) ヘッドホン

正解 B ❶で、デザインの修正版に目を通すことを依頼された男性は、❷「それは、当社がずっと取り組んでいる携帯電話の試作品用か」と聞き返し、女性は❸でそれを肯定している。2人は以降でもその携帯電話について話し合っている。よって、(B)が正解。mention「〜のことを述べる」。
(A) furniture「家具」。
(C) clothing「衣料品」。
(D) headset「(マイク付きの)ヘッドホン」。

---

40 What is causing a problem for the speakers?

(A) A supply issue
(B) A piece of software
(C) A material in a product
(D) An audio file

何が、話し手たちに問題をもたらしていますか。

(A) 供給トラブル
(B) ソフトウエア
(C) 製品に使われる素材
(D) 音声ファイル

正解 C 女性が❹「電話機を覆うプラスチック製カバーがあまり頑丈ではなく、簡単にひびが入った」と問題点に言及した後、❺でデザインの変更理由が新素材の使用にあることを伝えている。これを聞いた男性も、❻で、プラスチック製カバーが割れるようではいけない、と素材の問題に関して同意している。よって、(C)が正解。cause 〜 for …「…に〜をもたらす」。
(A) supply「供給」、issue「問題」。
(B) a piece of 〜「(不可算名詞を数えて)1つの〜」。
(D) audio「音声の」。

Words & Phrases　look over 〜　〜に目を通す　revision　修正されたもの　prototype　試作品
work on 〜　〜に取り組む　development　開発　examine　〜を調べる、〜を吟味する　shell　外殻、(機器類の)覆い
cover　〜を覆う　durable　耐久性のある　crack　ひびが入る　material　材料、素材
require 〜 to do　〜が…することを必要とする　have 〜 doing　〜に…させる　take a look at 〜　〜を見てみる

Questions 41 through 43 refer to the following conversation.

🇬🇧 W Hi, ❶this is Ji-Yeon Park from Minetti's Pet Supplies. ❷I recently placed an order for 30 bags of your premium dry cat food.

🇨🇦 M Hello, Ms. Park. Is there a problem with your order?

🇬🇧 W Well, ❸I've been selling a lot of this product recently, and I was hoping to change my order from 30 bags to 50. ❹I know it's technically too late to change, but I just thought I'd see.

🇨🇦 M You're in luck. We haven't finalized your shipment yet. I can send you 50 bags, no problem.

🇬🇧 W Wonderful, thanks. ❺I'll send the bank transfer as soon as we finish this call.

問題41-43は次の会話に関するものです。

もしもし、こちらはMinetti'sペット用品店のJi-Yeon Parkです。私はついこの間、そちらのプレミアムドライキャットフードを30袋注文しました。

こんにちは、Park様。そのご注文のことで問題がございますか。

ええと、私のところではこの製品が最近よく売れていまして、注文を30袋から50袋に変更したいと思っていました。変更するには技術的に遅過ぎるということは承知しているのですが、ちょっと確かめてみようと思ったのです。

お客さまは運が良いですね。私どもはまだ、お客さまへの発送品を最終確定しておりません。50袋をお送りできます、問題ありません。

素晴らしい、ありがとうございます。この電話が終わり次第、銀行振り込みをします。

TEST1 PART 3

---

41 Where does the woman work?

(A) At a pet store
(B) At a restaurant
(C) At a catering company
(D) At an accounting firm

女性はどこで働いていますか。

(A) ペット用品店
(B) レストラン
(C) ケータリング会社
(D) 会計事務所

正解 A 女性は❶で、Minetti'sペット用品店のJi-Yeon Parkだと名乗っている。また、❷「私はついこの間、そちらのプレミアムドライキャットフードを30袋注文した」と述べ、その製品について❸で、自分のところでよく売れていると伝えている。よって、女性はペット用品を販売する店で働いており、商品の仕入れ注文の電話をかけていると判断できるので、(A)が正解。
(B) (C) いずれもorderやfoodなどの語から連想され得る点に注意。
(D) accounting firm「会計事務所」。

---

42 Why does the woman call the man?

(A) To complain about a delay
(B) To update an order
(C) To acknowledge receipt of an item
(D) To explain a delivery method

女性はなぜ男性に電話をしていますか。

(A) 遅延についての苦情を伝えるため
(B) 注文内容を更新するため
(C) 品物の受領を知らせるため
(D) 配達方法について説明するため

正解 B 女性は注文済みの製品について、❸「私のところではこの製品が最近よく売れていて、注文を30袋から50袋に変更したいと思っていた」と注文数の変更を希望し、❹でそれが可能か確認しようと思ったと付け足している。よって、(B)が正解。update「〜を更新する」。
(A) complain about 〜「〜について苦情を言う」、delay「遅延」。
(C) acknowledge「〜を認める、〜(の受領)を知らせる」、receipt「受領」、item「品物」。
(D) explain「〜について説明する」、delivery「配達」、method「方法」。

---

43 What does the woman say she will do?

(A) Review a bill
(B) Contact another employee
(C) Help load a truck
(D) Send a payment

女性は何をすると言っていますか。

(A) 請求書を見直す
(B) 別の従業員に連絡する
(C) トラックに荷物を積むのを手伝う
(D) 支払金を送る

正解 D 注文数の変更が可能だと知った女性は、❺「この電話が終わり次第、銀行振り込みをする」と言っている。よって、(D)が正解。payment「支払金」。
(A) review「〜を見直す」、bill「請求書」。
(B) contact「〜に連絡する」、employee「従業員」。
(C) help do「〜するのを手伝う」、load「〜に荷物を積む」。

Words & Phrases

supplies 用品　recently 最近　place an order for 〜 〜を注文する　bag 袋　product 製品　hope to do 〜したいと思う　technically 技術的に、厳密に言えば　be in luck 運が良い　finalize 〜を最終決定する　shipment 発送(品)　transfer 移動、振り込み　as soon as 〜 〜するとすぐに、〜し次第

Questions 44 through 46 refer to the following conversation.

問題44-46は次の会話に関するものです。

W Hey, Stefan. ❶What did you think of the training session yesterday?

ねえ、Stefan。昨日の研修会についてどう思いましたか。

M Uh, ❷to speak frankly, I don't think it was very useful for me. ❸A lot of the sales techniques they explained were ones I've been using for years.

ええと、率直に言うと、私にとってはあまりためにならなかったと思います。彼らが説明してくれた販売テクニックの多くは、私が長年使っているものでした。

W Hmm, that's good to know. It's probably more suited to newer employees. Thanks for telling me. Information like this is so useful to management.

なるほど、それを知ってよかったです。おそらく、もっと新人の従業員により適しているのでしょうね。教えてくれてありがとうございます。このような情報は経営管理にとても役立ちます。

M No problem.

どういたしまして。

W ❹Could you e-mail me any ideas you have for training sessions that would be more suitable to experienced employees?

経験豊富な従業員により適すると思われる研修会について、あなたが持っているアイデアを何でも、私にEメールで送っていただけますか。

M ❺I'll do that, Sunita, thanks.

そうします、Sunita、ありがとうございます。

44 What event is being discussed?

(A) A training session
(B) A trade fair
(C) A job interview
(D) An investors' meeting

どんなイベントについて話し合われていますか。

(A) 研修会
(B) 見本市
(C) 就職面接
(D) 出資者会議

正解 A 女性が❶「昨日の研修会についてどう思ったか」と感想を尋ねているのに対し、男性は❷・❸で、自分の感想を伝えている。2人は以降でも、研修会について話し合っているので、(A)が正解。discuss「～について話し合う」。
(B) trade fair「見本市」。
(C) job interview「就職面接」。
(D) investor「投資家、出資者」。

45 Who most likely is the man?

(A) A salesperson
(B) A teacher
(C) A computer programmer
(D) A warehouse manager

男性は誰だと考えられますか。

(A) 販売員
(B) 教師
(C) コンピュータープログラマー
(D) 倉庫管理者

正解 A 男性は研修会の内容について、❸「彼らが説明した販売テクニックの多くは、私が長年使っているものだった」と述べている。この発言から、男性は販売テクニックを必要とする業務をしていると判断できるので、(A)が正解。salesperson「販売員」。
(D) warehouse「倉庫」は話題にされていない。会話に登場するmanagementという語から連想され得る点に注意。

46 What does the man agree to do?

(A) Make an apology
(B) Share some suggestions
(C) Modify a meeting time
(D) Postpone a trip

男性は何をすることに同意していますか。

(A) 謝罪する
(B) 提案を伝える
(C) 会議の時間を変更する
(D) 旅行を延期する

正解 B 女性は❹で、経験豊富な従業員により適した研修会についてのアイデアをEメールで送るよう頼み、男性はこれに対し❺「そうする」と引き受けている。よって、❹で依頼されている内容をshare「～を伝える」とsuggestion「提案」を用いて表している(B)が正解。agree to do「～することに同意する」。
(A) make an apology「謝罪する」。
(C) modify「～を変更する、～を修正する」。
(D) postpone「～を延期する」。

Words & Phrases
What did you think of ～? ～についてどう思いましたか。 ★感想を尋ねる表現
training session 研修会　to speak frankly 率直に言うと　useful 有用な　for years 何年も、長年
That's good to know. それを知ってよかったです。　be suited to ～ ～に適している　management 経営管理
e-mail ～ … ～に…をEメールで送る　be suitable to ～ ～に適している　experienced 経験豊かな

Questions 47 through 49 refer to the following conversation.

W Hello, ❶I'd like to buy this book, please.

M ❷Sure, I'll ring you right up. **Hey, you do know we're having a sale, right?** ❸You can get the entire series for half off.

W The fact is <u>I usually don't like science fiction.</u> ❹But my friend recommended this, so I thought I'd at least try the first book in the series.

M Fair enough. Have you got a rewards card?

W No, but I'd like to sign up for one, please.

M No problem. ❺Can you start by telling me your first and last name?

問題47-49は次の会話に関するものです。

こんにちは、この本を購入したいのですが。

はい、すぐにお会計します。あの、当店がセール中だということはご存じですよね？こちらのシリーズ全巻を半額でお求めになれますよ。

実のところ、私は普段はSFを好まないのです。でも、友人がこれを薦めてくれたので、せめてシリーズの第1巻は読んでみようと思ったのです。

分かりました。ポイントカードはお持ちですか。

いいえ、でも申し込みたいのでお願いします。

承知しました。まず、お客さまの姓名を教えていただけますか。

---

47 Where most likely are the speakers?

　(A) In a publisher's office
　(B) In a public library
　(C) In a bookstore
　(D) In a classroom

話し手たちはどこにいると考えられますか。

　(A) 出版社のオフィス
　(B) 公立図書館
　(C) 書店
　(D) 教室

正解 C ❶「この本を購入したい」と伝えている女性に対し、男性は❷でSureと了承し、「すぐに会計をする」と言っている。その後も書籍シリーズのセールやポイントカードの発行について話題が展開している。(C)が正解。bookstore「書店」。(A) (B) いずれも本に関連するが、本の購入に関して話題が展開しているので不適切。(A) publisher「出版社」、(B) public「公立の」。

---

48 Why does the woman say, "I usually don't like science fiction"?

　(A) To decline an offer
　(B) To give advice
　(C) To change the subject
　(D) To accept a compliment

女性はなぜ "I usually don't like science fiction" と言っていますか。

　(A) 申し出を断るため
　(B) 助言をするため
　(C) 話題を変えるため
　(D) 賛辞を受け入れるため

正解 A 女性が購入しようとしている本について❸で、シリーズ全巻を半額で買えると勧める男性に対し、女性は「実のところ」と言った後、下線部の発言で普段はSFを好まないと述べ、続けて❹で、シリーズの第1巻だけでも読んでみようと思ったと話している。よって、全巻を半額で購入するという男性の提案を断るために、女性はこの発言をしていると分かる。decline「～を（丁重に）断る」。(C) 下線部と❹の発言を聞いた男性は、納得してから話題を変えているが、女性は話題を変えるために下線部の発言をしたのではない。subject「話題」。(D) accept「～を受け入れる」、compliment「賛辞」。

---

49 What information does the man ask for?

　(A) A name
　(B) A phone number
　(C) A due date
　(D) An e-mail address

男性はどんな情報を求めていますか。

　(A) 名前
　(B) 電話番号
　(C) 期日
　(D) Eメールアドレス

正解 A ポイントカードを作りたいと述べる女性に対し、男性は了承してから❺「まず、あなたの姓名を教えてもらえるか」と頼んでいる。よって、(A)が正解。ask for ～「～を求める」。(C) due date「（支払いや返却などの）期日」。

Words & Phrases

ring up ～ ～をレジに記録する、～の会計をする　right 〈副詞などの前に置いて〉すぐに
entire 全ての　for half off 半額で　the fact is (that) ～ 実は～である　science fiction 空想科学小説、SF
recommend ～を推薦する　at least せめて　Fair enough. 結構です。まあいいでしょう。　★相手の意見を認める表現
rewards card （店などの）ポイントカード　sign up for ～ ～の登録申し込みをする　start by doing ～することから始める

Questions 50 through 52 refer to the following conversation with three speakers.

M Hello. It's nice to meet you both. ❶I understand you're looking to hire some support staff?

W Yes. ❷We're both physicians, and we're opening our own medical clinic this year. ❸We need a few good receptionists, which is why we've come to your hiring agency.

M Exciting! Yes, we have lots of experienced receptionists. ❹Any special requirements?

W ❺We definitely want someone who has filed insurance paperwork before.

W Absolutely. ❻We want someone who's no stranger to this kind of work.

M Got it.

問題50-52は3人の話し手による次の会話に関するものです。

こんにちは。お二方とも、初めまして。サポートスタッフを雇用しようとしていらっしゃると伺っておりますが?

はい。私たちは2人とも内科医で、今年自分たちの医院を開業することになっています。私たちには有能な受付係が数名必要で、そういう理由でこちらの人材派遣会社に伺いました。

素晴らしいですね! はい、当社には多数の経験豊かな受付係がおりますよ。何か、特別なご要件は?

以前に保険の事務処理をしたことのある人がぜひとも欲しいですね。

その通りです。この種の作業に精通している人を希望します。

承知しました。

---

50 What are the speakers discussing?

(A) Hiring new employees
(B) Merging two companies
(C) Investing money in a company
(D) Changing an employment contract

話し手たちは何について話し合っていますか。

(A) 新しい従業員を雇用すること
(B) 2社を合併すること
(C) 企業に投資すること
(D) 雇用契約を変更すること

正解 A ❶「サポートスタッフを雇用しようとしていると理解しているが」と述べる男性に対し、1人目の女性はYesと肯定した後、❷で、医院の開業について述べ、❸「私たちには有能な受付係が数名必要で、そういう理由でこちらの人材派遣会社に来た」と伝えている。以降でも、3人は新しい人材の要件について話し合っているので、(A)が正解。
(B) merge「~を合併する」。
(C) invest money in ~「~に投資する」。
(D) employment「雇用」、contract「契約」。

---

51 Who are the women?

(A) Lawyers
(B) Doctors
(C) Investors
(D) Receptionists

女性たちは誰ですか。

(A) 法律家
(B) 医者
(C) 投資家
(D) 受付係

正解 B 1人目の女性は、❷「私たちは2人とも内科医で、今年自分たちの医院を開業することになっている」と自分たちについて説明している。❷のbothは、1人目の女性と2人目の女性を指す。physiciansをdoctorsと表している(B)が正解。
(A) lawyer「法律家」。
(C) investor「投資家」。
(D) 受付係は女性たちが必要としている人材。

---

52 What do the women express concern about?

(A) Agency fees
(B) Insurance costs
(C) A filing system
(D) Work experience

女性たちは何についての関心を示していますか。

(A) 代理店手数料
(B) 保険料
(C) 文書管理システム
(D) 実務経験

正解 D ❹で、求める人材の要件を尋ねる男性に対し、2人目の女性は❺で、保険の事務処理の経験者が欲しいと答えている。1人目の女性も❺の発言を肯定し、❻でこの作業（＝保険の事務処理）に精通している人材が必要だと伝えている。よって、2人は実務経験を気にしていると分かる。express「~を表明する」、concern「懸念、関心」。
(A) agency「代理店」、fee「手数料」。
(B) 保険の事務処理経験に言及しているだけで、保険料は話題にされていない。

Words & Phrases
look to do ~しようとする　hire ~を雇用する　physician 内科医、医師
receptionist 受付係　~, which is why … ~が…の理由である　hiring agency 人材派遣会社　experienced 経験豊かな
requirement 要件　definitely 絶対に　file ~を整理保存する、~（文書など）を正式に提出する　insurance 保険
paperwork 事務書類　absolutely 全くその通り　be no stranger to ~ ~に精通している　Got it. 分かりました。

20

Questions 53 through 55 refer to the following conversation.

M Hi, my name's Abdel Hassoun. ❶I'm calling to reschedule my flight.

W I can help you with that. Do you have your booking confirmation number?

M Yes—it's T3JG5.

W One moment. OK, I can see your flight information, Mr. Hassoun. ❷As a gold star member of our airline, there's no charge for the change. What return date would work for you?

M Next Friday—any time would be OK.

W We have one available flight that departs at noon.

M That's great.

W OK, ❸you'll get an e-mail with your new flight information shortly.

問題53-55は次の会話に関するものです。

もしもし、Abdel Hassounと申します。私の乗る飛行機の日時を変更するためにお電話しています。

そのご用件について、お手伝いいたします。お客さまの予約確認番号はお分かりですか。

はい——T3JG5です。

少々お待ちください。はい、お客さまのフライト情報が確認できました、Hassoun様。当航空会社のゴールドスター会員様ですので、変更手数料はかかりません。お帰りは何日ですとご都合がよろしいでしょうか。

今度の金曜日です——何時でも構いません。

正午に出発する予約可能なフライトが1便ございます。

それはありがたいです。

それでは、新しいフライト情報が記載されたEメールが間もなくお客さまに届きます。

53 Why does the man call the woman?

(A) To change a reservation
(B) To extend a registration time
(C) To inquire about meal options
(D) To sign up for a special promotion

男性はなぜ女性に電話をしていますか。

(A) 予約を変更するため
(B) 登録期間を延長するため
(C) 食事の選択肢について問い合わせるため
(D) 特別キャンペーンに申し込むため

正解 A 男性は名前を言ってから、❶「私の乗る飛行機の日時を変更するために電話している」と電話の用件を伝えている。その後のやりとりもフライトの予約の変更に関するものなので、(A)が正解。reservation「予約」。
(B) extend「～を延長する」、registration「登録」。
(C) inquire about ～「～について尋ねる」、option「選択肢」。
(D) sign up for ～「～に申し込む」、promotion「(販売促進の)キャンペーン」。

54 What allows the man to avoid paying a fee?

(A) A coupon
(B) A computer error
(C) A membership program
(D) An early purchase date

何によって、男性は手数料の支払いをせずに済みますか。

(A) クーポン
(B) コンピューター上のエラー
(C) 会員プログラム
(D) 早期の購入日

正解 C 女性は男性のフライト情報を確認した後、❷「当航空会社のゴールドスター会員なので、変更手数料はかからない」と伝えている。よって、男性は会員であるために変更手数料を支払う必要がないと分かるので、(C)が正解。allow ～ to do「～が…することを可能にする」、avoid doing「～することを避ける」、fee「手数料」。
(D) purchase「購入」。

55 What will the man receive after the telephone call?

(A) A free sample
(B) A customer survey
(C) An updated invoice
(D) A confirmation e-mail

男性は通話の後、何を受け取りますか。

(A) 無料の試供品
(B) 顧客アンケート
(C) 更新済みの請求書
(D) 確認のEメール

正解 D 自分の希望に合った予約可能なフライトがあると知り、「ありがたい」と述べる男性に対し、女性は❸「新しいフライト情報が記載されたEメールが間もなくあなたに届く」と知らせている。❸のan e-mail with your new flight information を a confirmation e-mail「確認のEメール」と表した(D)が正解。receive「～を受け取る」。
(B) customer survey「顧客アンケート」。
(C) ❷より、変更手数料は無料と分かる。update「～を更新する」、invoice「請求書」。

Words & Phrases

reschedule ～の日時を変更する　　help ～ with … …のことで～を手伝う　　booking 予約
confirmation 確認　　One moment. 少々お待ちください。　　charge 料金、手数料　　work for ～ ～に都合がよい
available 利用可能な　　depart 出発する　　shortly すぐに、間もなく

Questions 56 through 58 refer to the following conversation.

問題56-58は次の会話に関するものです。

W　Good afternoon, this is Amina Qurashi. ❶I'm calling to check on the status of my mortgage loan application. Can you help me with that?

こんにちは、こちらは Amina Qurashi です。私の住宅ローン申請の状況を確かめるためにお電話しています。それに関して手伝ってもらえますか。

M　Of course, Ms. Qurashi. It looks like your employer verified your current salary yesterday. ❷Unfortunately, I haven't received a copy of the property appraisal yet. Can you tell me who I should call for that?

もちろんです、Qurashi 様。お客さまの雇用主は昨日、現在の給与を証明されたようですね。あいにくですが、私はまだ、不動産の査定書を受け取っておりません。その件はどなたに電話すればいいか教えていただけますか。

W　Oh, yes. ❸Kelly Ross did the appraisal. You can reach her at 555-0127. I'm sure she can send you a copy of the report right away.

ああ、はい。Kelly Ross が査定してくれました。555-0127 で彼女と連絡を取ることができます。彼女はきっと、すぐにあなたに報告書を送ってくれると思います。

M　Great! ❹I'll call her first thing tomorrow. ❺If all goes well, you should receive an approval letter for the loan next week.

よかったです！ 明日一番で彼女に電話します。万事順調に進めば、お客さまは来週ローンの承認書をお受け取りになるはずです。

---

56 What are the speakers discussing?

(A) A news article
(B) A fund-raiser
(C) A loan application
(D) A job interview

話し手たちは何について話し合っていますか。

(A) ニュース記事
(B) 資金集めのイベント
(C) ローンの申請
(D) 就職面接

正解 **C**　女性は❶「私の住宅ローン申請の状況を確かめるために電話している」と用件を伝えている。これに対し、男性は女性の給与証明や不動産の査定書に言及してローン申請に関する会話を続け、❺でローンの承認書の取得の見通しについて述べている。よって、(C)が正解。
(A) article「記事」。
(B) fund-raiser「資金集めのイベント」。

---

57 What problem does the man mention?

(A) A missing document
(B) A property dispute
(C) A project delay
(D) An accounting error

男性はどんな問題について述べていますか。

(A) 欠けている書類
(B) 不動産争議
(C) 計画の遅延
(D) 会計上の誤り

正解 **A**　男性は、女性の住宅ローン申請の状況について、❷「あいにくだが、私はまだ、不動産の査定書を受け取っていない」と問題点を伝えてから、この件は誰に電話すべきかと尋ねている。よって、必要な書類が男性の手元にないと分かるので、(A)が正解。missing「見当たらない、欠けている」、document「書類」。
(B) dispute「論争、紛争」。
(C) delay「遅延」。
(D) accounting「会計」、error「誤り」。

---

58 When will the man contact Ms. Ross?

(A) Later today
(B) Tomorrow
(C) Next week
(D) Next month

男性はいつ Ross さんに連絡を取りますか。

(A) 本日後ほど
(B) 明日
(C) 来週
(D) 来月

正解 **B**　女性は❸で、自分の不動産の査定をした Kelly Ross という人物の名前と電話番号を男性に教え、彼女から男性に報告書を送ることができるだろうと伝えている。これに対し、男性は❹「明日一番で彼女に電話する」と言っているので、(B)が正解。contact「〜と連絡を取る」。
(C) ❺に next week とあるのは、首尾よく進んだ場合に女性がローンの承認書を受け取れる時期として述べられている。

Words & Phrases　check on 〜 〜を確かめる　status 状況　mortgage loan 担保付き融資、住宅ローン　application 申請　it looks like 〜 〜のようである　employer 雇用主　verify 〜が正しいことを証明する　current 現在の　salary 給与　unfortunately あいにく　property 不動産、資産　appraisal 査定　reach 〜と連絡を取る　right away 直ちに　first thing まず第一に、真っ先に　go well うまくいく　approval 承認

Questions 59 through 61 refer to the following conversation with three speakers.

 W **①**Hi, Marco. Welcome to Shannak Associates. We're delighted you're interning with us this summer.

M Thanks—**②**I'm excited to get some practical experience in corporate law.

 W You'll learn a lot here, but things can move at a fast pace, so we're pairing you with a mentor. Now, you've already filled out most of the paperwork—**③**I just need you to sign this last form, which allows us to get your employee badge made.

M All right. Here you go.

 W Thanks—and **④**here's your mentor, Hiroki, now. Excellent timing—we just finished up here.

M Great. Hi, Marco. I hope your first day is off to a good start. **⑤**Let me take you to meet the rest of our team.

問題59-61は3人の話し手による次の会話に関するものです。

こんにちは、Marco。Shannak Associates社へようこそ。あなたがこの夏、うちでインターンとして働いてくれることをうれしく思います。

ありがとうございます——会社法の実務経験を積むのが楽しみです。

あなたにはここで多くのことを学んでもらうことになりますが、物事が速いペースで動く場合があるので、教育係とペアを組んでもらいます。さて、すでに大半の必要書類に記入を済ませていますね——あとはこの最後の用紙に署名してもらう必要があるだけです。それであなたの従業員バッジを作ってもらえるので。

分かりました。はい、どうぞ。

ありがとう——そして、ほら、ちょうどあなたの教育係のHirokiが来ました。素晴らしいタイミングですね——私たちはちょうど今終わったところですよ。

よかった。こんにちは、Marco。あなたの初出勤日が好調なスタートを切ることを願っています。うちのチームの残りのメンバーとの顔合わせにご案内しましょう。

---

59 Where does the conversation most likely take place?
- (A) At a law office
- (B) At a retail store
- (C) At an advertising agency
- (D) At a graphic design company

会話はどこで行われていると考えられますか。
- (A) 法律事務所
- (B) 小売店
- (C) 広告代理店
- (D) グラフィックデザイン会社

正解 A 女性は ① で、MarcoをShannak Associates社に歓迎し、インターンとして迎え入れている。これに対し、Marcoはお礼を言ってから、②「会社法の実務経験を積むのが楽しみだ」と述べているので、話し手たちがいるShannak Associates社は法律業務に関する会社だと判断できる。よって、(A)が正解。take place「行われる」。law office「法律事務所」。

---

60 Why does the woman request a signature?
- (A) To finalize a contract
- (B) To obtain an employee badge
- (C) To grant a parking permit
- (D) To process a payment

女性はなぜ署名を求めていますか。
- (A) 契約を仕上げるため
- (B) 従業員バッジを取得するため
- (C) 駐車許可証を与えるため
- (D) 支払金を処理するため

正解 B 女性は、Marcoが大半の必要書類に記入済みであることを確認してから、③「あとはこの最後の用紙に署名してもらう必要があるだけだ。それであなたの従業員バッジを作ってもらえる」と署名を求めて理由も述べている。よって、(B)が正解。signature「署名」。obtain「～を取得する」。
(A) finalize「～を仕上げる」、contract「契約」。
(C) grant「～を与える」、permit「許可証」。
(D) process「～を処理する」、payment「支払金」。

---

61 What does Hiroki say he is going to do next?
- (A) Greet a new client
- (B) Prepare a work space
- (C) Introduce staff members
- (D) Review some policy changes

Hirokiは次に何をするつもりだと言っていますか。
- (A) 新規顧客にあいさつする
- (B) 作業スペースを用意する
- (C) スタッフを紹介する
- (D) 方針の変更を見直す

正解 C 女性の ④ の発言から、HirokiとはMarcoの教育係と分かる。Hirokiは⑤「うちのチームの残りのメンバーとの顔合わせに案内しよう」と申し出ているので、HirokiがMarcoにチームのスタッフを紹介するつもりだと分かる。よって、(C)が正解。introduce「～を紹介する」。
(A) Marcoがチームのスタッフと顔合わせするのであり、Hirokiがclient「顧客」にあいさつするのではない。greet「～にあいさつする」。

Words & Phrases

be delighted (that) ～　～ということをうれしく思う　　pair ～ with …　～を…と組み合わせる
Here you go.　はい、どうぞ。　　finish up　終わる　　off to a good start　好調なスタートを切って　　the rest　その他の人々・もの

Questions 62 through 64 refer to the following conversation and receipt.

🍁 M Welcome to Blue Brook Outdoor Supplies. How can I help you?

🇺🇸 W ❶I'd like to return these binoculars. I bought them yesterday, but it turns out my husband had already ordered some online.

🍁 M No problem. ❷Do you have your receipt?

🇺🇸 W Yes, but ❸I also wanted to purchase a new water bottle and a few other things.

🍁 M OK, ❹I can hold on to these binoculars for you while you shop if you like. ❺When you're ready, you can just come back here, and I'll process the exchange.

問題62-64は次の会話とレシートに関するものです。

Blue Brookアウトドア用品店へようこそ。どのようなご用件でしょうか。

この双眼鏡を返品したいと思っています。昨日、これを買ったのですが、夫がすでにオンラインで注文していたということが判明しまして。

問題ございません。レシートはお持ちですか。

はい、ですが、新しい水筒と幾つか他の商品も購入したかったのです。

かしこまりました。もしよろしければ、お客さまがお買い物されている間、この双眼鏡をお預かりできますよ。ご準備ができましたら、こちらにお戻りくだされば交換の手続きをいたします。

Blue Brook Outdoor Supplies

Receipt	July 10
Binoculars	$30
Batteries	$ 7
Utensils	$20
Hiking poles	$65
Total	$122

Blue Brook アウトドア用品店

レシート	7月10日
双眼鏡	30ドル
バッテリー	7ドル
諸用具	20ドル
登山ポール	65ドル
合計	122ドル

62 Look at the graphic. What is the price of the item the speakers are mainly discussing?

(A) $30
(B) $7
(C) $20
(D) $65

図を見てください。話し手たちが主に話し合っている品物の値段は幾らですか。

(A) 30ドル
(B) 7ドル
(C) 20ドル
(D) 65ドル

正解 A　女性は❶「この双眼鏡を返品したいと思っている」と伝え、続けてその理由を説明している。男性は女性の要望に対応し、以降でも2人はこの双眼鏡について主に話し合っている。図を見ると、双眼鏡の値段は30ドルなので、(A)が正解。price「値段」、item「品物」、mainly「主に」。
(B)(C)(D) それぞれバッテリー、諸用具、登山ポールの値段だが、いずれの品物にも具体的な言及がない。

63 What does the man ask the woman for?

(A) An e-mail address
(B) A water bottle
(C) A bag
(D) A document

男性は女性に何を求めていますか。

(A) Eメールアドレス
(B) 水筒
(C) 袋
(D) 書類

正解 D　購入済みの双眼鏡を返品したいと伝える女性に対し、男性はNo problem.と了承した後、❷「レシートは持っているか」と尋ねている。よって、❷のyour receiptをa documentと表現している(D)が正解。ask ～ for … 「～に…を求める」。document「書類」。
(B) 水筒への言及はあるが、女性が購入したいと思っている商品の一つとして述べられているのであり、男性が女性に求めているわけではない。

64 What will the woman most likely do next?

(A) Look up some information online
(B) Shop for some items
(C) Go to a different store
(D) Call her husband

女性は次に何をすると考えられますか。

(A) オンラインで情報を調べる
(B) 幾つかの品物を買いに行く
(C) 別の店へ行く
(D) 夫に電話をかける

正解 B　女性は❸で、水筒を含めた商品を幾つか購入したいと伝えている。それに対して男性は承諾し、❹で、買い物をしている間は双眼鏡を預かると申し出て、続けて❺で、準備ができたら戻ってくるよう付け加えている。よって、女性はこれから、買いたい品物を探しに行くと考えられる。shop for ～ 「～を買いに行く」。
(A) look up ～ 「～を調べる」。
(C) 女性は別の品物を探しに行こうとしているが、返品する双眼鏡を預けて同店の中で買い物をしようとしており、別の店に行こうとしているわけではない。different「別の」。
(D) 女性は夫に言及しているが、電話をするとは言っていない。

Words & Phrases

receipt　領収書、レシート　　supplies　用品　　return　～を返品する　　binoculars　双眼鏡
turn out (that) ～　～であることが分かる　　order　～を注文する　　purchase　～を購入する　　water bottle　水筒
hold on to ～　～を手放さない　　while　～している間に　　shop　買い物をする　　if you like　もしよければ
process　～の手続きをする　　exchange　交換

レシート　battery　電池、バッテリー　　utensil　用具、用品　　hiking pole　登山ポール　★ハイキングや登山などの際に使う杖

Questions 65 through 67 refer to the following conversation and list of classes.

M Sang-Mi, ❶here's the schedule of classes they're offering at the Greenview Garden Center. ❷I think these would be helpful since we're both going to be working in the community garden this year.

W For sure. ❸But they're all on Saturdays? ❹I have to work every Saturday this month except the sixteenth. I could attend that one, though.

M Oh, that's too bad. I'm planning on attending all of them.

W I'd like to go to at least one other session. ❺I'm going to ask Hiroshi if he can work at least one Saturday for me. ❻I'll send him an e-mail.

問題65-67は次の会話と講座一覧表に関するものです。

Sang-Mi、これが、Greenviewガーデンセンターで開講される講座の予定表です。今年、私たちは2人とも市民農園で作業する予定なので、これらは役立つだろうと思います。

確かに。でも、それは全て土曜日にあるのですね? 私は、今月は16日以外は毎週土曜日に仕事をしなければならないのです。その講座には出席できそうですが。

ああ、それは残念ですね。私は講座の全てに出席するつもりです。

私は最低でももう1つ他の講座に行きたいです。Hiroshiに、私の代わりに少なくともどこか1つの土曜日に勤務できるか尋ねてみます。彼にEメールを送りますね。

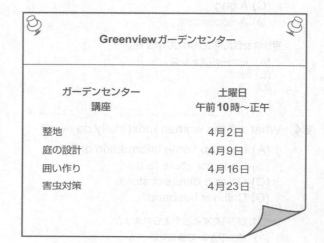

Garden center classes	Saturdays 10 A.M.–Noon
Soil preparation	April 2
Planning your garden	April 9
Building a frame	April 16
Dealing with pests	April 23

Greenview ガーデンセンター

ガーデンセンター 講座	土曜日 午前10時～正午
整地	4月2日
庭の設計	4月9日
囲い作り	4月16日
害虫対策	4月23日

65 Why does the man suggest attending gardening classes?

(A) He wants to start a gardening business.
(B) The speakers will be working in a garden.
(C) The classes were recommended to him.
(D) The classes are taught by his friend.

男性はなぜ、園芸講座に出席することを提案しているのですか。

(A) 彼は園芸の事業を始めたいと思っている。
(B) 話し手たちは農園で作業することになっている。
(C) その講座が彼に対して薦められた。
(D) その講座が彼の友人によって教えられている。

正解 **B**　男性は女性に、❶でGreenviewガーデンセンターの開講講座の一覧表を見せ、続けて❷「今年、私たちは2人とも市民農園で作業する予定なので、これらは役立つだろうと思う」と、園芸講座への参加を提案している。よって、(B)が正解。suggest *doing*「～することを提案する」、gardening「園芸」。
(A) start a business「事業を興す」。
(C) 男性は女性に講座を薦めているが、誰かが男性にそれを薦めたという言及はない。recommend「～を推奨する」。

66 Look at the graphic. Which class does the woman say she can attend?

(A) Soil preparation
(B) Planning your garden
(C) Building a frame
(D) Dealing with pests

図を見てください。女性はどの講座に出席することができると言っていますか。

(A) 整地
(B) 庭の設計
(C) 囲い作り
(D) 害虫対策

正解 **C**　講座一覧表を見た女性は、❸で講座が全て土曜日に開かれることに言及し、❹「私は、今月は16日以外は毎週土曜日に仕事をしなければならない。その講座には出席できそうだが」と自分の都合を述べている。16日の講座だけ出席できると言っているので、図を見ると4月16日に行われる囲い作りの講座に出席できると分かる。よって、(C)が正解。

67 What does the woman say she will do next?

(A) Contact a colleague
(B) Register online
(C) Buy equipment
(D) Research local suppliers

女性は次に何をすると言っていますか。

(A) 同僚に連絡する
(B) オンラインで登録する
(C) 用具を購入する
(D) 地元の納入業者を調べる

正解 **A**　女性は❺で、Hiroshiという人物に自分の代わりに少なくともどこか1つの土曜日に勤務可能か尋ねてみると言い、その直後に❻「彼にEメールを送る」と発言している。よって、同僚のHiroshiにEメールで連絡すると分かるので、send ～ an e-mailをcontactと、Hiroshiをa colleagueとそれぞれ表している(A)が正解。colleague「同僚」。
(B) register「登録する」、online「オンラインで」。
(C) equipment「用具」。
(D) research「～を調べる」、local「地元の」、supplier「納入業者」。

Words & Phrases　list 一覧表　class 講座　schedule 予定表　offer ～を提供する　helpful 役立つ
community garden 市民農園　for sure 確かに　except ～を除いて、～以外は　attend ～に出席する
though もっとも～ではあるが　plan on *doing* ～するつもりである　at least 少なくとも　session 集まり、会

講座一覧表　soil 土壌　preparation 準備　plan ～を設計する　frame （栽培用の）囲い　deal with ～ ～に対処する
pest 害虫

Questions 68 through 70 refer to the following conversation and schedule.

問題68-70は次の会話と予定表に関するものです。

🇬🇧 W Sorry, I just got here. I was starting to worry I'd miss the train!

すみません、ちょうど今着きました。電車に乗り遅れるのではないかと心配になってきたところでした！

🇦🇺 M No problem. ❶Our train to Middletown was actually rescheduled, so we have plenty of time. ❷Was it traffic that delayed you?

大丈夫ですよ。私たちが乗る予定のミドルタウン行きの列車は、実のところ時刻が変更になったので、時間はたっぷりあります。あなたが遅れたのは交通渋滞のせいですか。

🇬🇧 W No, ❸they're doing construction on Pioneer Bridge, and I had to take a detour.

いいえ、パイオニア橋で工事が行われていて、遠回りをしなければならなかったのです。

🇦🇺 M Oh, I heard about that roadwork, but I came from the other direction. Well, I'm glad you made it.

ああ、あの道路工事のことは聞きましたが、私は別の方向から来ました。とにかく、あなたが間に合ってよかったです。

🇬🇧 W Me too. ❹I'm going to get a coffee. ❺Can I buy one for you?

同感です。私はコーヒーを買いに行ってきます。あなたにも1杯買ってきましょうか。

🇦🇺 M No, thanks. I think I'll just wait here and finish reading the newspaper.

いいえ、結構です、ありがとう。私はここで待ちながら新聞を読み終えようと思います。

🚄 Departures		
Time	**Destination**	**Track**
10:00 A.M.	Branburg	1
11:20 A.M.	Middletown	2
12:10 P.M.	Pleasantville	3
1:00 P.M.	Cashmere	4

🚄 出発列車		
時刻	行き先	ホーム
午前10時00分	ブランバーグ	1
午前11時20分	ミドルタウン	2
午後12時10分	プレザントビル	3
午後 1時00分	カシミール	4

68 Look at the graphic. What track will the speakers' train leave from?

(A) Track 1
(B) Track 2
(C) Track 3
(D) Track 4

図を見てください。話し手たちの列車はどのホームから出発しますか。

(A) 1番ホーム
(B) 2番ホーム
(C) 3番ホーム
(D) 4番ホーム

TEST1 PART 3

正解 **B** 男性は、❶「私たちが乗る予定のミドルタウン行きの列車は、実のところ時刻が変更になった」と述べている。図によると、行き先がミドルタウンの列車のホームは2番。よって、(B)が正解。

69 What delayed the woman?

(A) Car problems
(B) A blocked railroad crossing
(C) A work emergency
(D) Bridge construction

何のせいで女性は遅れましたか。

(A) 車の不具合
(B) 遮断された踏切
(C) 業務上の緊急事態
(D) 橋の工事

正解 **D** ❷で、女性が遅れた原因は交通渋滞のせいかと確認する男性に対し、女性はNoと否定した後、❸「パイオニア橋で工事があり、遠回りをしなければならなかった」と遅れた理由を伝えている。よって、(D)が正解。
(A) problem「問題、支障」。
(B) block「～をふさぐ」、railroad crossing「踏切」。
(C) emergency「緊急事態」。

70 What does the woman offer to do?

(A) Purchase a beverage
(B) Exchange a ticket
(C) Reserve a rental car
(D) Buy a newspaper

女性は何をすることを申し出ていますか。

(A) 飲み物を購入する
(B) 乗車券を交換する
(C) レンタカーを予約する
(D) 新聞を買う

正解 **A** 女性は❹で、コーヒーを買いに行くと言ってから、❺「あなたにも1杯買ってこようか」と男性に申し出ている。よって、buyをpurchase、a coffeeをa beverage「飲み物」と表現している(A)が正解。offer to do「～することを申し出る」。
(B) exchange「～を交換する」、ticket「券、切符」。
(C) reserve「～を予約する」。
(D) newspaper「新聞」は男性の最後の発言に含まれるが、男性が読むと言っているだけであり、女性が購入を申し出ているものではない。

Words & Phrases   start to *do* ～し始める   worry (that) ～ ～だろうかと心配する   miss ～を逃す
actually 実は   reschedule ～の日時を変更する   plenty of ～ たくさんの～   traffic 交通(量)、交通渋滞
delay ～を遅らせる   construction 工事(作業)   take a detour 回り道をする   roadwork 道路工事   direction 方向
make it うまくいく、間に合って到着する   finish *doing* ～し終える

予定表 departure 出発、出発列車   destination 行き先   track 鉄道線路、プラットホーム

PART 4

Questions 71 through 73 refer to the following announcement.

🇨🇦 M

❶Welcome to the Fairtown Community outdoor farmers market. ❷Our local farmers are pleased to offer you fresh, local produce at affordable prices today. ❸Be advised that there is a silver pickup truck blocking one of the parking lot entrances. ❹If this is yours, please remove it now or it will be towed. And ❺shoppers, don't forget our exciting contest. ❻Enter your name in our drawing to win a twenty-dollar gift certificate good at any of our farmers' stands.

問題71-73は次のお知らせに関するものです。

フェアータウン地域の野外青物市へようこそ。地元農家は、本日皆さんに新鮮な地元の農産物を手頃な値段でご提供できることをうれしく思っています。駐車場の入り口の一つをふさいでしまっているシルバーの小型トラックがあることをお知らせします。この車がご自分のものである場合、今すぐにそれを移動させてください。でなければレッカー車で撤去されることになります。それから、お買い物中の皆さん、私たちの心躍るコンテストをお忘れなく。お名前を書いて抽選会に参加し、どの農家の売り場でも使える20ドルの商品券を当ててください。

---

71 Where is the announcement taking place?

(A) At a music festival
(B) At a car show
(C) At a sports arena
(D) At a farmers market

お知らせはどこで行われていますか。

(A) 音楽フェスティバル
(B) 自動車展示会
(C) 競技場
(D) 青物市

正解 D 話し手は、❶「フェアータウン地域の野外青物市へようこそ」と聞き手を歓迎している。また、❷で、地元の農家が農産物を提供できることを喜んでいると伝えている。よって、(D)が正解。
(B) 車への言及があるのは、入り口をふさいでいる小型トラックについて移動を要請するため。car show「自動車展示会」。
(C) sports arena「競技場」。

---

72 What problem does the speaker mention?

(A) A pathway needs repairs.
(B) A thunderstorm is predicted.
(C) A vehicle is blocking an entryway.
(D) A product is out of stock.

話し手はどんな問題について述べていますか。

(A) 通路は補修が必要である。
(B) 雷雨が予報されている。
(C) 車両が入り口の通路をふさいでいる。
(D) 生産品が品切れである。

正解 C 話し手は❸「駐車場の入り口の一つをふさいでしまっているシルバーの小型トラックがあることを知らせる」と伝えた後、❹でそのトラックの持ち主に、すぐに移動させないとレッカー車で撤去されると警告している。よって、❸のa silver pickup truckをa vehicle「車両」と表している(C)が正解。entryway「入り口の通路」。
(A) pathway「小道、通路」、repair「補修」。
(B) thunderstorm「雷雨」、predict「～を予報する」。
(D) product「生産品」、out of stock「品切れで」。

---

73 What are some of the listeners reminded to do?

(A) Pick up a flyer
(B) Enter a drawing
(C) Bring reusable bags
(D) Listen to a local performer

聞き手の一部は、何をするよう念を押されていますか。

(A) ちらしを受け取る
(B) 抽選会に参加する
(C) 再利用可能な袋を持参する
(D) 地元の演奏者に耳を傾ける

正解 B 話し手は❺でコンテストを忘れないようにと聞き手に念を押し、続けて❻「名前を書いて抽選会に参加し、どの農家の売り場でも使える20ドルの商品券を当ててください」と、抽選会への参加を勧めている。よって、(B)が正解。enter「～(コンテストなど)に参加申し込みをする」。
(A) pickupという語から連想され得る点に注意。pick up ～「～を受け取る」、flyer「ちらし」。
(C) reusable「再利用可能な」。
(D) 地元のperformer「演奏者」については述べられていない。

Words & Phrases　　announcement お知らせ　community 地域社会　outdoor 野外の
farmers market （農産物の)産地直売所、青物市　local 地元の　farmer 農家　be pleased to do ～することをうれしく思う
offer ～ … …に…を提供する　produce 農産物　affordable 金銭的に手頃な
Be advised that ～. ～ということをご承知おきください。　pickup truck （屋根のない)小型トラック　block ～をふさぐ
parking lot 駐車場　entrance 入り口　remove ～を移動させる　or さもなければ　★命令文などの後で使う
tow ～をレッカー車で撤去する　exciting 心躍るような　enter one's name （コンテストなどに)記名してエントリーする
drawing 抽選会　win ～を勝ち取る　gift certificate 商品券　good 有効な　stand 売り場

Questions 74 through 76 refer to the following telephone message.

🇺🇸 w

問題74-76は次の電話のメッセージに関するものです。

Hello, ❶this is Emiko Yamada from Southwest Furniture. ❷You called about renting furniture for your downtown office. ❸You did mention that you would require furniture that would meet a modest budget. We specialize in offering high-quality furniture at low prices. You can rent furniture for as few as ten days and see how it fits your needs. ❹We have a rent-to-buy option, so you can start by renting and then purchase the furniture whenever you are ready. Please call me back at 555-0112. I look forward to talking to you.

もしもし、こちらはSouthwest家具店のEmiko Yamadaです。お客さまは、中心街の事務所でお使いになる家具のレンタルの件でお電話をくださいましたね。低めのご予算に合う家具が必要だとおっしゃいました。当店は、高品質な家具を低価格でご提供することを専門としております。お客さまには、ほんの10日間だけ家具をレンタルして、ニーズにどのように合うかを確かめていただけます。当店はレンタル後購入の選択肢をご用意しておりますので、まずはレンタルから始めて、お気持ちが固まり次第、その家具をご購入いただけます。555-0112まで、折り返しお電話をください。お客さまとお話しできるのを心待ちにしております。

74 Where does the speaker work?

(A) At an investment firm
(B) At a furniture store
(C) At an accounting office
(D) At a manufacturing plant

話し手はどこで働いていますか。

(A) 投資会社
(B) 家具店
(C) 会計事務所
(D) 製造工場

正解 B　話し手は❶「こちらはSouthwest家具店のEmiko Yamadaだ」と名乗った後、❷で、聞き手から事務所用家具のレンタルの件で電話をもらったことを確認している。話し手は以降でも、自分たちが提供している家具について話をしているので、(B)が正解。
(A) investment「投資」、firm「会社」。
(C) accounting「会計」。
(D) manufacturing「製造(の)」、plant「工場」。

75 What requirement does the listener have?

(A) Low costs
(B) Quick delivery
(C) High quality
(D) Reliable customer service

聞き手にはどんな要件がありますか。

(A) 低コスト
(B) 迅速な配達
(C) 高品質
(D) 信頼できる顧客サービス

正解 A　話し手は、聞き手から家具のレンタルの件で電話をもらったことを確認してから、❸「あなたは、低めの予算に合う家具が必要だと言っていた」と聞き手の要望に言及している。よって、❸のa modest budgetをlow costsと表している(A)が正解。requirement「要件」。
(C) 話し手の店が扱う家具の品質の高さには言及されているが、聞き手の要件としては述べられていない。
(D) reliable「信頼できる」、customer service「顧客サービス」。

76 What financial option does the speaker mention?

(A) A free trial
(B) A low-interest loan
(C) Renting to buy
(D) Paying each month

話し手はどんな金銭上の選択肢について述べていますか。

(A) 無料のお試し
(B) 低利融資
(C) レンタル後購入
(D) 月払い

正解 C　話し手は、聞き手が家具を短期間レンタルして自分のニーズに合うかを確かめることが可能だと言った後、❹「当店はレンタル後購入の選択肢を用意しているので、まずはレンタルから始めて、気持ちが固まり次第、その家具を購入できる」と説明している。よって、(C)が正解。financial「財務の、金銭上の」。
(A) 無料で試せるとは述べられていない。trial「試し」。
(B) low-interest「低金利の」、loan「融資」。

TEST1 PART 4

Words & Phrases　furniture　家具(類)　rent　〜を有料で借りる　downtown　中心街の、商業地区の　mention that 〜　〜と述べる　require　〜を要求する、〜を必要とする　meet　〜(要求など)を満たす　modest　控えめの　budget　予算　specialize in 〜　〜を専門にする、〜に専念する　high-quality　高品質の　as few as 〜　わずか〜　★数の少なさを強調する表現　fit　〜に適合する、〜に合う　rent-to-buy　レンタル後購入(の)　option　選択肢　start by doing　〜することから始める　whenever　〜するときはいつでも　look forward to doing　〜することを心待ちにする

Questions 77 through 79 refer to the following excerpt from a meeting.

問題77-79は次の会議の抜粋に関するものです。

🇬🇧 W

Good afternoon. ❶At today's meeting I'd like to focus on ticket sales. As you know, ❷sales have been declining. We continue to offer top-quality films, but ❸the availability of online entertainment options is responsible for this decline. We've lost young moviegoers in particular. ❹So today I want you to brainstorm ways we could attract a greater turnout to our theater—especially a younger audience. But ❺before we begin, we'll take a look at the annual report to review our income and expenses. ❻Let me just bring the figures up on my laptop so we can all view them on the screen.

こんにちは。本日の会議では、チケットの売上に焦点を絞りたいと思います。ご存じのように、売上は減少してきています。私たちは最高品質の映画を提供し続けていますが、オンライン上のさまざまな娯楽を利用できることがこの減少の原因です。当館はとりわけ、若い映画ファンを失っています。そのため、本日皆さんには、当映画館にもっと多数の来館者——特に若年層の観客——を引き付けられそうな方法についてブレーンストーミングしていただきたいと思っています。ですが、始める前に、当館の収支を見直すために年次報告書を見ることにします。全員がスクリーンで見られるよう、まず私のノートパソコンに数値を表示します。

77 According to the speaker, what has recently happened?

(A) A building's lease has expired.
(B) A competing theater opened.
(C) Ticket sales have dropped.
(D) Loan payments have been late.

話し手によると、最近何が起こりましたか。

(A) 建物のリース契約が切れた。
(B) 競合する映画館がオープンした。
(C) チケットの売上が落ちた。
(D) ローンの返済が遅れている。

正解 C 話し手は❶で、今日の会議ではチケットの売上に焦点を絞ると伝えた後、❷「売上は減少してきている」と近況を述べ、❸ではその原因に言及している。よって、チケットの売上の減少をdrop「落ちる、下がる」を用いて表している(C)が正解。
(A) lease「リース契約」、expire「期限切れになる」。
(B) 競合の対象としては、オンライン上の娯楽に言及されているのみ。competing「競合する」。
(D) payment「支払い」。

78 What does the speaker want the listeners to do?

(A) Select a new food vendor
(B) Brainstorm alternative hiring practices
(C) Test new theater seating
(D) Discuss strategies to attract customers

話し手は聞き手に何をしてほしいと思っていますか。

(A) 新しい食品販売業者を選び出す
(B) 既存のものに代わる雇用活動についてブレーンストーミングする
(C) 新しい映画館の座席をテストする
(D) 顧客を引き付けるための戦略について話し合う

正解 D 話し手は、自分たちの映画館の客足が落ちていることに触れてから、❹で、来館者数を増やす方法についてブレーンストーミングしてもらいたいと、聞き手に求めている。よって、その内容を言い換えた(D)が正解。discuss「～について話し合う」、strategy「戦略」。
(A) select「～を選び出す」、vendor「販売業者」。
(B) ❹にあるbrainstormを含むが、聞き手に話し合ってほしいのはhiring practice「雇用活動」ではなく観客を引き付ける方法。alternative「代替の、既存のものに代わる」。

79 What will the speaker do next?

(A) Present an annual report
(B) Evaluate a film contract
(C) Introduce a guest speaker
(D) Review recycling policies

話し手は次に何をしますか。

(A) 年次報告書を提示する
(B) 映画の契約を評価する
(C) 招待講演者を紹介する
(D) リサイクルの方針を見直す

正解 A 話し手は次の流れとして❺で、年次報告書を見ると伝え、❻で、全員がスクリーンで見られるようにノートパソコンに数値を表示すると言っている。❻のthe figuresは❺のthe annual reportの数値を指すので、話し手はこれから、スクリーンに年次報告書を映し出すと分かる。よって、(A)が正解。present「～を提示する、～を発表する」。
(B) evaluate「～を評価する」、contract「契約」。
(D) policy「方針」。

Words & Phrases
excerpt 抜粋　focus on ～ ～に焦点を絞る　decline 減少する　top-quality 最高品質の
availability 入手・利用できること　option 選択肢　be responsible for ～ ～の原因である　decline 減少
moviegoer （映画館に足を運ぶ）映画ファン　in particular 特に
brainstorm ～についてブレーンストーミングする、～について自由に話し合う　attract ～を引き付ける　turnout 来場者
especially 特に　audience 観客　annual 年次の　income 収入　expenses 支出
bring up ～ on … ～を…の画面に表示する　figure 数　laptop ノートパソコン　view ～を見る

Questions 80 through 82 refer to the following telephone message.

W

Hi, my name is Kyung-Sook Lim. ❶I'm currently working on an art history documentary series. ❷Your museum has several paintings we'd like to feature in our episode on eighteenth-century portraits. However, the paintings we're interested in aren't on display in your galleries. I know they're not available to the public to view, but ❸could I make an appointment to film some of the paintings from your archives? ❹I can send you a list of the specific works we'd like to focus on, if that would help. I look forward to hearing from you.

問題80-82は次の電話のメッセージに関するものです。

こんにちは、Kyung-Sook Limと申します。私は現在、美術史のドキュメンタリーシリーズの制作に取り組んでいます。そちらの美術館は、私たちが18世紀の肖像画についての回で特集したい絵画を何点か所蔵していらっしゃいます。しかし、私たちが関心のある絵画は、貴館の展示室では展示されていません。それらが一般公開されていないことは承知していますが、貴館の保管庫の絵画の何点かを撮影するアポイントメントを取らせていただけないでしょうか。私たちが焦点を当てたいと思っている具体的な作品の一覧表をお送りできます、もしそれがお役に立つようであれば。ご連絡をお待ちしております。

80 Who most likely is the speaker?

(A) An art collector
(B) An advertising agent
(C) A librarian
(D) A filmmaker

話し手は誰だと考えられますか。

(A) 美術品収集家
(B) 広告代理業者
(C) 司書
(D) 映像制作者

正解 D 話し手は❶「私は現在、美術史のドキュメンタリーシリーズの制作に取り組んでいる」と自己紹介し、❷で、特集したい絵画が聞き手の美術館に所蔵されていると述べている。また、❸でその撮影の許可を求めている。よって、話し手は映像作品の制作者だと考えられるので、(D)が正解。filmmaker「映像制作者」。
(A) 話し手が作品を収集しているとは述べていない。art historyやmuseum、paintingsなどの語句から連想され得る点に注意。collector「収集家」。
(B) advertising agent「広告代理業者」。
(C) librarian「図書館員、司書」。

81 What is the purpose of the message?

(A) To confirm a project schedule
(B) To discuss a new art exhibit
(C) To request access to a collection
(D) To organize a youth-outreach program

メッセージの目的は何ですか。

(A) 計画の予定を確認すること
(B) 新しい美術展について話し合うこと
(C) 所蔵品に接する機会を求めること
(D) 若者向けの支援プログラムを企画すること

正解 C 話し手は、美術館の一般公開されていない絵画に言及し、❸「貴館の保管庫の絵画の何点かを撮影するアポイントメントを取らせてもらえないか」と、非公開の絵画の閲覧機会を求めている。よって、その内容をaccess「利用の機会」やcollection「所蔵品」という語を用いて表した(C)が正解。
(B) 新たなexhibit「展覧会」への言及はない。
(D) organize「~を企画する」、youth「若者」、outreach program「支援プログラム（美術館などが興味を持ってもらうために行う広報的プログラム）」。

82 What does the speaker offer to provide?

(A) A list of items
(B) A signed contract
(C) Professional certification
(D) Examples of past work

話し手は何を提供することを申し出ていますか。

(A) 物品の一覧表
(B) 署名済みの契約書
(C) 専門家の認定
(D) 過去の作品例

正解 A 話し手は❸で、撮影のアポイントを取れるかと尋ねた後、❹で、焦点を当てたいと考えている絵画作品の一覧表を送ることができると申し出ている。よって、❹のthe specific worksをitemsと表している(A)が正解。provide「~を提供する」。item「物品」。
(B) signed「署名済みの」、contract「契約書」。
(C) professional「専門的な」、certification「証明」。
(D) example「例」、past「過去の」。

TEST1 PART 4

Words & Phrases currently 現在　painting 絵画　feature ～を特集する
episode （連続番組などの）1回分の話　portrait 肖像画　on display 展示されて　gallery 展示室
the public 一般市民　make an appointment 会う約束をする、アポイントメントを取る　film ～（映画など）を撮影する
archive 保管所　specific 特定の、具体的な　work 作品　hear from ～ ～から連絡をもらう

Questions 83 through 85 refer to the following talk.

問題83-85は次の話に関するものです。

🇦🇺 M

Hi, everyone. You have probably heard that the city is holding its first-ever craft fair, and it will happen near our candle shop this summer. ❶I believe we will have much more business than usual at our store, selling handmade candles and candleholders. More customers means other changes will come. As you know, we've operated as a cash-only business, but ❷credit card payments are much quicker for everyone. So, to help with the added business, credit card readers will be installed at each of our cash registers next week. ❸The system may seem complicated, ❹but just so you know, there will be training for all staff.

こんにちは、皆さん。市が初の手工芸品市を開催する予定であることはおそらくお聞きでしょうが、それはこの夏、当ろうそく店の近くで行われます。当店ではきっと、手作りのろうそくやろうそく立ての販売で、普段よりもはるかに多くの商取引が発生するだろうと思います。顧客が増えれば他の変更も生じることになります。ご存じのように、当店は現金取引のみで営業してきましたが、誰にとってもクレジットカード払いの方がはるかに迅速です。そのため、増加する取引業務の助けとなるよう、来週、クレジットカードリーダーが当店の各レジに設置されます。このシステムは複雑に思えるかもしれませんが、念のためお知らせしますと、全従業員向けに研修がある予定です。

---

83 What is the speaker explaining?

(A) How to open a craft store
(B) How to make a display for a trade show
(C) How to prepare for extra business
(D) How to create new advertising

話し手は何について説明していますか。

(A) 手工芸品店の開き方
(B) 展示会用の陳列の仕方
(C) 追加の取引に向けた準備の仕方
(D) 新しい広告の作り方

正解 C　話し手は店の責任者であり、従業員に向けて話をしていると考えられる。手工芸品市が自分たちの店の近辺で開かれることに言及し、❶で、店では普段よりもずっと多くの商取引が発生するだろうと予測している。またそれ以降では、予想される業務増に向けた準備について具体的に説明している。よって、(C)が正解。prepare for ~「~に向けて準備する」、extra「余分な、追加の」。
(B) make a display「陳列をする」、trade show「展示会」。

---

84 According to the speaker, why will a new payment option be introduced?

(A) To reduce some costs
(B) To speed up customer service
(C) To meet a loan requirement
(D) To accept online purchases

話し手によると、新たな支払いの選択肢はなぜ導入される予定なのですか。

(A) 諸経費を削減するため
(B) 顧客サービスを迅速化するため
(C) 融資の要件を満たすため
(D) オンライン購入を受け付けるため

正解 B　話し手は、予想される顧客増と、これまで現金取引のみで営業してきたことに触れた後、❷で、クレジットカード払いの方がはるかに速いので専用リーダーを設置すると知らせている。つまり、クレジットカード払いという新たな支払いの選択肢を導入するのは、顧客対応をより迅速に行うためだと分かるので、(B)が正解。
(A) reduce「~を削減する」。
(C) meet「~を満たす」、loan「融資」、requirement「要件」。
(D) accept「~を受け入れる」。

---

85 Why does the speaker say, "There will be training for all staff"?

(A) To provide information about new products
(B) To reassure workers about a new process
(C) To remind staff of an upcoming holiday
(D) To apply for a booth at the craft fair

話し手はなぜ "There will be training for all staff" と言っていますか。

(A) 新製品についての情報を提供するため
(B) 新しい手順に関して従業員を安心させるため
(C) 今度の休日について従業員に念を押すため
(D) 手工芸品市でのブースの申請をするため

正解 B　話し手は、設置予定のクレジットカードリーダーについて、❸「このシステムは複雑に思えるかもしれない」と述べた後、❹で逆接のbutを続けて、念のため知らせると前置きをし、下線部の発言で全従業員向けに研修があることを伝えている。つまり、話し手は導入されるクレジットカード払いの対応手順について、研修があると知らせることで聞き手の従業員を安心させようとしていると判断できる。reassure ~ about …「…について~を安心させる」、process「手順」。
(C) upcoming「近づきつつある、今度の」。
(D) apply for ~「~を申請する」。

Words & Phrases

first-ever 初めての　craft fair 手工芸品市　business （商）取引　than usual いつもより　candleholder ろうそく立て　mean (that) ~ （結果として）~ということになる　operate 営業する　cash-only business 現金のみの取引　help with ~ ~の助けになる　added 追加の　reader 読み取り機、リーダー　install ~を設置する　cash register レジ　complicated 複雑な　just so you know 念のため知らせると

Questions 86 through 88 refer to the following telephone message.

問題86-88は次の電話のメッセージに関するものです。

🇨🇦 M

Hi, Akari. ❶I just learned that Santo Fantini was named executive chef at Keller Bistro. I don't need to tell you what a big deal this is in the culinary world. ❷I would like you to write a feature article about the restaurant and its new chef for the upcoming issue of the *Margate Guide*. ❸See if you can get an exclusive interview with Mr. Fantini. Direct statements always add more depth to features. ❹He doesn't always agree to give interviews, so be sure to mention the *Margate Guide*. ❺That should do the trick.

こんにちは、Akari。つい先ほど知ったのですが、Santo Fantiniが Kellerビストロの総料理長に任命されました。このことが料理界においていかに重大な出来事かについては、お伝えする必要はないですね。あなたには、『Margateガイド』誌の次号で、同レストランと新料理長についての特集記事を書いてもらいたいと思っています。Fantini氏の独占インタビューを取れるかどうか確かめてください。本人直々の発言は常に、特集記事により深みを与えますから。彼はいつもインタビューに応じるわけではないので、必ず『Margateガイド』誌の名前を出してください。それでうまくいくはずです。

86 According to the speaker, what has recently happened?

(A) A restaurant hired a new chef.
(B) A business received an award.
(C) A competitor announced a new project.
(D) An event schedule was updated.

話し手によると、最近何が起こりましたか。

(A) レストランが新しい料理長を雇った。
(B) 企業が受賞した。
(C) 競合会社が新しいプロジェクトを発表した。
(D) イベントの予定表が更新された。

正解 **A**　話し手は、❶「つい先ほど知ったのだが、Santo FantiniがKellerビストロの総料理長に任命された」と話を切り出し、❷では同レストランおよび新料理長についての記事を書くよう頼んでいる。よって、(A)が正解。hire「〜を雇用する」。
(B) business「企業、会社」、award「賞」。
(C) competitor「競合会社」、announce「〜を発表する」。
(D) schedule「予定表」、update「〜を更新する」。

87 Who most likely is the listener?

(A) A professor
(B) A photographer
(C) A software developer
(D) A journalist

聞き手は誰だと考えられますか。

(A) 教授
(B) 写真家
(C) ソフトウエア開発者
(D) ジャーナリスト

正解 **D**　話し手は❷で、雑誌の特集記事を書くよう聞き手に依頼し、❸では、その記事のために新料理長であるFantini氏の独占インタビューを取れるか確かめるよう伝えている。よって、聞き手は雑誌の取材記事を執筆する仕事をしていると考えられるので、(D)が正解。
(A) professor「教授」。
(B) photographer「写真家」。
(C) developer「開発者」。

88 What does the speaker imply when he says, "be sure to mention the *Margate Guide*"?

(A) Mr. Fantini was given some incorrect information previously.
(B) Mr. Fantini should subscribe to a local publication.
(C) Mr. Fantini will be more likely to agree to an interview.
(D) Mr. Fantini will appreciate some advice.

"be sure to mention the *Margate Guide*" という発言で、話し手は何を示唆していますか。

(A) Fantiniさんには以前、誤った情報が伝えられた。
(B) Fantiniさんは地元の刊行物を定期購読しているはずである。
(C) Fantiniさんがインタビューに応じてくれる可能性が高まるだろう。
(D) Fantiniさんは助言をありがたく思うだろう。

正解 **C**　Fantini氏の独占インタビューを取れるかどうかを確かめるよう依頼した話し手は、同氏について❹「彼はいつもインタビューに応じるわけではない」と言っている。直後に、so「だから」に続けて下線部の発言で、必ず雑誌名を話に出すよう伝え、❺では、そうすればうまくいくはずだと述べている。よって、話し手は、雑誌名に言及することで同氏がインタビューに応じる可能性が高まると示唆しているのだと判断できる。
(A) incorrect「誤った」、previously「以前に」。
(B) subscribe to 〜「〜を定期購読する」、publication「刊行物」。
(D) appreciate「〜をありがたく思う」、advice「助言」。

Words & Phrases

name 〜 …	〜を…に任命する
executive	幹部の
bistro	小規模のレストラン
big deal	一大事
culinary	料理の
feature	特集(記事)
issue	(雑誌などの)号
see if you can 〜	〜できるか確かめる
exclusive	独占的な
statement	声明、発言
depth	深み
do the trick	うまくいく

Questions 89 through 91 refer to the following talk.

🏳 M

Hi, everyone. ❶I just met with the Montclair City Council and have some unfortunate news. ❷They selected another business to do their park remodeling, so we're out of luck. However, ❸I just got news that a different park in Ridgewood is undergoing a big renovation: lots of tree planting and lawn installations, and the city is looking for a company to do it. ❹We'd be a perfect fit. ❺Nothing's been finalized yet, but I should know for sure in a couple of weeks.

問題89-91は次の話に関するものです。

こんにちは、皆さん。私はちょうどモントクレア市議会と会合したところで、残念なお知らせがあります。市は、公園の改修を行うのに別の企業を選出しました。ですので、当社は運がなかったです。しかしながら先ほど、リッジウッドにある別の公園でたくさんの植樹と芝生設置という大規模な改修工事が実施されるという新情報を入手しまして、市はそれを行う企業を探しているところです。当社こそ申し分なく適任でしょう。まだ何も最終決定されていませんが、数週間後には確実に分かるはずです。

---

89 What problem does the speaker mention?

(A) His company lost a business opportunity.
(B) A worker is leaving the business.
(C) The cost of materials is rising.
(D) A business trip was canceled.

話し手はどんな問題について述べていますか。

(A) 彼の会社は商機を逸した。
(B) 従業員が会社を退職する。
(C) 材料費が上がっている。
(D) 出張が中止された。

正解 A 話し手は❶で、市議会との会合を終えて残念な知らせがあると前置きしてから、❷「彼らは、公園の改修を行うのに別の企業を選出した」と知らせている。よって、話し手の会社が改修作業を行う企業に選ばれなかったという問題を lost a business opportunity「商機を逸した」と表現している(A)が正解。opportunity「機会」。
(C) material「材料」、rise「(価格などが)上がる」。

---

90 What type of work do the listeners most likely do?

(A) Landscaping
(B) Building construction
(C) Music production
(D) Web development

聞き手はどんな種類の仕事をしていると考えられますか。

(A) 造園
(B) 建物の建設
(C) 音楽制作
(D) ウェブ開発

正解 A 話し手は、❷で自分たちの会社が市の公園改修事業の請負業者として選ばれなかったことを伝えている。また、❸で、別の公園の植樹と芝生設置といった改修工事のために市が企業を探していると話し、❹では自分たちの会社が適任だと述べている。よって、聞き手は話し手と共に造園に携わる企業で働いていると考えられるので、(A)が正解。landscaping「造園」。
(B) 建物の建設には言及がない。remodeling や renovation などの語から連想され得る点に注意。
(C) production「制作」。
(D) development「開発」。

---

91 What does the speaker say he will know in a couple of weeks?

(A) Whether more workers will be hired
(B) Whether a payment was correct
(C) Whether the city council will hold an event
(D) Whether his business will do certain work

話し手は数週間後に何が分かると言っていますか。

(A) 追加の従業員が雇用されるかどうか
(B) 支払いが正しかったかどうか
(C) 市議会がイベントを開催するかどうか
(D) 彼の会社がある仕事を行うかどうか

正解 D 話し手は、❸・❹で、市が公園の改修工事を行う企業を探していること、および自分たちの会社がそれに適任であると述べてから、❺「まだ何も最終決定されていないが、数週間後には確実に分かるはずだ」と見込みを伝えている。つまり、話し手の会社が公園の改修工事を請け負えるかどうかが数週間後に分かると言っていると判断できるので、改修工事のことを certain work と表している(D)が正解。certain「ある、特定の」。
(B) payment「支払い」、correct「正しい」。
(C) 市議会への言及はあるが、イベントの開催については述べられていない。

Words & Phrases　meet with 〜　〜と会合する　city council　市議会　unfortunate　残念な　select　〜を選出する　business　企業　remodeling　改築、改修　out of luck　運が悪い　different　別の　undergo　〜(変化など)を受ける・被る　renovation　改修工事　tree planting　植樹　lawn　芝生　installation　設置　look for 〜　〜を探す　perfect fit　最適な人・もの　finalize　〜を最終決定する　for sure　確実に　a couple of 〜　2、3の〜、幾つかの〜

Questions 92 through 94 refer to the following excerpt from a meeting.

🇺🇸 w

Hello, my name is Lisa Lee. Thank you for inviting me to the management meeting. ❶I'm here to represent the front-desk workers at the company's veterinary clinics. ❷We have a request: we would like to wear scrubs, like the ones doctors wear, instead of formal clothing while on the job. ❸The requirement of wearing business-professional attire is problematic. ❹Since we handle so many animals, our clothes often get very dirty, and they tend to wear out quickly. <u>Formal clothes can be very expensive</u>.

問題92-94は次の会議の抜粋に関するものです。

こんにちは、Lisa Leeと申します。私を経営会議にお招きくださり、ありがとうございます。私は会社の動物診療所の受付係を代表してこちらに来ています。私たちからお願いがあります。私たちは、勤務中はフォーマルな衣服ではなく医師が着用するような手術着を着用したいと思っています。ビジネスのプロらしい服装をするという要件には問題があります。私たちは非常に多くの動物を扱うので、たびたび衣服がひどく汚れ、すぐに傷んでしまいがちです。<u>フォーマルな衣服は非常にお金がかかる可能性があるのです</u>。

---

92 Where does the speaker work?

(A) In a veterinary office
(B) In a pharmacy
(C) In a recording studio
(D) In an accounting office

話し手はどこで働いていますか。

(A) 動物診療所
(B) 薬局
(C) 録音スタジオ
(D) 会計事務所

正解 A 話し手は、経営会議の場に招かれた礼を述べ、❶「私は会社の動物診療所の受付係を代表してここに来ている」と、自分の立場を説明している。また❹でも、多くの動物を扱うことに言及している。よって、(A)が正解。
(B) clinicsやdoctorsなどの語から連想され得る点に注意。pharmacy「薬局」。
(C) recording「録音」。
(D) accounting「会計」。

---

93 What does the speaker say is problematic?

(A) A company policy
(B) A business expansion plan
(C) Press coverage of a recent event
(D) Competitors' market strategies

話し手は何に問題があると言っていますか。

(A) 会社の方針
(B) 事業拡大計画
(C) 最近の催しについてのメディア報道
(D) 競合会社の市場戦略

正解 A 話し手は❷で、勤務中にはフォーマルな衣服ではなく手術着を着用したいと要望を伝え、❸「ビジネスのプロらしい服装をするという要件には問題がある」と述べている。よって、話し手は会社の服装規定を問題視していると判断できるので、(A)が正解。policy「方針」。
(B) expansion「拡大」。
(C) press coverage「メディア報道」、recent「最近の」、event「出来事、催し」。
(D) market strategy「市場戦略」。

---

94 Why does the speaker say, "Formal clothes can be very expensive"?

(A) To indicate surprise at a recent trend
(B) To provide support for a request
(C) To correct an employee's mistake
(D) To acknowledge a change in price

話し手はなぜ "Formal clothes can be very expensive"と言っていますか。

(A) 最近の傾向に対する驚きを示すため
(B) 要求事項の裏付けを提示するため
(C) 従業員の誤りを訂正するため
(D) 価格の変更を認めるため

正解 B 話し手は、❷・❸で、会社の服装規定に関してフォーマルな衣服ではなく手術着を着用したいという要求を述べた後、❹で、フォーマルな衣服を着用することで生じる問題点に言及している。その直後に、フォーマルな衣服はお金がかかり得るという下線部の発言をしているので、話し手は自分たちの要求が妥当なものであるという裏付けを提示するために下線部の発言をしているのだと判断できる。support「裏付け」。
(A) indicate「~を示す」、trend「傾向」。
(C) correct「~を訂正する」、mistake「誤り」。
(D) acknowledge「~を認める」。

Words & Phrases

invite ~ to … ~を…に招く   management 経営(陣)   represent ~を代表する   front-desk 受付の   veterinary 獣医の   wear ~を着用する   scrubs 手術着   instead of ~ ~ではなく   clothing 衣類   on the job 勤務中に   requirement 必須条件、要件   business-professional ビジネスのプロの   attire 服装   problematic 問題のある、問題を含む   handle ~を扱う、~に手を触れる   dirty 汚れた   tend to *do* ~する傾向がある   wear out (服などが)擦り切れる、傷む   expensive 費用のかかる、高くつく

Questions 95 through 97 refer to the following advertisement and table.

問題95-97は次の広告と表に関するものです。

🇬🇧 w

❶Are you searching for work? ❷The Richardson Jobs Network can help! The Richardson Jobs Network offers opportunities from all types of businesses, from large corporations to local shops. ❸We have listings for jobs covering a wide range of skills. Are you a great salesperson, editor, or graphic designer? There are currently job openings for you! And ❹we recently added a huge number of listings for IT specialists. ❺Our largest number of jobs is in this field at the moment. And ❻we have several discounts; one service is 50 percent off right now! ❼Visit our Web site for our full list of discounts.

お仕事をお探しですか？ Richardson仕事ネットワーク社がお力になれます！ Richardson仕事ネットワーク社は、大企業から地域の商店に至るまで、あらゆる業種の会社からの雇用機会をご提供します。当社は、幅広い技能を網羅する募集職リストをご用意しています。あなたは腕利きの販売員、編集者、それともグラフィックデザイナーですか？ 現在、あなたに合った求人がございます！ それから、当社は最近、IT専門家向けのリストの項目を多数追加しました。現在、当社で最大の数を占める職はこの分野のものです。そして、当社は幾つかの割引もご用意しております。1つのサービスは、ちょうど今50パーセント引きです！ 割引の全リストについては、当社のウェブサイトにアクセスしてください。

Current Discounts	
Résumé support	10%
Cover letter editing	20%
Designing business cards	30%
Interview practice	50%

現在の割引	
履歴書作成サポート	10パーセント
カバーレターの編集	20パーセント
名刺のデザイン	30パーセント
面接の練習	50パーセント

95 What is the advertisement mainly about?

    (A) Providing job training
    (B) Starting a new business
    (C) Finding the right job
    (D) Understanding customer needs

広告は主に何についてのものですか。

    (A) 職業訓練を提供すること
    (B) 新事業を立ち上げること
    (C) 適した仕事を探すこと
    (D) 顧客のニーズを理解すること

正解 C 話し手は❶「仕事を探していますか」と切り出し、❷で、Richardson仕事ネットワーク社が手助けできること、および同社があらゆる業種の会社からの雇用機会を提供していることを伝えている。❸やそれ以降でも、さまざまな職の雇用機会について述べているので、(C)が正解。mainly「主に」。
(A) 広告で主に述べられているのは雇用機会についてであり、job training「職業訓練」ではない。provide「～を提供する」。
(B) 新事業の立ち上げへの言及はない。start a new business「新事業を立ち上げる」。

---

96 According to the speaker, which job has the most listings?

    (A) Salesperson
    (B) Editor
    (C) Graphic designer
    (D) IT specialist

話し手によると、どの職が最も多くリストに載っていますか。

    (A) 販売員
    (B) 編集者
    (C) グラフィックデザイナー
    (D) IT専門家

正解 D 話し手は❹で、最近、IT専門家向けのリストの項目が多数追加されたことを伝えてから、❺「現在、当社で最大の数を占める職はこの分野のものだ」と知らせている。❺のthis fieldとは直前の❹で言及されているIT分野を指すので、(D)が正解。
(A) (B) (C) いずれの職種にも言及があるが、募集している求人の例として挙げられているのみ。

---

97 Look at the graphic. Which service is mentioned in the advertisement?

    (A) Résumé support
    (B) Cover letter editing
    (C) Designing business cards
    (D) Interview practice

図を見てください。どのサービスが広告で述べられていますか。

    (A) 履歴書作成サポート
    (B) カバーレターの編集
    (C) 名刺のデザイン
    (D) 面接の練習

正解 D 話し手は、会社が提供している雇用機会の詳細について一通り述べた後、❻「当社は幾つかの割引も用意している。1つのサービスは、ちょうど今50パーセント引きだ」と割引情報を伝えている。続けて❼で、割引の全リストをウェブサイトで確認するよう聞き手を促している。現在提供中の割引情報を示している図を見ると、50パーセント引きになっているのは面接の練習。よって、(D)が正解。

Words & Phrases　　advertisement 広告　table 表　search for ～ ～を探す　opportunity （雇用）機会
large corporation 大企業　local 地元の、地域の　listing 一覧表・リスト(の記載項目)　cover ～を含む
a wide range of ～ 幅広い～　skill 技能　salesperson 販売員　editor 編集者　currently 現在
job opening 求人、就職口　recently 最近　add ～を追加する　a huge number of ～ 膨大な数の～
specialist 専門家　field 分野　at the moment 目下、現在のところ　several 幾つかの　discount 割引
off 割り引いて　right now ちょうど今　full 完全な、詳細な

表　current 現在の　résumé 履歴書　support 支援、サポート　cover letter カバーレター、添え状
   edit ～を編集する　design ～をデザインする　business card 名刺　interview 面接　practice 練習

Questions 98 through 100 refer to the following talk and map. 　問題98-100は次の話と地図に関するものです。

 M

Next week we'll have cooking demonstrations in our supermarket. ❶For those of you who are new, we offer cooking demos every month to encourage our customers to try products we're introducing. ❷This month, since we'll be highlighting some new bakery goods, we'll have the demo station in the bakery area. So, let's go there now to make space for the cooking equipment. And ❸if any of you are interested in helping our chef during a cooking demonstration, you can switch one of your regular shifts and do that instead. ❹Just let me know in advance.

来週、当スーパーマーケットでは調理実演を行う予定です。新人の方のために言いますと、当店では毎月、新発売の製品を試すようお客さまに勧めるために、調理実演を行っています。今月は新しいベーカリー商品を目玉にする予定なので、実演スペースをベーカリーエリアに用意します。というわけで、今からそこへ行って、調理器具用のスペースを作りましょう。それから、皆さんの中に調理実演中に当店の料理人を手伝うことに関心がおありの方がいましたら、ご自分の通常のシフトの一つを取り替えて、代わりにそれを行うことが可能です。前もって私に知らせてください。

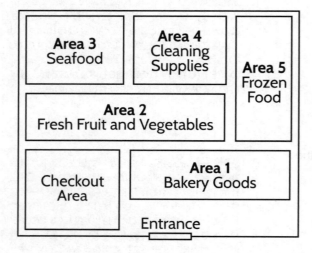

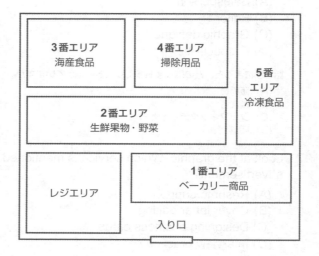

98 What is the purpose of the cooking demonstrations?

(A) To teach about healthy food choices
(B) To try out new cooking equipment
(C) To train some new staff
(D) To promote new store products

調理実演の目的は何ですか。

(A) 健康的な食べ物の選択肢について教えること
(B) 新しい調理器具を試しに使ってみること
(C) 新しい従業員を教育すること
(D) 店の新製品の販売を促進すること

> **正解 D** 話し手は、調理実演の予定について述べた後、❶「新人のために言っておくと、当店では毎月、新発売の製品を試すよう客に勧めるために、調理実演を行っている」と、実演の目的を伝えている。よって、この内容をto promote new store productsと表している(D)が正解。purpose「目的」。promote「～の販売を促進する」。
> (A) healthy「健康的な」。
> (B) 調理器具を試すことが目的ではない。try out ～「～を試しに使ってみる」。
> (C) 新人への言及はあるが、調理実演についてよく知らない人のために説明する文脈で話に出ているのみ。train「～を教育する」。

99 Look at the graphic. Where will a cooking demonstration be held this month?

(A) In Area 1
(B) In Area 2
(C) In Area 3
(D) In Area 4

図を見てください。今月、調理実演はどこで行われますか。

(A) 1番エリア
(B) 2番エリア
(C) 3番エリア
(D) 4番エリア

> **正解 A** 話し手は、調理実演の目的を説明した後、❷「今月は新しいベーカリー商品を目玉にする予定なので、実演スペースをベーカリーエリアに用意する」と調理実演の実施場所を知らせている。図を見ると、ベーカリー商品が置かれているのは1番エリア。よって、(A)が正解。

100 What does the speaker invite the listeners to do?

(A) Suggest some recipes
(B) Change a work shift
(C) Obtain an employee discount
(D) Use a break room

話し手は聞き手に何をするよう勧めていますか。

(A) レシピを提案する
(B) 勤務シフトを変更する
(C) 従業員向けの割引を取得する
(D) 休憩室を利用する

> **正解 B** 話し手は、❸「皆さんの中に調理実演中に当店の料理人を手伝うことに関心がある人がいれば、自分の通常のシフトの一つを取り替えて、代わりにそれを行うことが可能だ」と伝え、続けて❹で、その場合には事前に知らせるよう頼んでいる。よって、(B)が正解。❸にあるdo thatとはhelp our chef during a cooking demonstrationを表す。invite ～ to do「～に…するよう勧める」。
> (A) suggest「～を提案する」。
> (C) obtain「～を得る、～を獲得する」。
> (D) break room「休憩室」。

Words & Phrases

demonstration 実演 ★demoは略式の表現　　offer ～を提供する
encourage ～ to do ～に…することを勧める　　try ～を試す、～を試食・試飲する　　introduce ～を導入する、～を発売する
highlight ～を目玉にする　　goods 商品　　station （特定のサービスを提供するための）場所　　area 区域
make space for ～ ～のスペースを作る　　equipment 器具　　be interested in doing ～することに関心がある
switch ～を取り替える、～を変更する　　instead その代わりに　　in advance 前もって、事前に

地図　supplies 用品　　frozen food 冷凍食品　　checkout レジ　　entrance 入り口

101 Makiro Furniture customers can easily ------- the shelving units using only simple tools.

(A) assemble
(B) assembled
(C) assembling
(D) assembles

Makiro家具のお客さまは、簡便な工具だけを使って、そのユニット棚を簡単に組み立てることができます。

(A) ～を組み立てる
(B) ～を組み立てた
(C) ～を組み立てている
(D) ～を組み立てる

正解 **A** 　選択肢は動詞assemble「～を組み立てる」と変化形。この文には助動詞canがあるがそれに続く動詞がないので、原形の(A) assembleが適切。furniture「家具」、shelving unit「ユニット式ラック、ユニット棚」、tool「工具」。
(B) 過去形または過去分詞。
(C) 現在分詞または動名詞。
(D) 三人称単数現在形。

102 Mr. Zhao will ------- work on international accounts while Ms. Gutierrez is on leave.

(A) temporarily
(B) comparatively
(C) nearly
(D) highly

Gutierrezさんが休暇の間は、Zhaoさんが海外の顧客を一時的に担当します。

(A) 一時的に
(B) 比較的
(C) ほとんど
(D) 高く

正解 **A** 　選択肢は全て副詞であり、空所に続く動詞workを適切に修飾するものを選ぶ。文頭からaccountsまでが主節で、「Zhaoさんは海外の顧客を-------取り扱う予定である」という意味。while以下は従属節で、「Gutierrezさんが休みの間」という意味。(A) temporarily「一時的に」を入れると、Gutierrezさんの休暇中はZhaoさんが海外の顧客を一時的に担当するということになり、意味が通る。work on ～「～に取り組む」、account「顧客、取引先」、be on leave「休暇中である」。

103 According to the builder, the ------- of the main entrance will be completed in three weeks.

(A) renovate
(B) renovates
(C) renovated
(D) renovation

建築業者によれば、正面入り口の改装は3週間後に完了します。

(A) ～を改装する
(B) ～を改装する
(C) ～を改装した
(D) 改装

正解 **D** 　選択肢は動詞renovate「～を改装する」と変化形や派生語。the ------- of the main entranceが主語に当たり、空所の前には定冠詞the、後ろにはof the main entrance「正面入り口の」と修飾語句が続くので、空所には名詞が入る。名詞の(D) renovation「改装」が適切。builder「建築業者」、main entrance「正面入り口、正面玄関」、complete「～を完了させる」、in ～「～後に」。
(A) 原形または現在形。
(B) 三人称単数現在形。
(C) 過去形または過去分詞。

104 The park will remain open ------- the weather changes dramatically.

(A) by
(B) unless
(C) common
(D) fast

その公園は、天気が劇的に変わらない限り、開園したままの予定です。

(A) 〜によって
(B) 〜でない限り
(C) 一般的な
(D) 速く

> **正解 B** 空所の前後がともに〈主語＋動詞〉の形を含む節であり、文頭からopenまでは「その公園は開いたままの予定だ」、空所の後は「天気は劇的に変わる」という意味。空所にはこれらの節をつなぐ接続詞が入る。接続詞の(B) unless「〜でない限り」を入れると、天気が劇的に変わらない限り公園は開園したままだ、となって意味が通る。remain 〜「〜のままである」、dramatically「劇的に」。
> (A) 前置詞または副詞、(C) 形容詞、(D) 形容詞または副詞。いずれも節と節を接続する働きを持たない。

105 Ms. Ansah's ------- report was excellent and needed no further revisions.

(A) initial
(B) initially
(C) initiate
(D) initiates

Ansahさんの最初の報告書は素晴らしく、さらなる修正は一切必要ありませんでした。

(A) 最初の
(B) 最初に
(C) 〜を始める
(D) 〜を始める

> **正解 A** 主語はMs. Ansah's ------- report、述語動詞はwasとneededでそれらがandで接続されている。空所の前にMs. Ansah'sという所有格があり、後ろには名詞のreport「報告書」が続いているので、空所にはreportを修飾する語が入ると考えられる。形容詞の(A) initial「最初の」が適切。excellent「優れた、素晴らしい」、further「さらなる」、revision「修正」。
> (B) 副詞。
> (C) 動詞の原形または現在形。
> (D) 動詞の三人称単数現在形。

106 Parkfield Fruit Bars have been made ------- added sugar since 1950.

(A) between
(B) over
(C) without
(D) against

Parkfieldフルーツバーは、1950年以来、砂糖無添加で製造されています。

(A) 〜の間で
(B) 〜を越えて
(C) 〜なしで
(D) 〜に反して

> **正解 C** 選択肢は全て前置詞の働きを持つ語。空所直後のadded sugar「加えられた砂糖」は空所に入る前置詞の目的語であり、------- added sugarは述語動詞have been made「製造されてきた」を修飾する副詞句となると考えられる。空所に(C) without「〜なしで」を入れると、Parkfieldフルーツバーは1950年からずっと砂糖を加えずに作られてきた、ということになり、意味が通る。fruit bar「フルーツバー（刻んだ果物を混ぜて焼いた棒状のクッキー）」、add「〜を加える」。

TEST1 PART 5

107 The sales team has provided an ------- of customer preferences.

(A) analyze
(B) analytical
(C) analysis
(D) analytically

営業チームは、顧客の好みについての分析を提供しました。

(A) 〜を分析する
(B) 分析的な
(C) 分析
(D) 分析的に

正解 C 選択肢は動詞 analyze「〜を分析する」と派生語。主語は The sales team、述語動詞は has provided で an ------- of customer preferences はその目的語となる。空所の前は不定冠詞 an、後ろは of customer preferences「顧客の好みの」という修飾語句なので、空所には名詞が入る。名詞の (C) analysis「分析（結果）」が適切。sales「営業（の）、販売業務（の）」、provide「〜を提供する」、preference「好み、嗜好」。
(A) 原形または現在形。
(B) 形容詞。
(D) 副詞。

108 Ms. Sato is considered to be ------- talented for such a young painter.

(A) indirectly
(B) rapidly
(C) carefully
(D) exceptionally

Sato さんは、あれほど若い画家としては、並外れて才能があると考えられています。

(A) 間接的に
(B) 迅速に
(C) 慎重に
(D) 並外れて

正解 D 選択肢は全て副詞。文頭から talented までは「Sato さんは、------- 才能があると考えられている」という意味であり、空所に入る副詞は続く形容詞の talented を修飾すると考えられる。(D) exceptionally「例外的に、並外れて」を入れると、「並外れて才能がある」となって意味が通る。〈such a＋形容詞＋名詞〉は「あれほど〜な…」という意味なので、ここでは「あれほど若い画家」となる。consider 〜 to be …「〜（人・物・事）を…だと考える」、talented「才能のある」。

109 Next month's town festival will feature a ------- author.

(A) celebrate
(B) celebrates
(C) celebrated
(D) to celebrate

来月の町のお祭りは、著名な作家の参加を目玉にしています。

(A) 〜を祝う
(B) 〜を祝う
(C) 著名な
(D) 〜を祝うために

正解 C 選択肢は動詞 celebrate「〜を祝う」と変化形や派生語。a ------- author は動詞 feature の目的語。空所の前に不定冠詞 a があり、後ろに名詞の author「作家、著者」があるので、空所には名詞 author を修飾する語が入る。形容詞の (C) celebrated「著名な、有名な」が適切。festival「祭り」、feature「〜を目玉にする、〜を呼び物にする」。
(A) 原形または現在形。
(B) 三人称単数現在形。
(D) to 不定詞。

110 Car travel ------- the northern part of Willingboro will be difficult until the road repair projects are completed.

(A) through
(B) under
(C) among
(D) upon

Willingboro北部を通る車での移動は、その道路の修繕事業が完了するまで難しいでしょう。

(A) ～を通っての
(B) ～の下の
(C) ～の中の
(D) ～の上の

正解 A 選択肢は全て前置詞の働きを持つ語。文頭からdifficultまでが主節で、その主語は Car travel ------- the northern part of Willingboro「Willingboro北部-------車での移動」。空所からWillingboroまでの部分がCar travelを修飾すると考えられ、(A) through「～を通っての」を入れると意味が通る。until以下は、「その道路の修繕事業が完了するまで」という意味の時を表す副詞節なので、未来の内容だが現在形が使われている。travel「移動」、northern「北の」、repair「修理、修繕」。

111 Tonight's substitute ------- are listed on a separate piece of paper inserted in the theater program.

(A) perform
(B) performers
(C) performing
(D) performance

今夜の代演者たちは、劇場のプログラムに差し込まれた別紙に記載されています。

(A) 演じる
(B) 演者
(C) 演じること
(D) 演技

正解 B 選択肢は動詞perform「演じる」と変化形や派生語。述語動詞はare listedなので、主語は複数形の名詞と考えられる。(B) performers「演者」を入れると、主語が「今夜の代演者たち」という複数形になり、意味も通る。substitute「代理(の)」、be listed on ～「～(リスト・名簿)に載っている」、separate「別の」、insert ～ in …「～を…に差し込む」。
(A) 原形または現在形。
(C) 動名詞または現在分詞。動名詞だとしても、単数扱いなのでareと一致しない。
(D) 名詞。単数形なのでareと一致しない。

TEST1 PART 5

112 All cakes were ------- to customers as expected on Saturday morning.

(A) trusted
(B) delivered
(C) responded
(D) prevented

全てのケーキが、予定通り土曜日の午前中に顧客に配達されました。

(A) 信頼された
(B) 配達された
(C) 返答された
(D) 妨げられた

正解 B 選択肢は全て動詞の過去分詞。「全てのケーキが、予定通り土曜日の午前中に顧客に-------された」という内容なので、(B) deliveredを入れてwere delivered「(全てのケーキが)配達された」とすると、意味が通る。as expected「予定通りに」。

113 Beginning on August 1, the ------- Sunday lunch menu will be offered on Saturdays as well.

(A) popularity
(B) popularize
(C) popularly
(D) popular

8月1日から、人気のある日曜日のランチメニューが土曜日にも提供されます。

(A) 人気
(B) 〜を大衆化する
(C) 一般に
(D) 人気のある

正解 D the ------- Sunday lunch menu が文の主語に当たる。空所の前に定冠詞theがあり、後ろに名詞句Sunday lunch menu「日曜日のランチメニュー」が続いているので、空所には名詞句を修飾する語が入ると考えられる。よって、形容詞の(D) popular「人気のある」が適切。beginning on 〜「〜を初日として」、offer「〜を提供する」、as well「同様に」。
(A) 名詞。名詞には形容詞的用法もあるが、ここでは適さない。
(B) 動詞の原形または現在形。
(C) 副詞。名詞を修飾しない。

114 Please let Ms. Choi know which staff members we will be sending as ------- to the engineering trade show.

(A) techniques
(B) pieces
(C) debtors
(D) representatives

どの従業員を代表者として工学展示会に派遣する予定かChoiさんに知らせてください。

(A) 技術
(B) 部品
(C) 債務者
(D) 代表者

正解 D let 〜 know … は、「〜に…を知らせる」という意味。which以下の節がknowの目的語に相当する。空所の前のasは「〜として」という意味であり、which以下は「私たちがどの従業員を-------として工学展示会に派遣する予定か」という内容になる。(D) representatives「代表者」を入れると、代表者としてどの従業員を派遣するか、となって意味が通る。staff member「従業員、職員」、engineering「工学、エンジニアリング」、trade show「展示会、見本市」。

115 New patients are advised to arrive fifteen minutes ------- their appointment time in order to complete the required paperwork.

(A) into
(B) before
(C) beside
(D) within

新規患者の方は、必要な事務手続きを完了するために、予約時刻の15分前にご来院ください。

(A) 〜の中へ
(B) 〜の前に
(C) 〜のそばに
(D) 〜の範囲内で

正解 B 選択肢は全て前置詞の働きを持つ語。文頭からarriveまでの部分は、「新規患者は到着するよう勧められている」という意味で、ここでは患者への依頼事項を伝えている。in order to以下はその目的を表し、「必要とされる事務手続きを完了するために」という意味。空所に続くtheir appointment timeは空所に入る前置詞の目的語であり、空所に(B) before「〜の前に」を入れるとfifteen minutes before their appointment timeが「予約時刻の15分前に」となって、意味が通る。patient「患者」、advise 〜 to do「〜に…するよう助言する、〜するよう勧める」、appointment time「予約時刻」、required「必要とされる」、paperwork「事務手続き、文書業務」。

116 During his training period, Mr. Yun became ------- better at addressing the needs of customers.

(A) progress
(B) progressed
(C) progressive
(D) progressively

研修期間中に、Yunさんは顧客のニーズに対処することが次第にうまくなりました。

(A) 進歩する
(B) 進歩した
(C) 進歩的な
(D) 次第に

正解 D 選択肢は動詞progress「進歩する」と変化形や派生語。become better at ～ は「～が(以前)より上手になる」という意味であり、becameとbetterに挟まれている空所には、それを修飾する副詞が入る。副詞の(D) progressively「次第に、徐々に」が適切。training period「研修期間」、address「～(仕事・問題など)に対処する」。
(A) 原形または現在形。もしくは名詞で「進歩」。
(B) 過去形または過去分詞。
(C) 形容詞。

117 The flower-arranging workshop will be held in the large meeting room ------- over 30 people register by the May 1 deadline.

(A) at
(B) if
(C) even
(D) instead

5月1日の締め切りまでに30名を超える人が登録した場合は、生け花の講習会は大会議室で開催されます。

(A) ～で
(B) もし～なら
(C) ～でさえ
(D) その代わりに

正解 B 空所の前後がともに〈主語＋動詞〉の形を含む節なので、空所にはこれらの節をつなぐ接続詞が必要。接続詞の(B) if「もし～なら」を入れると、「締め切りまでに30名を超える人が登録した場合は」という条件を表すことになり、意味も通る。flower-arranging「生け花の、フラワーアレンジメントの」、workshop「講習会」、be held「(会などが)開催される」、register「登録する」、deadline「締め切り、最終期限」。
(A) 前置詞、(C) (D) 副詞。いずれも節と節を接続する働きを持たない。

118 Food display cases must be maintained at a ------- temperature to keep products fresh.

(A) steady
(B) mature
(C) punctual
(D) curious

食品陳列ケースは、商品を新鮮に保つため、一定の温度に維持されなければなりません。

(A) 一定の
(B) 成熟した
(C) 時間に正確な
(D) 好奇心の強い

正解 A 選択肢は全て形容詞。文頭からtemperatureまでの部分は、「食品陳列ケースは、------- 温度に維持されなければならない」という意味で、to keep products freshは「商品を新鮮に保つため」とその目的を表す。空所に入る形容詞は名詞temperature「温度」を修飾するので、商品を新鮮に保つために食品陳列ケースが維持されるべき温度を説明する語が入る。(A) steady「一定の、安定した」が適切。display「陳列」、maintain「～を維持する、～を保つ」、keep ～ …「～を…(の状態)に保つ」、fresh「新鮮な」。

119 The staff does not know ------- mobile phone was left behind in the conference room.

- (A) neither
- (B) whose
- (C) nobody
- (D) whoever

誰の携帯電話が会議室に置き忘れられていたのか、スタッフには分かりません。

- (A) どちらの〜も…でない
- (B) 誰の
- (C) 誰も〜ない
- (D) 誰であれ

正解 B The staff does not know は、「スタッフには分からない」という意味で、その分からない内容が空所以下に書かれていると考えられる。空所には名詞句 mobile phone が続いているので、所有格を示す疑問詞の (B) whose を入れると、空所以下が「誰の携帯電話が会議室に置き忘れられたのか」となって意味が通る。leave 〜 behind「〜を置き忘れる」、conference room「会議室」。
(A) 形容詞または代名詞または副詞、(C) 代名詞または名詞、(D) 代名詞。いずれも意味が通らない。

120 The first ------- of the Wilson Motors advertising campaign is to increase consumer awareness of the product.

- (A) plant
- (B) sound
- (C) goal
- (D) room

Wilson Motors 社の広告キャンペーンの第一目標は、その製品に対する消費者の認知度を上げることです。

- (A) 工場
- (B) 音
- (C) 目標
- (D) 部屋

正解 C 選択肢は全て名詞。主語は文頭から campaign までで、「Wilson Motors 社の広告キャンペーンの第一の-------」という意味。is 以下は、「その製品に対する消費者の認知度を上げることである」という意味。(C) goal「目標」を入れると、認知度を上げることが広告キャンペーンの目標ということになり、意味が通る。advertising「広告（の）」、increase「〜を増やす」、consumer「消費者」、awareness「知名度、認知度」。

121 The final cost ------- only slightly from the estimate we had received earlier in the year.

- (A) variety
- (B) varied
- (C) various
- (D) variation

最終的な費用は、私たちが本年先立って受け取っていた見積もりから、ほんのわずかだけ変わりました。

- (A) 多様性
- (B) 変化した
- (C) さまざまな
- (D) 変化

正解 B 文全体の構造を考える。述語動詞がないので空所には動詞が入り、The final cost がこの文の主語と考えられる。the estimate (which) we had received earlier in the year は、「私たちが本年先立って受け取っていた見積もり」という名詞句で、直前の前置詞 from の目的語。空所に動詞の過去形の (B) varied を入れると vary from 〜「〜から変化する」の形になり、最終的な費用が見積もりからわずかだけ変わった、となって意味が通る。final「最終的な」、cost「費用」、slightly「わずかに」、estimate「見積もり」。
(A) (D) 名詞。
(C) 形容詞。

122 Since Mr. Park has worked in ------- accounting and marketing, he will bring much-needed experience to Mr. Lee's team.

(A) both
(B) either
(C) whether
(D) although

Parkさんは会計とマーケティングの両方で仕事をしたことがあるので、大いに必要とされている知識をLeeさんのチームにもたらすでしょう。

(A) 両方とも
(B) どちらか
(C) ～かどうか
(D) ～だけれども

正解 A 空所の前には前置詞inがあり、後ろはaccounting「会計」とmarketing「マーケティング」がandで並列されている。both A and Bで「AとBの両方」を表すので、(A) bothを入れるとin both accounting and marketing「会計とマーケティングの両方で」となり、意味が通る。bring ～ to … 「…に～をもたらす」、much-needed「大いに必要とされている、待望の」、experience「経験、(経験によって得られた)知識」。
(B) either A or B で「AかBか」。
(C) (D) 接続詞。

123 The visitor center at Wengle corporate headquarters is located ------- across from the main entrance to the complex.

(A) direct
(B) direction
(C) directly
(D) directed

Wengle社の本社の案内所は、総合ビルの正面玄関の真向かいに位置しています。

(A) 直接の
(B) 方向
(C) まさに
(D) 向けられた

正解 C 空所の語がなくても文として成り立つので、空所には修飾語が入ると考えられる。空所に続くのは前置詞の働きを持つacross from ～「～の向かいに」で、これを修飾する副詞の(C) directly「ちょうど、まさに」が適切。directly across from the main entrance「正面玄関の真向かいに」となり意味も通る。visitor center「案内所」、corporate headquarters「本社」、be located「位置する」、main entrance「正面玄関」、complex「総合ビル、複合施設」。
(A) 形容詞で「直接の」、または動詞で「～を向ける」。副詞で「直接に、(寄り道せず)真っすぐに」という意味もあるが、意味が通らない。
(B) 名詞。
(D) 動詞の過去形または過去分詞。

124 Washly Architects submitted a particularly ------- bid to design the new city office building.

(A) imminent
(B) competitive
(C) abandoned
(D) heavier

Washly建築社は、新市庁舎の設計で際立って競争力のある入札を行いました。

(A) 差し迫った
(B) 競争力のある
(C) 見捨てられた
(D) より重い

正解 B 選択肢は全て形容詞。空所の後ろの名詞bid「入札」を適切に修飾する語を選ぶ。submit a bidは「入札を行う」の意味であり、続くto design the new city office buildingはこの会社の行った入札が何かを具体的に述べている。(B) competitive「(価格)競争力のある」を入れると、競争力のある入札、つまり他社に負けない価格の入札を行ったとなって意味が通る。architect「建築家、設計者」、particularly「際立って、特に」、design「～を設計する」、city office building「市庁舎」。

125 Farrier Auto Repair, ------- recently changed ownership, will expand its facilities considerably.

(A) about
(B) which
(C) so that
(D) not only

Farrier自動車修理店は、最近所有者が代わり、店の設備を大幅に拡張する予定です。

(A) 〜について
(B) そしてそれは
(C) 〜するように
(D) 〜だけでなく

正解 B 主語はFarrier Auto Repair、述語動詞はwill expand。カンマに挟まれた部分は主語に説明を加える形で挿入されていると考えられるので、主語Farrier Auto Repairを先行詞とする主格の関係代名詞の(B) whichが適切。カンマに挟まれた部分は「それ（＝Farrier自動車修理店）は最近、所有者を代えた」という意味になる。auto「自動車」、ownership「所有、所有権」、expand「〜を拡張する」、facilities「設備」、considerably「かなり」。
(C) that単独であれば主格の関係代名詞としても使われるが、その場合でも挿入用法（非制限用法）では用いない。

126 Our customized training sessions will show you how to make your business extremely -------.

(A) alternate
(B) existent
(C) negotiated
(D) profitable

当社の顧客特化型講習会は、御社の事業を極めて収益性の高いものにする方法をお教えします。

(A) 交互に起こる
(B) 現存する
(C) 協議された
(D) 収益性の高い

正解 D 選択肢は全て形容詞の働きを持つ語。make 〜 … は「〜を…にする」という意味で、空所の位置が…（補語）に当たるので、how to make your business extremely -------は「御社の事業を極めて-------にする方法」という意味になる。(D) profitable「収益性の高い」を入れると意味が通る。customized「注文に応じて作られた、カスタマイズされた」、training session「講習会」、show 〜 how to do「〜に…のやり方を教える」、extremely「極度に」。

127 Hotel guests who would like to ------- tomorrow's hike should contact the concierge, Ms. Jeong.

(A) play with
(B) look through
(C) participate in
(D) adapt to

明日のハイキングへの参加を希望されるホテル宿泊のお客さまは、コンシェルジュのJeongにご連絡ください。

(A) 〜と遊ぶ
(B) 〜に目を通す
(C) 〜に参加する
(D) 〜に順応する

正解 C 主語はHotel guests、述語動詞はshould contact。主語に続くwho would like to ------- tomorrow's hikeはHotel guestsを説明する関係代名詞節で「明日のハイキング-------ことを希望する（人）」という意味。(C) participate in「〜に参加する」を入れると意味が通る。hike「ハイキング」、concierge「コンシェルジュ（チケットの手配や店の予約など、宿泊客の要望に対応するホテルの接客係）」。

128 Here at the Jeju Financial Group, we pride ------- on offering personalized guidance to satisfy clients' needs.

(A) us
(B) our
(C) ourselves
(D) ours

こちらJejuファイナンシャル・グループでは、お客さまのニーズを満たす、お一人お一人に合わせたご案内を提供していることを誇りとしております。

(A) 私たちを
(B) 私たちの
(C) 私たち自身
(D) 私たちのもの

正解 C　選択肢は全て人称代名詞。空所の前にはwe prideとあり、後ろには前置詞onが続いている。動詞prideは再帰代名詞を目的語とするので、(C) ourselves「私たち自身」が適切。pride oneself on ～で「～を誇る」という意味になる。offer「～を提供する」、personalized「個人向けにした」、guidance「案内」、satisfy「～を満足させる」、client「顧客」。
(A) 目的格。
(B) 所有格。
(D) 所有代名詞。

129 ------- Ms. Lim finishes filing the receipts, she can start processing the new orders.

(A) Further
(B) Also
(C) Once
(D) Rather

Limさんは、領収書の整理保存を終えたら、新規注文の処理を始めることができます。

(A) さらに
(B) その上
(C) ひとたび～したら
(D) むしろ

正解 C　カンマの前後がともに〈主語＋動詞〉の形を含む節になっているので、空所には接続詞が必要。カンマの前は「Limさんは領収書の整理保存を終える」、カンマの後は「彼女は新規注文の処理を始めることができる」という意味。接続詞の(C) Once「ひとたび～したら」を入れると意味が通る。file「～(書類など)を整理保存する、ファイリングをする」、receipt「領収書」、process「～を処理する」、order「注文」。
(A) 副詞または形容詞。
(B) 副詞。口語では接続詞として使われる場合もあるが、文頭に置いて従属節は作らない。
(D) 副詞。

130 The conference center has recently become ------- with several local businesses.

(A) affiliated
(B) crafted
(C) given
(D) shown

そのコンファレンスセンターは最近、数社の地元企業と業務提携しました。

(A) 提携した
(B) 念入りに作られた
(C) 与えられた
(D) 見せられた

正解 A　選択肢は全て過去分詞。コンファレンスセンターが地元企業とどのような関係になり得るかを考える。become affiliated with ～で「～と提携する」という意味になるので、(A) affiliatedが適切。conference center「コンファレンスセンター(大会議場を備えた建物)」、business「企業」。

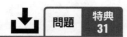

PART 6

Questions 131-134 refer to the following recipe.

How to Make Dried Orange Peel

❶ Many delicious recipes contain dried orange peel. Those cooking at home, though, will discover that dried orange peel can be difficult to find in grocery stores. Luckily, it is simple to make at home. ------- . After washing and drying the fruit, use a sharp paring knife or peeler and remove
131.
only the bright orange peel. ------- , arrange the peels on a dish in a sunny place for 2–3 days until
132.
dried and crispy. There is also a ------- way to make them. Some cooks ------- the peels in a
133.   134.
low-heat oven for a few hours instead.

問題131-134は次のレシピに関するものです。

乾燥オレンジピールの作り方

多くのおいしいレシピで乾燥オレンジピールが使われています。ですが、家庭で料理をする人は、食料品店で乾燥オレンジピールを見つけるのは難しい場合があると気付くでしょう。幸いなことに、それはご家庭で簡単に作れます。*傷がなくて柔らかくない新鮮なオレンジを使うことから始めてください。果物を洗って水分を拭き取った後、鋭利な果物ナイフかピーラーを使って鮮やかなオレンジ色の皮だけをむき取ってください。次に、その皮を皿の上に並べて、乾いてパリパリになるまで日当たりのいい場所に2～3日間置いてください。それをもっと速く作る方法もあります。料理人の中には、代わりに、皮を低温のオーブンに2～3時間入れる人もいます。

*問題131の挿入文の訳

Words & Phrases　　　　　recipe　レシピ、調理法　　dried orange peel　乾燥オレンジピール　　❶ contain　～を含む
those　人々　★those peopleのpeopleを略したもの　　though　でも　　grocery store　食料雑貨店、スーパー
simple　簡単な　　dry　～を乾かす、～の水気を取る　　sharp　鋭利な　　paring knife　果物ナイフ
peeler　ピーラー、皮むき器　　remove　～を取り除く　　bright　明るい、鮮やかな　　peel　皮　　arrange　～を並べる
crispy　パリパリの　　cook　料理人、コック　　low-heat　低温の　　instead　その代わりに

Expressions

〈until＋形容詞〉「～になるまで」（❶4～5行目）　★レシピなどでしばしば見られる表現。untilと形容詞の間に〈主語＋be動詞〉を補える
Sauté the chopped onions until brown.
刻んだタマネギをあめ色になるまで炒めてください。

131
(A) Dried lemon peel is also an excellent addition to many meals.
(B) You can purchase dried orange peels on our Web site.
(C) Start by using fresh oranges that are not bruised or soft.
(D) Check them every fifteen minutes to be sure they do not turn brown.

(A) 乾燥レモンピールもまた、多くの料理に加えられる素晴らしい材料です。
(B) 乾燥オレンジピールは、当社のウェブサイトでご購入いただけます。
(C) 傷がなくて柔らかくない新鮮なオレンジを使うことから始めてください。
(D) それらが茶色くならないように15分ごとに確認してください。

正解 C 空所直前の文で、乾燥オレンジピールは家で簡単に作ることができると述べられており、空所に続く文では、「果物を洗って拭き、皮をむき取ってください」と、具体的な作り方が述べられている。空所に(C)を入れると、直後の文のthe fruit「その果物」が(C)で言及されている「(傷がなくて柔らかくない新鮮な)オレンジ」を意味していることになり、自然なつながりになる。なお、orangesが複数形なのに対してfruitが複数形でないのは、このfruitが食材として不可算名詞扱いであるため。bruised「傷がついた」。
(A) 本文全体を通してオレンジピールについて述べられているので、途中でレモンピールについて言及するのは不自然。addition「加わった物、付加物」、meal「食事、料理」。
(B) 直前の文で乾燥オレンジピールは自宅で簡単に作れると述べられ、直後の文でその手順に言及されているので、購入できるという内容は不自然。
(D) be sure (that) ～「必ず～であるようにする」、turn「(色などが)変わる」。

132
(A) Nevertheless
(B) Besides
(C) Overall
(D) Next

(A) それにもかかわらず
(B) その上
(C) 全体としては
(D) 次に

正解 D 選択肢は全て副詞の働きを持つ語。空所を含む文は、「-------、その皮を皿の上に並べて、乾いてパリパリになるまで日当たりのいい場所に2～3日間置いてください」という意味。空所の直前の文では皮のむき方の手順と注意点が述べられているので、空所を含む文は作り方の説明の続きだと分かる。よって、順序を示す(D) Next「次に」が適切。空所を含む文のthe peels「その皮」は、前文で述べられている新鮮なオレンジからむき取った皮を指している。
(A) (B) (C) 前後の内容とうまくつながらない。

133
(A) cheaper
(B) quicker
(C) taller
(D) earlier

(A) より安い
(B) より速い
(C) より高い
(D) より早い

正解 B 選択肢は全て形容詞の比較級。空所を含む文の前文では、2～3日間天日干しをして乾燥オレンジピールを作る方法が説明されており、続く文ではオーブンを使って2～3時間で作る方法が述べられている。(B) quicker「より速い」を入れると、「それ(＝乾燥オレンジピール)をもっと速く作る方法もある」となって、意味が通る。
(A) 金額については述べられていない。
(D) earlyは「(時期が)早い、初期の」の意味であり、way「方法」を修飾する形容詞として不適切。また、空所の前の不定冠詞がanではなくaであることからも当てはまらないと分かる。

134
(A) place
(B) places
(C) to place
(D) had placed

＊選択肢の訳は省略

正解 A 動詞place「～を置く」の適切な形を選ぶ。空所を含む文はSome cooks「一部の料理人たち」が主語で、空所には述語動詞が入る。文脈から、習慣を表す現在形がふさわしいと考えられ、主語が複数形なので(A) placeが適切。
(B) 三人称単数現在形。主語が複数形なので不適切。
(C) to不定詞。述語動詞にならない。
(D) 過去完了形。述語動詞にはなるが、手順を説明する文脈に合わない。

Questions 135-138 refer to the following letter.

July 7

Camila and Rafael Martin
58 Hotspur Lane
Springfield, MO 63015

Dear Camila and Rafael,

① Everyone at Palmyra Realty hopes you are settling into your new home. In addition to getting to know both of you, I enjoyed meeting your children when we took our last look at the property. ------- . As a token of our thanks, we will be sending you a gift certificate from Imagi Designs. I
135.
hope ------- will help you put the finishing touches on your home.
136.

② Also, I have a small favor to ask of you. Palmyra Realty has been nominated for the Franklin County People's Choice Award for the best real estate agency. We love working with clients to find their ideal homes. We would certainly ------- your vote!
137.

③ I am always ------- for questions. And please consider Palmyra for any future transactions.
138.

All the best,

Elisa Lee
Real Estate Agent
Palmyra Realty

問題135-138は次の手紙に関するものです。

7月7日

Camila Martin 様、Rafael Martin 様
ホットスパー通り　58番地
スプリングフィールド、ミズーリ州　63015

Camila 様、Rafael 様

お二人が新居に落ち着かれつつあることを、Palmyra不動産社の全員が願っております。お二人と知り合いになったことに加え、物件の最終確認をした際にお二人のお子さまたちにお会いしたことも楽しい経験でした。＊Palmyra不動産社は、お二人とお取引ができたことに心から感謝しております。当社の感謝の印としまして、Imagiデザインズ社のギフト券をお送りいたします。それが、お二人のお宅に最後の仕上げをするのに役立つことを願っています。

それから、お二人にちょっとしたお願いがございます。Palmyra不動産社は、フランクリン郡民選択賞に、ベスト不動産会社部門でノミネートされております。当社は、理想の家を見つけるためにお客さま方と一緒に仕事をするのを楽しんでおります。ご投票いただければ大変ありがたく存じます。

私はいつでもご質問に対応いたします。また、今後も何かお取引の案件がございましたら、Palmyra社をご検討ください。

敬具

Elisa Lee
不動産代理人
Palmyra不動産社

＊問題135の挿入文の訳

135
(A) There are several design experts in your neighborhood.
(B) Palmyra Realty is sincerely grateful for your business.
(C) Renting apartments has become competitive in Franklin County.
(D) I have worked in real estate for twenty years.

(A) お二人の近隣には、何人かの設計の専門家がいます。
(B) Palmyra不動産社は、お二人とお取引ができたことに心から感謝しております。
(C) フランクリン郡では、マンションの賃借は競争が激しくなってきています。
(D) 私は不動産業界で20年間働いてきました。

正解 B	宛名や差出人名と❶ 1～2 行目から、この手紙は新居に入居したCamilaさんとRafaelさんに対して、Palmyra不動産社が送ったものだと分かる。空所直後に、「当社の感謝の印として、Imagiデザインズ社のギフト券を送る」とあることから、二人に礼を述べている(B)を入れると自然な流れになる。be grateful for ～「～を感謝している」、sincerely「心から」、business「取引」。

(A) expert「専門家」、neighborhood「近所」。
(C) rent「～を賃借りする」、competitive「競争的な」。
(D) real estate「不動産(業)」。

136
(A) he
(B) enough
(C) each
(D) it

(A) 彼
(B) 十分な量
(C) それぞれ
(D) それ

正解 D	空所には、続く動詞will helpの主語に相当する語が入り、空所を含む文は、「-------があなた方の家に最後の仕上げをするのに役立つことを私は願っている」という意味。直前の文でImagiデザインズ社のギフト券を送ると書かれていることから、(D) itを入れると、itがギフト券を指し、このデザイン会社のギフト券を使って新居に何らかの仕上げを施してほしいという趣旨になって意味が通る。

(A) (B) いずれも何を指すのか不明であり、不適切。
(C) 前の文にa gift certificateとあることから、ギフト券は1枚であると考えられるため、不適切。

137
(A) respond to
(B) consider
(C) appreciate
(D) understand

(A) ～に反応する
(B) ～を考慮する
(C) ～に感謝する
(D) ～を理解する

正解 C	❷では、Palmyra不動産社がフランクリン郡民選択賞のベスト不動産会社部門にノミネートされているため、同社に投票してほしいというお願いが述べられている。空所の語は条件や仮定を示すwouldに続き、your voteを目的語とするので、(C) appreciate「～に感謝する」を入れると「投票してくれたらありがたい」となり、意味が通る。

(A) (B) (D) いずれも文脈に合わない。

138
(A) avails
(B) availing
(C) available
(D) availability

(A) 役に立つ
(B) 役に立っている
(C) 対応できる
(D) 対応できること

正解 C	選択肢は動詞avail「役に立つ」の変化形や派生語。空所を含む文は「私はいつでも質問に-------」という意味。空所は〈主語＋be動詞〉の形に続いているので、補語が入ると考えられる。形容詞の(C) available「対応できる」を入れると、「いつでも質問に対応できる」ということになり、適切。

(A) 三人称単数現在形。be動詞には続かない。
(B) 現在分詞または動名詞、(D) 名詞。いずれもbe動詞に続き得るが、意味が通らない。

Words & Phrases

lane　通り、小道　　MO　ミズーリ州　★アメリカの郵便の略号　　❶ realty　不動産
settle into ～　～(新居など)に落ち着く　　in addition to ～　～に加えて　　take a look at ～　～を見る、～を調べる
property　不動産、地所　　token　印　　gift certificate　ギフト券　　put the finishing touches on ～　～に最後の仕上げをする
❷ nominate ～ for …　～を…に推薦する　　county　郡　　real estate agency　不動産会社　　ideal　理想の　　vote　投票
❸ consider　～を考慮する、～を検討する　　transaction　取引、売買

Expressions

have a favor to ask of ～　「～に頼み事がある」(❷ 1行目)

I have a favor to ask of you: could you check this financial report?
お願いがあるのですが、この会計報告書を確認していただけませんか。

Questions 139-142 refer to the following excerpt from a guidebook.

❶ Coming into the city of Dahlberg, you will see that the skyline is dominated by a tall, pyramid-shaped ------- . This unusual building was designed by Finnish architect Erno Tuokkola.
139.
Although he is best known for designing private residences, Mr. Tuokkola also designed several public buildings in Dahlberg. ------- . Five stories tall and ------- in 2003, it contains nearly a
140. **141.**
million books. It is hard to believe that the building received ------- reviews when it was first built.
142.
Architects now rightly praise the building, and it has since become one of the city's best-loved landmarks.

問題139-142は次のガイドブックからの抜粋に関するものです。

　ダールバーグ市に入ると、ピラミッド型の高い建造物がスカイラインで最も目立っているのに気付くでしょう。この風変わりな建物は、フィンランド人建築家のErno Tuokkolaによって設計されました。Tuokkola氏は個人の邸宅の設計で最もよく知られていますが、ダールバーグの公共建造物も幾つか設計しました。*しばしばピンク・ピラミッドと呼ばれるそれは、市の中央図書館の所在地です。5階建てで2003年に完成し、100万冊近い本を所蔵しています。建てられた当初、この建物が批判的な評価を受けたというのは信じ難いことです。建築家たちは今ではこの建物を正当に称賛しており、その後ずっと、それは市で最も愛されるランドマークの一つとなっています。

*問題140の挿入文の訳

Words & Phrases
❶ skyline　スカイライン　★空を背景とした、山や高層建築物などの輪郭
dominate　～を支配する、～を特色付ける　　-shaped　～の形をした　　unusual　普通でない、まれな
Finnish　フィンランド(人)の　　architect　建築家　　although　～ではあるが　　private　個人の　　residence　住宅
public　公共の　　story　階　　contain　～を含む　　review　評価　　rightly　正しく、正当に　　praise　～を称賛する
since　その後ずっと　　best-loved　最も愛される　　landmark　ランドマーク、目印になる建物

Expressions
see that ～　「～ということに気付く」（❶ 1～2行目）
　At first, our development team didn't see that the issue was so complicated.
　最初は、私たち開発チームはその問題がそれほど複雑だとは気付きませんでした。

139
(A) statue
(B) structure
(C) sign
(D) hill

(A) 像
(B) 建造物
(C) 標識
(D) 丘

正解 B 空所を含む文は、「ダールバーグ市に入ると、ピラミッド型の高い-------がスカイラインで最も目立っているのにあなたは気付くだろう」という意味。続く文は This unusual building「この風変わりな建物」を主語として、建造物が誰によって設計されたかを述べているので、空所に(B) structure「建造物」を入れると、This unusual building が「ピラミッド型の高い建造物」を指すことになり、自然なつながりになる。なお、Coming into the city of Dahlberg は分詞構文で、「あなたがダールバーグ市に入るとき」といった意味合い。
(A) (C) (D) 直後の文に「この風変わりな建物は」とあり、それ以降も建造物を説明する内容が続いているため、いずれも不適切。

140
(A) The Pink Pyramid, as it is often called, is home to the city's Central Library.
(B) His custom-designed homes can be seen throughout Finland.
(C) Dahlberg is located on a thin strip of land between two lakes.
(D) Mr. Tuokkola never achieved the fame of some other Finnish architects.

(A) しばしばピンク・ピラミッドと呼ばれるそれは、市の中央図書館の所在地です。
(B) 彼の特注設計による住宅はフィンランドの至る所で見られます。
(C) ダールバーグは2つの湖に挟まれた細長い土地に位置しています。
(D) Tuokkola 氏は他の何人かのフィンランド人建築家のような名声を得ることはありませんでした。

正解 A 空所直前の文で、フィンランド人建築家の Erno Tuokkola 氏が市の公共建物を設計したことについて述べられており、また直後の文では、100万冊近い本を所蔵していることが説明されている。よって空所には、公共建物の紹介であり、本を所蔵するという説明につながる(A)を入れると、流れとして自然。home「本拠地」。
(B) 直前の文で Tuokkola 氏が住宅の設計で有名だと述べられているが、住宅に関する文を入れると次の文に自然につながらないため不適切。custom-designed「特注で設計された」、throughout「〜の至る所で」。
(C) ダールバーグ市の案内としてあり得る一文だが、具体的な建造物について述べる2つの文の間に入る文としては不自然。a strip of land「細長い土地」、thin「細い、細長い」。
(D) 直前の文は Tuokkola 氏について述べているが、同氏について補足する文を入れると次の文に自然につながらないため不適切。achieve「〜を獲得する」、fame「名声」。

141
(A) completing
(B) completely
(C) completed
(D) completeness

(A) 〜を完成させる
(B) 完全に
(C) 完成した
(D) 完全さ

正解 C 選択肢は動詞 complete「〜を完成させる」の変化形や派生語。空所を含む文は、カンマ以降の it contains nearly a million books「それは100万冊近い本を所蔵している」の部分が主節で、it は Tuokkola 氏が設計したピラミッド型の建造物を指す。Five stories tall and ------- in 2003 の部分は分詞構文と考えられ、過去分詞の(C) completed を入れると completed in 2003「2003年に完成して」と付帯状況を表し、意味が通る。なお、Five stories tall の部分は、Being five stories tall の Being が省略されたものと解釈できる。
(A) 現在分詞または動名詞。現在分詞だとしても、文の主語は it(建物)であり、建物が「完成させる」というつながりは不適切。
(B) 副詞。
(D) 名詞。

142
(A) important
(B) independent
(C) numerous
(D) critical

(A) 重要な
(B) 独立した
(C) 非常に多くの
(D) 批判的な

正解 D 選択肢は全て形容詞の働きを持つ語。空所を含む文は、「建てられた当初、その建物が-------評価を受けたことは信じ難い」という意味。続く文で、今ではその建物が称賛されていることが述べられているので、空所に現在の肯定的評価とは逆の意味を表す(D) critical「批判的な」を入れると、自然な流れになる。
(A) (B) (C) いずれも、今では称賛されているという流れに合わない。

Questions 143-146 refer to the following article.

❶ SEOUL (May 2)—Experienced local business leader Ms. Binna Hyeon will ------- Chin-Hae
143.
Communications in the role of chief operations officer. Ms. Hyeon began her career at Chin-Hae
Communications. Five years ago, she left the company to serve ------- an area manager for
144.
Bishop Technology's North American division. ------- .
145.

❷ "I'm pleased to welcome Ms. Hyeon back to Chin-Hae Communications to lead operations," said
Geon Kim, president and CEO of Chin-Hae. "Based on her record at Bishop Technology, I
believe Ms. Hyeon will be instrumental in helping Chin-Hae Communications achieve its goal of
becoming the communications leader in Asia."

❸ Chin-Hae Communications is a major ------- of IT services for businesses in South Korea.
146.

問題143-146は次の記事に関するものです。

ソウル（5月2日）── 経験豊富な地元のビジネスリーダーであるBinna Hyeon氏が、最高執行責任者としてChin-Haeコミュニケーションズ社に復帰する。Hyeon氏は自身のキャリアをChin-Haeコミュニケーションズ社でスタートさせた。5年前、同氏はBishopテクノロジー社の北米事業部で地域統括マネジャーとして勤務するため、Chin-Haeコミュニケーションズ社を退職した。＊Hyeon氏は、自身の担当地域でBishopテクノロジー社の市場シェアを大きく拡大させた。

Chin-Hae社の社長兼最高経営責任者であるGeon Kimは、「私は、Hyeon氏がChin-Haeコミュニケーションズ社に復帰して業務の指揮を執ってくれることをうれしく思います」と述べた。「Bishopテクノロジー社での彼女の実績を考えれば、Hyeon氏は、Chin-Haeコミュニケーションズ社がアジアにおける通信技術分野のリーダーになるという目標を達成するのを助けてくれることと思います」。

Chin-Haeコミュニケーションズ社は、韓国における企業向けITサービスの主要プロバイダーの一つである。

＊問題145の挿入文の訳

Words & Phrases ❶ experienced 経験豊富な　communications 通信技術
in the role of ～ ～の役割で、～として　chief operations officer 最高執行責任者、COO　serve 勤務する
division 事業部、部局　❷ be pleased to *do* 喜んで～する、～してうれしい　welcome ～を迎える、～を歓迎する
lead ～を指揮する　operation 業務、運営　CEO 最高経営責任者　★chief executive officerの略
based on ～ ～を考えれば、～に基づいて言えば　record 実績、業績　achieve ～を達成する　goal 目的、目標
❸ major 主要な　IT 情報技術　★information technologyの略

Expressions

be instrumental in *doing* 「～するのに役立つ」（❷3行目）

Our strategy was instrumental in completing the project on time.
当社の戦略は、プロジェクトを時間通りに完了するのに役立ちました。

143
(A) rejoin
(B) affect
(C) recommend
(D) visit

(A) 〜に復帰する
(B) 〜に影響を及ぼす
(C) 〜を推薦する
(D) 〜を訪れる

正解 **A**　選択肢は全て動詞の働きを持つ語。空所を含む文は、「経験豊富な地元のビジネスリーダーであるBinna Hyeon氏が、最高執行責任者としてChin-Haeコミュニケーションズ社-------」という意味であり、空所の語はChin-Hae Communicationsという社名を目的語としている。それに続く❶2〜4行目で、彼女が同社でキャリアをスタートしたが5年前に他社に移ったことが述べられており、また、❷1〜2行目では彼女を再び迎えられてうれしいというChin-Haeコミュニケーションズ社の社長兼CEOの発言が述べられている。よって、(A) rejoin「〜に再び加わる、〜に復帰する」を入れるのが、流れとして自然。

144
(A) of
(B) in
(C) as
(D) to

(A) 〜の
(B) 〜の中で
(C) 〜として
(D) 〜へ

正解 **C**　選択肢は全て前置詞の働きを持つ語。空所の直前は自動詞serve「勤務する」、空所に入る前置詞の目的語はan area managerであり、空所を含む文は、「5年前、彼女はBishopテクノロジー社の北米事業部で地域統括マネジャー-------勤務するため、Chin-Haeコミュニケーションズ社を退職した」という意味。(C) as「〜として」を入れると、serve as 〜「〜として勤務する」となり、意味が通る。
(A) (B) (D) いずれも空所前後のserve、an area managerとうまくつながらない。

145
(A) Bishop Technology plans to close several facilities worldwide.
(B) Ms. Hyeon greatly expanded Bishop Technology's market share in her area.
(C) Bishop Technology plans to interview Ms. Hyeon.
(D) The two companies once considered forming a partnership.

(A) Bishopテクノロジー社は、世界中で幾つかの施設を閉鎖する計画である。
(B) Hyeon氏は、自身の担当地域でBishopテクノロジー社の市場シェアを大きく拡大させた。
(C) Bishopテクノロジー社はHyeon氏を面接する予定である。
(D) その2社はかつて、提携関係を結ぶことを検討した。

正解 **B**　空所の直前の文で、Hyeon氏が5年前にBishopテクノロジー社の北米事業部の地域統括マネジャーになったことに言及されている。空所に続く段落の❷ではHyeon氏を迎えるChin-Hae社のCEOの言葉が述べられ、同2〜3行目には「Bishopテクノロジー社での彼女の実績を考えれば、Hyeon氏は、Chin-Haeコミュニケーションズ社が目標を達成するのを助けてくれることと思う」とある。空所に(B)を入れると、担当地域でBishopテクノロジー社の市場シェアを拡大させたのが「彼女の実績」ということになり、自然な流れになる。expand「〜を拡大させる」、market share「市場シェア」。
(A) ❷2〜4行目で、Hyeon氏のBishopテクノロジー社での実績について肯定的に述べられており、Bishopテクノロジー社が施設を閉鎖する計画という内容は文脈に合わない。facility「施設」、worldwide「世界中で」。
(C) ❶より、Hyeon氏はBishopテクノロジー社からChin-Hae社に移ることが分かるので不自然な内容。interview「〜を面接する」。
(D) ❶ではHyeon氏個人の経歴が述べられているので、2社の提携に関する話題は唐突で不自然。form「〜(関係など)を結ぶ」、partnership「提携関係、パートナーシップ」。

146
(A) provide
(B) provided
(C) providing
(D) provider

(A) 〜を供給する
(B) 供給された
(C) 〜を供給している
(D) プロバイダー

正解 **D**　選択肢は動詞provide「〜を供給する」と変化形や派生語。空所の前には不定冠詞aと形容詞major「主要な」があり、直後にはof IT services for businesses「企業向けITサービスの」という修飾語句が続くので、空所には前後の語句に修飾される名詞が入ると考えられる。よって、名詞の(D) provider「プロバイダー、供給業者」が適切。
(A) 原形または現在形。
(B) 過去分詞または過去形。
(C) 現在分詞または動名詞。動名詞「供給すること」だとしても、前後の語句とのつながりが不自然で、意味が通らない。

PART 7

Questions 147-148 refer to the following coupon.

Silver Sprint Grill
Home of the Mega Fun Burger

Date: May 7

❶ Congratulations! As a winner of our Wednesday night trivia quiz, you are entitled to a free appetizer or dessert. Exclusions apply. You must present this coupon to claim your prize. Coupon expires six months from the date shown above.

❷ The weekly trivia quiz is presented by DJ D'Shaun. To book D'Shaun for a private event, visit www.djdshaun.com or call 777-555-0109.

問題147-148は次のクーポンに関するものです。

Silver Sprint グリル料理店
メガファンバーガーの発祥地

日付：5月7日

おめでとうございます！当店の水曜夜の雑学クイズの勝者として、お客さまは無料の前菜またはデザートをお受け取りになれます。対象外のものもあります。賞品をお受け取りになるには、このクーポンを提示する必要がございます。クーポンは上記の日付から6カ月で有効期限が切れます。

毎週の雑学クイズはDJ D'Shaunによって出題されます。私的なイベントにD'Shaunの出演を予約するには、www.djdshaun.comにアクセスするか、777-555-0109にお電話ください。

147 Who is D'Shaun?

    (A) A waiter at Silver Sprint Grill

    (B) The winner of a trivia quiz

    (C) The inventor of the Mega Fun Burger

    (D) The host of a contest

D'Shaunとは誰ですか。

    (A) Silver Sprintグリル料理店のウエーター

    (B) 雑学クイズの勝者

    (C) メガファンバーガーの考案者

    (D) コンテストの司会者

> **正解 D** D'Shaunについては、❷1行目に、The weekly trivia quiz is presented by DJ D'Shaun. とある。the weekly trivia quizをa contest「コンテスト、競争」と表し、presentを用いて説明されている内容をhost「司会者」と表現している(D)が正解。
> (A) waiter「給仕係、ウエーター」。
> (C) inventor「考案者」。

148 What is most likely true about the coupon?

    (A) It expires on May 7.

    (B) It can be exchanged for cash.

    (C) It can be used for any side order or drink.

    (D) It was issued on a Wednesday night.

クーポンについて正しいと考えられることは何ですか。

    (A) 5月7日で有効期限が切れる。

    (B) 換金することができる。

    (C) どんなサイドオーダーや飲み物にも使用することができる。

    (D) 水曜日の夜に発行された。

> **正解 D** ❶1〜2行目に、「当店の水曜夜の雑学クイズの勝者として、あなたは無料の前菜またはデザートを受け取れる」とある。よって、水曜日の夜にクイズの勝者に対してクーポンが発行されると考えられるので、(D)が正解。issue「〜を発行する」。
> (A) 5月7日は、クーポンが発行された日付。❶3〜4行目より、その日付から6カ月で有効期限が切れることが分かる。
> (B) 換金については述べられていない。exchange 〜 for …「〜を…と交換する」、cash「現金」。
> (C) ❶1〜2行目より、前菜またはデザートが対象であることが分かる。サイドオーダーや飲み物に関する記述はない。side order「添え料理、サイドオーダー」。

Words & Phrases

grill　グリル料理、網焼き料理　　home　発祥地　　burger　ハンバーガー
❶ Congratulations!　おめでとう!　　trivia　雑学、豆知識　　appetizer　前菜　　dessert　デザート　　exclusion　除外事項
apply　適用される　　present　〜を提供する、〜を紹介する　　claim　〜を要求する　　prize　賞、賞品
expire　期限切れになる、失効する　　❷ DJ　★disc jockey「ディスクジョッキー」の略　　book　〜を予約する　　private　私的な

Expressions

be entitled to 〜　「〜を持つ権利がある、〜を持つ資格がある」(❶1〜2行目)

The software creator is entitled to a share in the profits.
そのソフトウエア制作者は利益の分配を受ける資格があります。

Questions 149-150 refer to the following memo.

MEMO

To: All Staff
From: Maintenance
Date: Monday, March 9

❶ Because of a delay in the delivery of some materials, repairs to the roof will not be made today. The work has been postponed until Thursday, March 12.

❷ As previously noted, the building will remain fully accessible while the repairs are being made. However, you may experience some distractions from the sound of power tools and maintenance workers overhead. Because we are in a slow period in our production cycle, we expect the impact to be minimal.

❸ Thank you for your cooperation as we ensure that our building is a safe and comfortable place to work. Please contact the maintenance department directly with any questions.

問題149-150は次のメモに関するものです。

メモ

宛先：従業員各位
差出人：保守管理部
日付：3月9日 月曜日

幾つかの資材の配送が遅れているため、本日、屋根の修理作業は行われません。作業は3月12日（木曜日）まで延期されました。

以前に述べた通り、修理作業が行われている間も、建物は引き続き完全に利用できます。しかし、頭上から聞こえる電動工具や保守作業員の音のせいで、多少気が散ることがあるかもしれません。現在当社は生産サイクルの閑散期にあるため、影響は最小限になると考えています。

当社の建物を確実に安全かつ快適な仕事場にするに際して、ご協力をお願いいたします。何かご質問がございましたら、保守管理部に直接ご連絡ください。

149 What is the purpose of the memo?

    (A) To announce a schedule change

    (B) To warn about hazardous conditions

    (C) To seek input about needed repairs

    (D) To offer a reminder about workplace safety

メモの目的は何ですか。

    (A) 予定の変更を知らせること

    (B) 危険な状況について警告すること

    (C) 必要とされる修理作業について意見を求めること

    (D) 仕事場の安全性について注意を与えること

正解 A　メモは、保守管理部が全従業員に宛てたもの。❶に、「幾つかの資材の配送が遅れているため、本日、屋根の修理作業は行われない。作業は3月12日(木曜日)まで延期された」とあり、この内容を知らせることがメモの目的と考えられる。よって、修理作業の延期をa schedule changeと表した(A)が正解。announce「～を知らせる」、schedule「予定」。
(B) 修理作業中の注意事項への言及はあるが、危険については警告されていない。warn「警告する」、hazardous「危険な」、condition「状況」。
(C) 修理作業の話題ではあるが、必要な修理作業について意見は求められていない。seek「～を求める」、input「意見」。
(D) 仕事場の安全性への言及はあるが、それについてのreminder「あらためて思い出させるための注意」を与えてはいない。workplace「仕事場」、safety「安全性」。

150 How is the work expected to affect employees?

    (A) It will cause part of the building to be closed.

    (B) It will create some loud noise.

    (C) It will lead to some power outages.

    (D) It will disrupt package deliveries.

作業はどのように従業員に影響を与えると見込まれていますか。

    (A) 建物の一部の閉鎖をもたらすだろう。

    (B) 大きな騒音を生じさせるだろう。

    (C) 停電を引き起こすだろう。

    (D) 荷物の配送を混乱させるだろう。

正解 B　工事作業について、❷2～3行目に、However, you may experience some distractions from the sound of power tools and maintenance workers overhead. とある。このthe sound of power tools and maintenance workers overheadをloud noise「大きな騒音」と表している(B)が正解。affect「～に影響を与える」。create「～を創り出す、～を引き起こす」。
(A) ❷1～2行目で、建物は作業中も完全に利用できることが述べられているので、閉鎖されることはない。cause ～ to do「～に…させる」。
(C) lead to ～「～を引き起こす、～につながる」、power outage「停電」。
(D) ❶1～2行目で資材の配送の遅れに言及されているが、屋根の修理作業の延期の原因として述べられているのであり、今後起こり得ることとしてではない。disrupt「～を混乱させる」、package「荷物」。

Words & Phrases
maintenance 保守管理　❶ because of ～　～のせいで、～のために　delay 遅れ
material 資材　repairs 修理作業　roof 屋根　postpone ～を延期する　❷ previously 以前に
note ～と述べる　remain ～　～のままである　fully 完全に　accessible 行きやすい、利用できる
distraction 気を散らすこと　power tool 電動工具　overhead 頭上で　in a slow period 閑散期で
production cycle 生産サイクル　expect ～ to do　～が…するものと予期する　impact 影響　minimal 最小限の
❸ cooperation 協力　comfortable 快適な　directly 直接に

Expressions

ensure that ～　「～であることを確実にする」(❸1～2行目)

The government needs to ensure that workers' rights are respected.
政府は労働者の権利が尊重されることを確実にする必要があります。

Questions 151-152 refer to the following text-message chain.

Sarah Fuller (8:48 A.M.)
Are you going to be in the office this afternoon?

Jack Bennett (8:49 A.M.)
I am. What's going on?

Sarah Fuller (8:50 A.M.)
I just got a call that the new furniture for the lobby can be delivered early if someone is there to sign for it. I'm working from home today because my car is in the repair shop. I can't be there to sign for the furniture and show them where to put it.

Jack Bennett (8:53 A.M.)
Do you know what time it would be delivered? I was planning to leave at 4 this afternoon.

Sarah Fuller (8:55 A.M.)
Let me check.

Sarah Fuller (9:13 A.M.)
The delivery company says between 1 and 2 p.m.

Jack Bennett (9:15 A.M.)
That works for me.

Sarah Fuller (9:16 A.M.)
Thank you so much. I'll e-mail you the layout, so you can tell them where to place the furniture. It will be nice to finally get some new furniture. The lobby has looked so empty since we removed the old furniture.

問題 151-152 は次のテキストメッセージのやりとりに関するものです。

Sarah Fuller（午前8時48分）　　今日の午後オフィスにいますか。

Jack Bennett（午前8時49分）　　いますよ。どうしたのですか。

Sarah Fuller（午前8時50分）　　ちょうど電話を受けたところなのですが、もし誰か受け取りの署名をする人がいるならロビー用の新しい家具を早く配達できるとのことです。私は、車が修理工場にあるので今日は在宅勤務をしています。そちらで家具の受け取りの署名をしたり置き場所を指示したりできないのです。

Jack Bennett（午前8時53分）　　何時に配達されそうか分かりますか。私は今日の午後は4時に退社するつもりでした。

Sarah Fuller（午前8時55分）　　確認させてください。

Sarah Fuller（午前9時13分）　　配送会社は午後1時から2時の間だと言っています。

Jack Bennett（午前9時15分）　　それなら大丈夫です。

Sarah Fuller（午前9時16分）　　どうもありがとうございます。レイアウトをEメールで送るので、彼らに家具をどこに置けばいいか伝えてください。ついに新しい家具が入るのはうれしいですね。古い家具を撤去してから、ロビーはとてもがらんとした感じでしたから。

151 What is indicated about Ms. Fuller? Fullerさんについて何が示されていますか。

    (A) She works for a furniture delivery company.   (A) 家具配送会社に勤務している。

    (B) She has to leave work at 4:00 P.M.   (B) 午後4時に退社しなければならない。

    (C) She is unable to come to the office today.   (C) 今日オフィスに行くことができない。

    (D) She has not yet removed the old furniture.   (D) まだ古い家具を撤去していない。

正解 C Fullerさんは❶で、Bennettさんに「今日の午後オフィスにいるか」と尋ねており、❸で、「私は、車が修理工場にあるので今日は在宅勤務をしている」と述べ、続けて I can't be there to sign for the furniture and show them where to put it. と伝えている。このthereは話の流れからオフィスを指すので、Fullerさんは今日はオフィスには行けないと分かる。よって、(C)が正解。be unable to *do*「~することができない」。

(A) 家具の配送に関連する話題だが、Fullerさんは配送される家具を受け取るための手配をしているのであり、家具配送会社に勤務しているという記述はない。

(B) ❸より、Fullerさんは在宅勤務をしており、❹より、午後4時に退社する予定なのはBennettさんと分かる。

(D) ❽より、古い家具はすでに撤去されたと分かる。

152 At 9:15 A.M., what does Mr. Bennett most likely mean when he writes, "That works for me"? 午前9時15分に、"That works for me" という発言で、Bennettさんは何を意図していると考えられますか。

    (A) He plans to work late today.   (A) 今日遅くまで仕事をするつもりである。

    (B) He will accept a furniture shipment.   (B) 家具の配達品を受け取るつもりである。

    (C) He can drive Ms. Fuller to the office.   (C) Fullerさんを車でオフィスまで送ることができる。

    (D) He likes the style of the new furniture.   (D) 新しい家具の様式が好きである。

正解 B Bennettさんは❹で、「何時に配達されそうか分かるか。私は今日の午後は4時に退社するつもりだった」と家具の配達時間を尋ね、4時にはオフィスを退出する旨を伝えている。Fullerさんが❻で、配達予定時間を午後1時から2時の間だと答えたことに対し、Bennettさんは午前9時15分に❼で、That works for meという発言をしている。ここでのwork for ~は「(日時などが)~にとって都合がいい」という意味なので、Bennettさんはその時間であれば問題ないと判断し、家具の受け取りを承諾したと考えられる。よって、(B)が正解。accept「~を受け取る」、shipment「出荷品」。

(C) drive「~を車で送る」。

Words & Phrases   text-message　テキストメッセージの　chain　一続き　❷ What's going on?　どうしたのですか。
❸ furniture　家具　sign for ~　~の受領証明として署名をする　work from home　在宅勤務をする
repair shop　修理工場　❻ between *A* and *B*　*A*と*B*の間に　❽ e-mail ~ …　~に…をEメールで送る
layout　レイアウト　place　~を置く　finally　ついに　look　~に見える　empty　空の、空虚な
remove　~を撤去する

Expressions

where to *do*　「どこで~すべきか」（❸6行目）

    I have so many things to tell you that I don't know where to start.
    話すべきことが多過ぎて、どこから始めればいいのか分かりません。

Questions 153-155 refer to the following Web page.

https://www.dublinwaxzoo.ie

| **Home** | About Us | Tickets | Contact |

① The Dublin Wax Zoo is the world's first museum zoo. Visitors can see life-size wax replicas of all their favourite animals. Both children and adults are amazed when they compare their own size to the enormous replicas of the blue whale and the African elephant. The wax zoo's newest additions are now open as well: the wax primate house and the African safari trolley ride.

② Tickets are €20 for adults, €14 for youths aged 12–18, and €10 for children under 12. See the Web site's ticket page to order.

③ And remember, parking is always free at the Dublin Wax Zoo!

問題153-155は次のウェブページに関するものです。

https://www.dublinwaxzoo.ie

<u>ホーム</u>　当園について　チケット　お問い合わせ

ダブリンろう人形動物園は世界初の博物館型動物園です。ご来園の皆さまは、お気に入りのあらゆる動物の実物大ろう製レプリカを見ることができます。自分自身の大きさとシロナガスクジラやアフリカゾウの巨大なレプリカを比べると、子どもも大人も驚きます。また、当ろう人形動物園の最新の追加設備も、このたびオープンしました。ろう人形霊長類園とアフリカンサファリ・トロリー・ライドです。

チケットは、大人が20ユーロ、12～18歳の若者が14ユーロ、12歳未満の子どもは10ユーロです。ご注文はウェブサイトのチケットのページをご覧ください。

そしてどうぞお忘れなく、ダブリンろう人形動物園では駐車場がいつも無料です！

Words & Phrases
contact　問い合わせ　❶ wax　ろう、ろう(製)の　life-size　実物大の　replica　レプリカ、複製
favourite　お気に入りの　★米国表記は favorite　amazed　驚いて　enormous　巨大な　blue whale　シロナガスクジラ
newest　最新の　addition　追加(された人・物)　as well　なお、その上　primate　霊長類の動物
trolley　路面電車、トロリー　ride　乗り物　★遊園地や大きい公園などにあるアトラクション
❷ €(euro)　ユーロ　★EU共通通貨単位　youth　若者　aged ～　～歳の

153 What is suggested about the replica of the blue whale?

    (A) It is the same size as a real blue whale.
    (B) It has been copied for display in another wax zoo.
    (C) It is exhibited outdoors.
    (D) Viewing it requires an additional fee.

シロナガスクジラのレプリカについて何が分かりますか。

    (A) 本物のシロナガスクジラと同じ大きさである。
    (B) 別のろう人形動物園での展示のために複製が作られた。
    (C) 屋外で展示されている。
    (D) それを見るには追加料金が必要である。

正解 A ❶ 1〜2行目に、Visitors can see life-size wax replicas of all their favourite animals. とあるので、この動物園は実物大のろう製レプリカを展示していると分かる。シロナガスクジラのレプリカについては、同2〜4行目に、「自分自身の大きさとシロナガスクジラやアフリカゾウの巨大なレプリカを比べると、子どもも大人も驚く」とあり、シロナガスクジラのレプリカも実物大のものが展示されていると判断できる。よって、life-sizeをthe same size as a real blue whaleと表している(A)が正解。
(B) 別のろう人形動物園への言及はない。copy「〜を複製する」。
(C) 展示場所に関する言及はない。exhibit「〜を展示する」、outdoors「屋外で」。
(D) 追加料金への言及はない。view「〜を見る」、require「〜を必要とする」、additional fee「追加料金」。

154 What is indicated about the wax zoo?

    (A) It includes replicas of famous people.
    (B) There are two new areas.
    (C) The safari trolley ride has live animals.
    (D) The parking garage will open soon.

ろう人形動物園について何が示されていますか。

    (A) 有名な人物のレプリカを含んでいる。
    (B) 2つの新しいエリアがある。
    (C) サファリ・トロリー・ライドでは本物の動物がいる。
    (D) 立体駐車場が間もなくオープンする予定である。

正解 B ❶ 4〜5行目に、「また、当ろう人形動物園の最新の追加設備も、このたびオープンした」とあり、続けて、ろう人形霊長類園とアフリカンサファリ・トロリー・ライドという2つが紹介されている。よって、新たに2つのエリアが追加されていると分かるので、(B)が正解。
(A) 人物のろう人形には言及されていない。include「〜を含む」。
(C) 本物の動物の有無には言及されていない。live「生きている、本物の」。
(D) ❸に駐車場が無料であるとの記載があるだけで、新たにオープンする駐車場については述べられていない。parking garage「立体駐車場、屋内駐車場」。

155 How much is a ticket for someone who is 12 years old?

    (A) €10
    (B) €14
    (C) €16
    (D) €20

12歳の人のチケットは幾らですか。

    (A) 10ユーロ
    (B) 14ユーロ
    (C) 16ユーロ
    (D) 20ユーロ

正解 B チケットの料金については、❷ 1〜2行目に、「大人が20ユーロ、12〜18歳の若者が14ユーロ、12歳未満の子どもは10ユーロ」とある。よって、12〜18歳の若者の料金である(B)が正解。children under 12は「12歳未満の子ども」という意味なので、12歳の人は含まれない。

Expressions

compare 〜 to …　「〜を…と比べる」(❶ 2〜4行目)
  Click the "History Record" button to compare the edited version of your file to the original version.
  ファイルの編集済みのバージョンを元のバージョンと比較するには、「履歴の記録」ボタンをクリックしてください。

Questions 156-157 refer to the following form.

Joyous Mode Fashions
Job Application

Name: Regina Riyad
E-mail address: reginariyad@myemail.com

❶ **Question: Explain in detail why you would be a good manager at Joyous Mode Fashions. Describe relevant experience and anything else that qualifies you for the position.**

❷ Applicant Answer: I understand how challenging it can be to find clothing that is both fashionable and affordable. As a salesperson at Boutique Cecilia, where I worked for three years, I specialized in helping customers find flattering clothing within their price range. Although I was not in management, with the owner's permission I launched a text-messaging program. I notified customers of the arrival of new merchandise that I thought would suit them. In this way, I built a loyal base of repeat customers, increasing store profits by almost 20 percent per month.

❸ I believe my retail background and the initiative I have shown make me a good choice for the manager role at Joyous Mode Fashions.

問題156-157は次の用紙に関するものです。

Joyousモードファッションズ社
就職応募用紙

氏名：Regina Riyad
Eメールアドレス：reginariyad@myemail.com

質問：Joyousモードファッションズ社でご自分が良いマネジャーになるだろうと思う理由を詳しく説明してください。関連のある経験や、あなたをこの職に適任とするその他どんなことでも述べてください。

応募者の回答：ファッショナブルかつ手頃な値段の衣服を見つけるのがいかに大変な場合があるか、私は理解しています。Ceciliaブティックの販売員として、そこでは3年間働きましたが、私は、お客さまが予算内で魅力を引き立てる衣服を見つけるよう手助けすることを専門としていました。経営の立場ではありませんでしたが、オーナーの許可をもらって私はテキストメッセージを送るプログラムを始めました。似合うだろうと思った新商品の入荷をお客さまにお知らせしたのです。このようにして、常連客の忠実な基盤を築き、店の利益を1カ月につき20パーセント近く増やしました。

小売業での経歴とここに示した自発的取り組みによって、私はJoyousモードファッションズ社のマネジャーの役割にふさわしい人材であると思います。

Words & Phrases
application 申込書、応募　❶ in detail 詳しく　describe ～を述べる　relevant 関連した　qualify ～ for … ～に…(地位)の資格を与える、～を…に適任とする　position 職　❷ applicant 応募者　challenging やりがいのある、困難な　clothing 衣類、衣服　fashionable 流行の　affordable 手頃な値段の　salesperson 販売員　boutique ブティック　★婦人服などを売る小さな洋品店　specialize in ～ ～を専門とする　help ～ do ～が…するのを手伝う　flattering 魅力を引き立てる　range 範囲　management 経営　owner 所有者、オーナー　permission 許可　launch ～を始める　text-messaging テキストメッセージ送信(の)　arrival 到着、到来　merchandise 商品　suit ～に似合う、～を満足させる　loyal 忠実な　base 基盤　repeat customer 常連客　profit 利益　per ～につき　❸ retail 小売業　background 経歴　initiative 自発性、主導権　choice 選ばれた人　role 役割

156 What is true of Ms. Riyad?

    (A) She is applying for a bookkeeping position.

    (B) She previously worked at Joyous Mode Fashions.

    (C) She has several years of experience working in retail.

    (D) She specializes in designing clothing.

Riyadさんに当てはまることは何ですか。

    (A) 経理の職に応募している。

    (B) 以前Joyousモードファッションズ社で働いていた。

    (C) 小売業での数年間の勤務経験がある。

    (D) 衣服のデザインを専門にしている。

> **正解 C** 冒頭の氏名欄より、Riyadさんとは応募書類を書いている人物と分かる。自身の経歴として❷2～3行目で、As a salesperson at Boutique Cecilia, where I worked for three yearsと述べているので、彼女は3年間販売員として働いた経験があると分かる。また、この経験について、❸1行目でもmy retail backgroundと言及している。よって、(C)が正解。
> (A) 見出しより、就職応募用紙であることが分かるが、❷で販売員としての経験をアピールしているので、bookkeeping「経理」職への応募とは考えにくい。apply for ～「～に応募する」。
> (B) Joyousモードファッションズ社はRiyadさんが応募している会社。❷2～3行目より、以前働いていたのはCeciliaブティックと分かる。previously「以前に」。
> (D) 応募用紙で説明されているのは衣服の販売に関連した職であり、デザイン職への言及はない。design「～をデザインする」。

157 Why did Ms. Riyad text customers at her previous job?

    (A) To alert them to new items they might like

    (B) To notify them that payments were due

    (C) To offer them discounts on merchandise

    (D) To notify them that their orders were ready

Riyadさんは前職でなぜ顧客にテキストメッセージを送りましたか。

    (A) 彼らが気に入るかもしれない新しい品物を通知するため

    (B) 支払期日がきたことを知らせるため

    (C) 商品に対する割引を提供するため

    (D) 注文品の用意ができたことを知らせるため

> **正解 A** 前職での経験として、❷4～5行目でテキストメッセージを送るプログラムを始めたことが述べられ、続く同5～6行目に、I notified customers of the arrival of new merchandise that I thought would suit them.とある。よって、これが前職で顧客にテキストメッセージを送った理由だと判断できる。notifyをalert、merchandiseをitemsと言い換えて説明した(A)が正解。alert ～ to …「～に…について注意喚起する」。
> (B) due「支払期日になって」。
> (C) offer ～ …「～に…を提供する」、discount「割引」。
> (D) ready「用意ができて」。

Expressions

notify ～ of … 「～に…を知らせる」（❷5～6行目）

The hiring team will notify each applicant of the interview results by e-mail.
採用チームは、各応募者に面接の結果をEメールで通知する予定です。

Questions 158-160 refer to the following e-mail.

To:	Seema Singh <ssingh@jademail.com>
From:	Jenny Paek <jpaek@kotarusengineering.com>
Date:	28 October
Subject:	Invoice 58202

Dear Ms. Singh,

❶ — [1] —. On behalf of the Kotarus Engineering Company, I want to thank you for the work you did performing some much-needed data entry. Without contributions from freelance workers such as yourself, our project managers would not be able to check easily on the progress of projects or plan their schedules. We were very impressed with how quickly and accurately you were able to complete your assignments. — [2] —.

❷ I have received and approved your invoice. It is being processed, and payment will be mailed to you within 30 days. — [3] —. If you would prefer to receive future payments by direct deposit, contact our accounts payable department. — [4] —.

❸ Please let me know at your earliest convenience when you are available to take on additional work for Kotarus Engineering. I look forward to working with you again.

Sincerely,

Jenny Paek

問題158-160は次のEメールに関するものです。

受信者：Seema Singh <ssingh@jademail.com>
送信者：Jenny Paek <jpaek@kotarusengineering.com>
日付：10月28日
件名：請求書58202

Singh様

Kotarus Engineering社を代表して、あなたが行ってくださった非常に必要性の高いデータ入力のお仕事についてお礼を申し上げます。あなたのようなフリーランスの方々の貢献がなければ、当社のプロジェクトマネジャーたちは、プロジェクトの進行を簡単に確認したり予定を立てたりすることはできないでしょう。私どもは、あなたがいかに迅速かつ正確に仕事を完了できたかということに、非常に感心いたしました。*実際、あなたは当社が協業した最も素晴らしいコンサルタントのお一人です。

私はあなたのご請求書を受け取り、承認いたしました。現在処理中で、お支払いは30日以内にあなたに郵送される予定です。もし、今後のお支払いを口座振込で受け取られることをご希望なら、当社の買掛金部門にご連絡ください。

Kotarus Engineering社からのさらなる仕事をお受けになれるときは、ご都合がつき次第私にお知らせください。また一緒にお仕事ができることを楽しみにしております。

敬具

Jenny Paek

*問題160の挿入文の訳

Words & Phrases

invoice 送り状、請求書　　❶ on behalf of ～　～を代表して
thank ～ for … …について～に感謝する　　perform ～を実行する　　much-needed 大いに必要とされた
data entry データ入力　　contribution 貢献　　freelance フリーランスの　　check on ～　～の様子を見る、～を調べる
progress 進行　　be impressed with ～　～に感心している　　accurately 正確に　　assignment 仕事、業務
❷ approve ～を承認する　　process ～を処理する　　mail ～を郵送する　　prefer to do ～する方を好む
direct deposit （給料の）口座振込　　account payable 買掛金　★取引で発生した代金の未払い分。支払債務
❸ available 手が空いている、応じられる　　take on ～　～を引き受ける　　look forward to doing ～することを楽しみにする

158 What is a purpose of the e-mail?

    (A) To process a request for direct deposit

    (B) To acknowledge receipt of an invoice

    (C) To invite a vendor to bid on a job

    (D) To negotiate a payment amount

Eメールの一つの目的は何ですか。

    (A) 口座振込の依頼を処理すること

    (B) 請求書の受領を知らせること

    (C) 仕事に入札するよう販売業者に勧めること

    (D) 支払金額を交渉すること

> **正解 B** 件名に Invoice 58202 とあり、❶で Singh さんの行った仕事に対して謝意を示した後、❷ 1行目で、I have received and approved your invoice. と述べている。これが E メールの目的の一つと判断できるので、この内容を acknowledge「~（の受け取り）を知らせる」と receipt「受領」を用いて表した (B) が正解。
> (A) 口座振込は、今後の支払いで用いることができる手段として挙げているだけ。request「依頼」。
> (C) invite ~ to do「~に…するように勧める」、vendor「販売業者」、bid on ~「~に入札する」。
> (D) 支払いについて話題にされているが、金額の交渉はしていない。negotiate「~を交渉する」、amount「金額」。

159 What is indicated about Ms. Singh?

    (A) She works in the accounts payable department.

    (B) She is a project manager.

    (C) She inputs data.

    (D) She travels frequently.

Singh さんについて何が示されていますか。

    (A) 買掛金部門で働いている。

    (B) プロジェクトマネジャーである。

    (C) データを入力する。

    (D) 頻繁に旅行する。

> **正解 C** Singh さんとは E メールの受信者。送信者の Paek さんが、❶ 1~2 行目で、I want to thank you for the work you did performing some much-needed data entry と書き、Singh さんの行ったデータ入力業務にお礼を述べている。data entry を input「~を入力する」を用いて表した (C) が正解。
> (A) ❶ 2~3 行目より、Singh さんはフリーランスで働いていると分かる。買掛金部門は、支払金の受け取り手段の変更を希望する場合の連絡先として述べられている。
> (B) ❶ 2~4 行目で、Singh さんの貢献によってプロジェクトマネジャーたちが仕事をしやすくなっていることが述べられているが、Singh さん自身がプロジェクトマネジャーだとは述べられていない。
> (D) frequently「頻繁に」。

160 In which of the positions marked [1], [2], [3], and [4] does the following sentence best belong?

"In fact, you are among the finest consultants we have worked with."

    (A) [1]   (C) [3]

    (B) [2]   (D) [4]

[1]、[2]、[3]、[4] と記載された箇所のうち、次の文が入るのに最もふさわしいのはどれですか。

「実際、あなたは当社が協業した最も素晴らしいコンサルタントのお一人です」

> **正解 B** 挿入文では、相手への賛辞が述べられている。❶ 4~5 行目に、「私たちは、あなたがいかに迅速かつ正確に仕事を完了できたかということに、非常に感心した」とあり、Singh さんの仕事ぶりを称賛している。この直後の (B) [2] に挿入文を入れると、前文に続き Singh さんに対して賛辞を述べる内容が続くことになり、流れとして適切。in fact は「実際に、実のところ」という意味で、ここでは前言を補足するために使われている。among「~の（中の）一人で」、consultant「コンサルタント（専門的な意見などを提供する相談相手・顧問）」。

Expressions

at _one's_ earliest convenience　「~の都合がつき次第」（❸ 1~2 行目）

Could you send the document at your earliest convenience?
ご都合がつき次第、その文書を送っていただけませんか。

Questions 161-163 refer to the following advertisement.

About the Eierdorff Bio Company

❶ Do you have a plastic product you want to bring to market? Let Eierdorff Bio help you! Whether you are searching for a new manufacturer of plastic materials or looking to switch to a more Earth-friendly option, we can help. Eierdorff Bio is one of the world's most trusted manufacturers of compostable plastic. We have worked with companies around the globe to produce everything from disposable cutlery to cell phone cases and more.

❷ We can work with you at any stage of your business process, including designing and drafting. At our central facility in Denmark, we can <u>meet</u> multiple manufacturing needs, including polymer casting, 3-D printing, and injection molding. Contact one of our certified technicians today to begin bringing your product to reality!

❸ Visit our Web site at productintros@eierdorffbio.dk for more information.

問題161-163は次の広告に関するものです。

Eierdorff Bio社について

市場に出したいプラスチック製品はありますか？ Eierdorff Bio社にお手伝いさせてください！ 貴社が新しいプラスチック素材メーカーをお探しであれ、より地球に優しい選択肢に切り替えようとしていらっしゃるのであれ、当社はお手伝いすることができます。Eierdorff Bio社は、世界で最も信頼されている、堆肥化可能プラスチックのメーカーの一つです。当社は、使い捨てカトラリーから携帯電話ケースやその他まで、あらゆるものを生産する世界中の会社と協業してまいりました。

当社は、設計や製図を含め、貴社の事業プロセスのいかなる段階においても協業できます。デンマークにある当社の中心施設では、ポリマー鋳造、3D印刷、射出成形をはじめ、多様な製造ニーズを<u>満たす</u>ことができます。貴社の製品の実現に着手するために、当社の認定技術者に今すぐご連絡ください！

さらなる情報は当社のウェブサイトproductintros@eierdorffbio.dkにアクセスしてください。

Words & Phrases

bio 生物学 ★biologyの略　❶ bring ~ to market ~を市場に出す、~を売り出す
search for ~ ~を探す　manufacturer メーカー、製造業者　material 材料、素材　be looking to do ~する予定である
switch to ~ ~に切り替える　Earth-friendly 地球に優しい　option 選択肢　trust ~を信頼する
compostable 堆肥化可能な　around the globe 世界中の　produce ~を生産する　disposable 使い捨ての
cutlery 食卓用金物類 ★ナイフ・フォーク・スプーンなどの総称　cell phone 携帯電話　and more その他いろいろ
❷ stage 段階　business process 事業過程　including ~を含めて、~をはじめ　draft 下図を書く　central 中心の
facility 施設　multiple 多数の、多様な　manufacturing 製造(の)　needs ニーズ、要望
polymer ポリマー、高分子化合物　casting 鋳造　3-D 3次元の ★three-dimensionalの略
injection molding 射出成形 ★金型を用いた成形法の一つ　certified 認定の　technician 技術者、技師　reality 現実

Expressions

whether A or B　「AであれBであれ」（❶ 2~3行目）

Whether we succeed or fail, we must do our best to become more competitive.
成功しようと失敗しようと、私たちはより競争力をつけるために最善を尽くさなければなりません。

161 What service does Eierdorff Bio offer?

(A) Overseas moving and storage
(B) Waste management consultation
(C) Electronics repair
(D) Plastics manufacturing

Eierdorff Bio社はどんな業務を行っていますか。

(A) 海外への引っ越しと保管
(B) 廃棄物処理の相談
(C) 電子機器の修理
(D) プラスチック製品の製造

> **正解 D** 見出しより、この広告はEierdorff Bio社についてのものと分かる。❶ 1〜2行目で「市場に出したいプラスチック製品はあるか？ Eierdorff Bio社がお手伝いする」と述べ、同2〜3行目で「あなたが新しいプラスチック素材メーカーを探しているのであれ、より地球に優しい選択肢に切り替えようとしているのであれ、当社は手伝うことができる」と売り文句を続けている。そして同3〜4行目で、Eierdorff Bio is one of the world's most trusted manufacturers of compostable plastic. と述べていることから、同社は環境に配慮したプラスチックの製造会社だと判断できる。よって、(D)が正解。
> (A) overseas「海外の」、storage「保管」。
> (B) waste「廃棄物」、management「管理、処理」、consultation「相談」。
> (C) electronics「電子機器」、repair「修理」。

162 Who most likely is the intended audience for the advertisement?

(A) Business owners
(B) Chemical engineers
(C) Environmental activists
(D) Phone technicians

誰が広告の対象者だと考えられますか。

(A) 事業主
(B) 化学エンジニア
(C) 環境保護活動家
(D) 電話技師

> **正解 A** 冒頭の❶ 1〜2行目で「市場に出したいプラスチック製品はあるか？ Eierdorff Bio社がお手伝いする」とプラスチック製品を売り出したい事業者に訴えかけており、同4〜6行目では「当社は、使い捨てカトラリーから携帯電話ケースやその他まで、あらゆるものを生産する世界中の会社と協業してきた」と述べられている。また、❷ 1〜2行目に「当社は、設計や製図を含め、貴社の事業プロセスのいかなる段階においても協業できる」とあり、事業主に向けて自社の宣伝をしている。よって、(A)が正解。intended「意図した、狙った」、audience「視聴者、読者」。business owner「事業主」。
> (B) chemical「化学の」、engineer「エンジニア」。
> (C) 地球に優しい素材への言及はあるが、環境保護活動に関することが広告のメインではない。environmental「環境の、環境保護の」、activist「活動家」。

163 The word "meet" in paragraph 2, line 2, is closest in meaning to

(A) encounter
(B) satisfy
(C) connect
(D) present

第2段落・2行目にある "meet" に最も意味が近いのは

(A) 〜に出会う
(B) 〜を満たす
(C) 〜をつなぐ
(D) 〜を提示する

> **正解 B** ❷ 1〜2行目で、Eierdorff Bio社は取引相手の事業プロセスのいかなる段階でも協業可能であることを述べている。続く同2〜3行目の該当の語を含む文は、「デンマークにある当社の中心施設では、ポリマー鋳造、3D印刷、射出成形をはじめ、多様な製造ニーズ------ことができる」という意味。つまりこの文では、Eierdorff Bio社がプラスチック製造に関するさまざまな要求に対応できることを前文に続き詳しく述べている。よって、(B) satisfy「〜を満たす」が正解。

Questions 164-167 refer to the following e-mail.

```
╔══════════════════════════════════════════════════════════╗
║                         *E-mail*                          ║
╠══════════════════════════════════════════════════════════╣
```

To:	gmccafferty@greyharbor.ca
From:	mtoskala@norston.ca
Date:	2 June
Subject:	News from Norston

Dear Mr. McCafferty,

① Thank you for being a loyal customer for the past three years. As the premier business-to-business provider of office supplies for North America, we at Norston are constantly renewing our stock. Although our annual catalogue shipped out two months ago, we wanted to alert you to some product updates that have occurred since then.

② • Our Eikennen office chair is now priced at $149 instead of $179.

• The Votna desk now comes in mahogany and oak in addition to cedar.

• The Bygden filing cabinet is available in white and grey in addition to black.

• Our Glamnor videoconference camera now includes a built-in microphone.

③ We also want to announce the long-awaited launch of our new Web site: www.norston.ca. There you can sign up for our weekly newsletter, which is full of updates and great deals. The first 50 subscribers are eligible to win a new Tyrgo laser printer worth $350!

Sincerely,

Mia Toskala
Norston

問題164-167は次のEメールに関するものです。

受信者：gmccafferty@greyharbor.ca
送信者：mtoskala@norston.ca
日付：6月2日
件名：Norston社からのお知らせ

McCafferty様

過去3年にわたって当社をご愛顧いただきありがとうございます。北アメリカを対象とする企業向けオフィス用品のトップ供給会社として、当Norston社は絶えず在庫を更新しております。当社の年刊カタログが2カ月前に発送されましたが、それ以降に発生した商品の最新情報についてお客さまにお知らせしたいと思っていました。

• 当社のEikennenオフィスチェアーは現在、179ドルではなく149ドルというお値段になっております。
• Votnaデスクは現在、ヒマラヤスギ材に加えてマホガニー材とオーク材がございます。
• Bygden書類整理キャビネットは、黒色に加えて白色と灰色のものをご用意しております。
• 当社のGlamnorテレビ会議用カメラは現在、内蔵マイクを搭載しています。

また当社は、待望の新しいウェブサイトwww.norston.caの開始をお知らせしたいと思います。そちらで当社の週刊会報にお申し込みいただくことができ、そこには最新情報とお買い得品がたくさんございます。最初の50名の定期購読ご加入者は350ドル相当の新しいTyrgoレーザープリンターを勝ち取る資格があります！

敬具

Mia Toskala
Norston社

Words & Phrases

① loyal customer　常連客、得意客　　past　これまでの　　premier　首位の、一流の　business-to-business　企業間の　　constantly　絶えず　　renew　〜を更新する　　catalogue　カタログ　★米国表記はcatalog　ship out　発送される　　alert 〜 to …　〜に…に対して注意喚起する　　occur　起こる　**②** be priced at 〜　〜の値段が付いている　come in 〜　〜の形で売られる　　mahogany　マホガニー（材）　　oak　オーク（材）　　cedar　ヒマラヤスギ（材）　videoconference　テレビ会議　　built-in　内蔵の　　microphone　マイク　**③** long-awaited　長く待ち望まれた　great deal　お買い得品　　subscriber　定期購読者　　be eligible to *do*　〜する資格がある　　worth　〜の価値がある

164 What is the main purpose of the e-mail?

(A) To thank a customer for a recent purchase
(B) To announce some inventory changes
(C) To request a contract renewal
(D) To apologize for a delayed release

Eメールの主な目的は何ですか。

(A) 顧客に最近の購入についてお礼を言うこと
(B) 在庫品の変更点を知らせること
(C) 契約更新を求めること
(D) 発売の遅れを謝罪すること

正解 B 件名に「Norston社からのお知らせ」とあり、❶1行目で得意客へのお礼が述べられているので、このEメールはNorston社が顧客に宛てたお知らせと分かる。同3～4行目で、年刊カタログ発送後だがという前置きに続いて、「私たちは商品の最新情報についてあなたに知らせたかった」と述べられている。続く❷で、在庫品に関する変更点が具体的に記されてい

ることから、(B)が正解。inventory「(商品の)目録、在庫品」。
(A) 得意客へのお礼は述べられているが、最近の購入に対するお礼ではない。thank ～ for …「…について～に感謝する」。
(C) request「～を求める」、contract「契約」、renewal「更新」。
(D) apologize for ～「～について謝罪する」、delayed「遅れた」、release「発売」。

165 What is indicated about Norston?

(A) It manages many retail outlets.
(B) It mails catalogs every two months.
(C) It sells primarily to other companies.
(D) It sells office furniture exclusively.

Norston社について何が示されていますか。

(A) 多くの小売店を運営している。
(B) 2カ月ごとにカタログを郵送している。
(C) 主として他の会社に販売している。
(D) オフィス家具のみを販売している。

正解 C ❶1～2行目に、Norston社についてAs the premier business-to-business provider of office suppliesとある。business-to-business providerとは企業に対して販売を行う供給会社なので、それをsells primarily to other companiesと表している(C)が正解。primarily「主に」。
(A) retail outlet「小売店」を運営しているといった記述はない。

manage「～を運営する」。
(B) ❶3～4行目より、カタログは年刊だと分かる。mail「～を郵送する」、every two months「2カ月ごとに」。
(D) ❷の4つ目より、オフィス家具のみではなく、テレビ会議用カメラも販売していることが分かる。exclusively「もっぱら、全く～のみ」。

166 What is indicated about the Eikennen chair?

(A) Its price was lowered.
(B) Its materials were changed.
(C) Its color options were increased.
(D) Its design became sturdier.

Eikennenチェアーについて何が示されていますか。

(A) 値段が下げられた。
(B) 素材が変更された。
(C) 色の選択肢が増やされた。
(D) 設計がより頑丈になった。

正解 A Eikennenチェアーについては、❷の1つ目に、「当社のEikennenオフィスチェアーは現在、179ドルではなく149ドルという値段になっている」と書かれている。つまり、値段が下げられているので、(A)が正解。lower「～を下げる」。

(B) ❷の2つ目より、素材に言及があるのはVotnaデスクであり、素材の種類が増えている。material「素材」。
(C) ❷の3つ目より、色に言及があるのはBygden書類整理キャビネット。option「選択肢」、increase「～を増やす」。
(D) 設計がより頑丈になったという記載はない。sturdy「頑丈な」。

167 How can Norston customers potentially receive a free promotional item?

(A) By placing an order from the catalog
(B) By subscribing to a newsletter
(C) By giving feedback on a new Web site
(D) By purchasing three or more products

Norston社の顧客はどうすれば無料の販促品を受け取れる可能性がありますか。

(A) カタログから注文することによって
(B) 会報を定期購読することによって
(C) 新しいウェブサイトについての意見を提供することによって
(D) 3つ以上の製品を購入することによって

正解 B ❸1～3行目で、ウェブサイトで申し込める週刊会報に言及し、続く同3～4行目で、「最初の50名の定期購読加入者は350ドル相当の新しいTyrgoレーザープリンターを勝ち取る資格がある」と述べている。つまり、顧客は会報を定期購読することで、プリンターを無料でもらえるチャンスが得られ

ると分かる。よって、(B)が正解。potentially「可能性として」、promotional「販売促進の」。subscribe to ～「～を定期購読する」。
(A) place an order「注文する」。
(C) feedback「意見、感想」。

Questions 168-171 refer to the following article.

NORTH CITY NEWS
Local shoe store thrives in digital age

① NORTH CITY (October 18)—It is uncommon for independent retailers to stay viable long enough to celebrate their sixtieth anniversary. One of these rare businesses is Morro's Shoe Store, a popular athletic footwear seller on Twelfth Avenue owned by resident Stan Morro. It has even thrived amid competition from online retailers. — [1] —. Mr. Morro's father, Patrick, established the store after he moved from Detmar Valley to North City. The elder Morro had learned about the shoe industry from working in several shoe stores in Detmar Valley. After moving, he opened his store in North City on Fortieth Avenue. When the younger Morro took over the business, he moved the shop to its current location on Twelfth Avenue.

② Stan Morro received a stroke of luck when North University built a new regional campus in the city. "Thanks to the university's sports programs, demand for athletic shoes really took off," he said. "We also expanded our selection of merchandise to offer shoes in all sizes and styles." — [2] —. To keep up with business trends, he launched an online shop a few years ago. However, he noted that most of his regular customers prefer to visit the store and try on shoes for themselves. He explained that online shoppers get "satisfactory" results when they order shoes made by the same brand as the worn-out shoes they are replacing. — [3] —.

③ Earlier in the month, *Shoe Retailing Horizons*, an industry trade magazine, named Morro's Shoe Store the third-best retailer in the region. — [4] —. Mr. Morro said that "attentive customer service" is the key to his store's success.

問題168-171は次の記事に関するものです。

ノースシティーニュース
地元の靴店がデジタル時代に成功

ノースシティー（10月18日）──独立小売業者が長く生き残って60周年を祝うというのはなかなかないことだ。こういった希少な店の一つが、住民のStan Morroが所有する12番街の人気運動靴販売店、Morro's靴店である。同店はオンライン小売業者との競争の中にあっても成功してきた。Morro氏の父Patrickはデトマーバレーからノースシティーに移ってきた後、この店を創業した。父親のMorroはデトマーバレーの幾つかの靴店で働いて靴業界について学んだ。引っ越し後、彼はノースシティーの40番街に自分の店を開いた。息子のMorroは、事業を引き継いだ際、店を12番街の現在地に移した。

ノース大学が市内に新しい地域キャンパスを建設したとき、Stan Morroは思いがけない幸運を手にした。「大学のスポーツプログラムのおかげで、運動靴の需要が非常に急増しました」と彼は述べた。「当店もまた、あらゆるサイズとスタイルの靴を提供するために商品の品ぞろえを拡大しました」。ビジネスの動向に遅れずについていくために、彼は数年前にオンラインショップを立ち上げた。しかし彼は、常連客の大半は店を訪れて自ら靴を試し履きする方を好むと述べた。オンラインショップの買い物客は、履き古した靴の買い替えで同じブランドの靴を注文する場合に「満足のいく」結果を得るのだと説明した。*それでも、多くの客がオンラインで購入した靴を交換するために店にやって来る。

今月先立って、業界誌『靴小売業の地平』はMorro's靴店を地域で3番目に優れた小売業者に選んだ。Morro氏は「こまやかな顧客サービス」が自店の成功の秘訣だと述べた。

*問題171の挿入文の訳

Words & Phrases

thrive 繁栄する　age 時代　**①** uncommon 珍しい、まれな　independent 独立した　viable 生存できる、存続し得る　anniversary 周年記念日　rare まれな　athletic 運動用の　avenue 大通り　amid 〜の中で　competition 競争　establish 〜を設立する　the elder 〜 （2人の人物の）年長の方の〜　take over 〜 〜を引き継ぐ　**②** a stroke of luck 思いがけない幸運　thanks to 〜 〜のおかげで　demand for 〜 〜への需要　take off （売り上げなどが）急上昇する　expand 〜を拡大する　regular customer 常連客　try on 〜 〜を試着する　for *oneself* 自分で　satisfactory 満足のいく　worn-out 使い古した　replace 〜を取り換える　**③** horizons （思考・知識などの）地平・範囲　trade 商売　name 〜 … 〜を…（賞など）に選ぶ　region 地域　attentive 気を配る、親切な

Expressions

keep up with 〜　「〜に遅れずについていく」（**②**8〜10行目）

Technology changes so fast that it is difficult for some businesses to keep up with it.
技術はあまりにも速く変化するので、それに遅れずについていくのが困難な事業者もいます。

168 What is mentioned about Patrick Morro?

(A) He designed a line of sports shoes.
(B) He opened a store after relocating.
(C) He designed a store's Web site.
(D) He was hired to work in his son's store.

Patrick Morro について何が述べられていますか。

(A) 運動靴のシリーズをデザインした。
(B) 転居後に店を開いた。
(C) 店のウェブサイトをデザインした。
(D) 自分の息子の店で働くために雇用された。

正解 B Patrick Morroについては、❶ 10〜12行目に、「Morro氏の父PatrickはデトマーバレーからノースシティーにⅠ移ってきた後、この店を創業した」とある。よって、(B)が正解。relocate「転居する」。
(A) ❶ 12〜15行目より、靴店で働いて業界について学んだこと

は分かるが、靴のデザインをしたとは述べられていない。design「〜をデザインする」、line「製品シリーズ」。
(C) ❷ 8〜10行目より、息子のStan Morroがオンラインショップを始めたと分かるが、ウェブサイトのデザインについては言及がない。

---

169 According to the article, what is true about North City?

(A) It has two stadiums for sporting events.
(B) It has a factory that manufactures athletic footwear.
(C) It hosts conventions for the athletic apparel industry.
(D) It is the site of a university campus.

記事によると、ノースシティーについて正しいことは何ですか。

(A) スポーツイベントのためのスタジアムが2つある。
(B) 運動靴を製造する工場がある。
(C) 運動用衣料品業界のための大会を主催している。
(D) 大学キャンパスの所在地である。

正解 D ❷ 2〜3行目に、North University built a new regional campus in the cityとあり、このthe cityはMorro's靴店のあるノースシティーのこと。よって、(D)が正解。site「所在地」。
(A) 大学のスポーツプログラムへの言及があるだけで、stadium

「スタジアム」については述べられていない。
(B) factory「工場」への言及はない。manufacture「〜を製造する」。
(C) convention「大会、協議会」やapparel「衣服、衣料品」に関する言及はない。host「〜を主催する」。

---

170 What is indicated about Morro's Shoe Store?

(A) It will soon return to its original location.
(B) It is currently hiring new staff members.
(C) It has recently been recognized in another publication.
(D) It will expand in the upcoming year.

Morro's靴店について何が示されていますか。

(A) 間もなく元の場所に戻る予定である。
(B) 現在、新しい従業員を雇用しようとしている。
(C) 最近、別の出版物で評価された。
(D) 次年度に拡大する予定である。

正解 C ❸ 1〜4行目に、「今月先立って、業界誌『靴小売業の地平』はMorro's靴店を地域で3番目に優れた小売業者に選んだ」とある。この文書の記事とは異なる出版物である業界誌で、Morro's靴店は優れた店舗として評価されているので、

(C)が正解。recognize「〜を高く評価する」、publication「出版物」。
(D) 店が評価されていることは述べられているが、拡大に関する言及はない。expand「拡大する」、upcoming「近く起こる」。

---

171 In which of the positions marked [1], [2], [3], and [4] does the following sentence best belong?

"Even so, many customers come to the store to exchange shoes they purchased online."

(A) [1]　　　　(C) [3]
(B) [2]　　　　(D) [4]

[1]、[2]、[3]、[4]と記載された箇所のうち、次の文が入るのに最もふさわしいのはどれですか。

「それでも、多くの客がオンラインで購入した靴を交換するために店にやって来る」

正解 C 挿入文では、オンラインで靴を購入した客について述べられている。❷ 8〜10行目で靴店のオンラインショップについて紹介した後、同11〜13行目で、常連客の多くは直接店に来ると述べている。さらに同13〜16行目で、オンラインショップの買い物客が満足を示す同一ブランドの靴の買い替えという購買行動について伝えている。この直後の(C)[3]に挿入文を入れると、そうは言っても、オンラインで購入した多くの顧客が靴の交換に実店舗に来店する、という自然な流れになる。even so「そうであっても」、exchange「〜を交換する」。

Questions 172-175 refer to the following online chat discussion.

❶ Sharon Li [10:55 A.M.]
Have you both entered your department's July data in the monthly sales spreadsheet yet?

❷ Juan Ayers [10:58 A.M.]
I have not entered it yet for the mobile phone department. Why?

❸ Sharon Li [10:59 A.M.]
Each department is supposed to enter its data by tomorrow, and I can only find the spreadsheet from the last fiscal year. Where can I find the current one? I need to enter the data for the kitchen appliance department.

❹ Linda Davies [11:00 A.M.]
I just entered the data for the camera department. The new spreadsheet is on the company shared drive. Do you want me to send you the link?

❺ Sharon Li [11:02 A.M.]
No—I can find it. I just didn't think to look there. Thanks so much!

❻ Linda Davies [11:12 A.M.]
My pleasure.

問題172-175は次のオンラインチャットの話し合いに関するものです。

Sharon Li（午前10時55分）
お二人はもうご自身の部門の7月のデータを月間売上高スプレッドシートに入力しましたか。

Juan Ayers（午前10時58分）
携帯電話部門についてはまだ入力していません。どうしてですか。

Sharon Li（午前10時59分）
各部門が明日までにデータを入力することになっていますが、昨年度のスプレッドシートしか見つかりません。どこに現在のものがありますか。私は台所家電部門のデータを入力しなければならないのです。

Linda Davies（午前11時00分）
私はちょうどカメラ部門のデータを入力したところです。新しいスプレッドシートは会社の共有ドライブ上にあります。リンクをお送りしましょうか。

Sharon Li（午前11時02分）
いいえ——自分で見つけられます。そこを見ることを思い付かなかっただけです。どうもありがとうございます！

Linda Davies（午前11時12分）
どういたしまして。

172 What type of business do the writers most likely work for?

    (A) An electronics store
    (B) A sporting goods store
    (C) A clothing shop
    (D) An auto repair shop

書き手たちはどのような店で働いていると考えられますか。

    (A) 電子機器店
    (B) スポーツ用品店
    (C) 衣料品店
    (D) 自動車修理店

正解 A	各部門のデータ入力について、Ayersさんは❷で、I have not entered it yet for the mobile phone department.と、Liさんは❸で、I need to enter the data for the kitchen appliance department.と、Daviesさんは❹で、I just entered the data for the camera department.とそれぞれ述べている。mobile phone、kitchen appliance、cameraの部門があることから、書き手たちは電子機器を扱う店で働いていると考えられる。(A)が正解。electronics「電子機器」。 (B) sporting goods「スポーツ用品」。 (C) clothing「衣料品」。 (D) auto「自動車」、repair「修理」。

173 What does Mr. Ayers need to do soon?

    (A) Write a sales report
    (B) Update a document
    (C) Send Ms. Li a link to the shared drive
    (D) Open a new desktop calendar

Ayersさんは間もなく何をする必要がありますか。

    (A) 売上報告書を書く
    (B) 文書ファイルを更新する
    (C) Liさんに共有ドライブのリンクを送る
    (D) 新しいデスクトップカレンダーを開く

正解 B	Liさんの❶の「もう自身の部門の7月のデータを月間売上高スプレッドシートに入力したか」という問い掛けに対し、Ayersさんは❷で、「携帯電話部門についてはまだ入力していない」と述べている。Liさんは❸で、「各部門が明日までにデータを入力することになっている」と発言していることから、Ayersさんは、明日までにデータを入力してスプレッドシートを更新する必要があると判断できる。よって、スプレッドシートにデータを入力することをupdate a documentと表した(B)が正解。update「〜を更新する」、document「文書ファイル」。 (A) 月間売上高スプレッドシートへのデータ入力について話しているが、売上報告書を書くことについては述べられていない。sales report「売上報告書」。 (C) Liさんが❺で、Daviesさんによるリンク送付の申し出を断っている。 (D) desktop「デスクトップの」。

Words & Phrases		
chat チャット discussion 話し合い ❶ enter 〜を入力する department 部門		
monthly 月間の spreadsheet スプレッドシート、表計算ソフト ❸ fiscal year 会計年度 current 現在の、最新の		
kitchen appliance 台所家電 ❹ shared drive 共有ドライブ		
Do you want me to *do*? 〜しましょうか。 ★自分が何かを行うことを申し出る表現 send 〜 … 〜に…を送る		
❺ think to *do* 〜することを思い付く ❻ My pleasure. どういたしまして。		

174 What does Ms. Li want to know about a new spreadsheet?

    (A) Its password
    (B) Its length
    (C) Its location
    (D) Its owner

Liさんは新しいスプレッドシートについて何を知りたいのですか。

    (A) パスワード
    (B) 長さ
    (C) 場所
    (D) 所有者

> **正解 C** Liさんは❸で、昨年度のスプレッドシートしか見つからないと発言した後、Where can I find the current one?と、現在のスプレッドシートの保存場所を尋ねている。よって、(C)が正解。location「場所」。

175 At 11:12 A.M., what does Ms. Davies most likely mean when she writes, "My pleasure"?

    (A) She is pleased that a company initiative was successful.
    (B) She is happy to train some new colleagues.
    (C) She feels relieved that a workday is ending.
    (D) She is happy to help Ms. Li with her request.

午前11時12分に、"My pleasure"という発言で、Daviesさんは何を意図していると考えられますか。

    (A) 会社の新構想が成功したことを喜んでいる。
    (B) 新しい同僚を教育できてうれしい。
    (C) 勤務時間が終了することにほっとしている。
    (D) Liさんの頼み事を手伝えてうれしい。

> **正解 D** Liさんは❸で、現在のスプレッドシートの在りかを尋ねている。その直後にDaviesさんが❹で、「新しいスプレッドシートは会社の共有ドライブ上にある。リンクを送ろうか」と保存されている場所を教え、リンクの送付を申し出ている。それに対して、Liさんは❺で、リンクの送付は不要であることを伝えてから、「そこを見ることを思い付かなかっただけだ」と言い、お礼を述べている。下線部のDaviesさんの発言は、このお礼に対する返礼で、Liさんがスプレッドシートを見つける手助けができて喜んでいると判断できるので、(D)が正解。help ~ with …「…に関して~を手伝う」。
> (A) be pleased that ~「~ということを喜んでいる」、initiative「新構想、新政策」、successful「成功した」。
> (B) DaviesさんにとってLiさんが新しい同僚であるといった情報はない。train「~を教育する、~を訓練する」、colleague「同僚」。
> (C) feel relieved that ~「~ということにほっとしている」、workday「一日の勤務時間」。

Expressions

be supposed to do 「~することになっている」（❸ 2行目）

What time is the guest speaker supposed to arrive?
ゲストスピーカーは何時に到着することになっていますか。

Questions 176-180 refer to the following article and e-mail.

News Team Continues to Grow

❶ PORTLAND (January 25)—Beginning next month, Chelsea Lee will join *Quetic News*. Ms. Lee spent the past ten years of her career at the *Singleton Times*. While there, she developed its podcast platform, both producing and hosting some of the most widely streamed news podcasts in the country. The podcast she hosted, *News Now*, focused on detailing each day's top stories.

❷ Her experience with digital media was one reason that *Quetic News* wanted to bring Ms. Lee on board. Last year, it announced that it would be branching out into video and audio in addition to its print news. While Ms. Lee is among a number of journalists new to the network, she is perhaps the most well-known. She already has a large and loyal following. "We are thrilled that Ms. Lee will be joining *Quetic News*. Her extensive experience, creativity, and ability to connect with listeners will make her a valued part of our team," said Daniel Koblin, editor in chief.

❸ Ms. Lee is developing a weekly podcast, yet to be named. Unlike her daily podcast, this show will take an in-depth look into one news story at a time. The premiere episode is scheduled for April 20.

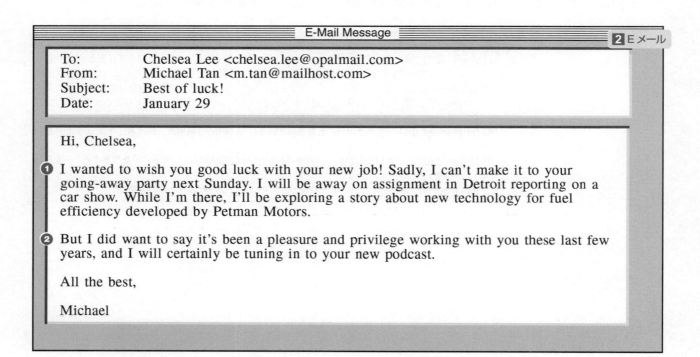

E-Mail Message

To: Chelsea Lee <chelsea.lee@opalmail.com>
From: Michael Tan <m.tan@mailhost.com>
Subject: Best of luck!
Date: January 29

Hi, Chelsea,

❶ I wanted to wish you good luck with your new job! Sadly, I can't make it to your going-away party next Sunday. I will be away on assignment in Detroit reporting on a car show. While I'm there, I'll be exploring a story about new technology for fuel efficiency developed by Petman Motors.

❷ But I did want to say it's been a pleasure and privilege working with you these last few years, and I will certainly be tuning in to your new podcast.

All the best,

Michael

問題176-180は次の記事とEメールに関するものです。

ニュースチームは成長し続ける

ポートランド（1月25日）——来月から、Chelsea Lee が『Queticニュース』に加わる。Lee氏は『Singleton タイムズ』でこの10年間のキャリアを築いた。在職中、彼女は同社のポッドキャスト・プラットフォームを開発し、国内で最も広くストリーミング配信されているニュースポッドキャストの幾つかの制作と司会の両方を行った。彼女が司会をしたポッドキャストである『今のニュース』は毎日の主要ニュースを詳しく述べることに焦点を絞っていた。

Lee氏のデジタルメディアでの経験は、『Queticニュース』が彼女の入社を望んだ一つの理由であった。昨年、同社は紙媒体のニュースに加えて、動画とオーディオに進出する予定だと発表した。Lee氏は同ネットワークの新顔である多数のジャーナリストの一人だが、おそらく最も有名だろう。彼女にはすでに多くの忠実な支持者がいる。「私たちはLee氏が『Queticニュース』に加わるということに興奮しています。広範な経験、創造性、リスナーと信頼関係を結ぶ能力によって、彼女は私たちのチームの大切な一員となるでしょう」と編集長のDaniel Koblin は述べた。

Lee氏は、まだ名称は決まっていないが、週刊ポッドキャストを制作する。彼女が行っていた毎日配信のポッドキャストとは違って、この番組は一度に一つのニュースを徹底的に掘り下げる。初回の放送は4月20日に予定されている。

受信者：Chelsea Lee <chelsea.lee@opalmail.com>
送信者：Michael Tan <m.tan@mailhost.com>
件名：幸運を祈る！
日付：1月29日

Chelseaさん

新しい仕事での成功をお祈りします！ 残念ながら、私は次の日曜日あなたの送別会に行けません。自動車展示会についての記事を書く仕事でデトロイトにいる予定です。そこにいる間、Petman Motors社によって開発された燃費の新技術にまつわる話を調査することになっています。

でも、この数年間あなたと一緒にお仕事をしたことは喜びであり名誉であると、どうしてもお伝えしたかったのです。それから私は、あなたの新しいポッドキャストを必ず聞きますね。

幸運をお祈りして。

Michael

176 What is the purpose of the article?

(A) To announce a new employee at *Quetic News*
(B) To advertise a new service at the *Singleton Times*
(C) To detail a famous musician's career
(D) To discuss the trend of podcasting

記事の目的は何ですか。

(A) 『Queticニュース』の新しい従業員を発表すること
(B) 『Singletonタイムズ』の新しいサービスを宣伝すること
(C) 有名な音楽家の経歴を詳しく述べること
(D) ポッドキャスト配信の動向について詳しく述べること

> **正解 A** 記事の目的が問われているので、❶記事を確認する。冒頭の❶ 1～2行目に、「来月から、Chelsea Leeが『Queticニュース』に加わる」とあり、続けてLeeさんの前職での活躍が述べられている。❷では1～3行目で、『Queticニュース』がLeeさんを入社させたいと思った理由が挙げられ、また❸では、Leeさんの『Queticニュース』での仕事の予定が書かれている。以上より、記事は『Queticニュース』の新しい従業員であるLeeさんについて発表するのが目的と分かるので、(A)が正解。announce「～を発表する」。
> (B) 『Singletonタイムズ』はLeeさんの経歴を伝えるために言及されているにすぎず、同社のポッドキャストはすでに運用されているので、新しいサービスでもない。advertise「～を宣伝する」。
> (D) ポッドキャストには言及されているが、その動向について述べることが記事の目的とは言えない。discuss「～について詳しく述べる」、trend「流行、動向」。

177 What is mentioned about *Quetic News*?

(A) It was founded ten years ago.
(B) It has a fellowship program for emerging journalists.
(C) It is expanding its digital media platforms.
(D) It hosts a popular daily podcast.

『Queticニュース』について何が述べられていますか。

(A) 10年前に設立された。
(B) 新進ジャーナリスト向けの奨励金プログラムがある。
(C) 同社のデジタルメディア・プラットフォームを拡大することになっている。
(D) 毎日配信の人気ポッドキャストを提供している。

> **正解 C** 『Queticニュース』については、❶記事の❷ 3～5行目に、Last year, it announced that it would be branching out into video and audioとある。branching outをexpand「～を拡大する」、video and audioをdigital media platformsという語句を用いて表した(C)が正解。
> (A) ❶の❶にLeeさんが『Singletonタイムズ』に10年間勤務していたという記述があるだけで、『Queticニュース』の設立時期については述べられていない。found「～を設立する」。
> (B) fellowship「研究奨励金」、emerging「新興の、新生の」。
> (D) 毎日配信のポッドキャストは『Queticニュース』によるものではなく、Leeさんが『Singletonタイムズ』在職時に制作と司会を行っていた『今のニュース』。

178 What is mentioned in the article about a new podcast?

(A) It will be titled *News Now*.
(B) It will be aired every day of the week.
(C) Each episode will focus on one topic.
(D) Some episodes will have a guest host.

新しいポッドキャストについて、記事で何が述べられていますか。

(A) それは『今のニュース』と名付けられる予定である。
(B) それは毎日放送される予定である。
(C) 各放送回では一つの話題に焦点を絞る予定である。
(D) ゲスト司会者を迎える放送回もある予定である。

> **正解 C** ❶記事を確認する。新しいポッドキャストとは❸ 1～2行目で言及されている『Queticニュース』でLeeさんが制作予定の週刊ポッドキャストのこと。続く同3～4行目に、this show will take an in-depth look into one news story at a timeとある。take an in-depth look into ～「～を徹底的に調べる」をfocus on ～「～に焦点を絞る」を使って表現した(C)が正解。
> (A) 『今のニュース』は、Leeさんが『Singletonタイムズ』在職時に制作と司会を行っていたポッドキャスト。❶の❸ 1～2行目より、新しいポッドキャストはまだ名称が決まっていないと分かる。title ～ …「～を…と名付ける」。
> (B) ❶の❸ 1～2行目より、新しいポッドキャストは週1回の配信と分かる。air「～を放送する」、every day of the week「毎日(欠かさず)」。
> (D) host「司会者」。

179 According to the e-mail, what will Ms. Lee most likely do next Sunday?

(A) Travel to Detroit
(B) Report on new technology
(C) Go to a car show
(D) Attend a party

Eメールによると、Leeさんは次の日曜日に何をすると考えられますか。

(A) デトロイトに旅行する
(B) 新しい技術について記事を書く
(C) 自動車展示会に行く
(D) パーティーに出席する

正解 D ❷Eメールを確認する。これはTanさんがLeeさんに宛てたもの。❶1～2行目に、Sadly, I can't make it to your going-away party next Sunday. とある。❶記事の❶1～4行目から、Leeさんは『Singletonタイムズ』を退職して、来月から『Queticニュース』に加わると分かる。Tanさんが言うyour going-away partyとは、Leeさんが『Singletonタイムズ』を退職するにあたっての送別パーティーと考えられるので、Leeさん本人はこれに出席すると判断できる。よって、(D)が正解。
(A) (B) (C) ❷の❶より、いずれもTanさんの予定。

---

180 What is likely true about Michael Tan?

(A) He is a reporter at *Quetic News*.
(B) He is Ms. Lee's new boss.
(C) He will host a television news show premiering in April.
(D) He works at the *Singleton Times*.

Michael Tanについて正しいと考えられることは何ですか。

(A) 『Queticニュース』の記者である。
(B) Leeさんの新しい上司である。
(C) 4月に初回放送されるテレビのニュース番組の司会をする予定である。
(D) 『Singletonタイムズ』で働いている。

正解 D Leeさん宛ての❷Eメールの送信者であるMichael Tanは、同❶で送別会に行けないことを説明し、続けて同❷1～2行目で「この数年間あなたと一緒に仕事をしたことは喜びであり名誉であると、どうしても伝えたかった」と書いている。❶記事の❶3～4行目から、Leeさんは『Singletonタイムズ』でこの10年間働いてきたと分かるので、Michael Tanも『Singletonタイムズ』でLeeさんと共に仕事をしたと判断できる。よって、(D)が正解。
(A) (B) 『Queticニュース』はLeeさんの新しい所属先なので、送別のEメールを書いているTanさんが所属しているとは考えられない。
(C) ❶の❸より、4月に開始するのはLeeさんの週刊ポッドキャスト。premiere「封切りされる、初演される」。

Words & Phrases

❶記事
continue to *do* ～し続ける　❶ career キャリア、経歴　develop ～を開発する、～を制作する
podcast ポッドキャスト ★オンライン上の音声・動画番組
platform プラットフォーム ★システムの基盤となる運用環境　produce ～を制作する　host ～の司会をする
stream ～をストリーミング配信する ★音声や動画をインターネット上で配信する際に、読み込みながら再生する方法
focus on ～ ～に焦点を絞る　detail ～を詳しく述べる　story 記事、ニュース
❷ bring ～ on board ～を(仕事・組織に)加える　announce that ～ ～ということを発表する
branch out into ～ ～に活動範囲を広げる　print 活字(の)、印刷(の)　while ～だけれども
a number of ～ 多数の～　following 〈集合的に〉支持者　be thrilled that ～ ～ということに興奮している
extensive 広範囲にわたる　creativity 創造性　ability to *do* ～する能力
connect with ～ ～とつながる、～と気持ちが通じる　valued 大切な、貴重な　editor in chief 編集長
❸ (be) yet to *do* まだ～していない　name ～に名を付ける　unlike ～と違って
take a look into ～ ～を調査する　in-depth 徹底的な　premiere 初日(の)、初演(の)
episode (番組などの)1回分

❷Eメール
Best of luck 幸運をお祈りします　❶ going-away party 送別会　on assignment 仕事で
report on ～ ～について記事を書く　car show 自動車展示会　explore ～を調査する
fuel efficiency 燃料効率　❷ pleasure 喜び　privilege 名誉　certainly 必ず
tune in to ～ ～(局・番組)に周波数・チャンネルを合わせる　All the best, ごきげんよう、幸運を祈ります

Expressions

make it to ～ 「～に都合がつく、～に参加できる」(❷の❶1～2行目)

I hope you can make it to the reception on Friday.
あなたが金曜日のレセプションに出られるとよいのですが。

Questions 181-185 refer to the following order form and review.

More Coffee Please
Online Store Checkout

Name: James Faure
Mailing address: 3450 Pollard St., Conway, NH 03813
Order date: September 3

Order:

Code	Product	Description	Price
W025	Dancing beans mug	Ceramic coffee mug	$11.00
J999	Decca coffee grinder	Electric, 7 grind settings	$28.99
P838	Whole coffee beans, regular	5 pounds Captain dark roast	$38.99
A636	Whole coffee beans, decaffeinated	5 pounds Colombia decaffeinated	$42.99
		Shipping	$0.00
		Total	$121.97

All items are shipped from our California facility.
We offer free shipping to addresses in the United States with orders over $100.
Our products are also available in our seventeen stores throughout the United States.

Review: More Coffee Please
Reviewer: James Faure
October 8
Rating: ★★★★★

More Coffee Please opened only a few years ago, and their business has grown quickly. It is easy to see why. Their Decca coffee grinder is the best ever. I am very particular about my coffee and have used electric coffee grinders that were more expensive than this one. With the Decca grinder, whatever setting I use, the grinds are perfectly consistent. Also, their decaffeinated coffee is rich and flavorful. On top of that, their dancing beans mug looks great. Many at my office admire it. Everything they sell is worth a try.

More Coffee Please社
オンラインストア精算

氏名：James Faure
郵送先住所：ポラード通り3450番地、コンウェイ、ニューハンプシャー州 03813
注文日：9月3日

注文：

コード	商品	明細	価格
W025	Dancing beansマグカップ	陶器のコーヒー用マグカップ	11.00ドル
J999	Deccaコーヒーグラインダー	電動、7段階のひき方設定	28.99ドル
P838	ひいていないコーヒー豆、レギュラー	Captain深煎り　5ポンド	38.99ドル
A636	ひいていないコーヒー豆、カフェイン抜き	Colombiaカフェイン抜き　5ポンド	42.99ドル
		配送料	0.00ドル
		合計	121.97ドル

全ての品物は当社のカリフォルニアの施設から出荷されます。
100ドルを超えるご注文でアメリカ合衆国のご住所に無料配送いたします。
当社の商品はアメリカ合衆国内の17店舗でもお求めいただけます。

レビュー：More Coffee Please社
レビュー執筆者：James Faure
10月8日
評価：★★★★★

More Coffee Please社はほんの数年前に開業し、同社の事業は急成長しました。その理由を理解するのは簡単です。同社のDeccaコーヒーグラインダーはこれまでで最高のものです。私は自分のコーヒーについて好みがとてもうるさくて、これよりも高価な電動コーヒーグラインダーを今まで使ってきました。Deccaグラインダーを使えば、どんな設定を使用しても、豆のひき具合は申し分なく安定しています。また、カフェイン抜きコーヒーはコクがあって風味豊かです。それに加えて、同社のdancing beansマグカップは見た目が素晴らしいです。職場の同僚の多くがそれを褒めてくれます。同社が販売しているものは全て試す価値があります。

181 What is indicated on the order form?

(A) Mr. Faure ordered both tea and coffee.
(B) Mr. Faure did not pay for shipping.
(C) Mr. Faure visited a store in California.
(D) Mr. Faure used a coupon with his order.

注文書に何が示されていますか。

(A) Faureさんは紅茶とコーヒーの両方を注文した。
(B) Faureさんは配送料を支払わなかった。
(C) Faureさんはカリフォルニアの店舗を訪れた。
(D) Faureさんは注文でクーポンを使用した。

正解 B **1**注文書を確認すると、氏名欄から、Faureさんとは注文をした人物と分かる。**1**の注文明細表のShippingについてPriceの欄に＄0.00とあり、Faureさんは配送料を支払わなかったと分かるので、(B)が正解。**2** 2行目に「100ドルを超える注文でアメリカ合衆国の住所に無料配送する」とあり、これに当てはまっていることが分かる。pay for ～「～の代金を支払う」。
(A) **1**の**1**の注文明細表に、紅茶は載っていない。
(C) **1**の**2** 3行目から実店舗もあることが分かるが、**1**の冒頭にOnline Store Checkout「オンラインストア精算」とあるので、Faureさんはオンラインで購入したと分かる。
(D) クーポンに関する記載はない。

182 Why did Mr. Faure write a review?

(A) To describe a More Coffee Please store
(B) To complain about an order he made
(C) To recommend More Coffee Please products
(D) To advise people to drink only decaffeinated coffee

Faureさんはなぜレビューを書きましたか。

(A) More Coffee Please社の店舗を説明するため
(B) 彼がした注文について不満を述べるため
(C) More Coffee Please社の商品を薦めるため
(D) 人々にカフェイン抜きコーヒーだけを飲むように助言するため

正解 C **2**レビューを確認する。Faureさんは、More Coffee Please社の商品について、**1** 2行目でTheir Decca coffee grinder is the best ever.と書き、続けて具体的にこのコーヒーグラインダーの特長を述べている。さらに同5～6行目でtheir decaffeinated coffee is rich and flavorfulとカフェイン抜きコーヒーを称賛し、同6行目でtheir dancing beans mug looks greatとマグカップの良さに触れている。最後には、同7行目でEverything they sell is worth a try.と締めくくり、同社の販売する商品を薦めているので、(C)が正解。
(A) 商品については述べられているが、店舗についての説明はない。describe「～を説明する」。
(B) 注文した品を褒めており、不満は述べていない。complain about ～「～について不満を述べる」。
(D) カフェイン抜きコーヒーを褒めてはいるが、それだけを飲むように助言しているわけではない。advise ～ to do「～に…するよう助言する」。

183 What does Mr. Faure indicate about the Decca product?

(A) It arrived quickly.
(B) It runs quietly.
(C) It has a low price.
(D) It grinds beans evenly.

FaureさんはDeccaという商品について何を示していますか。

(A) 迅速に届いた。
(B) 静かに作動する。
(C) 低価格である。
(D) 豆を均一にひく。

正解 D **1**注文書の**1**および**2**レビューの**1** 2行目にあるように、Deccaとは、Deccaコーヒーグラインダーのこと。Faureさんは、**2**の**1** 2行目からこのコーヒーグラインダーを取り上げ、4～5行目でWith the Decca grinder, whatever setting I use, the grinds are perfectly consistent.と書いている。the grinds are perfectly consistent「ひき具合は申し分なく安定している」という内容をgrinds beans evenly「豆を均一にひく」と言い換えた(D)が正解。grind「～をひく」。
(B) run「作動する」。
(C) Faureさんは**2**の**1** 2～4行目で、Deccaより高価な電動コーヒーグラインダーを使用してきたことに言及しているが、Deccaが低価格であるとは述べていない。

184 What does Mr. Faure say about the decaffeinated coffee?

(A) It has a light color.
(B) It is delicious.
(C) It was sent by mistake.
(D) It was too expensive.

Faureさんはカフェイン抜きコーヒーについて何と言っていますか。

(A) 明るい色をしている。
(B) おいしい。
(C) 間違って送られた。
(D) 高価過ぎた。

> **正解 B** カフェイン抜きコーヒーについて、Faureさんは、**2**レビューの**❶**5〜6行目で、Also, their decaffeinated coffee is rich and flavorful.と述べている。このrichは「(味が)濃厚な、コクのある」、flavorfulは「風味に富む、味の良い」という意味。よって、(B)が正解。
> (A) カフェイン抜きコーヒーの色についての説明はない。light「明るい」。
> (C) by mistake「間違って」。
> (D) **1**の**❶**より、注文した商品項目の中ではカフェイン抜きコーヒー豆の金額が最も高額と分かるが、Faureさんはそれを高価過ぎるとは述べていない。

185 How much did Mr. Faure pay for the product that his coworkers like?

(A) $11.00
(B) $28.99
(C) $38.99
(D) $42.99

Faureさんは同僚が気に入っている商品に幾ら支払いましたか。

(A) 11.00 ドル
(B) 28.99 ドル
(C) 38.99 ドル
(D) 42.99 ドル

> **正解 A** **2**レビューの**❶**6行目で、dancing beansマグカップの見た目が素晴らしいと述べ、続く同6〜7行目で「職場の同僚の多くがそれ（＝マグカップ）を褒めてくれる」とある。つまり、Faureさんの同僚が好んでいる商品とは、dancing beansマグカップのことと判断できる。**1**注文書の**❶**から、Dancing beansマグカップの価格は11ドルと分かるので、(A)が正解。

Words & Phrases

1 注文書 checkout （買い物の）精算　mailing address 郵送先住所　NH ニューハンプシャー州 ★アメリカの郵便の略号　**❶** description 明細、説明　bean 豆　mug マグカップ ★mug cupとは通常言わない　ceramic 陶器の　coffee grinder コーヒーグラインダー、コーヒーミル　electric 電動の　grind （粉の）ひき具合　setting 設定　whole （豆が）丸ごとの　regular （コーヒーが）レギュラーの ★ここでは、カフェイン抜きでない通常のコーヒーを指す　pound ポンド ★重量の単位。1ポンド＝約454グラム　dark roast 深煎り　decaffeinated カフェイン抜きの　shipping 配送(料)　**❷** ship 〜を出荷する　facility 施設　throughout 〜中の至る所に

2 レビュー rating 評価　**❶** the best ever これまでで最高のもの　be particular about 〜 〜に関して好みがうるさい　whatever たとえどんな〜でも　consistent 不変の、安定した　rich （味が）濃厚な　flavorful 風味に富む　admire 〜を称賛する　be worth a try 試す価値がある

Expressions

on top of that 「それに加えて」（**2**の**❶**6行目）

Our boss missed his flight, and on top of that he had to wait ten hours for the next one.
私たちの上司は乗る予定のフライトを逃し、それに加えて、次のフライトを10時間待たなければなりませんでした。

Questions 186-190 refer to the following form, e-mail, and flyer.

① フォーム

The Black Hinge—Booking Form

① **Name of Main Act**	*The Rick Candies*
Musical Genre	*Rhythm and Blues*
Date(s) of Performance(s)	*April 29*
Contact Name	*Santiago Martinez*
Contact E-mail	*smartinez@rapidonet.com*
Main acts must arrange their own opening acts. Who will your opening act be?	*DJ Cosmic Center, techno music*
Questions or special requests?	*Do you offer any services or amenities? We would like dressing rooms for both the main act and the opening act.*

② E メール

To:	Santiago Martinez <smartinez@rapidonet.com>
From:	Yuko Miura <ymiura@theblackhinge.com>
Subject:	Booking your performance
Date:	January 17

Dear Santiago,

① We've received your booking form and are delighted to welcome The Rick Candies to The Black Hinge on April 29! Regarding your special request, we can only accommodate the main act.

② Here are some show details to note:

• Performance time at The Black Hinge is 7–11 P.M.

• The desired stage-time split is up to the main and opening acts, but typically the opening act plays 7–8 P.M. and the main act plays 8:30–11 P.M.

• Regarding payment, you may choose one of the following two options:

1. A $300 flat payment to be divided among the two musical acts as they see fit.

2. The proceeds of a $10-per-guest cover charge. Acts may keep the money collected at the door minus a 10% fee, which will be paid to the person who collects the cover charge from guests. This person will be provided by The Black Hinge.

• We can provide a table for you to sell your band's merchandise, but no staff from The Black Hinge will be available to supervise the table.

Sincerely,

Yuko Miura

③ チラシ

THE RICK CANDIES
featuring special guest DJ Cosmic Center

① April 29 @ The Black Hinge, Chicago
Cover Charge: $10
7–8 P.M.: DJ Cosmic Center
8:30–11 P.M.: The Rick Candies

② Join us for an unforgettable night with The Rick Candies, four soulful rhythm and blues performers from Peoria. The quartet takes its inspiration from the legends who pioneered the music we love. Come early to hear DJ Cosmic Center kick things off with an eclectic techno music set. Merchandise will be available for sale after the show.

問題186-190は次のフォーム、Eメール、チラシに関するものです。

The Black Hinge —— 出演予約フォーム

主公演者名	The Rick Candies
音楽ジャンル	リズム＆ブルース
公演日	4月29日
連絡担当者	Santiago Martinez
連絡先Eメール	smartinez@rapidonet.com
主公演者は前座公演者を手配しなければなりません。	DJ Cosmic Center、テクノ音楽
誰が前座公演者になりますか？	
質問または特別な要望	何かサービスや特典は提供されますか。主公演者と前座公演者の両方に楽屋を希望します。

受信者：Santiago Martinez <smartinez@rapidonet.com>
送信者：Yuko Miura <ymiura@theblackhinge.com>
件名：ご公演の予約
日付：1月17日

Santiago様

私どもはあなたの出演予約フォームを受領し、4月29日に The Rick Candies を The Black Hinge に喜んでお迎えします。特別なご要望に関しましては、私どもは主公演者さまにのみ場所を提供することができます。

以下はご留意いただきたい公演詳細情報です：
・The Black Hinge での公演時間は午後7時から11時までです。
・望ましいステージ時間の配分は主公演者さまと前座公演者さま次第ですが、通常は前座公演者さまが午後7時から8時に演奏し、主公演者さまが午後8時半から11時に演奏します。
・支払いに関しまして、次の2つの選択肢の1つをお選びいただけます：
1. 2つの公演者さま間で適切と思われるよう分配していただく300ドルの一定額でのお支払い。
2. 観客1人当たり10ドルのカバーチャージの収益。公演者さまは入り口で徴収する代金から10パーセントの手数料を差し引いた分をお受け取りになれます。この手数料は観客からカバーチャージを徴収する人員に支払われます。この人員は The Black Hinge が用意します。
・私どもは公演者さまがバンドの商品を販売するテーブルをご提供することはできますが、テーブルを管理するために The Black Hinge がスタッフをご用意することはできません。

敬具

Yuko Miura

THE RICK CANDIES
特別ゲストのDJ Cosmic Centerを迎えて

4月29日、シカゴ　The Black Hinge にて
カバーチャージ：10ドル
午後7〜8時：DJ Cosmic Center
午後8時30分〜11時：The Rick Candies

ピオリア出身の情感あふれる4人のリズム＆ブルースの演奏者、The Rick Candies との忘れ難い夜にぜひご参加ください。この4人組は、私たちの愛するこの音楽の草分けである伝説的人物からインスピレーションを受けています。早くお越しになって、DJ Cosmic Center がさまざまなジャンルをミックスしたテクノ音楽で幕を開けるのをお聞きください。公演後に商品がお買い求めいただけます。

186 In the e-mail, what is indicated about selling merchandise?

(A) The Black Hinge prohibits sales of merchandise inside the venue.
(B) The Black Hinge takes a percentage of sales.
(C) The band can sell T-shirts through The Black Hinge's Web site.
(D) The band must provide its own staff to sell any merchandise.

Eメールで、商品の販売について何が示されていますか。

(A) The Black Hingeは会場内での商品の販売を禁止している。
(B) The Black Hingeは売り上げから手数料を取る。
(C) バンドはThe Black Hingeのウェブサイトを通してTシャツを販売することができる。
(D) バンドは商品を販売するために自分たちでスタッフを用意しなければならない。

正解 D **2**Eメールを確認する。これはMartinezさんに宛てたものであり、**1**フォームの**❶**1つ目と4つ目の項目より、MartinezさんとはThe Rick Candiesというバンドの関係者と分かり、**1**のタイトルおよび**2**の**❶**から、The Black Hingeとはバンドが演奏するライブハウスなどの店舗だと考えられる。**2**の**❷**最後の項目で、The Black Hingeはバンドが商品を販売するテーブルを提供することはできるが、テーブルを管理するためにスタッフを用意することはできないと説明されている。よって、(D)が正解。
(A) **2**の**❷**最後の項目よりバンドの商品販売用のテーブルは用意されることが分かるので、販売は禁止されていない。prohibit「~を禁止する」、venue「会場」。
(B) **2**の**❷**7~9行目に店側がカバーチャージの10パーセントを取るという支払いの選択肢について記載があるが、商品の売り上げから手数料を取るとは書かれていない。percentage「割合、(パーセントで示す)手数料」。

187 What amenity will the main act receive?

(A) Snacks
(B) Beverages
(C) A dressing room
(D) Transportation to and from the venue

主公演者はどんな特典を受け取りますか。

(A) 軽食
(B) 飲み物
(C) 楽屋
(D) 会場の行き帰りの送迎

正解 C **1**フォームの**❶**のQuestions or special requests? の欄で、記入者のMartinezさんは特典が提供されるか質問し、続けてWe would like dressing rooms for both the main act and the opening act. と述べ、主公演者と前座公演者の両方に楽屋を要望している。これに対し、**2**Eメールの**❶**2~3行目で、Regarding your special request, we can only accommodate the main act. と回答されているので、主公演者のみに楽屋が用意されると分かる。よって、(C)が正解。

188 Who most likely is Ms. Miura?

(A) A cook at The Black Hinge
(B) A social media consultant
(C) A security officer
(D) A booking manager

Miuraさんは誰だと考えられますか。

(A) The Black Hingeの料理人
(B) ソーシャルメディア・コンサルタント
(C) 警備員
(D) 出演予約マネジャー

正解 D Miuraさんとは、**2**Eメールの送信者。**2**の件名に、Booking your performanceとあり、本文冒頭の**❶**1~2行目で、出演予約フォームを受け取ったと述べてから、「4月29日にThe Rick CandiesをThe Black Hingeに喜んで迎える」と書いている。また、同**❶**2~3行目で、出演予約フォームの特別な要望に対して回答し、同**❷**で、公演の注意事項について箇条書きで説明している。以上のことから、Miuraさんは公演者からの出演の申し込みに対応する人物だと判断できるので、(D)が正解。

Expressions

be up to ~ 「~次第である」(**2**の**❷**3~4行目)
It is up to the manager to make the final decision.
最終決定を下すかはマネジャー次第です。

189 What decision did The Rick Candies make about the performance?

    (A) To replace the opening act
    (B) To include dancers in the performance
    (C) To take payment from a cover charge
    (D) To have a different time split than Ms. Miura recommended

The Rick Candiesは公演についてどんな決定をしましたか。

    (A) 前座公演者を取り換えること
    (B) 公演にダンサーを含めること
    (C) カバーチャージから支払いを受けること
    (D) Miuraさんが推奨したのとは異なる時間の配分をすること

> **正解 C** ❸チラシは、The Rick CandiesというバンドのThe Black Hingeという会場における公演の案内。同❶2行目には「カバーチャージ：10ドル」と記載がある。一方、❷Eメールの❷5〜9行目ではThe Black Hingeから公演者への2つの支払い方法の選択肢が提示されており、2つ目の選択肢として同7〜9行目で、観客1人当たり10ドルのカバーチャージを課してその収益から手数料を引いた分を公演者が得られることが説明されている。つまり、The Rick Candiesは各観客に10ドルのカバーチャージを支払ってもらい、そこから公演料の支払いを受けることにしたと分かるので、(C)が正解。
> (A) ❶の❶6行目にあるのと同じ前座公演者名が❸の❶3行目にもあるので、前座公演者は変更されていないと分かる。replace「〜を取り換える」。
> (D) ❷の❷3〜4行目でMiuraさんが例示したのと同じ時間配分が、❸の❶に反映されている。よって、The Rick CandiesはMiuraさんの提案を受け入れたと分かる。different 〜 than …「…とは異なる〜」、recommend「〜を推奨する」。

190 What does the flyer indicate about The Rick Candies?

    (A) The group consists of four performers.
    (B) The group's members are from Chicago.
    (C) The group plays techno music.
    (D) The group's members are performing together for the first time.

チラシはThe Rick Candiesについて何を示していますか。

    (A) グループは4名の演奏者から成る。
    (B) グループのメンバーはシカゴ出身である。
    (C) グループはテクノ音楽を演奏する。
    (D) グループのメンバーは初めて一緒に演奏する。

> **正解 A** ❸チラシを確認する。❷1〜2行目に、The Rick Candies, four soulful rhythm and blues performers from Peoriaとあるので、The Rick Candiesは4名の演奏者で構成されていると分かる。また、続く文でこのバンドをthe quartet「4人組、カルテット」と紹介していることからも(A)が正解と分かる。consist of 〜「〜から成る」。
> (B) ❸の❷1〜2行目に、メンバーはピオリア出身とある。なお、同❶1行目より、シカゴはThe Black Hingeの所在地。
> (C) ❸の❷1〜2行目で、The Rick Candiesはリズム＆ブルースのグループとして紹介されている。同3〜4行目より、テクノ音楽を演奏するのは、前座公演者のDJ Cosmic Center。
> (D) for the first time「初めて」。

Words & Phrases

❶フォーム booking 出演予約 ❶ main act 主公演者 ★ライブやコンサートなどで目玉となる出演者 genre ジャンル
rhythm and blues リズム＆ブルース ★1940年代に生まれた米国黒人ポピュラー音楽。R&Bと略す
arrange 〜を手配する opening act 前座公演者
techno テクノ音楽 ★シンセサイザーなどを多用した電子音楽
amenities アメニティー ★快適にするための物品や設備 dressing room 楽屋

❷Eメール book 〜を予約する ❶ be delighted to *do* 〜してうれしい regarding 〜に関して
accommodate 〜を収容できる、〜(要求など)に応じる ❷ desired 望ましい split 分割
typically 典型的に、通常は flat 均一の、固定の divide 〜を配分する see fit 適当と思う
proceeds 収入、売上高 per 〜につき cover charge カバーチャージ、席料 collect 〜を集める
minus 〜を引いた supervise 〜を管理する

❸チラシ ❷ unforgettable 忘れられない soulful 感情を込めた performer 演奏者 quartet 4人組
inspiration ひらめき legend 伝説、伝説的な人物 pioneer 〜の先駆者となる kick off 〜 〜を始める
eclectic 折衷的な ★幾つかの要素の良い点を取り合わせているさま set (音楽の)1セッション、1ステージ

Questions 191-195 refer to the following flyer, article, and e-mail.

1 チラシ

Breeman's Bakery

❶ *We bake with the freshest fruits! No artificial flavoring or preservatives!*

❷ **Muffins**—We offer bran, blueberry, and banana nut. Buy ten and get one for free!
Cakes—Try our chocolate, vanilla, and lemon flavors with your choice of icing and fruit filling. All cakes are made to order. Please allow two days for orders to be filled.
Cookies—We only make chocolate chip, but they are the best!
Pies—Choose from five fruit fillings. Pies are available both fresh and frozen.

❸ A full product list is available at www.breemansbakery.com. Order online or call (208) 555-0112.

Early Winter Storm

2 記事

❶ IDAHO FALLS (November 14)—The area's first winter storm arrived early today, Thursday morning, leaving significant snowfall. Many highways and local roads will be closed throughout Thursday. By Friday morning, most major roads should be open again. The cold spell will not last long, as the forecast for Friday, Saturday, and Sunday is for temperatures slightly above freezing.

❷ On a positive note, winter sports enthusiasts can prepare to enjoy themselves earlier than usual this year. According to meteorologist Elizabeth Merkot, residents can expect heavy snows to occur early this winter. "Last year, the region's winter sports facilities did not open until the middle of December, but this year they plan to open at the end of November. Get your gear ready and make your reservations!"

3 E メール

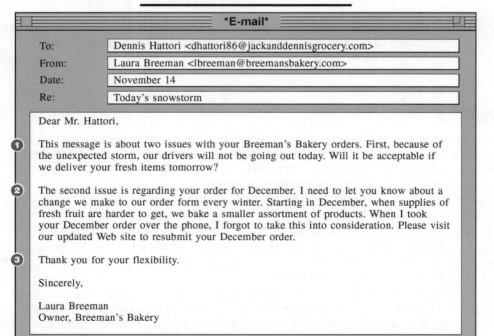

E-mail	
To:	Dennis Hattori <dhattori86@jackanddennisgrocery.com>
From:	Laura Breeman <lbreeman@breemansbakery.com>
Date:	November 14
Re:	Today's snowstorm

Dear Mr. Hattori,

❶ This message is about two issues with your Breeman's Bakery orders. First, because of the unexpected storm, our drivers will not be going out today. Will it be acceptable if we deliver your fresh items tomorrow?

❷ The second issue is regarding your order for December. I need to let you know about a change we make to our order form every winter. Starting in December, when supplies of fresh fruit are harder to get, we bake a smaller assortment of products. When I took your December order over the phone, I forgot to take this into consideration. Please visit our updated Web site to resubmit your December order.

❸ Thank you for your flexibility.

Sincerely,

Laura Breeman
Owner, Breeman's Bakery

問題191-195は次のチラシ、記事、Eメールに関するものです。

Breeman'sベーカリー

当店は最高に新鮮な果物を使って焼いています！　人工の調味料や保存料は使っていません！

マフィン —— ブラン、ブルーベリー、バナナナッツをご用意しています。10個お買い上げいただくと、1個無料で差し上げます！
ケーキ —— お好みのアイシングと果物の具材を使った、チョコレート、バニラ、レモン風味のケーキをお試しください。全てのケーキ
は受注生産しております。ご注文品の納品には2日間みてください。
クッキー —— 当店はチョコレートチップのみを作っておりますが、最高です！
パイ —— 5つの果物の具材からお選びください。パイは焼きたてと冷凍の両方で用意がございます。

全商品のリストはwww.breemansbakery.comでご覧になれます。オンラインでご注文されるか、(208) 555-0112にお電話ください。

初冬の嵐

アイダホフォールズ（11月14日）——本日、木曜日の朝、地域で最初となる冬の嵐が到来し、かなりの降雪となった。多くの幹線道路と
地方道が木曜日いっぱいは閉鎖されるだろう。金曜日の朝までには、ほとんどの主要な道路が再び通行可能になるはずである。金曜日、
土曜日、日曜日の予報では気温が氷点よりわずかに高く、この寒波の期間は長くは続かないだろう。

明るい話題としては、ウインタースポーツのファンは今年はいつもより早く楽しむ準備をすることができる。気象学者のElizabeth
Merkotによれば、住民はこの冬早くに大雪が降ることを期待できる。「昨年、地域のウインタースポーツ施設は12月半ばまで開きませ
んでしたが、今年は11月末に開く予定です。装備の用意をして、予約をしてください！」

受信者：Dennis Hattori <dhattori86@jackanddennisgrocery.com>
送信者：Laura Breeman <lbreeman@breemansbakery.com>
日付：11月14日
件名：本日の吹雪

Hattori様

このメッセージはお客さまのBreeman'sベーカリーへのご注文に関する2つの問題についてです。1つ目ですが、突然の嵐のせいで、当
店の運転手は本日出て行くことができません。お客さまへの作りたて商品を明日配達するとしたら、それをご了承いただけるでしょうか。

2つ目の問題はお客さまの12月のご注文に関してです。当店が毎年冬に行う注文書の変更についてお知らせする必要がございます。12
月からは、新鮮な果物の供給を確保するのがより困難になるので、当店の焼き菓子の品ぞろえが少なくなります。私が電話でお客さまの
12月のご注文を受けたとき、この点を考慮するのを忘れておりました。更新済みの当店ウェブサイトにアクセスして、12月の注文を再
度お出しください。

お客さまの柔軟なご対応に感謝いたします。

敬具

Laura Breeman
Breeman'sベーカリーオーナー

191 According to the flyer, how do the pies differ from other Breeman's Bakery items?

    (A) They must be ordered two days in advance.
    (B) The minimum order for them is ten.
    (C) They are sold in various sizes.
    (D) They are available frozen as well as fresh.

チラシによると、パイは他のBreeman'sベーカリーの品物とどのように異なりますか。

    (A) 2日前に注文しなければならない。
    (B) 最小注文数は10個である。
    (C) さまざまな大きさで売られている。
    (D) 焼きたてだけでなく冷凍でも売られている。

正解 D ❶チラシを確認する。❷にBreeman'sベーカリーの商品が記載されている。パイについては、同7〜8行目に、「5つの果物の具材から選んでください。パイは焼きたてと冷凍の両方で用意がある」とある。同1〜6行目のマフィン、ケーキ、クッキーについての説明には冷凍に関する記載がないので、(D)が正解。A as well as B「Bだけでなく Aも」。
(A) ❶の❷ 4〜5行目より、納品まで2日みる必要があるのはケーキ。in advance「事前に、前もって」。
(B) ❶の❷ 1〜2行目に、マフィンは10個買うと1個無料でもらえるという記載があるだけ。最小注文数に関する記載はない。minimum「最小の」。
(C) パイの大きさに関する記載はない。various「さまざまな」。

192 What does the article recommend that local residents do?

    (A) Participate in outdoor activities
    (B) Go to a movie theater
    (C) Learn to bake at home
    (D) Visit Idaho Falls on Thursday

記事は地元住民が何をすることを勧めていますか。

    (A) 野外の活動に参加する
    (B) 映画館に行く
    (C) 自宅で焼くことを学ぶ
    (D) 木曜日にアイダホフォールズを訪れる

正解 A ❷記事を確認する。❷3〜8行目で、地元住民は今年は早くに大雪を期待でき、地域のウインタースポーツ施設も早く開く予定だと報じられている。続く同9〜10行目で、「装備の用意をして、予約をしてください」と記事が締めくくられている。よって、記事は地元住民に雪を使った野外の活動に参加することを勧めていると判断できるので、(A)が正解。participate in 〜「〜に参加する」、outdoor「野外の」、activity「活動」。
(D) 記事は、冒頭にアイダホフォールズとあり、その地の地元住民に向けて書かれていると考えられるので不適切。

193 According to the e-mail, why does Breeman's Bakery change its order form every winter?

    (A) Its drivers need more time to make deliveries.
    (B) It begins selling special holiday items.
    (C) It is unable to obtain a wide variety of fresh fruits.
    (D) It increases the assortment of items for sale.

Eメールによると、なぜBreeman'sベーカリーは毎冬注文書を変更するのですか。

    (A) 同店の運転手が配達するのにより多くの時間が必要である。
    (B) 特別な祝日用の品物を売り始める。
    (C) 多種多様な新鮮な果物を手に入れることができない。
    (D) 販売する品物の品ぞろえを増やす。

正解 C ❸Eメールを確認する。これはBreeman'sベーカリーのオーナーが書いたもので、❷1〜2行目で、毎年冬に行う注文書の変更について言及し、続けてStarting in December, when supplies of fresh fruit are harder to getと、扱う焼き菓子の品ぞろえが少なくなる理由を述べている。よって、この内容を言い換えた(C)が正解。be unable to do「〜することができない」、obtain「〜を手に入れる」、a wide variety of 〜「多種多様な〜」。
(A) ❸の❶ 1〜3行目で嵐で配達ができないことが述べられているが、配達の問題が冬の注文書の変更理由ではない。
(B) holiday「祝日、休日」。
(D) 冬には品ぞろえが減ることが述べられている。for sale「売りに出されて」。

194 What products are NOT affected by the change in the order form?

(A) Muffins
(B) Cakes
(C) Cookies
(D) Pies

注文書の変更によって影響を受けないものはどの商品ですか。

(A) マフィン
(B) ケーキ
(C) クッキー
(D) パイ

> **正解 C** 　3Eメールの❷1～3行目で、注文書の変更について、新鮮な果物の入手が困難になるためだと理由が述べられている。1チラシの❷のBreeman'sベーカリーの商品のうち、クッキーについては「チョコレートチップのみを作っている」とあり、新鮮な果物を使用していないことが分かる。よって、注文書の変更によって影響を受けないものはクッキーだと判断できるので、(C)が正解。
> (A) (B) (D) 1の❷より、具材に果物が使われているので影響を受けると考えられる。

195 According to Ms. Breeman, when can the driver deliver Mr. Hattori's order?

(A) On Thursday
(B) On Friday
(C) On Saturday
(D) On Sunday

Breemanさんによると、運転手はいつHattoriさんの注文を配達できますか。

(A) 木曜日
(B) 金曜日
(C) 土曜日
(D) 日曜日

> **正解 B** 　3Eメールのヘッダー、本文、署名から、Breemanさんはこのメールの送信者でBreeman'sベーカリーのオーナー、HattoriさんはEメールの受信者で同店の顧客と分かる。3の❶1～3行目で、Breemanさんは突然の嵐のせいで本日の配達ができないと述べ、続けて「あなたへの作りたて商品を明日配達するとしたら、それを了承してもらえるか」と尋ねている。3の日付は11月14日となっている。同じ11月14日付けの❷記事の❶1～4行目には、「本日、木曜日の朝、地域で最初となる冬の嵐が到来し、かなりの降雪となった」とある。よって、Breemanさんの言う「本日」は木曜日で、配達できると言う「明日」は金曜日と分かるので、(B)が正解。

Words & Phrases

| 1チラシ | bakery ベーカリー、パン・菓子類販売店　❶ bake パン・菓子を焼く　fresh 新鮮な、作りたての artificial 人工の　flavoring 調味料　preservative 防腐剤　❷ bran ブラン、ふすま　flavor 風味 icing アイシング　★菓子にかける糖衣　filling 詰め物、具　made to order 受注生産の allow ～ for … …のために～(時間の猶予)をみておく　fill ～(注文)に応じて提供する　frozen 冷凍された |

| 2記事 | storm 嵐　❶ leave ～を残す　significant 重要な、かなりの　snowfall 降雪　highway 幹線道路 throughout ～の間じゅう　major 主要な　cold spell 寒さの続く期間、寒波の期間　last 続く forecast 予報　temperature 気温　slightly わずかに　above ～より上で　freezing 氷点、セ氏0度 ❷ on a positive note 明るい話題としては　★ニュース報道などで使われる　enthusiast ファン、熱狂者 prepare to do ～する準備をする　enjoy oneself 楽しむ　than usual いつもより　meteorologist 気象学者 resident 住民　occur 起こる　get ～ ready ～を準備する　gear 用具一式、装備　reservation 予約 |

| 3Eメール | snowstorm 吹雪　❶ issue 問題　unexpected 予期しない、不意の acceptable 受け入れられる、承認できる　❷ regarding ～に関して　make a change to ～ ～に変更を加える supply 供給物　assortment 取り合わせ、品ぞろえ　resubmit ～を再提出する　❸ flexibility 柔軟性 |

Expressions

take ～ into consideration 「～を考慮に入れる」(3の❷3～4行目)

In these fast-changing situations, we should take every possibility into consideration.
この目まぐるしく変化する状況の中で、私たちは全ての可能性を考慮に入れるべきです。

Questions 196-200 refer to the following sign and e-mails.

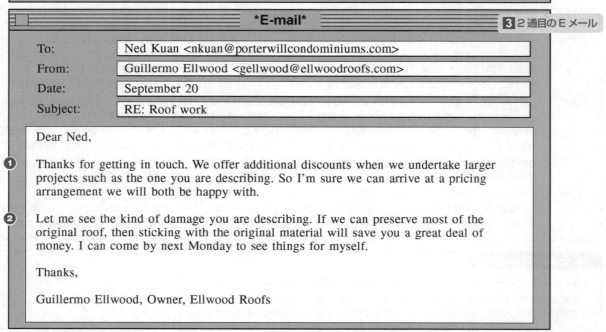

1 看板

Free Roofing Estimates from Ellwood Roofs!

❶ The roof on this building was recently repaired by Ellwood Roofs. Does your roof need work? We can help you with the following.

- Damage from hail or falling tree branches
- Leaks from age and normal wear
- Problems arising from poorly installed roofing

❷ When you contact us for an appointment, mention the address where you saw this sign and get a 10 percent discount!

Contact Ellwood Roofs at 202-555-0116 or info@ellwoodroofs.com.

2 1通目のEメール

To:	Information <info@ellwoodroofs.com>
From:	Ned Kuan <nkuan@porterwillcondominiums.com>
Date:	September 19
Subject:	Roof work

To Whom It May Concern:

❶ I manage Porterwill Condominiums, and we have had some damage from the recent storms. I saw your sign at 124 Sagamore Drive in Carnville.

❷ I was wondering what kind of a price you could offer me for repairing the roofs of six buildings. All the roofs have the same dimensions, and they all have asphalt shingles. However, in cases where the damage is serious, I would consider replacing those roofs with metal, wooden, or composite shingles.

❸ Please let me know when we can meet to discuss this.

Thanks,

Ned Kuan, Porterwill Condominiums

3 2通目のEメール

E-mail

To:	Ned Kuan <nkuan@porterwillcondominiums.com>
From:	Guillermo Ellwood <gellwood@ellwoodroofs.com>
Date:	September 20
Subject:	RE: Roof work

Dear Ned,

❶ Thanks for getting in touch. We offer additional discounts when we undertake larger projects such as the one you are describing. So I'm sure we can arrive at a pricing arrangement we will both be happy with.

❷ Let me see the kind of damage you are describing. If we can preserve most of the original roof, then sticking with the original material will save you a great deal of money. I can come by next Monday to see things for myself.

Thanks,

Guillermo Ellwood, Owner, Ellwood Roofs

問題196-200は次の看板と2通のEメールに関するものです。

Ellwood Roofs社の屋根ふき工事無料見積もり!

この建物の屋根は最近Ellwood Roofs社によって修理されました。お宅の屋根は工事が必要ですか? 当社は下記についてお客さまをお手伝いできます。

・あられや木の枝の落下による被害
・経年や通常の摩耗による雨漏り
・粗雑に取り付けられた屋根ふき材から生じる問題

ご予約について当社にご連絡される際にこの看板を見た場所の住所を言っていただくと、10パーセントの割引が受けられます!

Ellwood Roofs社に、202-555-0116またはinfo@ellwoodroofs.comまでご連絡ください。

受信者:インフォメーション <info@ellwoodroofs.com>
送信者:Ned Kuan <nkuan@porterwillcondominiums.com>
日付:9月19日
件名:屋根の工事

ご担当者さま

私はPorterwillコンドミニアムを管理しています。こちらでは最近の嵐によって一部被害を受けました。貴社の看板をカーンビルのサガモア通り124番地で見ました。

6棟の建物の屋根を修理するのに、貴社がどのような価格を提示してくださるのか知りたいと思っていました。屋根は全て同じ寸法で、全てアスファルトの屋根板があります。しかし、被害が深刻な場合は、それらの屋根を金属、木材、または複合材の屋根板と交換することを検討するかもしれません。

本件について話し合うためにいつお会いできるかお知らせください。

よろしくお願いします。

Porterwillコンドミニアム　Ned Kuan

受信者:Ned Kuan <nkuan@porterwillcondominiums.com>
送信者:Guillermo Ellwood <gellwood@ellwoodroofs.com>
日付:9月20日
件名:RE:屋根の工事

Ned様

ご連絡ありがとうございます。当社はお客さまがご説明されているような大きめの案件をお受けする際には、追加の割引をご提示します。ですので、私は双方が納得する価格設定で合意に達することができると確信しています。

お客さまがご説明されている被害がどのようなものか拝見させてください。もし元の屋根の大部分を保持することができるのであれば、元の材料のままでいくことがお客さまにとって多額の費用の節約になるでしょう。私は自分で状況を確認するために次の月曜日に伺うことができます。

よろしくお願いします。

Ellwood Roofs社オーナー　Guillermo Ellwood

196 Where is the sign for Ellwood Roofs most likely located?

(A) On a highway billboard
(B) In a bus station
(C) In a hotel lobby
(D) In front of a building

Ellwood Roofs 社の看板はどこにあると考えられますか。

(A) 幹線道路の広告板
(B) バスターミナル
(C) ホテルのロビー
(D) 建物の前

> **正解 D** **1**看板の❶1行目に、The roof on this building was recently repaired by Ellwood Roofs.とある。続けて同社の宣伝が書かれているので、看板は実際に修理された屋根を見てもらう意図で、建物の前に設置されていると考えられる。よって、(D)が正解。
> (A) billboard「(屋外の大型)広告・掲示板」。

197 According to the first e-mail, how were the condominium roofs damaged?

(A) By animals
(B) By storms
(C) By age
(D) By inexperienced workers

1通目のEメールによると、コンドミニアムの屋根はどのようにして損傷を受けましたか。

(A) 動物によって
(B) 嵐によって
(C) 経年によって
(D) 未熟な作業員によって

> **正解 B** **2**1通目のEメールを確認する。これはヘッダー、本文冒頭、署名から、Porterwillコンドミニアムの管理者のNed KuanがEllwood Roofs社に宛てたものと判断できる。❶1～2行目で、we have had some damage from the recent stormsと嵐による被害を述べ、屋根の修理について相談を続けている。よって、(B)が正解。damage「～に損傷を与える」。
> (C) (D) **1**看板の❶に記述があるが、コンドミニアムの屋根の損傷の原因として**2**には書かれていない。
> (D) inexperienced「未熟な」。

198 Why most likely did Mr. Kuan mention where he had seen the sign?

(A) To get a 10 percent discount
(B) To provide a reason for moving the sign
(C) To show where his condominiums are located
(D) To specify the type of roof he would like

Kuanさんはなぜ看板を見た場所を述べたと考えられますか。

(A) 10パーセントの割引を受けるため
(B) 看板を移動する理由を示すため
(C) 自分のコンドミニアムの所在地を示すため
(D) 自分が望む屋根の種類を指定するため

> **正解 A** **2**1通目のEメールの送信者Kuanさんは、❶2行目で看板を見た場所の住所を述べた後、❷1～2行目で、「6棟の建物の屋根を修理するのに、貴社がどのような価格を提示するのか知りたいと思っていた」と書いている。**1**看板の❷には、「予約について当社に連絡する際にこの看板を見た場所の住所を言うと、10パーセントの割引が受けられる」とある。これらから、Kuanさんは10パーセントの割引を受けるために看板を見た場所を伝えたと考えられるので、(A)が正解。
> (C) be located「位置している」。
> (D) **2**の❷3～4行目に屋根板の種類への言及はあるが、種類を指定してはいない。specify「～を指定する、～を特定する」。

Expressions

get in touch 「連絡を取る」(**3**の❶1行目)

I will get in touch with you if I have any questions about my account.
私のアカウントについて何か分からないことがあれば、あなたに連絡を取ります。

199 Why does Mr. Ellwood express certainty about an arrangement?

　(A) Because Mr. Kuan needs to have his roofs repaired immediately
　(B) Because he and Mr. Kuan have already settled on a material
　(C) Because Ellwood Roofs offers discounts on large projects
　(D) Because he and Mr. Kuan have already spent a lot of time negotiating

Ellwoodさんはなぜ合意について確信を表明しているのですか。

　(A) Kuanさんは今すぐ屋根を修理してもらう必要があるから
　(B) 彼とKuanさんはすでに材料を決めたから
　(C) Ellwood Roofs社は大きな案件に割引を提供するから
　(D) 彼とKuanさんはすでに交渉に多くの時間を費やしたから

> **正解 C** EllwoodさんがKuanさんに宛てた**3**2通目のEメールの**❶**2～3行目に、So I'm sure we can arrive at a pricing arrangement we will both be happy with.とある。設問のexpress certaintyとは、このI'm sure (that) ～「～ということを確信している」という表現のことであり、about an arrangement「合意について」とはa pricing arrangement「価格設定の合意」のこと。Ellwoodさんは、この直前の同1～2行目で「当社はあなたが説明しているような大きめの案件を受ける際には追加の割引を提示する」と書いており、それに続けてSo「従って」で次の文を始めているので、これが合意を確信する根拠だと判断できる。よって、(C)が正解。express「～を表現する」。
> (A) 修理を急いでいるといった言及はない。have ～ done「～を…してもらう」、immediately「今すぐ」。
> (B) **3**の**❷**で、元の材料を使うことで得られるメリットは述べられているが、材料はまだ決まっていない。settle on ～「～を決める」。
> (D) **2**と**3**より、KuanさんはEllwood Roofs社に見積もりを依頼したばかりであり、交渉は始めていない。spend ～ doing「…するのに～(時間)を費やす」、negotiate「交渉する」。

200 What shingle material would enable Mr. Kuan to save the most money?

　(A) Asphalt
　(B) Wood
　(C) Metal
　(D) Composite

どんな屋根板材であれば、Kuanさんは費用を最も節約することができますか。

　(A) アスファルト
　(B) 木材
　(C) 金属
　(D) 複合材

> **正解 A** Ellwoodさんは、Kuanさんに宛てた**3**2通目のEメールの**❷**1～3行目で、「もし元の屋根の大部分を保持することができるなら、元の材料のままでいくことがあなたにとって多額の費用の節約になるだろう」と述べている。Ellwoodさんの言う屋根の元の材料については、Kuanさんによる**2**1通目のEメールの**❷**2行目に、「屋根は全て同じ寸法で、全てアスファルトの屋根板がある」とある。以上のことから、Kuanさんが費用を最も節約することができる屋根板材はアスファルトだと判断できるので、(A)が正解。

Words & Phrases

　　sign　看板

1 看板　roofing　屋根ふき(の工事)、屋根ふき材料　　estimate　見積もり　　❶ help ～ with …　…に関して～を手伝う
　　the following　次のこと　　damage　被害、損傷　　hail　あられ、ひょう　　branch　枝　　leak　漏れ
　　age　老齢、古くなること　　wear　摩耗、消耗　　arise from ～　～から生じる　　poorly　下手に
　　install　～を設置する

2 Eメール　To Whom It May Concern　担当者の方へ　　❶ condominium　コンドミニアム、分譲マンション
　　drive　(小さな)通り　　❷ dimensions　寸法　　asphalt　アスファルト(の)　　shingle　屋根板　　case　場合
　　consider doing　～することを検討する　　replace ～ with …　～を…と交換する　　metal　金属(の)
　　wooden　木製の　　composite　合成物(の)、複合材(の)

3 Eメール　❶ undertake　～を引き受ける　　describe　～を説明する　　arrive at ～　～(合意・結論)に到達する
　　arrangement　合意　　be happy with ～　～に満足している　　❷ preserve　～を保持する、～を保存する
　　original　元の　　stick with ～　～を続ける　　material　材料　　save ～ …　～の…(金・時間)を節約できる
　　a great deal of ～　たくさんの～　　come by　立ち寄る　　for oneself　自分で

TEST 2 の正解一覧

リスニングセクション

問題番号	正解
Part 1	
1	D
2	C
3	C
4	B
5	B
6	A
Part 2	
7	B
8	A
9	C
10	B
11	C
12	A
13	C
14	B
15	C
16	A
17	A
18	B
19	C
20	C
21	A
22	A
23	B
24	C
25	B
26	B
27	C
28	A
29	C
30	C
31	A
Part 3	
32	C
33	D
34	B
35	C
36	D
37	B
38	A
39	D
40	C
41	D
42	A
43	C
44	A
45	C
46	D
47	B
48	A
49	D
50	C

問題番号	正解
51	D
52	B
53	C
54	D
55	B
56	D
57	C
58	A
59	D
60	C
61	D
62	B
63	C
64	D
65	C
66	D
67	B
68	D
69	C
70	B
Part 4	
71	D
72	A
73	B
74	C
75	A
76	D
77	D
78	C
79	D
80	B
81	D
82	A
83	D
84	C
85	A
86	A
87	C
88	B
89	A
90	C
91	D
92	C
93	B
94	B
95	A
96	B
97	B
98	A
99	C
100	D

リーディングセクション

問題番号	正解
Part 5	
101	B
102	A
103	B
104	D
105	A
106	C
107	C
108	B
109	A
110	A
111	B
112	A
113	D
114	B
115	D
116	B
117	C
118	D
119	D
120	D
121	A
122	A
123	C
124	A
125	A
126	C
127	D
128	B
129	D
130	D
Part 6	
131	C
132	A
133	B
134	D
135	A
136	C
137	B
138	D
139	A
140	D
141	C
142	D
143	B
144	C
145	C
146	A
Part 7	
147	C
148	D
149	D
150	C

問題番号	正解
151	B
152	A
153	C
154	B
155	D
156	C
157	B
158	B
159	C
160	B
161	A
162	D
163	A
164	B
165	B
166	A
167	D
168	C
169	A
170	C
171	A
172	D
173	A
174	A
175	B
176	C
177	A
178	B
179	D
180	A
181	C
182	A
183	A
184	D
185	B
186	D
187	C
188	C
189	B
190	D
191	B
192	B
193	A
194	A
195	D
196	B
197	D
198	A
199	C
200	B

1

2

3

---

1 🇺🇸 W

(A) He's cutting grass.
(B) He's planting seeds.
(C) He's gathering branches.
(D) He's raking leaves.

(A) 彼は草を刈っている。
(B) 彼は種をまいている。
(C) 彼は枝を集めている。
(D) 彼は葉を熊手でかき集めている。

正解 D 男性は熊手を使って落ち葉をかき集めている。leavesはleaf「葉」の複数形。rake「～を熊手でかき集める」。
(A) grass「草、芝」は写っているが、男性は草刈りをしてはいない。cut「～を刈る」。
(B) seed「種」は確認できない。plant「～を植える、～(種)をまく」。
(C) 男性が集めているのはbranch「枝」ではなく、落ち葉である。gather「～を集める」。

2 🇦🇺 M

(A) Some people are trying on shoes.
(B) Some people are entering a market.
(C) Clothes are displayed on racks.
(D) A floor is being polished.

(A) 人々が靴の試し履きをしている。
(B) 人々が市場に入っていくところである。
(C) 衣服がラックに陳列されている。
(D) 床が磨かれているところである。

正解 C 多数のclothes「衣服」がrack「ラック」に掛けられ、陳列されている。display「～を陳列する」。
(A) 2人の人物は衣服を見ており、靴の試し履きはしていない。try on ～「～を試着する」。
(B) 衣料品店の店内の様子が写っており、2人はmarket「市場、食料品店」に入っていくところではない。enter「～に入る」。
(D) floor「床」は写っているが、磨かれているところではない。polish「～を磨く」。

3 🇨🇦 M

(A) They're looking at a road sign.
(B) They're trying to stop a taxi.
(C) They're standing near a busy street.
(D) They're opening a car door.

(A) 彼らは道路標識を見ている。
(B) 彼らはタクシーを止めようとしている。
(C) 彼らは交通量の多い車道のそばに立っている。
(D) 彼らは車のドアを開けているところである。

正解 C 2人の人物が車の多い車道のすぐそばに立っている。busy「混雑した、交通量の多い」。
(A) 2人が見ているのは男性の手元であり、road sign「道路標識」ではない。
(B) 2人が車を止めようとしている様子はない。try to do「～しようと努める」、stop「～を停止させる」。
(D) 車は写っているが、2人はそのドアを開けているところではない。

4

5

6

---

4 🇬🇧 W

(A) She's paying for some groceries.
(B) She's shopping for vegetables.
(C) She's cooking a meal.
(D) She's taking off her coat.

(A) 彼女は食料雑貨類の代金を支払っている。
(B) 彼女は野菜を買おうと見て回っている。
(C) 彼女は食事を作っている。
(D) 彼女は上着を脱いでいるところである。

> **正解 B** 女性は、さまざまなvegetables「野菜」が並べられた場所で買い物かごを持ちながら野菜を見ている。shop for ～「～を買いに行く、～を買おうと見て回る」。
> (A) 女性はgroceries「食料雑貨類」を見ているが、代金を支払っているところではない。pay for ～「～の代金を支払う」。
> (C) meal「(1回分の)食事」。
> (D) 女性はcoat「上着」を着用しており、それを脱いでいるところではない。take off ～「～を脱ぐ」。

---

5 🇨🇦 M

(A) He's inspecting a crack in a wall.
(B) He's building wooden containers.
(C) He's removing some tiles on a patio.
(D) He's recycling some cardboard boxes.

(A) 彼は壁にある割れ目を調べている。
(B) 彼は木製の入れ物を作っている。
(C) 彼はテラスのタイルを剥がしている。
(D) 彼は段ボール箱をリサイクルしている。

> **正解 B** 男性は木のcontainer「入れ物」に向かい、作業をしている。wooden「木製の」。
> (A) 外壁は写っているが、男性はそれを調べてはいない。inspect「～を調べる」、crack「割れ目、ひび」。
> (C) 男性はpatio「中庭、テラス」のタイルらしきものの上にしゃがんでいるが、それを剥がしてはいない。remove「～を取り除く」。
> (D) 男性はcardboard box「段ボール箱」をリサイクルしている様子はない。recycle「～をリサイクルする」。

---

6 🇺🇸 W

(A) Handrails have been installed along some steps.
(B) Potted plants have been placed next to an open door.
(C) Some gravel has been poured into a pile.
(D) A walkway is being cleaned by a machine.

(A) 手すりが階段に沿って設置されている。
(B) 鉢植えが、開いたドアの隣に置かれている。
(C) 砂利が注がれて山になっている。
(D) 歩道が機械で清掃されているところである。

> **正解 A** 階段伝いに設置されたhandrail「手すり」が写っている。install「～を設置する」、along「～に沿って」、steps「階段」。
> (B) 開いたドアは確認できるが、potted plant「鉢植え」は写っていない。place「～を置く」。
> (C) gravel「砂利」のようなものは写っているが、山になってはいない。pour ～ into …「～を…へ注ぐ」、pile「山、積み重ね」。
> (D) walkway「歩道」は写っているが、清掃中のmachine「機械」は写っていない。

PART 2

7 🇺🇸 W　Which sales presentation are you going to?

🇦🇺 M　(A) The flight arrives at noon.
　　　(B) Jennifer's morning session.
　　　(C) Everything went smoothly.

あなたはどの営業プレゼンに出ますか。
(A) その便は正午に到着します。
(B) Jenniferの午前の会です。
(C) 万事、順調に運びました。

| 正解 B | Which ～?でどの営業プレゼンに出る予定かと尋ねている。これに対し、「Jenniferの午前の会だ」と、特定のプレゼンを答えている(B)が正解。session「会、集まり」は、ここではプレゼンが行われる会合を指している。 |

(A) flight「(飛行機の)便」の到着時刻は尋ねられていない。noon「正午」。
(C) 予定について尋ねられているので、過去について述べる発言は応答にならない。smoothly「順調に」。

8 🇨🇦 M　When can we tour the new factory?

🇬🇧 W　(A) The day after tomorrow.
　　　(B) I finished counting the tickets.
　　　(C) No more than five at a time.

私たちはいつ、その新工場を見学することができますか。
(A) あさってです。
(B) 私はチケットを数え終えました。
(C) 一度に5人までです。

| 正解 A | When ～?で新工場を見学可能な時を尋ねているのに対し、「あさって」と具体的な日程を答えている(A)が正解。tour「～を見学する」、factory「工場」。 |

(B) 質問にあるtourと関連し得るticketsが含まれるが、応答になっていない。count「～を数える」。
(C) 数は尋ねられていない。no more than ～「～だけ、～以下」、at a time「一度に」。

9 🇦🇺 M　Where should I store these files?

🇺🇸 W　(A) By five o'clock at the latest.
　　　(B) The budget meeting last week.
　　　(C) In the cabinet near Tomoko's office.

どこにこれらのファイルを保管すればいいですか。
(A) 遅くとも5時までに。
(B) 先週の予算会議です。
(C) Tomokoの執務室のそばにある収納棚の中に。

| 正解 C | Where ～?でファイルを保管すべき場所を尋ねているのに対し、「Tomokoの執務室のそばにある収納棚の中」と場所を具体的に答えている(C)が正解。store「～を保管する」。cabinet「収納棚」。 |

(A) 期限は尋ねられていない。at the latest「遅くとも」。
(B) budget「予算」。

10 🇬🇧 W　Why did you cancel your trip?

🇨🇦 M　(A) Not until we get approval.
　　　(B) Because the seminar got postponed.
　　　(C) We notified them yesterday.

なぜ旅行を中止したのですか。
(A) 私たちが承認を得てからです。
(B) セミナーが延期されたからです。
(C) 私たちは昨日、彼らに知らせました。

| 正解 B | Why ～?でなぜ旅行を中止したのかと尋ねている。これに対し、Because ～でセミナーの延期という理由を答えている(B)が正解。cancel「～を中止する」。postpone「～を延期する」。 |

(A) 時期やタイミングは尋ねられていない。not until ～「～までは(…)ない、～して初めて(…する)」、approval「承認」。
(C) themが誰を指すか不明であり、応答になっていない。notify「～に知らせる」。

11 🇦🇺 M　Would you like to join us for lunch?

🇺🇸 W　(A) Profits are at an all-time high.
　　　(B) Andrew manages our health-care plan.
　　　(C) Sure, that sounds wonderful.

私たちと一緒に昼食をいかがですか。
(A) 収益は史上最高値です。
(B) Andrewが私たちの健康管理プランを管理しています。
(C) はい、それはすてきですね。

| 正解 C | Would you like to do ～?は「～したいですか」と相手の意向を丁寧に尋ねる表現。昼食を一緒に食べないかと尋ねているのに対し、Sureと賛成し、「それ(＝一緒に昼食を取ること)はすてきだ」と続けている(C)が正解。sound ～「～に聞こえる、～と思われる」。 |

(A) profit「収益」、all-time「これまでで一番の、空前の」。
(B) manage「～を管理する」、health-care「健康管理の」。

12 W Who's organizing the benefit concert?

M (A) Elizabeth and her colleagues in marketing.
(B) The piano needs tuning.
(C) Please put the flowers in the auditorium.

誰が慈善コンサートを企画していますか。
(A) マーケティング部のElizabethとその同僚たちです。
(B) そのピアノは調律が必要です。
(C) 花は講堂に置いてください。

正解 **A** Who ～?でコンサートの企画者を尋ねているのに対し、「マーケティング部のElizabethとその同僚たちだ」と、具体的な人物名と部署名を答えている(A)が正解。Who'sはWho isの短縮形。benefit「慈善興行」。colleague「同僚」、marketing「マーケティング」。
(B) コンサートが話題にされているが、ピアノには言及されていない。tuning「調律」。
(C) 質問にあるconcertと関連し得るauditorium「講堂、公会堂」が含まれるが、応答になっていない。

13 M How did you find your new designer?

W (A) I finished the survey ahead of schedule.
(B) About two months ago.
(C) A colleague recommended her.

あなたはどうやって新しいデザイナーを見つけたのですか。
(A) 私は予定より早くアンケートを仕上げました。
(B) 約2カ月前です。
(C) 同僚が彼女を推薦してくれました。

正解 **C** How ～?でどうやって新しいデザイナーを見つけたのかと尋ねているのに対し、「同僚が彼女を推薦してくれた」と、見つけた経緯を伝えている(C)が正解。herは質問にあるyour new designerを指す。recommend「～を推薦する」。
(A) survey「調査、アンケート」は話題にされていない。ahead of schedule「予定より早く」。
(B) 方法が尋ねられているので、時期を答える発言は応答にならない。

14 W Which apartment would you like to rent?

M (A) I spent about twenty euros on it.
(B) I have a few more to look at.
(C) Mr. Yasui started a new job recently.

どの部屋を借りたいですか。
(A) 私はそれに約20ユーロを費やしました。
(B) あと幾つか見るところがあります。
(C) Yasuiさんは最近、新しい仕事を始めました。

正解 **B** Which ～?でどの部屋を借りたいかと尋ねている。これに対し、具体的な物件には言及せず、「あと幾つか見るところがある」と他の物件も見るつもりであり、まだ決めていないということを暗に伝えている(B)が正解。moreはmore apartmentsを表す。apartment「共同住宅の住戸」、rent「～を賃借する」。
(A) かかった費用を伝える発言は応答にならない。spend「～を費やす」、euro「ユーロ」。
(C) recently「最近」。

15 M Would you prefer a laptop or desktop computer?

W (A) Because the lecture was too long.
(B) Yes, that would be ideal.
(C) I'm fine with either type.

ノートパソコンの方がいいですか、それともデスクトップコンピューターの方がいいですか。
(A) その講演が長過ぎたからです。
(B) はい、それだったら理想的です。
(C) どちらの種類でも結構です。

正解 **C** A or B?の形で、ノートパソコンとデスクトップコンピューターのどちらを希望するかと尋ねている。これに対し、一方を選択せずに、どちらの種類でも構わないことを伝えている(C)が正解。prefer「～の方を好む」、laptop「ノートパソコン」。either「どちらの～でも」、type「型、種類」。
(A) 理由を述べる発言は応答にならない。lecture「講演」。
(B) 二者択一の質問に対し、Yesで何を肯定しているか不明。また、thatが何を指すかも不明。ideal「理想的な」。

16 W Let's submit our research proposal.

M (A) I think we need more time.
(B) The station is just around the corner.
(C) I have always enjoyed reading.

私たちの研究計画を提出しましょう。
(A) 私はもっと時間が必要だと思います。
(B) 駅は角を曲がったところです。
(C) 私は常々、読書を楽しんできました。

正解 **A** Let's ～で研究計画の提出を提案しているのに対し、「私はもっと時間が必要だと思う」と述べ、提出は時期尚早であると示唆している(A)が正解。submit「～を提出する」、research「研究」、proposal「提案、計画」。
(B)駅の場所は話題にされていない。just around the corner「角を曲がったところに、すぐ近くに」。

17 🇦🇺 M　Which conference room is available?

🇬🇧 W　(A) The one near the lobby is free.
　　　(B) Please order five for me.
　　　(C) Your package has been sent.

どの会議室が利用可能ですか。
(A) ロビーの近くのものが空いています。
(B) 私の分を5つ注文してください。
(C) あなた宛ての小包が発送されました。

正解 **A**　Which ～?でどの会議室が利用可能か
と尋ねているのに対し、「ロビーの近く
のものが空いている」と、利用可能な会議室を伝えて
いる(A)が正解。oneはconference roomを表す。
conference room「会議室」、available「利用可能
な」、free「(場所が)空いている」。
(B) 何を5つ注文するよう依頼しているか不明であ
り、応答になっていない。order「～を注文する」。
(C) package「小包」に関することは話題にされてい
ない。

---

18 🇺🇸 W　We should review the latest round of résumés.

🇦🇺 M　(A) Not while I was there.
　　　(B) The position has been filled.
　　　(C) It costs twenty pounds per ounce.

私たちは最新到着分の履歴書を吟味すべきです。
(A) 私がそこにいた間ではありません。
(B) その職は埋まりました。
(C) それは1オンス当たり20ポンドかかります。

正解 **B**　最新到着分の履歴書を吟味すべきだと
いう発言に対し、その職はすでに埋まっ
たと伝え、履歴書を吟味する必要がないことを示唆
している(B)が正解。review「～を検討する、～を
吟味する」、latest「最新の、最近の」、round「(仕事
の)一区切り、一つの過程」、résumé「履歴書」。
position「職」、fill「～を埋める」。
(A) thereがどこを指すか不明。
(C) 発言にあるroundと似た音のpound「ポンド(英
国の通貨単位)」に注意。cost「～(費用)がかかる」、
per「～当たり」、ounce「オンス(重さの単位)」。

---

19 🇨🇦 M　Did you order new business cards?

🇬🇧 W　(A) We're taking a bus.
　　　(B) Has Thomas seen the grant application?
　　　(C) Yes, I included the company logo this time.

新しい名刺を注文しましたか。
(A) 私たちはバスに乗ります。
(B) Thomasは助成金の申請書に目を通しましたか。
(C) はい、私は今回、会社のロゴを入れました。

正解 **C**　新しい名刺を注文したかと尋ねているの
に対し、Yesと肯定し、会社のロゴを入
れたと付け加えている(C)が正解。business card
「名刺」。include「～を含める」、logo「ロゴ」。
(A) 質問にあるcardsと似た音のcars「車両」からの
連想に注意。
(B) grant「助成金」やapplication「申請書」などは話
題にされていない。

---

20 🇺🇸 W　Who will lead the training session?

🇨🇦 M　(A) The office is open in August.
　　　(B) That makes sense to me.
　　　(C) I didn't know one was planned.

誰が研修会で指導役をする予定ですか。
(A) 8月、そのオフィスは開いています。
(B) 私はそれで納得がいきます。
(C) それが計画されているとは知りませんでした。

正解 **C**　Who ～?で研修会で指導役をする人物
を尋ねているのに対し、そもそも研修会
が行われること自体を把握していなかったことを伝え
ている(C)が正解。oneはa training sessionを表す。
lead「～を主導する」、session「会、集まり」。plan「～
を計画する」。
(A) オフィスについては言及されていない。
(B) make sense「道理にかなう、なるほどと思え
る」。

---

21 🇦🇺 M　How is the new printer performing?

🇬🇧 W　(A) It's much faster than the old one.
　　　(B) Yes, Sofia made that spreadsheet.
　　　(C) Lunch will be delivered shortly.

新しいプリンターの性能はどうですか。
(A) 前のものよりもはるかに速いです。
(B) はい、Sofiaがそのスプレッドシートを作成しました。
(C) 昼食が間もなく届く予定です。

正解 **A**　How ～?で新しいプリンターの性能は
どうかと尋ねている。これに対し、前の
プリンターと比較して高速である点を伝えている
(A)が正解。itは質問にあるthe new printerを指し、
the old oneはthe old printerを表す。perform「機
能する」。
(B) 性能はどうかと尋ねられているので、Yes/No
では応答にならない。spreadsheet「スプレッドシ
ート」。
(C) deliver「～を配達する、～を届ける」、shortly「間
もなく」。

22 🇺🇸 W Why did Ms. Kim oppose funding our new project?

🇦🇺 M (A) Did you see the latest budget cuts?
(B) I'm looking forward to the opening of the new café.
(C) I will have it sent to her.

Kimさんはなぜ、私たちの新規プロジェクトへの資金提供に反対したのですか。
(A) 直近の予算削減は見ましたか。
(B) 新しいカフェの開店を楽しみにしています。
(C) それを彼女宛てに送ってもらいます。

正解 **A** Why ～?でKimさんが資金提供に反対した理由を尋ねている。これに対し、「直近の予算削減は見たか」と聞き返し、理由が予算削減にあることを示唆している(A)が正解。oppose *doing*「～することに反対する」、fund「～に資金提供する」。budget「予算」、cut「削減」。
(B) 質問にあるnewを含むが、カフェは話題にされていない。look forward to ～「～を心待ちにする」。
(C) herがMs. Kimを、itがour new projectを指すとしても、理由を尋ねる質問の応答にならない。have ～ *done*「～を…してもらう」。

---

23 🇬🇧 W Would you like the staff to set up for the party now?

🇺🇸 W (A) No, he doesn't like speaking in public.
(B) Yes, that'd be great.
(C) Can the client send another draft?

今からスタッフにパーティーの準備をしてもらいましょうか。
(A) いいえ、彼は人前で話をするのが好きではありません。
(B) はい、そうしていただけるとありがたいです。
(C) その顧客は別の草稿を送ってくれますか。

正解 **B** Would you like ～ to *do* ?「～に…してほしいですか」で、スタッフにパーティーの準備をさせようかと申し出ている。これに対し、Yesと答え、「そうしてもらえるとありがたい」と付け加えている(B)が正解。that'dはthat wouldの短縮形。staff「〈集合的に〉職員」、set up「準備する」。
(A) Noと答えているが、続く内容のheが誰を指すか不明。in public「人前で」。
(C) client「顧客」やdraft「草稿」に関することは話題にされていない。

---

24 🇨🇦 M I can't find the latest version of the art layout.

🇬🇧 W (A) We should see that museum exhibit.
(B) We could use the garden to host the fund-raiser.
(C) I have a copy on my desk.

最新版の美術品配置図が見つかりません。
(A) 私たちはあの美術館の展示を見た方がいいですね。
(B) 資金集めのイベントを開催するのに庭園を使ってもよいのではないでしょうか。
(C) 私の机の上に1部ありますよ。

正解 **C** 最新版の配置図が見つからないという発言に対し、自分の机の上にそれが1部あると述べて、それを参照できることを示している(C)が正解。a copyはa copy of the latest version of the art layoutを表す。version「版」、layout「配置図」。copy「写し、(本や書類の)部・冊」。
(A) 発言にあるartと関連するmuseum exhibit「美術館の展示」が含まれるが、応答になっていない。
(B) host「～を催す」、fund-raiser「資金集め行事」。

---

25 🇦🇺 M When will you send the brochures for the concert series?

🇨🇦 M (A) With the singer.
(B) As soon as they are back from the printer.
(C) While we were at the theater.

いつそのコンサートシリーズのパンフレットを発送する予定ですか。
(A) その歌手と一緒にです。
(B) 印刷業者から戻ってきたらすぐにです。
(C) 私たちがその劇場にいた間にです。

正解 **B** When ～?でパンフレットを発送する予定の時を尋ねている。これに対し、印刷業者から納品され次第すぐという発送のタイミングを答えている(B)が正解。theyは質問にあるthe brochures for the concert seriesを指す。brochure「パンフレット」、series「一連のもの」。as soon as ～「～するとすぐに」、printer「印刷業者」。
(C) 未来について尋ねられているので、過去の時点についての発言は応答にならない。

---

26 🇬🇧 W We're using Tanaka Catering, aren't we?

🇺🇸 W (A) The engineers revised the process.
(B) Let's discuss it when Martina is back.
(C) I'll schedule an additional workshop.

私たちはTanakaケータリング社を利用するのですよね？
(A) エンジニアたちはその工程を修正しました。
(B) Martinaが戻ったらそれについて話し合いましょう。
(C) 私は追加の講習会の予定を入れます。

正解 **B** 肯定文の文末に ～, aren't we?を付けて「～ですよね」と、利用するケータリング会社を確認している。これに対し、Yes/Noでは答えずに「Martinaが戻ったらそれについて話し合おう」と提案している(B)が正解。itは、ケータリング会社の利用に関する話題を指す。catering「仕出し業、ケータリング」。discuss「～について話し合う」。
(A) revise「～を修正する」、process「工程」。
(C) schedule「～を予定に入れる」、additional「追加の」、workshop「講習会」。

27 🇨🇦 M Isn't the dance studio opening a second location next month?

🇬🇧 W (A) A wonderful dance routine.
(B) No, the botanical gardens are closed today.
(C) The first classes begin in three weeks.

そのダンス教室は来月、第2教室をオープンするのではありませんか。
(A) 見事なダンスステップです。
(B) いいえ、植物園は今日閉まっています。
(C) 最初のクラスが3週間後に始まります。

正解 C 否定疑問文で、そのダンス教室は来月、第2教室をオープンするのではないかと尋ねているのに対し、Yes/Noでは答えていないが、新教室での最初のクラスが3週間後に始まると答えて開始時期を知らせている(C)が正解。studio「練習場」、location「所在地、店舗」。
(A) 質問にあるdanceを含む点や、関連するroutine「(ダンスの)定まった一連のステップ」に注意。
(B) Noと答えているが、botanical garden「植物園」は話題にされていない。

28 🇺🇸 W Should we discuss the proposed park expansion next week?

🇨🇦 M (A) The director wants an answer tomorrow.
(B) The trails hadn't been cleared.
(C) I'd say about a month.

私たちは、提案されている公園の拡張について来週話し合えばいいでしょうか。
(A) 所長は明日返事を欲しがっています。
(B) 小道はきれいにされていませんでした。
(C) 1カ月くらいでしょうね。

正解 A 公園の拡張について来週話し合えばいいかという質問に対し、「所長は明日返事を欲しがっている」と伝えることで、来週では遅く、明日に間に合うよう話し合うべきだと暗に伝えている(A)が正解。propose「～を提案する」、expansion「拡張」。director「管理者、所長」。
(B) 質問にあるparkと関連するtrailsを含むが、応答にならない。trail「小道、自然歩道」、clear「～(場所)を片付ける」。
(C) 期間については尋ねられていない。I'd say ～「まあ～でしょうね」は断定を避けた婉曲な表現。

29 🇦🇺 M Has the equipment arrived for tonight's performance?

🇨🇦 M (A) The orchestra was excellent last night.
(B) Has Ms. Gutierrez recorded her performance?
(C) The driver texted that he'll be here soon.

今夜の公演に向けて、機材は到着しましたか。
(A) そのオーケストラは昨夜、見事でした。
(B) Gutierrezさんは自分の演奏を録音しましたか。
(C) ドライバーが、間もなくこちらに着くとメッセージを送ってきました。

正解 C 今夜の公演に使う機材が到着したかと尋ねているのに対し、ドライバーから連絡があったことに言及して、機材が間もなく到着することを伝えている(C)が正解。equipment「機器、機材」、performance「公演、演奏」。text that ～「～とメッセージを送る」。
(A) 質問にあるperformanceと関連するorchestra「オーケストラ」を含むが、感想は尋ねられていない。
(B) 質問にあるperformanceを含むが、機材が到着したかどうかの応答になっていない。

30 🇦🇺 M Should our annual sale last for one week or two weeks?

🇺🇸 W (A) Let's go next month.
(B) Their sale prices are quite low.
(C) Customers prefer longer sale periods.

当店の毎年恒例のセールは1週間続けるべきですか、それとも2週間ですか。
(A) 来月行きましょう。
(B) 彼らのセール価格はかなり低いです。
(C) 顧客はセール期間がより長い方を好みます。

正解 C A or B?の形で、セール期間を1週間と2週間のどちらにするべきかと尋ねている。これに対し、具体的な期間には言及せず、顧客はセール期間がより長い方を好むと述べ、後者の選択を示唆している(C)が正解。annual「年に一度の、毎年恒例の」、last「続く」。period「期間」。
(A) 質問にあるweekと関連するmonthを含むが、来月行こうという提案は期間に関する質問への応答にならない。
(B) 質問にあるsaleを含むが、theirが指す内容が不明で、価格も話題にされていない。quite「かなり」。

31 🇺🇸 W Where's the best place to get a quick meal?

🇦🇺 M (A) I don't think we have time before the meeting.
(B) The contractor has responded with an offer.
(C) With a tax bill.

さっと食事を取るのに最適な場所はどこですか。
(A) 会議前に時間はないと思います。
(B) 請負業者は提示価格を添えて返答してきました。
(C) 税金の請求と一緒にです。

正解 A Where ～?でさっと食事を取るのに最適な場所を尋ねているのに対し、そもそも食事を取る時間はないと思うという考えを述べた(A)が正解。Where'sはWhere isの短縮形。quick「短時間の」、meal「食事」。
(B) contractor「請負業者」、respond「応じる」、offer「申し出、付け値」。
(C) tax「税金」、bill「請求書」。

PART 3

Questions 32 through 34 refer to the following conversation.

W **❶Hello, Laurelton Health Care. How can I help you today?**

M Hi, I'm Murad Malik. **❷I'm calling about my physical therapy appointment this week.**

W OK. Let me just look up your information. There we go. So what can we do for you today, Mr. Malik?

M **❸I'm looking to change my appointment with Dr. Ramsey. ❹I'd like to move it to next week, if possible.**

W Certainly. **❺Could you please give me your six-digit patient ID number?**

M **❻Yes. I have it here. One minute.**

問題32-34は次の会話に関するものです。

もしもし、Laurelton診療所です。本日はどのようなご用件でしょうか。

こんにちは、Murad Malikと申します。今週の理学療法の予約の件でお電話しています。

はい。まずあなたの情報をお調べしますね。見つかりました。それで、本日はどうなさいましたか、Malik様。

Ramsey先生の予約を変更したいと思っています。可能なら、それを来週にずらしたいのですが。

かしこまりました。6桁の患者さまID番号を教えていただけますか。

はい。ここにあります。少しお待ちください。

---

32 Where does the woman work?

(A) At a museum
(B) At a corporate headquarters
(C) At a health clinic
(D) At a television studio

女性はどこで働いていますか。

(A) 博物館
(B) 企業の本社
(C) 診療所
(D) テレビスタジオ

正解 C 女性は❶「もしもし、Laurelton診療所です」と告げ、続けて用件を尋ねている。またこれに対して男性は自分の名前を伝えた後、❷「今週の理学療法の予約の件で電話している」と述べているので、女性は理学療法を提供する医療施設で働いていると分かる。よって、(C)が正解。health clinic「診療所」。
(B) corporate「企業の」、headquarters「本社」。

33 Why is the man calling?

(A) To confirm a business trip
(B) To cancel an interview
(C) To discuss some test results
(D) To reschedule an appointment

男性はなぜ電話をしているのですか。

(A) 出張を確認するため
(B) 面談をキャンセルするため
(C) 検査結果について話し合うため
(D) 予約の日程を変更するため

正解 D 用件を尋ねられた男性は、❸「Ramsey先生の予約を変更したいと思っている」と述べ、続けて❹「可能なら、それを来週にずらしたい」と付け加えている。❹のitはmy appointment with Dr. Ramseyを指す。予約の日程変更をreschedule「～の日時を変更する」を用いて表した(D)が正解。
(A) confirm「～を確認する」、business trip「出張」。
(B) interview「面接、面談」。
(C) test「検査」、result「結果」。

34 What will the man do next?

(A) Download some files
(B) Provide an identification number
(C) Check a calendar
(D) Complete a payment

男性は次に何をしますか。

(A) ファイルをダウンロードする
(B) 識別番号を伝える
(C) 日程表を確認する
(D) 支払いを完了する

正解 B 予約の変更を承諾した女性は、❺「6桁の患者ID番号を教えてもらえるか」と尋ねている。これに対し、男性は❻でYesと答えてそれが手元にあることを伝えている。❻のitは、❺の(your) six-digit patient ID numberを指し、これをan identification numberと言い換えている(B)が正解。provide「～を提供する」。
(C) calendar「カレンダー、日程表」。
(D) complete「～を完了する」、payment「支払い」。

Words & Phrases

health care 医療、健康管理　physical therapy 理学療法　★物理療法と運動療法を組み合わせた治療法　appointment 予約　look up ～ ～を調べる　information 情報　There we go. （探しているものが）ありました。　★探し物を発見したときや、意図したことを遂行できたときに使うカジュアルな表現　look to do ～しようと思っている　move ～を移動させる、～（日時）を変更する　if possible 可能ならば　six-digit 6桁の　patient 患者　ID number ID番号　★IDはidentification「身元確認、身元証明書」の略

Questions 35 through 37 refer to the following conversation.

問題35-37は次の会話に関するものです。

🇺🇸 w Hi, Yoshio. I want to thank you for speaking on behalf of the product-development teams. ❶Are you pleased with the budget increase?

こんにちは、Yoshio。製品開発チームを代表して話をしてくれたことに感謝したいと思います。予算の増額に満足していますか。

🇦🇺 m Certainly! You know, ❷it's great that with this increase we'll be able to poll consumers and do more market research!

もちろんです！ なにしろ、この増額で私たちが消費者意識調査やさらなる市場調査を実施できるようになるのは素晴らしいことですから！

🇺🇸 w You're right. ❸Heading the budget committee was more work than I thought it would be. ❹I'm glad the position rotates annually and next year it will be someone else's turn.

その通りですね。予算委員会の委員長を務めるのは私が思っていたよりも大変な仕事でした。その役目は1年交替制で、来年は別の誰かの番になるのでよかったです。

TEST 2 PART 3

---

35 What are the speakers mainly discussing?

(A) A staff training initiative
(B) A sales call
(C) A funding increase
(D) A business trip

話し手たちは主に何について話し合っていますか。

(A) 従業員研修の新構想
(B) 営業の電話
(C) 資金の増額
(D) 出張

正解 C ❶「予算の増額に満足しているか」と女性が尋ねているのに対し、男性はCertainlyと強く肯定してから、❷で、増額によって可能となることに言及し、喜びを表している。よって、話し手たちは主に予算の増額について話し合っていると分かる。❶のbudgetをfunding「資金」と表している(C)が正解。
(A) initiative「新構想」。
(B) sales call「営業の電話」。

---

36 What is the man looking forward to?

(A) A signing ceremony
(B) A quarterly meeting
(C) Interviewing job applicants
(D) Conducting market research

男性は何を心待ちにしていますか。

(A) 調印式
(B) 四半期会議
(C) 求職者と面接すること
(D) 市場調査を実施すること

正解 D 男性は予算の増額に満足していることを強く肯定してから、❷で、増額によって消費者意識調査やさらなる市場調査を実施できるようになるのは素晴らしいことだと述べている。よって、(D)が正解。look forward to ~「~を心待ちにする」。conduct「~を実施する」。
(A) signing ceremony「調印式」。
(B) quarterly「四半期の」。
(C) interview「~と面接する」、job applicant「求職者」。

---

37 What does the woman say about a budget committee?

(A) She is not happy with the committee's decision.
(B) She will not head the committee next year.
(C) The committee has hired new staff.
(D) The committee should meet more often.

女性は予算委員会について何と言っていますか。

(A) 彼女は委員会の決定に満足していない。
(B) 彼女は来年、委員会の委員長を務めない。
(C) 委員会は新しい従業員を雇用した。
(D) 委員会はもっと頻繁に開かれるべきだ。

正解 B 女性は、❸で予算委員会の委員長は大変な仕事だったと述べ、❹「その役目は1年交替制で、来年は別の誰かの番になるのでよかった」と続けている。よって、女性は来年は自分が委員長を務めないと言っていることが分かるので、(B)が正解。
(A) 女性は、男性の❷の発言に同意しているので、委員会の決定には満足していると考えられる。be happy with ~「~に満足している」、decision「決定」。
(C) 新しい従業員については述べられていない。
(D) 委員会の開催頻度への言及はない。meet「(会などが)開かれる」。

Words & Phrases

thank ~ for *doing* …してくれたことについて~に感謝する　　on behalf of ~　~を代表して
product-development　製品開発の　　be pleased with ~　~に満足している　　budget　予算　　increase　増加
be able to *do*　~することができる　　poll　~に世論調査をする　　consumer　消費者　　market research　市場調査
head　~のリーダーを務める　　committee　委員会　　be glad (that) ~　~ということをうれしく思う、~ということに喜んでいる
position　役職　　rotate　(仕事などが)交替で行われる　　annually　毎年、1年ごとに　　turn　順番

Questions 38 through 40 refer to the following conversation.

W Hi, Klaus. ❶Is this a good time to discuss the seasonal menu we're introducing?

M Actually, ❷there's a problem in the kitchen. ❸A refrigerator isn't cooling properly. Fortunately, it's the overflow one and there were just some bottled drinks in it. Anyway, I just called the technician, and he should be able to get here in about two hours.

W OK, in that case, can you transfer those bottles over to the bigger fridge?

M Sure, and ❹in the meantime you might want to call and see if the vendor can delay this morning's beverage shipment, though it may already be on the way.

問題38-40は次の会話に関するものです。

こんにちは、Klaus。当店が導入予定の季節限定メニューについて話し合うのに今はご都合いいですか。

実は、厨房で問題が生じています。冷蔵庫が1台きちんと冷えないのです。幸い、それは余剰のもので、中にはボトル入り飲料が幾つか入っているだけでした。ともかく、ちょうど技術者に電話したところで、彼は約2時間後にここに到着できるはずです。

分かりました。それなら、それらのボトルを向こうの大きい方の冷蔵庫に移してもらえますか。

はい。それからその一方で、納入業者が今日の午前中の飲料の発送を遅らせることが可能かどうか電話して確かめてみてはどうでしょうか。すでに配達中かもしれませんが。

---

38 Where most likely do the speakers work?

(A) At a restaurant
(B) At a grocery store
(C) At a factory
(D) At a shipping company

話し手たちはどこで働いていると考えられますか。

(A) レストラン
(B) 食料雑貨店
(C) 工場
(D) 運送会社

正解 A 女性は❶「当店が導入予定の季節限定メニューについて話し合うのに今は都合がいいか」と男性に尋ねている。これに対し、男性は❷で、厨房で問題が生じていると述べた後、❸で、1台の冷蔵庫がうまく冷えないと説明している。これらのことから、2人はレストランで働いていると考えられるので、(A)が正解。
(B) 季節限定メニューに言及があるので、grocery store「食料雑貨店」での会話とは考えにくい。
(D) shipmentなどの語から連想され得る点に注意。shipping company「運送会社」。

---

39 What problem does the man discuss?

(A) Some product information is incorrect.
(B) Some items arrived broken.
(C) Some expenses have increased.
(D) Some equipment is not working.

男性はどんな問題について話していますか。

(A) 製品情報が誤っている。
(B) 品物が破損した状態で届いた。
(C) 経費が増加した。
(D) 機器が作動していない。

正解 D 男性は❷で、厨房で問題が生じていると知らせた後、❸「冷蔵庫が1台きちんと冷えない」と伝えている。よって、❸のa refrigeratorをsome equipmentと、isn't cooling properlyをis not workingとそれぞれ表している(D)が正解。equipment「機器」、work「(正常に)機能する」。
(A) product「製品」、incorrect「誤った」。
(B) item「品物」、arrive「到着する」。
(C) expenses「経費」、increase「増加する」。

---

40 What does the man suggest that the woman do?

(A) Conduct an interview
(B) Update a payment method
(C) Contact a supplier
(D) Update some staff members

男性は女性に何をするよう提案していますか。

(A) 面談を実施する
(B) 支払い方法を更新する
(C) 仕入れ先に連絡する
(D) 従業員に最新の情報を教える

正解 C 冷蔵庫の不具合に関連し、男性は、❹「その一方で、納入業者が今日の午前中の飲料の発送を遅らせることが可能かどうか電話して確かめてみてはどうか」と女性に対して提案している。よって、❹のcallをcontactと、the vendorをa supplierとそれぞれ表現している(C)が正解。supplier「納入業者、仕入れ先」。
(A) conduct「～を実施する」。
(B) update「～を更新する」、method「方法」。
(D) update「～に最新の情報を提供する」。

Words & Phrases

seasonal 季節的な　introduce ～を導入する　refrigerator 冷蔵庫　★fridgeは略式の表現
cool 冷える　properly 適切に　fortunately 幸いなことに　overflow あふれること、過剰　anyway ともかく
technician 技術者　in that case それなら、その場合は　transfer ～を移す　in the meantime その間に、その一方で
you might want to do （あなたは）～してもよいかもしれない　★控えめな提案や助言の表現　see if ～ ～かどうか確かめる
delay ～を遅らせる　beverage 飲料　though もっとも～ではあるが　on the way 途中で、輸送中で

Questions 41 through 43 refer to the following conversation.

🇨🇦 M I appreciate you showing me this room, but it's really not suitable. ❶There will be 50 trainees in attendance.

🇬🇧 W Oh, that many? I'll have to check and see what other conference rooms are available.

🇨🇦 M ❷How about the room across the hall? It's nicer and it seems quite a bit larger.

🇬🇧 W We're having new flooring installed. ❸It's going to take a few weeks. ❹But the patio conference room might not be booked. Let me make a quick phone call.

🇨🇦 M OK. Thanks.

問題41-43は次の会話に関するものです。

この部屋を見せていただいたことに感謝しますが、ここはあまり適していません。50名の研修生が出席予定なのです。

ああ、そんなに大勢なのですか。他のどの会議室が利用可能か確認しなければなりませんね。

廊下を挟んで向かいにある部屋はどうですか。そこの方が立派で、かなり広いようですが。

新しい床材を設置してもらっているところでして。それに数週間かかる予定なのです。でも、中庭の会議室なら予約が入っていないかもしれません。ちょっと電話させてください。

分かりました。ありがとうございます。

---

41 What is the man planning to do?

(A) Renovate a home
(B) Attend a concert
(C) Purchase a building
(D) Hold a training seminar

男性は何をすることを計画中ですか。

(A) 家をリフォームする
(B) コンサートに行く
(C) 建物を購入する
(D) 研修セミナーを開催する

正解 D 男性は、見せてもらった部屋が適していないと述べた後、❶「50名の研修生が出席予定だ」と伝えている。よって、男性は研修生が出席するイベントを開こうとしていると考えられるので、(D)が正解。hold「~を開催する」。
(A) 女性が新しい床材の設置に言及しているが、会議室の改修であって家のリフォームではない。renovate「~をリフォームする」。
(B) attendanceなどの語から連想され得る点に注意。

42 Why does the woman say, "We're having new flooring installed"?

(A) To reject a suggestion
(B) To explain a benefit
(C) To make a request
(D) To provide directions

女性はなぜ "We're having new flooring installed" と言っていますか。

(A) 提案を断るため
(B) メリットを説明するため
(C) 依頼をするため
(D) 指示を与えるため

正解 A ❷で、廊下を挟んで向かいの部屋はどうかと尋ねる男性に対し、女性は下線部の発言で「新しい床材を設置してもらっているところだ」とその部屋の状況を述べている。続けて、❸で設置作業に日数がかかることを補足し、❹で別の部屋を提案している。よって、女性は、向かいの部屋を使用するという男性からの提案を断るために下線部の発言をしていると分かる。reject「~を断る」、suggestion「提案」。
(B) benefit「便益、利益」。
(C) make a request「依頼をする」。
(D) directions「指示、命令」。

43 What will the woman do next?

(A) Write a letter
(B) Clean a patio
(C) Check a booking schedule
(D) Cancel a reservation

女性は次に何をしますか。

(A) 手紙を書く
(B) 中庭を掃除する
(C) 予約のスケジュールを確認する
(D) 予約をキャンセルする

正解 C 女性は、尋ねられた部屋が当面利用できないことを示唆した後、❹「でも、中庭の会議室なら予約が入っていないかもしれない。ちょっと電話させてほしい」と伝えている。よって、女性はこれからその部屋の予約状況を電話で確認すると考えられるので、(C)が正解。booking「予約」。
(B) 中庭は、会議室のある場所として挙げられているだけ。
(D) 女性は予約を確認するために電話をするのであり、キャンセルするためではない。cancel「~をキャンセルする」、reservation「予約」。

Words & Phrases

appreciate ~をありがたく思う　　suitable 適した　　trainee 研修生
in attendance 出席して　　check and see ~ ~を確認する　　available 利用可能な　　across ~の向こう側に
hall 集会場、廊下　　seem ~に見える　　quite a bit かなり　　have ~ done ~を…してもらう　　flooring 床材
install ~を設置する　　patio 中庭　　book ~を予約する

Questions 44 through 46 refer to the following conversation with three speakers.

🇺🇸 W **❶** Can I help you with your trip today?

🇨🇦 M **❷** I'm scheduled for the Express 2312 with my colleague Sara here. **❸** We'd like to take a later train because our meeting was pushed back a few hours.

🇬🇧 W That's right, we have business class tickets to Boston.

🇺🇸 W **❹** I should be able to transfer your reservations to the train that leaves at 12:40. You'd be in Boston about 2:30.

🇨🇦 M That would be perfect.

🇺🇸 W **❺** May I have your tickets? Give me just a moment to make the change.

🇨🇦 M **❻** Sara, we have extra time now. What should we do?

🇬🇧 W **❼** Maybe we should go over our sales demonstration again. Let's find a café where we can work.

問題44-46は3人の話し手による次の会話に関するものです。

本日は、ご旅行について何かお手伝いいたしましょうか。

私はここにいる同僚のSaraと一緒に、急行2312号に乗車予定です。会議が数時間後ろにずれたので、私たちはもっと後の列車に乗りたいと思っています。

そうなんです、私たちはボストン行きのビジネスクラスの乗車券を持っています。

ご予約を12時40分発の列車に移すことができるはずです。ボストンには2時30分頃のご到着となります。

それなら完璧ですね。

乗車券を頂けますか。変更するのに少々お時間をください。

Sara、私たちには余分な時間ができましたね。何をすべきでしょうか。

営業の実演をもう一度おさらいした方がいいかもしれません。作業できるカフェを見つけましょう。

---

44 Where is the conversation taking place?

(A) At a train station
(B) In a restaurant
(C) In a conference room
(D) At a shopping center

会話はどこで行われていますか。

(A) 鉄道駅
(B) レストラン
(C) 会議室
(D) ショッピングセンター

> **正解 A** 1人目の女性が❶で、旅行に関して用件を尋ね、男性は❷・❸で乗車予定の列車を変更したい旨を伝えている。1人目の女性は❹で予約を別の列車に変更できると伝え、❺でチケットを預かり、その手続きを進めている。よって、1人目の女性は鉄道の係員で、会話は鉄道駅で行われていると考えられる。
> (C) 男性がこの後の予定として会議があることを述べているだけ。

45 Why does the man request a change?

(A) An event was moved.
(B) A product was not delivered.
(C) A meeting was postponed.
(D) A service was canceled.

男性はなぜ変更を依頼しているのですか。

(A) イベントが変更になった。
(B) 製品が配達されなかった。
(C) 会議が延期された。
(D) サービスが中止された。

> **正解 C** 男性は、乗車予定の列車を伝えた後、❸「会議が数時間後ろにずれたので、私たちはこれより後の列車に乗りたい」と、予約を変更したい理由を伝えている。❸の our meeting was pushed back を a meeting was postponed と表現している(C)が正解。postpone「～を延期する」。
> (A) move「～(の日時・場所など)を変更する」。

46 What does Sara suggest?

(A) Visiting a tourist attraction
(B) Making a dinner reservation
(C) Rescheduling a meeting
(D) Working on a presentation

Saraは何を提案していますか。

(A) 観光名所を訪れること
(B) 夕食の予約を入れること
(C) 会議の日時を変更すること
(D) 発表の作業に取り組むこと

> **正解 D** 男性が❻で、同僚のSaraに空いた時間に何をすべきかと尋ねているのに対し、Saraは、❼「営業の実演をもう一度おさらいした方がいいかもしれない」と提案している。よって、❼の go over our sales demonstration を working on a presentation と表している(D)が正解。work on ～「～に取り組む」、presentation「発表」。
> (A) Saraが訪れることを提案しているのはカフェであり、tourist attraction「観光名所」ではない。
> (C) reschedule「～の日時を変更する」。

Words & Phrases

express 急行列車　　colleague 同僚　　push back ～ ～(予定など)を遅らせる
transfer ～ to … ～を…に移す　　reservation 予約　　extra 余分な　　go over ～ ～を見直す　　demonstration 実演

Questions 47 through 49 refer to the following conversation.

🇬🇧 w ❶The assembly room looks ready for Mr. Larson's retirement celebration. **The florist just delivered the centerpieces.**

🇨🇦 M It looks great. But I was thinking, ❷maybe we should change the audio system. ❸The audio in this room is never very good.

🇬🇧 w You're right. ❹There's another room on the second floor that has a new system. I wonder if we could use it here.

🇨🇦 M ❺You know Eiko Sasaki, right? ❻She's very good with equipment like this. Maybe she can help you.

🇬🇧 w That's a good idea. ❼I'll go talk to her now.

問題47-49は次の会話に関するものです。

集会室は、Larsonさんの退職祝いパーティーの準備が整ったようですね。花屋がつい先ほど、テーブル中央に置く装飾品を届けてくれました。

とてもすてきに見えますね。でも、考えていたのですが、私たちは音響装置を変えるべきかもしれませんよ。この部屋の音響は決して良好ではありませんから。

その通りですね。2階にある別の部屋には新しい装置があります。それをここで使えたらいいかと思うのですが。

Eiko Sasakiをご存じですよね? 彼女はこの手の機器の扱いに精通しています。彼女が手助けしてくれるかもしれません。

それは名案ですね。今から彼女に話をしに行ってみます。

---

47 Where does the conversation take place?

(A) In a florist shop
(B) In an assembly room
(C) In an electronics store
(D) In a restaurant

会話はどこで行われていますか。

(A) 花屋
(B) 集会室
(C) 電子機器店
(D) レストラン

正解 **B** 女性は❶「集会室は、Larsonさんの退職祝いパーティーの準備が整ったようだ」と述べている。男性も部屋の準備に言及し、❸でこの部屋の音響が良好ではないと伝え、女性は❹で、新しい装置をここで使うことを提案している。よって、会話は集会室で行われていると分かる。
(A) 女性は花屋から届いた装飾品に言及しているだけ。
(C) 音響装置について話しているが、電子機器店にいるわけではない。electronics「電子機器」。

---

48 What problem does the man mention?

(A) A poor sound system
(B) Bad lighting
(C) Not enough seats
(D) A late delivery

男性はどんな問題について述べていますか。

(A) 性能の悪い音響装置
(B) 劣悪な照明
(C) 不十分な座席数
(D) 配達の遅延

正解 **A** 男性は❷で、部屋の音響装置を変更するべきかもしれないと述べ、❸「この部屋の音響は決して良好ではない」と問題点に言及している。❸のnever very goodをpoor「(品質の)劣った」と表している(A)が正解。sound system「音響装置」。
(B) 男性が問題を指摘しているのは音響装置であり、lighting「照明(装置)」ではない。
(D) 花屋からの配達物への言及はあるが、それが遅延しているとは述べられていない。

---

49 Why will the woman talk to Ms. Sasaki?

(A) To help prepare a speech
(B) To reserve a meeting room
(C) To check on a florist-shop order
(D) To get help with some equipment

女性はなぜSasakiさんと話をするつもりなのですか。

(A) スピーチの準備を手伝うため
(B) 会議室を予約するため
(C) 花屋の注文を確認するため
(D) 機器について助力を得るため

正解 **D** ❹で、別の部屋の音響装置をここで使用する案について話す女性に対し、男性は❺でEiko Sasakiという人物を挙げ、❻「彼女はこの手の機器の扱いに精通している。彼女が手助けしてくれるかもしれない」と述べている。これに対し、女性は名案だと言い、❼で、今から彼女に話をしに行ってみると述べている。つまり、女性は音響機器について手助けを得るためにSasakiさんと話すつもりだと判断できる。(D)が正解。
(A) help do「~するのを手伝う」、prepare「~を準備する」。
(B) reserve「~を予約する」。
(C) check on ~「~を確かめる」。

Words & Phrases

assembly room 集会室 retirement 退職 celebration 祝賀会 florist 花屋
centerpiece (食卓などの中央に置く花などの)装飾物 audio 音響(の) wonder if ~ ~かなと思う
be good with ~ ~の扱いが上手である equipment 機器 go (and) do ~しに行く

Questions 50 through 52 refer to the following conversation.

🇨🇦 M Hi, Bianca. ❶Have you heard anything about budget cuts? ❷Ms. Han was supposed to let everyone know after the meeting with the directors.

🇬🇧 W The meeting isn't over yet. I really hope funding for our research on long-life batteries isn't cut.

🇨🇦 M I think everyone understands how important that research is to the future of the company.

🇬🇧 W You're right. ❸There might not be immediate profits from our long-life battery project, but I think we need to continue doing it.

問題50-52は次の会話に関するものです。

こんにちは、Bianca。予算削減について何か聞きましたか。重役陣との会議後に、Hanさんが皆に知らせてくれるはずでしたが。

会議はまだ終わっていません。長寿命バッテリーに関する私たちの研究への資金が削減されないことを切に望みます。

あの研究が当社の将来にとっていかに重要なものであるかについては、誰もが理解していると思いますよ。

その通りですね。私たちの長寿命バッテリーのプロジェクトからすぐに利益は出ないかもしれませんが、当社はその研究を継続する必要があると思います。

50 What does the man want to know?

(A) Whether an applicant was hired
(B) Whether a deadline was extended
(C) Whether an announcement was made
(D) Whether a research project has begun

男性は何を知りたいと思っていますか。

(A) 応募者が採用されたかどうか
(B) 最終期限が延長されたかどうか
(C) 発表が行われたかどうか
(D) 研究プロジェクトが開始したかどうか

正解 C 男性は女性に❶「予算削減について何か聞いたか」と尋ね、❷で、Hanさんが皆に周知することになっていたと続けている。このことから、男性は予算についての発表が行われたかどうかを知りたいと判断できるので、(C)が正解。make an announcement「発表する」。
(A) applicant「応募者」、hire「～を雇用する」。
(B) deadline「最終期限」、extend「～を延長する」。
(D) 研究プロジェクトはすでに進行中のものとして言及されている。

51 What does the woman imply when she says, "The meeting isn't over yet"?

(A) A suggestion will be used.
(B) A technical problem has been resolved.
(C) A security office has not been contacted.
(D) A decision has not been revealed.

"The meeting isn't over yet" という発言で、女性は何を示唆していますか。

(A) 提案が採用されるだろう。
(B) 技術的な問題が解決された。
(C) 保安課は連絡を受けていない。
(D) 決定事項が明らかにされていない。

正解 D 男性は、❶で予算削減について何か聞いたかと女性に尋ね、続けて❷「重役陣との会議後に、Hanさんが皆に知らせてくれるはずだった」と付け加えている。それに対して女性は下線部の発言で、会議がまだ終了していないことを伝えている。よって、女性は予算削減に関する決定事項はまだ知らされていないことを示唆していると考えられるので、未発表の状態を現在完了形で表している(D)が正解。decision「決定」、reveal「～を明らかにする」。
(A) suggestion「提案」。
(B) technical「技術的な」、resolve「～を解決する」。
(C) security office「保安課」。

52 What does the woman suggest about the battery project?

(A) It was originally her idea.
(B) It may not make money at first.
(C) It is nearly completed.
(D) It will be sold to another company.

女性はバッテリーのプロジェクトについて何を示唆していますか。

(A) それは、元々は彼女のアイデアだった。
(B) それは、最初はもうからないかもしれない。
(C) それは完了目前である。
(D) それは別の会社に売却される予定である。

正解 B 研究の重要性について話す男性に対し、女性は肯定した後、❸「私たちの長寿命バッテリーのプロジェクトからすぐに利益は出ないかもしれない」と、プロジェクトが最初はもうけを出さない可能性を示唆している。よって、(B)が正解。suggest「～を示唆する」。make money「利益を得る」、at first「最初は」。
(A) プロジェクトの発案者は話題にされていない。originally「元々は」。
(C) nearly「ほぼ、もう少しで」。

Words & Phrases
budget 予算　be supposed to do ～するはずである　let ～ know ～に知らせる
director 重役　over 終わって　funding 資金　research 研究　long-life （バッテリーなどが）長持ちする
immediate 即座の　profit 利益　continue doing ～することを続ける

Questions 53 through 55 refer to the following conversation with three speakers.

🇺🇸 W Excuse me, ❶I was looking at the smartphones that your store sells. ❷I'd really like to see the way that they display information. Can I turn any of them on?

🇨🇦 M ❸These are just for display and they're not charged. I do have some charged ones, though. Is there one, in particular, you'd like to see?

🇺🇸 W ❹This blue one. ❺It looks like it's being discounted.

🇨🇦 M OK, this shouldn't be a problem. ❻I'll get the manager. Murat?

🇦🇺 M Hi, I'm Murat, the manager. I overheard the conversation, and I have the model you're interested in right here. ❼You should know that the sales discount ends Sunday. ❽After that the price will go up.

問題53-55は3人の話し手による次の会話に関するものです。

すみません、こちらのお店で販売しているスマートフォンを見ていました。それが情報を表示している状態をぜひ見たいのですが。どれかの電源を入れてみてもいいですか。

これらは陳列専用でして、充電されておりません。ですが、充電済みのものが幾つかございますよ。特にご覧になりたいものはございますか。

この青いものです。それは割引中のようですね。

かしこまりました、こちらは問題ないはずです。店長を呼んでまいります。Murat?

こんにちは、店長のMuratと申します。お話を耳にしたのですが、ちょうどこちらにお客さまがご関心をお持ちの機種がございます。特別割引は日曜日に終了するということをご承知おきください。その後は値段が上がります。

---

53 Where does the conversation most likely take place?

(A) In a classroom
(B) In an automobile dealership
(C) In an electronics store
(D) In a newspaper office

会話はどこで行われていると考えられますか。

(A) 教室
(B) 自動車の販売代理店
(C) 電子機器店
(D) 新聞社

正解 C 女性はExcuse meと男性に声を掛けてから、❶「こちらのお店で販売しているスマートフォンを見ていた」と述べ、続けて❷では、画面表示の確認のために電源を入れてもいいか許可を求めている。これに対して1人目の男性は❸で、その商品は陳列専用であると伝えている。よって、会話はスマートフォンを販売する店で行われていると考えられる。electronics「電子機器」。
(B) automobile「自動車」、dealership「販売代理店」。

---

54 Why does the man get the manager?

(A) To address a complaint
(B) To report some damage
(C) To unlock a display case
(D) To show a sample product

男性はなぜ、店長を呼んでいるのですか。

(A) 苦情に対処するため
(B) 損傷を報告するため
(C) 陳列ケースを解錠するため
(D) 製品の見本を見せるため

正解 D スマートフォンの画面表示を見てみたいと述べた女性に、1人目の男性は特に見たい機種はあるかと尋ね、女性は❹「この青いものだ」と指し示している。1人目の男性はそれを受けて、❻で店長を呼んでいる。よって、女性の示したスマートフォンの見本を見せるために店長を呼んでいると分かるので、(D)が正解。
(A) address「～に対処する」、complaint「苦情」。
(B) report「～を報告する」、damage「損傷」。
(C) unlock「～を解錠する」。

---

55 What will happen after Sunday?

(A) A new shipment will arrive.
(B) A discount will no longer be in effect.
(C) A repair will be completed.
(D) A new employee will start work.

日曜日の後に何が起こりますか。

(A) 新たな発送品が到着する。
(B) 割引がもはや有効ではなくなる。
(C) 修理作業が完了する。
(D) 新しい従業員が就業を開始する。

正解 B ❹・❺より、女性は割引中の青いスマートフォンに興味を持っていると分かる。その充電済みの見本を示しながら、男性は❼「特別割引は日曜日に終了するのを知っておいてほしい」と述べ、続けて❽で、その後には値段が上がると補足している。よって、(B)が正解。no longer ～「もはや～ではない」、in effect「有効で」。
(C) repair「修理(作業)」。

Words & Phrases

display ～を表示する　　turn on ～ ～の電源を入れる　　display 陳列　　charge ～を充電する
though でも　　in particular 特に　　it looks like ～ ～のようである　　manager 責任者、店長
overhear ～を偶然耳にする　　be interested in ～ ～に関心を持っている　　go up (値段などが)上がる

Questions 56 through 58 refer to the following conversation.

問題56-58は次の会話に関するものです。

W Hey, Ozan. ❶Are you going to attend the company-wide dinner tomorrow?

ねえ、Ozan。あなたは明日の全社夕食会に出席する予定ですか。

M ❷Probably not. It should be fun, though, and ❸I know all sales professionals like us are encouraged to attend.

おそらく出席しません。でも、それは楽しいはずですし、私たちのような営業専門職の者は皆、出席するよう奨励されているということは知っています。

W That's right. The entire business-development team will be there.

その通りです。事業開発チームは全員出席する予定ですよ。

M ❹I'd like to, but I'm working late. We have an important new client who needs a lot of attention.

私も出席したいのですが、残業することになっています。私たちは大変な気配りを必要とする重要な新規顧客を抱えているので。

W Oh, are you assigned to the Crystal Communications account?

ああ、あなたはCrystal通信社の担当なのですか。

M That's right. Didn't I hear more staff would be assigned to this account?

そうなんです。この顧客にもっと多くのスタッフが割り当てられる予定だと聞いたんじゃなかったかな。

W I think there was a meeting about it. ❺I'll check the meeting minutes and see if a decision was made.

それに関する会議があったと思います。会議の議事録を確認して、決定が下されたかどうか見てみますね。

---

56 What part of the company do the speakers work in?

(A) Finance
(B) Product development
(C) Information technology
(D) Sales

話し手たちは会社のどんな部門で働いていますか。

(A) 財務
(B) 製品開発
(C) 情報技術
(D) 営業

正解 D ❶で全社夕食会に出席する予定かと尋ねる女性に対し、男性は❷でおそらく出席しないと言い、❸「私たちのような営業専門職の者は皆、出席するよう奨励されているということは知っている」と述べている。よって2人は同じ会社の営業部門で働いていると判断できる。part「部分」。
(A) finance「財務」。
(B) product development「製品開発」。
(C) information technology「情報技術」。

---

57 What does the man say about a company dinner?

(A) He will meet a new client there.
(B) He is helping with preparations for it.
(C) He may not be able to attend.
(D) He would like to bring a guest.

男性は会社の夕食会について何と言っていますか。

(A) 彼はそこで新規顧客と会う予定である。
(B) 彼はその準備を手伝うことになっている。
(C) 彼は出席できないかもしれない。
(D) 彼は招待客を連れて行きたいと思っている。

正解 C ❶で、全社夕食会に出席予定かと尋ねられている男性は、❷で、おそらく出席しないと伝えており、❹でも、出席したいが残業する予定だと述べている。よって、夕食会に出席できない見込みであることを、可能性を示す助動詞mayを使って表現している(C)が正解。
(A) 新規顧客への言及はあるが、夕食会で会うとは述べられていない。
(B) preparation「準備」への言及はない。

---

58 What does the woman say she will check?

(A) Some meeting notes
(B) A guest list
(C) Some company policies
(D) A corporate calendar

女性は何を確認すると言っていますか。

(A) 会議の記録
(B) 招待客名簿
(C) 会社の方針
(D) 会社の予定表

正解 A 女性は、Crystal通信社の顧客担当の増員についての会議があったと思うと述べてから、❺「会議の議事録を確認して、決定が下されたかどうか見てみる」と伝えている。よって、❺のthe meeting minutesをsome meeting notesと表している(A)が正解。notes「メモ、記録」。

Words & Phrases

company-wide 全社規模の　　professional 専門職の人
encourage ~ to do ~に…するよう奨励する　　entire 全体の　　business-development 事業開発の　　attention 注意、配慮
assign ~ to … ~を…に配属する　　account 得意先、顧客　　minutes 議事録　　make a decision 決定を下す

Questions 59 through 61 refer to the following conversation.

M ❶Have you had time to review the results of the testing we've been conducting?

W Not all of them yet. ❷We've completed most of the independent tests involving our new line of vacuum cleaners. We'll have enough data to write a formal review soon.

M I have to say, ❸I think this new line looks really sharp. I'm impressed. ❹They'll be the most attractive models on the market.

W ❺I agree. The design department did a great job with these.

M I hope the performance results will be equally successful.

W I think they will. ❻I'll send you some of the preliminary results from some tests, if you'd like. Look for it in an e-mail later today.

問題59-61は次の会話に関するものです。

私たちが実施してきた試験の結果を精査する時間はありましたか。

まだ全部はできていません。私たちは、当社の電気掃除機の新シリーズに関わる個別試験のほとんどを完了しました。間もなく、正式な審査結果を書くのに十分なデータがそろうでしょう。

本当に、この新シリーズはすごく見栄えがいいと思います。私は感心しています。これは市場で最も魅力的なモデルになりそうです。

同感です。デザイン部はこれに関して素晴らしい仕事をしてくれました。

性能試験結果も同様に好成績になるといいのですが。

そうなると思いますよ。もしよければ、試験の中間結果の一部をお送りしますよ。本日後ほど、Eメールの中にそれを探してみてください。

---

59 What are the speakers mainly discussing?

(A) Media coverage of their company's products
(B) Advertising options for new products
(C) Additional employees for a product launch
(D) Testing of a new product line

話し手たちは主に何について話し合っていますか。

(A) 自社の製品についてのメディア報道
(B) 新製品のための広告の選択肢
(C) 製品の発売開始に向けた従業員の増員
(D) 新しい製品シリーズの試験

正解 D ❶で、試験の結果を精査する時間があったかと尋ねる男性に対し、女性は全部はできていないと伝えた後、❷で、電気掃除機の新シリーズに関わる個別試験のほとんどが完了したと述べている。❻でも、その新しい製品シリーズの試験結果に言及している。よって、(D)が正解。
(A) coverage「報道」。
(B) advertising「広告」、option「選択肢」。
(C) additional「追加の」、launch「発売開始」。

60 What are the speakers impressed with?

(A) The durability of a product
(B) Cost-saving measures
(C) The visual appeal of a product
(D) The positive reputation of a company

話し手たちは何に感心していますか。

(A) 製品の耐久性
(B) コスト削減の方策
(C) 製品の視覚的な魅力
(D) 会社についての好意的な評判

正解 C 男性は❸で、新シリーズの見栄えの良さに感心していることを伝え、❹では市場で最も魅力的なものになるだろうと述べている。この発言に対し、女性も❺で同意し、デザイン部の仕事ぶりを称賛している。よって、2人は新製品の見た目の魅力に感心していると分かるので、(C)が正解。visual「視覚の」、appeal「魅力」。
(A) durability「耐久性」。
(B) cost-saving「コスト削減の」、measures「方策」。
(D) positive「肯定的な」、reputation「評判」。

61 What does the woman offer to do?

(A) Organize a meeting
(B) Take some pictures
(C) Conduct some interviews
(D) Send some results

女性は何をすることを申し出ていますか。

(A) 会議を企画する
(B) 写真を撮る
(C) 面談を実施する
(D) 結果を送付する

正解 D 女性は、新しいシリーズ製品の性能試験結果も好成績になると思うと述べてから、❻「もしよければ、試験の中間結果の一部を送る」と申し出て、後でEメールを見てみるよう伝えている。よって、(D)が正解。
(A) organize「〜を企画する」。
(C) interview「面談、面接」。

Words & Phrases

conduct 〜を実施する　independent 独立した　involve 〜を含む、〜に関連する
vacuum cleaner 電気掃除機　I have to say 本当に ★意見を強調する際に使う　sharp 粋な、スマートな
impress 〜に感銘を与える　performance 性能　equally 同様に　preliminary 準備の、予備段階の　look for 〜 〜を探す

TEST 2 PART 3

Questions 62 through 64 refer to the following conversation and table.

W Hi, ❶I'm calling about a job posting I saw on the Law Offices of Crawford and Touloun Web site. ❷I have a question about one of the positions.

M OK, but first I need to know the office location of the job you are interested in.

W It's at the downtown office. I would like to apply for a position, but ❸I wanted to find out if remote work is possible. ❹I live far from the city, and a daily commute would be challenging for me.

M ❺Which position are you interested in?

W ❻The one for a paralegal.

M ❼Let me connect you with the manager of that department.

W Thank you very much.

問題62-64は次の会話と表に関するものです。

もしもし、Crawford and Touloun法律事務所のウェブサイトで見た求人の件でお電話を差し上げています。職の一つに関して質問があります。

分かりました。ですが先に、ご関心をお持ちの職のオフィス所在地を教えていただく必要があります。

中心街のオフィスのものです。ある職に応募したいと思っているのですが、遠隔勤務が可能かどうかを知りたく思いました。私はその市から遠い所に住んでいまして、日々の通勤が私にとって大変になりそうなのです。

どの職にご関心がおありですか。

弁護士補助員のものです。

担当部署の責任者におつなぎします。

ありがとうございます。

Downtown Office	
Role	**Main Contact**
Technology support	Emily Kalkhof
Case-intake lead	Lucas Betz
Office manager	Eun-Young Jun
Paralegal manager	Joyce Reno

中心街のオフィス	
職務	主たる連絡先
技術サポート	Emily Kalkhof
案件受入窓口主任	Lucas Betz
オフィス責任者	Eun-Young Jun
弁護士補助員責任者	Joyce Reno

62 What is the woman calling about?

(A) A shipment
(B) A job listing
(C) A product review
(D) A schedule change

女性は何について電話をしていますか。

(A) 発送品
(B) 求人情報
(C) 製品レビュー
(D) 予定の変更

正解 **B** 女性は❶「Crawford and Touloun法律事務所のウェブサイトで見た求人の件で電話している」と用件を切り出した後、❷で、そのうちの一つの職について質問があると付け足している。よって、女性は、求人情報が掲載されているウェブサイトを見て、その件で電話していると分かるので、(B)が正解。listing「一覧表」。
(A) shipment「発送品」。
(C) review「批評、レビュー」。

63 What problem does the woman mention?

(A) A flaw in a product
(B) Difficulty finding a building
(C) A long commute
(D) A Web site error

女性はどんな問題について述べていますか。

(A) 製品の欠陥
(B) 建物を見つけることの困難さ
(C) 長時間の通勤
(D) ウェブサイト上のエラー

正解 **C** 女性は、中心街のオフィスの職に応募したい旨を伝え、❸で遠隔勤務が可能かどうかを知りたいと述べている。その理由として❹「私はその市から遠い所に住んでおり、日々の通勤が私にとって大変になりそうなのだ」と、長時間の通勤という懸念点に言及している。よって、(C)が正解。
(A) flaw「欠陥」。
(B) difficulty「困難」。
(D) ウェブサイトへの言及はあるが、エラーについては述べられていない。

64 Look at the graphic. Who will the woman speak with next?

(A) Emily Kalkhof
(B) Lucas Betz
(C) Eun-Young Jun
(D) Joyce Reno

図を見てください。女性は次に誰と話をしますか。

(A) Emily Kalkhof
(B) Lucas Betz
(C) Eun-Young Jun
(D) Joyce Reno

正解 **D** 中心街のオフィスでの職について、❺でどの職に関心を抱いているかと尋ねる男性に対し、女性は❻「弁護士補助員のものだ」と答えている。この返答に対して男性は、❼で担当部署の責任者につなぐと伝えている。図を見ると、「弁護士補助員責任者」の連絡先は「Joyce Reno」とあるので、(D)が正解。

Words & Phrases table 表　posting 投稿、掲示　law office 法律事務所　position 職　first 最初に、まず
location 位置、所在地　be interested in ～ ～に関心を持っている　downtown 中心街(の)、商業地区(の)
apply for ～ ～に応募する　find out if ～ ～かどうかを知る　remote work 遠隔勤務　far from ～ ～から遠くに
commute 通勤(時間)　challenging 骨の折れる　paralegal 弁護士補助員　connect ～ with … (電話で)～を…につなぐ

表　role 役割、職務　main 主な　technology 技術　case-intake (訴訟)案件受け入れの　lead 首位の人

Questions 65 through 67 refer to the following conversation and building directory.

W Hi, ❶I'm here to visit Maria Gaines. ❷Her office is in the newsroom. I believe I need to check in here at the front desk.

M Yes, I'll call up to the newsroom and let Maria know she has a visitor. ❸I have to warn you, there's a large tour group in the building. ❹It's very crowded and noisy.

W Oh, I've heard that the building is of historical interest to architecture enthusiasts. If it's OK, I'll take a look around after my appointment!

M No problem. ❺While I'm ringing Maria, please fill out this form so I can create your temporary ID.

W Sure thing.

問題65-67は次の会話と建物案内板に関するものです。

こんにちは、Maria Gainesさんを訪ねてこちらへ伺いました。彼女の執務室はニュース編集室にあります。こちらの受付で記帳する必要があるかと思いまして。

はい、ニュース編集室に電話をして、Mariaにお客さまがお見えだと知らせますね。申し上げておきますが、建物内には大人数の団体ツアー客がいらっしゃいます。それで非常に混雑していて騒がしくなっております。

ああ、この建物は建築ファンにとって歴史的に興味深いものだと聞いています。もし構わなければ、面会の約束の後に私も見て回ろうかと思います!

問題ございません。Mariaに電話をかけている間、お客さまの臨時IDをお作りできるよう、この用紙にご記入をお願いします。

もちろんです。

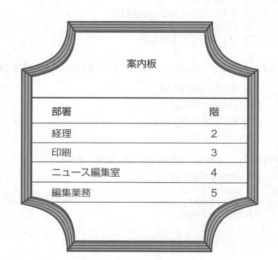

Directory	
Department	**Floor**
Accounting	2
Printing	3
Newsroom	4
Editorial Services	5

案内板	
部署	階
経理	2
印刷	3
ニュース編集室	4
編集業務	5

65 Look at the graphic. Where is the woman's appointment?

(A) On floor 2
(B) On floor 3
(C) On floor 4
(D) On floor 5

図を見てください。女性の面会の約束の場所はどこですか。

(A) 2階
(B) 3階
(C) 4階
(D) 5階

正解 **C**　女性は❶でMaria Gainesを訪ねに来たと訪問目的を伝えた後、❷「彼女の執務室はニュース編集室にある」と述べている。図を見ると、ニュース編集室が位置するのは4階なので、(C)が正解。
(A) (B) (D) それぞれ経理、印刷、編集業務の部署が位置する階だが、いずれにも言及がない。

66 What does the man warn the woman about?

(A) A broken air conditioner
(B) A canceled delivery
(C) Employee absences
(D) Crowds in the building

男性は女性に、何について注意喚起していますか。

(A) 故障中のエアコン
(B) キャンセルされた配達
(C) 従業員の不在
(D) 建物内の人混み

正解 **D**　男性は❸で、建物内に大人数の団体ツアー客がいることについて女性に注意喚起し、続けて❹「それで非常に混雑していて騒がしくなっている」と補足している。よって、(D)が正解。crowd「人混み」。
(A) broken「故障した」、air conditioner「エアコン」。
(C) absence「不在」。

67 What does the man ask the woman to do?

(A) Submit a payment
(B) Fill out a form
(C) Book an appointment
(D) Call a coworker

男性は女性に何をするよう頼んでいますか。

(A) 支払金を差し出す
(B) 用紙に記入する
(C) 面会を予約する
(D) 同僚に電話する

正解 **B**　男性は、❺「Mariaに電話をかけている間、あなたの臨時IDを作れるよう、この用紙に記入してほしい」と女性に頼んでいる。よって、(B)が正解。
(C) 女性がMariaと会う予定はすでに設定済みだと考えられるので、不適切。book「～を予約する」。
(D) 男性は今から自分がMariaに電話すると言っているのであり、女性に電話するよう頼んではいない。coworker「同僚」。

TEST 2　PART 3

Words & Phrases　building　建物　directory　（建物の）案内板　newsroom　ニュース編集室、報道室
check in　（受付などで）到着を記録する　front desk　受付　call up to ～　～に電話する　warn　～に注意喚起する
group　団体　crowded　混雑した　noisy　騒がしい
be of interest to ～　～にとって興味深いものである　★〈of＋名詞〉で性質を表す　historical　歴史的な　architecture　建築
enthusiast　愛好家　take a look around　見て回る　appointment　会う約束、面会　ring　～に電話をかける
fill out ～　～に記入する　temporary　臨時の　ID　身元証明書　★identificationの略

建物案内板　accounting　経理　printing　印刷　editorial　編集の　service　サービス、業務

Questions 68 through 70 refer to the following conversation and graph.

🇨🇦 M I'm really happy the four new retail outlets our company opened in the metropolitan area are bringing in lots of shoppers. ❶Have you seen the quarterly average-customer numbers?

🇬🇧 W Yes, ❷the store I went to earlier today is the second-most visited. It almost seemed overcrowded!

🇨🇦 M Well, that's a good problem to have! The regional operations manager should be pleased when we present these numbers.

🇬🇧 W I agree. ❸I'm just a little concerned that the rapid expansion leaves us without enough workers. ❹All those shoppers I saw made me think we could use more staff.

🇨🇦 M ❺I suggest we advertise some positions.

問題68-70は次の会話とグラフに関するものです。

当社が大都市圏にオープンした4つの新しい小売店が大勢の買い物客を集めていることをとても喜ばしく思います。四半期の平均顧客数は見ましたか。

はい、私が今日先立って行った店舗は来店客数が2番目に多い所です。超満員と言ってもいいくらいに見えましたよ!

おや、それはうれしい問題ですね! その地域の運営責任者は、私たちがこれらの数値を見せたら喜ぶでしょうね。

同感です。ただ、急速な拡大によって当社が従業員不足に陥ることが少し心配です。あの大勢の買い物客を見て、もっと多くの従業員がいれば助かるだろうと思わせられました。

幾つかの職の求人広告を出してはどうでしょう。

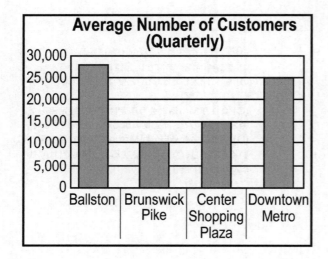

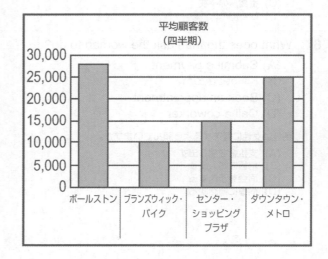

68 Look at the graphic. Which store did the woman visit today?

(A) Ballston
(B) Brunswick Pike
(C) Center Shopping Plaza
(D) Downtown Metro

図を見てください。女性は今日、どの店舗を訪れましたか。

(A) ボールストン
(B) ブランズウィック・パイク
(C) センター・ショッピングプラザ
(D) ダウンタウン・メトロ

正解 **D** 新規オープンした4店舗について❶で、四半期の平均顧客数を見たかと尋ねる男性に対し、女性はYesと肯定した後、❷「私が今日先立って行った店舗は来店客数が2番目に多い所だ」と伝えている。図を見ると、平均顧客数が2番目に多いのはダウンタウン・メトロなので、(D)が正解。

69 Why is the woman concerned?

(A) A facility failed a test.
(B) A store closed early.
(C) More staff may be needed.
(D) New designs are not approved.

女性はなぜ心配しているのですか。

(A) 施設が審査に不合格だった。
(B) 店が早く閉店した。
(C) より多くの従業員が必要かもしれない。
(D) 新しい設計案が承認されない。

正解 **C** 女性は店舗の集客の多さを喜びながらも、❸で、急速な拡大によって従業員不足に陥ることが心配だと懸念を述べ、続けて❹「あの大勢の買い物客を見て、もっと多くの従業員がいれば助かるだろうと思わせられた」と話している。よって、(C)が正解。
(A) facility「施設」、fail「～に不合格になる」。
(D) design「設計、デザイン」、approve「～を承認する」。

70 What does the man suggest?

(A) Visiting more stores
(B) Creating some advertisements
(C) Launching an online survey
(D) Purchasing more inventory

男性は何を提案していますか。

(A) もっと多くの店舗を訪問すること
(B) 広告を作成すること
(C) オンライン上のアンケート調査を開始すること
(D) もっと多くの在庫を仕入れること

正解 **B** ❸・❹で、自分たちの会社の人手不足について懸念する女性に対し、男性は❺「幾つかの職の求人広告を出してはどうか」と提案している。よって、この提案内容をcreating some advertisementsと表現している(B)が正解。create「～を作成する」、advertisement「広告」。
(C) launch「～を開始する」、survey「アンケート調査」。
(D) inventory「在庫(品)」。

Words & Phrases　　be happy (that) ～　～ということをうれしく思う　　retail outlet　小売店
metropolitan　主要都市の、大都市の　　bring in ～　～をもたらす、～を呼び込む　　shopper　買い物客　　quarterly　四半期の
average-customer number　平均顧客数　　second-most　2番目に多く　　almost　ほぼ～、～に近い　　seem　～に見える
overcrowded　超満員の、すし詰めの　　regional　地域の　　operations manager　運営責任者　　be pleased　喜ぶ
present　～を提示する、～を見せる　　be concerned that ～　～ということを心配している　　rapid　急速な　　expansion　拡大
leave ～ …　～を…のままにしておく　　could use ～　～があるとありがたい、～が必要である
suggest (that) ～　～ということを提案する　　advertise　～の広告を出す

グラフ　average　平均の

Questions 71 through 73 refer to the following telephone message.

🇬🇧 W

Good afternoon, Ms. Alamri. I'm calling from the Warlington Film Office. ❶The city has accepted your application for a permit to film here. Since you need some streets to be closed while you're making your movie, ❷you now need to submit a traffic-control plan for approval. ❸Given how soon you aim to film, I recommend using the online portal—you'll just need to set up a username and password. ❹It gets processed much faster than mail. If you have any questions, call me at 555-0199.

問題71-73は次の電話のメッセージに関するものです。

こんにちは、Alamri様。Warlington映画事務所からお電話しています。市は、あなたが出された当地での映画撮影の許可証の申請を受諾しました。映画製作中に幾つかの通りを通行止めにすることを必要とされているので、これから、交通規制計画書を提出して承認を得る必要があります。撮影のご希望時期まで間がないことを考慮しますと、オンラインポータルの利用をお勧めします——ユーザーネームとパスワードを設定すればいいだけです。その方が郵便よりもはるかに速く処理されます。ご質問があれば、555-0199まで私にお電話ください。

71 What information does the speaker give the listener?

(A) A policy has changed.
(B) A construction plan is being reviewed.
(C) An advertising campaign has started.
(D) A permit request was approved.

話し手は聞き手にどんな情報を提供していますか。
(A) 方針が変更になった。
(B) 建設計画書が見直されているところである。
(C) 広告キャンペーンが始まった。
(D) 許可証の要請が承認された。

> **正解 D** 話し手は、❶「市は、あなたが出した当地での映画撮影の許可証の申請を受諾した」と知らせている。よって、この通知内容をa permit requestを主語にし、approve「～を承認する」を用いて言い換えた(D)が正解。
> (B) 交通規制計画書に言及されているだけで、建設計画書は話題にされていない。construction「建設」、review「～を見直す」。
> (C) advertising「広告」。

72 What does the speaker say the listener should do next?

(A) Submit a traffic-control plan
(B) Write a summary of the film's story
(C) Confirm a project schedule
(D) Attend an information session

話し手は、聞き手が次に何をすべきだと言っていますか。
(A) 交通規制計画書を提出する
(B) 映画のあらすじを書く
(C) プロジェクトの予定を確認する
(D) 説明会に出席する

> **正解 A** 話し手は、聞き手が映画の製作中に通りを通行止めにする必要があることを理由に、❷「これから、交通規制計画書を提出して承認を得る必要がある」と説明している。よって、(A)が正解。
> (B) 話題は映画の撮影だが、あらすじへの言及はない。summary「要約」。
> (C) confirm「～を確認する」。
> (D) information session「説明会」。

73 What can the listener do to make the process happen more quickly?

(A) Pay an additional fee
(B) Use an online portal
(C) Make an in-person delivery
(D) Provide an e-mail address

手続きをより速めるために、聞き手は何をすることができますか。
(A) 追加料金を支払う
(B) オンラインポータルを利用する
(C) 自ら直接届ける
(D) Eメールアドレスを提供する

> **正解 B** 話し手は❷で、聞き手が交通規制計画書を提出する必要があると伝えてから、❸「撮影の希望時期まで間がないことを考慮すると、オンラインポータルの利用を勧める」と言い、❹で、その方が郵便よりも速く処理されると勧める理由を述べている。よって、(B)が正解。process「処理、手続き」。
> (A) additional「追加の」、fee「料金」。
> (C) make a delivery「配達する」、in-person「本人による、直接の」。
> (D) ポータルの利用にはユーザーネームとパスワードの設定が必要であると説明されているだけで、Eメールアドレスへの言及はない。

Words & Phrases		
accept ～を受諾する	application 申請	permit 許可証　traffic-control 交通規制の
approval 認可　given ～ ～を考慮に入れると	aim to *do* ～することを目指す	recommend *doing* ～することを勧める
portal ポータル ★入り口の役割を担うウェブサイト	process ～を処理する	mail 郵便

Questions 74 through 76 refer to the following instructions.

🇺🇸 W

❶Thank you all for volunteering to work this extra shift on a Saturday to help relocate our offices. ❷I really appreciate that you all volunteered for the work. ❸First, we're going to load the boxes and crates into the trucks outside. Be sure to use the carts that are in the lobby to move everything outside. If you have any questions, please ask me at any time. At about noon, we'll break for lunch. ❹Lunch is on the company today, so please let Mary know what you'd like to eat.

問題74-76は次の説明に関するものです。

当社オフィスの移転を手伝うために、土曜日にこの追加シフトの勤務を進んで引き受けてくださり、皆さんありがとうございます。皆さんがこの仕事を買って出てくださったことに、心より感謝いたします。まず、私たちは箱と木箱を外にあるトラックに積む予定です。必ずロビーにある台車を使用して全部を外に運び出してください。何かご質問があれば、いつでも私にお尋ねください。正午頃に、作業を中断して昼食にします。今日の昼食は会社持ちなので、ご自分が食べたいものをMaryに知らせてください。

---

74 Why does the speaker thank the listeners?

(A) For participating in a survey
(B) For carpooling to work
(C) For taking an additional shift
(D) For attracting new customers

話し手はなぜ聞き手に感謝しているのですか。

(A) 調査への参加に対して
(B) 自動車の相乗り通勤に対して
(C) 追加シフトを引き受けたことに対して
(D) 新規顧客の集客に対して

正解 **C** 話し手は❶「当社オフィスの移転を手伝うために、土曜日にこの追加シフトの勤務を進んで引き受けてくれて、皆さんありがとう」と聞き手に謝意を伝え、❷でも、仕事を買って出たことに対して重ねて感謝している。よって、(C)が正解。thank「～に感謝する」。additional「追加の」。
(A) participate in ～「～に参加する」、survey「調査」。
(B) carpool「(通勤などのために交替で)自家用車の相乗りをする」。
(D) attract「～を引き付ける」。

---

75 What will the listeners do first?

(A) Load some trucks
(B) Paint an office
(C) Complete a sale
(D) Design a new product

聞き手はまず何をする予定ですか。

(A) トラックに荷物を積む
(B) オフィスを塗装する
(C) 売却を完了する
(D) 新製品を設計する

正解 **A** 話し手は、❸「まず、私たちは箱と木箱を外にあるトラックに積む予定だ」と、聞き手に対して作業の流れを説明しているので、(A)が正解。load「～に荷物を積む」。
(B) オフィス移転の話題だが、塗装作業への言及はない。paint「～を塗装する」。
(D) design「～を設計する」。

---

76 Why should the listeners speak to Mary?

(A) To sign in
(B) To request an identification card
(C) To arrange payment details
(D) To give a lunch order

聞き手はなぜMaryと話をすべきなのですか。

(A) 出勤を記録するため
(B) 身元証明書を要請するため
(C) 支払いの詳細を取り決めるため
(D) 昼食の注文をするため

正解 **D** 話し手は、昼休憩に言及し、❹「今日の昼食は会社持ちなので、自分が食べたいものをMaryに知らせてください」と聞き手に伝えている。よって、(D)が正解。give an order「注文する」。
(A) sign in「(署名して)到着を記録する」。
(B) request「～を依頼する、～を要請する」、identification card「身元証明書」。
(C) arrange「～を取り決める、～を整える」、details「詳細情報」。

Words & Phrases

instructions 説明　volunteer to *do*　～することを進んで引き受ける、～することを買って出る
extra 追加の　help *do*　～するのを手伝う　relocate　～を移転させる
appreciate that ～　～ということを正しく認識する、～ということに感謝する　load　～を積む　crate　(運搬用の)木箱、木枠
be sure to *do*　必ず～する　move　～を移動させる　at any time　いつでも　break　(作業などを)中断する

TEST 2 PART 4

127

Questions 77 through 79 refer to the following introduction.

問題77-79は次の紹介に関するものです。

🍁 M

Good morning, visitors! ❶Thank you for joining me on a guided tour of the Fallburg City Museum. ❷This building holds countless treasures from the city's past and is especially well-known for its collection of eighteenth-century artifacts. We will concentrate on those galleries. Before we get started, ❸I recommend that you conclude your visit by enjoying a short film that covers the history of this magnificent building, which is itself a work of art. For now, ❹let's open our guidebooks and get started on the tour.

おはようございます、来館者の皆さま! フォールバーグ市立博物館のガイド付きツアーにご参加いただきありがとうございます。本館は当市の過去からの無数の貴重な品々を所蔵しており、特に18世紀の工芸品のコレクションでよく知られています。私たちはそれらの陳列室を集中的に見る予定です。開始前に申し上げておきますが、それ自体が芸術作品であるこの立派な建物の歴史を取り上げた短編映画を鑑賞してご来館を締めくくることをお勧めします。では、ガイドブックを開いてツアーを始めましょう。

77 Where does the speaker work?

(A) At a restaurant
(B) At a shopping mall
(C) At a concert hall
(D) At a museum

話し手はどこで働いていますか。

(A) レストラン
(B) ショッピングモール
(C) コンサートホール
(D) 博物館

正解 D 話し手は、❶「フォールバーグ市立博物館のガイド付きツアーに参加してくれてありがとう」と礼を述べ、❷ではその建物が所蔵する工芸品について言及している。よって、話し手はガイドとして博物館で働いていると判断できるので、(D)が正解。

78 What does the speaker recommend?

(A) Reading a biography
(B) Taking a break
(C) Watching a film
(D) Purchasing souvenirs

話し手は何を勧めていますか。

(A) 伝記を読むこと
(B) 休憩を取ること
(C) 映画を見ること
(D) 記念品を購入すること

正解 C 話し手は、これから行う博物館のツアーについてざっと説明し、❸「それ自体が芸術作品であるこの立派な建物の歴史を取り上げた短編映画を鑑賞して来館を締めくくることを勧める」と、最後に映画を見ることを勧めている。よって、(C)が正解。
(A) biography「伝記」。
(B) take a break「休憩を取る」。
(D) souvenir「記念品、土産」。

79 What does the speaker tell the listeners to do?

(A) Remain silent
(B) Take some notes
(C) Scan their tickets
(D) Open some books

話し手は聞き手に何をするよう伝えていますか。

(A) ずっと静かにしている
(B) メモを取る
(C) チケットをスキャンする
(D) 本を開く

正解 D 話し手は、❹「ガイドブックを開いてツアーを始めよう」と聞き手に呼び掛けている。よって、❹のopen our guidebooksをopen some booksと表現している(D)が正解。
(A) remain「〜のままである」、silent「静かな、無言の」。
(B) take notes「メモを取る」。
(C) scan「〜をスキャンする」。

Words & Phrases introduction 紹介　join 〜と(行動などを)共にする　guided ガイド付きの　building 建物　hold 〜を所有する　countless 無数の　treasure 宝物、(美術的・史的価値のある)貴重品　past 過去　be well-known for 〜 〜でよく知られている　especially 特に　collection 収蔵品、コレクション　eighteenth-century 18世紀の　artifact 工芸品、(史的価値のある)人工物　concentrate on 〜 〜に焦点を当てる　gallery 陳列室　get started 始める　recommend that 〜 〜ということを勧める　conclude 〜 by *doing* 〜を…することで締めくくる　cover 〜を取り扱う　magnificent 壮大な、立派な　itself それ自体　work of art 芸術作品　for now 差し当たり、では

Questions 80 through 82 refer to the following excerpt from a meeting.

🇬🇧 w

❶Let's start with a discussion about our participation in the upcoming trade show. ❷I have some questions about which devices our company should include in the product-demonstration session. **This is a major trade show, and it's important that we impress the audience.** ❸Some staff have suggested starting with our latest smartphone. <u>The phone has easily passed all internal testing.</u> ❹But I'd like to hear from more of you. ❺After this meeting, I want everyone in this room to send me a list of what new products you would most like to see demonstrated.

問題80-82は次の会議の抜粋に関するものです。

今度の見本市への当社の参加に関する話し合いから始めましょう。当社が製品実演会にどの機器を含めるべきかについて質問があります。これは主要な見本市であり、観衆に強い印象を与えることが重要です。一部のスタッフは当社の最新スマートフォンから始めることを提案しています。その電話機はあらゆる社内テストにすんなりと合格しました。でも、もう少し多くの皆さんから意見をもらいたいと思っています。この会議の後、この部屋にいる皆さんには、どの新製品の実演を最も見たいかについてのリストを私に送ってもらいたいと思います。

---

80 What does the speaker want to discuss?

(A) A television program
(B) A product demonstration
(C) A hiring event
(D) A store opening

話し手は何について話し合いたいと思っていますか。

(A) テレビ番組
(B) 製品の実演
(C) 雇用イベント
(D) 店の開店

正解 B 話し手は❶で、見本市への参加に関する話し合いから会議を始めることを述べ、続けて❷「当社が製品実演会にどの機器を含めるべきかについて質問がある」と話を切り出している。また、以降も製品実演に関する話を進めているので、(B)が正解。
(A) program「番組」。
(C)イベントに関連した話題だが、雇用関連のイベントではない。hiring「雇用」。

---

81 What does the speaker imply when she says, "The phone has easily passed all internal testing"?

(A) She thinks sales targets will be met.
(B) She hopes to receive good reviews.
(C) She believes a program needs changes.
(D) She agrees with a staff suggestion.

"The phone has easily passed all internal testing" という発言で、話し手は何を示唆していますか。

(A) 彼女は売り上げ目標が達成されるだろうと考えている。
(B) 彼女は高評価のレビューをもらうことを望んでいる。
(C) 彼女はプログラムに変更が必要であると考えている。
(D) 彼女はスタッフの提案に賛成である。

正解 D 話し手は、製品実演会で扱う機器の選択の話題で、❸「一部のスタッフは最新スマートフォンから始めることを提案している」と述べ、続けて下線部の発言で、同製品が社内テストを容易に通ったことを伝えている。よって、話し手は、製品の品質の高さを伝えることで、実演会では同製品の実演から始めるというスタッフの提案に賛成していると判断できる。suggestion「提案」。
(A) target「達成目標」、meet「～を満たす」。
(B) hope to do「～することを望む」。
(C) programが実演会の予定を表しているとしても、予定変更の必要性については述べられていない。

---

82 What does the speaker ask the listeners to do?

(A) Send a list of preferences
(B) Attend a training
(C) View a presentation
(D) Test a product

話し手は聞き手に何をするよう頼んでいますか。

(A) 望ましい製品のリストを送付する
(B) 研修に出席する
(C) 発表を見る
(D) 製品のテストをする

正解 A 話し手は製品実演会に含めるべき機器について、❹で、聞き手の意見が欲しいと伝えた後、❺で、どの新製品の実演を最も見たいかについてのリストを送るよう頼んでいる。よって、この内容をpreference「好み（のもの）、選択」を用いて表している(A)が正解。
(D) すでに行われた最新スマートフォンのテストへの言及はあるが、これからテストをするように頼んではいない。

TEST 2 PART 4

Words & Phrases

start with ～　～から始める　　participation　参加　　trade show　展示会、見本市
device　端末、機器　　product-demonstration　製品実演の　　major　大きい方の、主要な
impress　～に強い印象を与える、～を感心させる　　audience　観衆　　suggest doing　～することを提案する　　latest　最新の
pass　～に合格する　　internal　内部の、社内の　　see ～ done　～が…されるのを見る
demonstrate　～を実演する、～を実例で説明する

Questions 83 through 85 refer to the following telephone message.

問題83-85は次の電話のメッセージに関するものです。

🇺🇸 W

Hello, ❶I'm calling to ask about some tickets I purchased for the baseball game at City Stadium next weekend. I received an e-mail confirmation about this purchase, but I have a few questions. ❷It looks like we were charged for parking. Can you provide a refund for this part of the charge? <u>We plan to take public transportation</u>. Also, ❸the tickets were not attached to the e-mail. ❹Could you resend the e-mail with the tickets attached? Thanks for your help with these issues.

もしもし、私が購入した来週末の市営スタジアムでの野球の試合のチケットについてお尋ねするためにお電話しています。この購入に関する確認のEメールを受信しましたが、幾つか質問があります。私たちは駐車料金を請求されたようです。請求料金のこの部分を返金してもらえますか。<u>私たちは公共交通機関を利用するつもりです</u>。それから、チケットがEメールに添付されていませんでした。チケットを添付してEメールを再送していただけますか。これらの問題についての手助けをよろしくお願いします。

---

83 What will the speaker most likely attend?

(A) A museum opening
(B) A concert
(C) An awards ceremony
(D) A sports event

話し手は何に参加すると考えられますか。

(A) 博物館の開館式
(B) コンサート
(C) 表彰式
(D) スポーツイベント

正解 D 話し手は、❶「私が購入した来週末の市営スタジアムでの野球の試合のチケットについて尋ねるために電話している」と述べているので、(D)が正解。
(A) opening「オープニング式典」。
(C) awards ceremony「表彰式」。

---

84 Why does the speaker say, "<u>We plan to take public transportation</u>"?

(A) To suggest that there will be good weather
(B) To show that a distance is very short
(C) To explain a request
(D) To indicate that some traffic is expected

話し手はなぜ "We plan to take public transportation" と言っていますか。

(A) 天気がいいだろうということを示唆するため
(B) 距離が非常に短いということを示すため
(C) 要求の理由を説明するため
(D) ある程度の交通量が予想されるということを示すため

正解 C 話し手は❷で、請求された駐車料金を返金するよう聞き手に求めた後、下線部の発言で、自分たちが当日には公共交通機関を利用するつもりであることを伝えている。よって、話し手は、駐車料金を返金してほしいという要求の裏付けとなる理由を説明しているのだと判断できる。explain「～(の理由・意味など)を説明する」。
(A) suggest that ～「～ということを示唆する」。
(B) distance「距離」。
(D) indicate that ～「～ということを示す」、traffic「交通量、渋滞」、expect「～を予想する」。

---

85 What does the speaker mention about an e-mail?

(A) Some documents were not included.
(B) Some links to certain Web sites did not work.
(C) It should be forwarded to others.
(D) It contained clear instructions for a task.

話し手はEメールについて何と述べていますか。

(A) 幾つかの書類が含まれていなかった。
(B) 特定のウェブサイトへのリンクが機能しなかった。
(C) それは他の人々に転送されるべきである。
(D) それには、ある業務についての明確な指示が含まれていた。

正解 A 話し手は、購入に関する確認のEメールについて、❸「チケットがEメールに添付されていなかった」と問題点に言及し、続けて❹で、チケットを添付してEメールを再送するよう依頼している。よって、❸のthe ticketsをsome documentsと表現している(A)が正解。document「書類、文書」、include「～を含む」。
(B) certain「特定の」、work「正常に機能する」。
(C) forward ～ to …「～を…へ転送する」。
(D) contain「～を含む」、clear「明確な」、instructions「指示」、task「(課された)業務」。

Words & Phrases receive ～を受信する confirmation 確認(書) it looks like ～ ～のようである
charge ～ for … ～に…の料金を請求する parking 駐車 refund 返金 charge 料金
public transportation 公共交通機関 attach ～ to … ～を…に添付する resend ～を再送する
with ～ done ～が…された状態で ★withは付帯状況を表す issue 問題

Questions 86 through 88 refer to the following excerpt from a meeting.

[+] M

Thanks, everyone, for attending this meeting. **❶The factory received a rush order for 75 additional Kinslee desk chairs from an important retail client.** They want these chairs in two weeks. Shift managers tell me that we may not have enough staff available to meet this deadline. Plus, ❷I've learned that an automated fabric-cutting machine hasn't been working properly. Some of that work must be done by hand. So, I need volunteers for fabric cutting. There is a sign-up sheet to my left. ❸I have also reached out to Human Resources about hiring temporary staff.

問題86-88は次の会議の抜粋に関するものです。

皆さん、この会議にご出席いただきありがとうございます。当工場は、小売業の重要顧客から追加で75脚のKinsleeデスクチェアーの急ぎの注文を受けました。先方は2週間後にこれらの椅子をお望みです。シフト管理者たちは、この納期に間に合わせるのに十分なスタッフがいないかもしれないと言っています。その上、自動布地裁断機が正常に作動していないということが分かりました。その作業の一部は手で行う必要があります。そのため、布地の裁断をしてくれる有志を必要としています。私の左側に参加登録用紙があります。また、私は臨時スタッフの雇用に関して人事部に働きかけました。

---

86 What does the factory produce?

(A) Furniture
(B) Automobiles
(C) Clothing
(D) Appliances

工場は何を製造していますか。

(A) 家具
(B) 自動車
(C) 衣料品
(D) 家電製品

正解 A 話し手は、❶「当工場は、小売業の重要顧客から追加で75脚のKinsleeデスクチェアーの急ぎの注文を受けた」と受注内容を知らせているので、話し手たちの工場では家具を製造していると分かる。produce「～を製造する」。furniture「家具」。
(B) automobile「自動車」。
(C) fabric-cuttingなどの語から連想され得る点に注意。clothing「衣料品」。
(D) appliance「家庭用電化製品」。

---

87 What does the speaker say about a machine?

(A) It is new.
(B) It has been ordered.
(C) It is malfunctioning.
(D) It requires special training.

話し手は機械について何と言っていますか。

(A) それは新しい。
(B) それは注文済みである。
(C) それは故障している。
(D) それは特殊な研修を必要とする。

正解 C 話し手は、❷「自動布地裁断機が正常に作動していないということが分かった」と述べ、続けてそのために一部手作業で行う必要があると説明している。よって、❷の問題点を、malfunction「正常に作動しない、機能不全である」を用いて表している(C)が正解。
(D) require「～を必要とする」。

---

88 According to the speaker, what might human resources do next?

(A) Arrange for promotions
(B) Hire some additional workers
(C) Allow staff to work overtime
(D) Provide additional health benefits

話し手によると、人事部は次に何をする可能性がありますか。

(A) 昇格の手はずを整える
(B) 追加の作業員を雇用する
(C) スタッフに残業を認める
(D) 追加の健康保険給付金を支給する

正解 B 話し手は、布地の裁断作業を行う有志を求めていることを伝え、❸「また、私は臨時スタッフの雇用に関して人事部に働きかけた」と報告している。このことから、人事部は話し手の要請を受けて、急ぎの注文に対応するための臨時スタッフを雇用する可能性があると考えられるので、(B)が正解。
(A) arrange for ～「～の手はずを整える」、promotion「昇格」。
(C) allow ～ to do「～が…することを認める」、work overtime「残業する」。
(D) health benefits「健康保険給付金」。

TEST 2 PART 4

Words & Phrases

rush 大急ぎの additional 追加の meet ～(条件など)を満たす deadline 納期
plus その上 automated 自動の fabric-cutting 布地裁断の machine 機械 by hand 手で volunteer 有志
sign-up 登録(の) to one's left ～の左側に reach out to ～ ～に接触しようとする human resources 人事(部)
temporary 臨時の

Questions 89 through 91 refer to the following advertisement.

■ M

Hello, Marion County! Looking for something fun and family friendly to do this weekend? ❶Come to the annual marathon in downtown Clarke City. Everyone looks forward to this event all year long, especially runners! ❷This year's race is very special: it's the fiftieth annual Clarke City marathon. To celebrate this milestone, county officials will have free souvenirs available at the finish line area. ❸Please note: marathon runners should be sure to arrive early in order to get to the starting line before the race begins at 8 A.M.

問題89-91は次の広告に関するものです。

こんにちは、マリオン郡の皆さま! 今週末に行う楽しくて家族向きの何かをお探しですか? クラーク市の中心街での毎年恒例のマラソン大会にお越しください。誰もが一年中このイベントを心待ちにしています、特にランナーの皆さんは! 今年のレースは非常に特別です。今回はクラーク市民マラソンの50周年です。この節目を祝して、郡の職員がゴールラインのエリアで無料の記念品をご用意しています。以下にご注意ください。マラソン走者の方々は、午前8時のレース開始の前にスタートラインにつけるよう、必ず早めにご到着ください。

---

89 What type of event is being held?

(A) A running race
(B) A holiday parade
(C) A speech
(D) A seasonal sale

どんな種類のイベントが開催されますか。

(A) ランニングのレース
(B) 祝日のパレード
(C) 講演
(D) 季節限定セール

正解 **A** 話し手は今週末のイベントを話題にし、❶で、毎年恒例のマラソン大会に来るよう聞き手に呼び掛けている。また、❷で、今回はクラーク市民マラソンの50周年だと述べ、❸ではマラソン走者に早めの到着を呼び掛けている。よって、marathonをa running raceと表した(A)が正解。hold「～を開催する」。
(D) seasonal「季節の」。

---

90 According to the speaker, why is the event special?

(A) More people are expected to participate than in the past.
(B) It features local products.
(C) It has happened for 50 years.
(D) Admission is free.

話し手によると、イベントはなぜ特別なのですか。

(A) 過去よりも大勢の人々が参加すると見込まれている。
(B) それは地元の生産品を目玉としている。
(C) それは50年間行われてきた。
(D) 参加費が無料である。

正解 **C** 話し手は、開催予定のイベントの特別な点について、❷「今年のレースは非常に特別だ。今回はクラーク市民マラソンの50周年だ」と伝えている。よって、期間を表すfor 50 yearsを用いて50周年を表現している(C)が正解。
(A) be expected to do「～すると見込まれている」、participate「参加する」、in the past「過去に」。
(B) feature「～を目玉とする」、product「生産品」。
(D) 無料の記念品への言及はあるが、イベントのadmission「参加料」については述べられていない。

---

91 What does the speaker recommend some of the listeners do?

(A) Try some new equipment
(B) Select seats online
(C) Bring a friend
(D) Arrive early

話し手は聞き手の一部に何をするよう勧めていますか。

(A) 新しい機器を使ってみる
(B) オンラインで座席を選択する
(C) 友人を連れてくる
(D) 早く到着する

正解 **D** 話し手は、❸「注意してください。マラソン走者は、午前8時のレース開始の前にスタートラインにつけるよう、必ず早めに到着してください」と、マラソンに参加する聞き手に注意点を伝えている。よって、(D)が正解。recommend (that) ～「～ということを勧める」。
(A) equipment「機器」。
(C) 話し手はイベントが家族向きであることを示唆しているが、友人を誘うことには言及していない。

Words & Phrases　county 郡　look for ～ ～を探す　family friendly 家族向きの
annual 年に一度の、毎年恒例の　downtown 中心街の　look forward to ～ ～を心待ちにする　all year long 一年中
especially 特に、とりわけ　celebrate ～を祝う　milestone 重要な出来事、節目　official 役人、職員
souvenir 記念品　finish line （競技の）ゴールライン、決勝線 ★米国表現。英国表現はfinishing line　note ～に留意する
be sure to do 必ず～する　arrive 到着する　in order to do ～するために　get to ～ ～に到着する
starting line （競技の）スタートライン

Questions 92 through 94 refer to the following broadcast.

🇺🇸 W

❶Thank you for listening to Griflin City News! ❷We are the leader in local news. ❸One of our top stories today is the opening of the modern art museum in the city center. ❹This event has attracted many visitors. ❺Go to our Web site to watch short discussions with these people and hear all the wonderful things they have to say about the museum and the city! Up next, we have a live interview with Sung-Hee Kwon, one of the artists whose work is being exhibited at the museum. ❻We already have callers waiting to ask her some questions. <u>You could be next!</u> ❼We'd love to hear your voice on Griflin City News!

問題92-94は次の放送に関するものです。

グリフリン市ニュースをお聞きいただきありがとうございます！ 私たちは地元ニュースのリーダーです。今日のトップニュースの一つは、市の中心部における近代美術館の開館記念イベントです。このイベントは多くの来館者を集めました。当番組のウェブサイトにアクセスして、これらの方々の短い談話をご覧になり、彼らが美術館や市について語りたいと思っているもろもろの素晴らしい話をお聞きください！ さて次は、同美術館で作品展示中の芸術家の一人、Sung-Hee Kwon さんの生放送インタビューです。彼女に質問するために電話をかけてくださった方々にすでにお待ちいただいています。次はあなたかもしれません！ グリフリン市ニュースであなたの声をぜひお聞かせください。

92 What is the topic of the broadcast?

(A) International sports
(B) Classical music
(C) Community news
(D) Home-improvement advice

放送の話題は何ですか。

(A) 国際的なスポーツ
(B) クラシック音楽
(C) 地域のニュース
(D) 住宅リフォームについての助言

正解 **C** 話し手は❶で、グリフリン市ニュースの聞き手にあいさつをしてから、❷「私たちは地元ニュースのリーダーだ」と番組について紹介している。続けて❸～❺では市内の美術館の開館記念イベントを報じている。これらのことから、放送はグリフリン市の地域ニュースを話題にしていると分かるので、(C)が正解。topic「話題」。community「地域社会」。
(D) home-improvement「住宅リフォームの」。

93 According to the speaker, what should the listeners do on a Web site?

(A) Submit reviews
(B) View interviews with visitors
(C) Download information about the museum
(D) Read about local art classes

話し手によると、聞き手はウェブサイト上で何をするといいですか。

(A) レビューを投稿する
(B) 来館者へのインタビューを見る
(C) 美術館についての情報をダウンロードする
(D) 地元の美術講座について読む

正解 **B** 話し手は❹で、美術館の開館記念イベントが多くの人々を集めたことに言及した後、❺で、ウェブサイト上で来館者の談話の動画を見るよう聞き手を促している。よって、❺のshort discussionsをinterviewsと言い換えた(B)が正解。
(A) submit「～を投稿する」。
(C) 美術館の話題だが、情報のダウンロードについては述べられていない。

94 Why does the speaker say, "You could be next"?

(A) To suggest that the listeners enter a contest
(B) To encourage the listeners to call in
(C) To recommend a local restaurant
(D) To promote a job fair

話し手はなぜ "You could be next" と言っていますか。

(A) 聞き手に、コンテストに参加申し込みするよう勧めるため
(B) 聞き手に、電話を入れるよう勧めるため
(C) 地元のレストランを薦めるため
(D) 就職説明会を宣伝するため

正解 **B** 話し手は、Kwonさんの生放送インタビューが始まることを知らせた後、❻「彼女に質問するために電話をかけてくれた人々にすでに待ってもらっている」と今の状況を伝え、下線部の発言で聞き手に、次はあなたかもしれないと述べている。またその直後の❼で、番組内で聞き手の声を聞きたいと言っているので、番組に電話で参加するよう聞き手に勧めているのだと判断できる。encourage ～ to do「～に…することを勧める」、call in「電話を入れる」。
(A) enter「～に参加申し込みをする」。
(D) promote「～を宣伝する」、job fair「就職説明会」。

Words & Phrases broadcast 放送　leader リーダー、先導的な役割を担う人・もの　top story トップニュース　opening オープン記念イベント　modern 近代的な　Up next, さて次は ★番組などで使われる表現　live 生放送の　have ～ doing ～に…させている

Questions 95 through 97 refer to the following talk and map.

🇦🇺 M

❶This is our final preparation meeting before the Carsonville street fair this weekend. ❷Remember, this is a huge opportunity for us at Marko Kitchen Supplies. ❸Attendees will have the chance to get hands-on experience with our newest small appliances and cooking utensils. I need all of you to arrive by 9 A.M. to set up our tables and displays. ❹The town council told me that parking for the fair is always difficult. The public will be able to park in the municipal garages close to Mercer Square and on the riverfront, but ❺we'll need to park in the lot near Spruce Street. Happily, it's a short walk to the fair site.

問題95-97は次の話と地図に関するものです。

今回が、今週末のカーソンビル街頭フェアの前の最後の準備会議です。いいですか、これは、私たちMarko台所用品店にとっては非常に大きな機会です。参加者は、当店の最新の小型電化製品や調理用具を実際に体験する機会を得るでしょう。当店のテーブルと陳列物の準備をするため、皆さん全員に午前9時までに到着してもらう必要があります。町議会は、フェアのために駐車するのはいつも困難だと教えてくれました。一般の人々は、マーサー広場近くの川に面した町営駐車場に駐車可能ですが、私たちはスプルース通りに近い区画に駐車する必要があります。幸いにも、そこはフェアの会場まで歩いてすぐの所です。

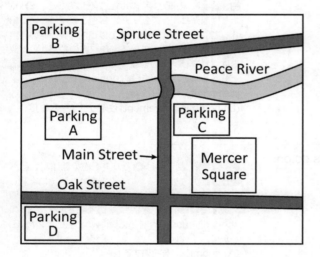

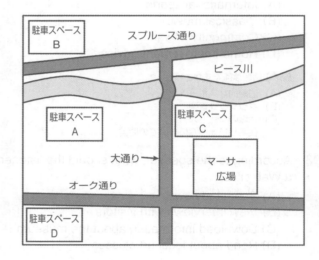

95 What kind of event is the speaker discussing?

(A) A local festival
(B) An art exhibition
(C) An automobile show
(D) A bicycle race

話し手はどんな種類のイベントについて話していますか。

(A) 地元の催し
(B) 美術展
(C) 自動車展示会
(D) 自転車レース

正解 **A** 話し手は❶「今回が、今週末のカーソンビル街頭フェアの前の最後の準備会議だ」と述べている。また❹でイベントのための駐車場所について町議会と話した内容を伝えているので、地元で開かれる催しについての話と考えられる。よって、(A)が正解。festival「(定期的な)催し」。
(B) (C) fair、displaysなどの語から連想され得る点に注意。(B) exhibition「展覧会」。(C) automobile「自動車」。

96 What kind of company do the listeners work for?

(A) A catering company
(B) A cookware retailer
(C) An art supply store
(D) A parking facility

聞き手はどんな種類の会社で働いていますか。

(A) ケータリング会社
(B) 調理用具の小売店
(C) 美術用品店
(D) 駐車施設

正解 **B** 話し手は、❷「いいですか、これは、私たちMarko台所用品店にとっては非常に大きな機会だ」と聞き手に念を押し、続けて❸で、フェアを訪れる人々が自店の小型電化製品や調理用具を実際に体験する機会を得るだろうと話している。よって、話し手と聞き手は調理用具を販売する店で働いていると考えられるので、(B)が正解。cookware「調理用具」、retailer「小売店」。
(C) art supply store「美術用品店」。
(D) 話し手は催しの駐車スペースについて説明しているのみ。facility「施設」。

97 Look at the graphic. Where are the listeners told to park?

(A) Parking A
(B) Parking B
(C) Parking C
(D) Parking D

図を見てください。聞き手はどこに駐車するよう言われていますか。

(A) 駐車スペースA
(B) 駐車スペースB
(C) 駐車スペースC
(D) 駐車スペースD

正解 **B** 話し手はフェアのための駐車が困難なことと一般の人々向けの駐車スペースの位置を伝えた後、❺「私たちはスプルース通りに近い区画に駐車する必要がある」と、催しの当日に自分たちが駐車すべき場所を教えている。図を見ると、スプルース通りの近くにあるのは駐車スペースBなので、(B)が正解。
(C) マーサー広場近くの川に面した駐車場は一般向けと述べられている。

TEST 2 PART 4

Words & Phrases		

preparation 準備　　street fair 街頭フェア　　Remember, ～. 念のために言っておきますが、～。
huge 莫大な、巨大な　　opportunity 機会　　supplies 用品　　attendee 参加者　　hands-on 実際に体験できる、実地の
experience 体験　　appliance (家庭用)電化製品　　cooking utensils 調理用具　　arrive 到着する
town council 町議会　　the public 一般の人々　　municipal 地方自治の、市・町営の　　garage 公共駐車場
close to ～ ～に近い　　square 広場　　riverfront 川岸　　lot (特定の目的のための)一区画　　happily 幸いにも
walk 歩行距離　　site 敷地、予定地

Questions 98 through 100 refer to the following excerpt from a meeting and table.

問題98-100は次の会議の抜粋と表に関するものです。

🇬🇧 W

As you know, ❶the company is preparing to launch a new line of luxury sedans. **The advertising campaign is substantial.** ❷You can see here in the table on the screen that we have been working in stages to create the content for the advertisements, and So-Hyoon's team has already created some excellent content for broadcast media. ❸Now we need to focus on Internet ads, which will have the widest reach. ❹We have plenty of experience with Internet ads after launching the new light truck last year. **Please use your experience with these ads to create new advertising content for the new sedans.** ❺Everyone should develop a sample ad by the end of the week.

ご存じのように、当社は高級セダンの新シリーズを発売する準備をしているところです。広告キャンペーンはかなり充実したものです。このスクリーン上の表から、当社が広告の内容制作に段階的に取り組んできていることがお分かりになるでしょう。そしてSo-Hyoonのチームはすでに、放送メディア向けの素晴らしい内容を制作済みです。今私たちは、最も広範囲に届くだろうインターネット広告に集中的に取り組む必要があります。昨年新型の小型トラックを発売してから、当社はインターネット広告の経験が豊富です。これらの広告の経験を生かして新型セダンの新広告の内容を制作してください。全員、今週中にサンプル広告を作成してください。

Advertisement Stage	Advertisement Type
1	TV
2	Radio
3	Internet
4	Newspaper

広告の段階	広告の種類
1	テレビ
2	ラジオ
3	インターネット
4	新聞

98 What product category is being discussed?

    (A) Vehicles
    (B) Electronics
    (C) Appliances
    (D) Clothes

どの製品分野について話されていますか。

    (A) 車両
    (B) 電子機器
    (C) 家電製品
    (D) 衣服

正解 A 話し手は、❶「当社は高級セダンの新シリーズを発売する準備をしているところだ」と話を切り出し、以降でもその新型セダン用の広告キャンペーンについて話を続けているので、(A)が正解。❹で話し手たちの会社が昨年発売した新型の小型トラックに言及している点もヒントになる。category「分野」。vehicle「乗り物、車両」。
(B) electronics「電子機器」。
(C) appliance「家庭用電化製品」。

99 Look at the graphic. Which stage is the group in?

    (A) Stage 1
    (B) Stage 2
    (C) Stage 3
    (D) Stage 4

図を見てください。グループはどの段階にありますか。

    (A) 第1段階
    (B) 第2段階
    (C) 第3段階
    (D) 第4段階

正解 C 話し手は❷で、広告制作の段階を示す表に言及し、放送メディア向けの制作が完了していることを述べた後、❸「今私たちは、最も広範囲に届くだろうインターネット広告に集中的に取り組む必要がある」と、今取り組もうとしている段階を伝えている。図を見ると、広告の種類としてインターネットが位置しているのは3つ目の段階なので、(C)が正解。
(A) (B) それぞれテレビ、ラジオという放送メディアが位置する段階だが、放送メディア向けの広告は制作済みと述べられている。
(D) 新聞については言及されていない。

100 What does the speaker ask the listeners to do?

    (A) Interview a colleague about their work experience
    (B) Evaluate some advertising submissions from a vendor
    (C) Test a product
    (D) Produce some work samples

話し手は聞き手に何をするよう求めていますか。

    (A) 実務経験について同僚にインタビューする
    (B) 供給業者からの広告の提案書を評価する
    (C) 製品のテストをする
    (D) 作品サンプルを作る

正解 D 話し手はインターネット広告に関する豊富な経験を生かすよう聞き手に求め、❺「全員、今週中にサンプル広告を作成してください」と指示している。❺のa sample adをsome work samplesと表している(D)が正解。
(A) 実務経験を生かすよう伝えているが、経験について同僚にインタビューすることは求めていない。colleague「同僚」。
(B) 広告制作は業者に依頼するのではなく、自社で行おうとしている。evaluate「～を評価する」、submission「(提出された)提案書」、vendor「販売業者、供給業者」。

Words & Phrases		
prepare to *do* ～する準備をする	luxury 高級品	sedan セダン ★自動車のタイプの一つ
substantial (量や程度などが)かなりの、相当な	in stages 段階的に	create ～を作成する	content 内容

excellent 素晴らしい   broadcast 放送   ad 広告 ★advertisementの略   wide 広範囲にわたる   reach 届く範囲
plenty of ～ たくさんの～   develop ～を開発する

101 Ms. Choi will explain some of the ------- features of the new marketing software.

(A) excite
(B) exciting
(C) excitedly
(D) excitement

Choiさんは、新しいマーケティング用ソフトウエアのわくわくするような特徴の幾つかについて説明する予定です。

(A) 〜を興奮させる
(B) 興奮させるような
(C) 興奮して
(D) 興奮

正解 B 選択肢は動詞 excite「〜を興奮させる」と派生語。空所の前に定冠詞 the があり、後ろに名詞の features「特徴」があるので、空所には名詞を修飾する語が入る。形容詞の (B) exciting「興奮させるような、刺激的な」が適切。explain「〜を説明する」、marketing「マーケティング（の）、市場調査（の）」。
(A) 原形または現在形。
(C) 副詞。
(D) 名詞。名詞には形容詞的用法もあるがここでは適さない。

---

102 The admission ------- at the Altkirch Museum is €13 for nonmembers.

(A) fee
(B) view
(C) curve
(D) doorway

Altkirch博物館の入館料は、非会員は13ユーロです。

(A) 料金
(B) 眺め
(C) 曲線
(D) 出入り口

正解 A 選択肢は全て名詞の働きを持つ語。文頭から Museum までが主語に当たり、at the Altkirch Museum「Altkirch博物館での」が The admission ------- を修飾している。is €13 for nonmembers は「非会員に対しては13ユーロである」という意味。空所に (A) fee「料金」を入れると、admission fee「入館料」は非会員は13ユーロである、となり意味が通る。admission「入場（料金）」、nonmember「非会員」。

---

103 Topscore Auto Parts uses modern inventory systems to replenish its stock -------.

(A) continue
(B) continually
(C) continuation
(D) continual

Topscore自動車部品社は、在庫を切れ目なく補充するために、最新式の在庫管理システムを使っています。

(A) 続く
(B) 絶えず
(C) 続けること
(D) 連続的な

正解 B 選択肢は動詞 continue「続く」と派生語。空所に何も入れなくても文として成り立つので、空所には修飾語が入る。副詞の (B) continually「絶えず、切れ目なく」を入れると、それが動詞 replenish「〜を再び満たす、〜を補充する」を修飾する形となり、在庫を切れ目なく補充する、となって意味も通る。auto part「自動車部品」、modern「現代の、最新式の」、inventory system「在庫管理システム」、stock「在庫（品）」。
(A) 原形または現在形。
(C) 名詞。
(D) 形容詞。

104 A new market will be located ------- Mason's Automobile Dealership and the Grace Theater.

(A) down
(B) along
(C) across
(D) between

新しい市場が、Mason's自動車販売店とGrace劇場の間に設置される予定です。

(A) ～の下に
(B) ～に沿って
(C) ～を横切って
(D) ～の間に

正解 D 選択肢は全て前置詞の働きを持つ語。空所以下の部分で新しい市場の場所を説明していると考えられる。空所の後は場所を示す2つの語句がandでつながれているので、(D) betweenを入れるとbetween A and B「AとBの間に」という形で位置を説明することになり、適切。market「市場」、locate「～を設置する」、dealership「販売店」。
(A) (B) (C) いずれも場所を表す前置詞だが、場所を示す2つの語句がandでつながれているという空所に続く要素とうまく合わない。

105 Marketing has not yet decided ------- sandals to feature during Folberg Shoes' spring sale.

(A) which
(B) that
(C) this
(D) those

マーケティング部はまだ、Folberg靴店の春季セール期間中にどのサンダルを目玉商品にするかを決定していません。

(A) どの
(B) あの
(C) この
(D) それらの

正解 A 文頭からdecidedまでは「マーケティング部はまだ決定していない」という意味。------- sandals to featureの部分がhas not decidedの目的語に当たり、マーケティング部がまだ決定していない内容と考えられる。疑問詞の(A) whichを入れると、その目的語に当たる部分が「どのサンダルを目玉商品にするか」となり、意味が通る。feature「～を目玉にする、～を呼び物にする」。
(B) (C) 単数名詞を続ける指示代名詞。複数形のsandalsを続けられない。
(D) 意味の通る文にならない。

106 The principal of Wilson Oak Primary School ------- students as they arrived for their first day.

(A) depended
(B) planned
(C) greeted
(D) wondered

Wilson Oak小学校の校長は、児童たちが初日に登校した際、彼らを出迎えました。

(A) 頼った
(B) ～を計画した
(C) ～を迎えた
(D) ～を不思議に思った

正解 C 選択肢は全て動詞の過去形。主語はThe principal of Wilson Oak Primary School「Wilson Oak小学校の校長」で、空所にはstudentsを目的語とする他動詞が入る。(C) greeted「～を迎えた、～にあいさつした」が適切。principal「校長」、primary school「小学校」。
(A) 自動詞なので目的語を直後に続けない。
(B) (D) 他動詞だが、意味の通る文にならない。

107 Zelwick Fashions will open its outlet in the suburbs ------- in the center of the city.

    (A) out of
    (B) by far
    (C) rather than
    (D) less than

Zelwickファッションズ社は、市の中心部ではなく郊外に販売店をオープンします。

    (A) ～から
    (B) はるかに
    (C) ～ではなく
    (D) ～より少なく

正解 C 文頭からsuburbsまでの部分は「Zelwickファッションズ社は、郊外に販売店をオープンする予定だ」という意味。また、空所の後ろの部分は「市の中心部に」という意味。*A* rather than *B*で「*B*ではなくむしろ*A*」となる(C) rather than「～ではなく」を入れると、in the suburbsが*A*に、in the center of the cityが*B*に相当し、市の中心部と郊外を対比する内容となって意味が通る。outlet「販売店、直営店」、the suburbs「〈集合的に〉郊外」。

---

108 Although some water from the storm entered the shop's basement, there was no -------.

    (A) recount
    (B) damage
    (C) caution
    (D) bargain

嵐による水が店舗の地階に流れ込みましたが、被害はありませんでした。

    (A) 再計算
    (B) 被害
    (C) 注意
    (D) 特価品

正解 B 選択肢は全て名詞の働きを持つ語。カンマの前後がともに〈主語＋動詞〉の形を含む節であり、文頭からカンマまでは逆接を示す接続詞Although「～だが」に導かれる従属節で「嵐による水が店の地階に流れ込んだが」という意味。主節であるカンマより後ろの部分は、従属節に対して逆接の内容になる。空所に(B) damage「被害」を入れると、水が流れ込んだが被害はなかったという内容になり、適切。basement「地階」。

---

109 Irons and ironing boards are available to Stennett Hotel guests upon -------.

    (A) request
    (B) to request
    (C) requested
    (D) requester

Stennettホテルに宿泊のお客さまは、ご要望に応じてアイロンとアイロン台をご利用いただけます。

    (A) 依頼
    (B) ～を依頼すること
    (C) 依頼された
    (D) 依頼者

正解 A 選択肢は動詞request「～を依頼する」の変化形や派生語。空所の直前に前置詞uponがあるので、ここにはその目的語となる名詞が入る。upon requestで「依頼のあり次第、要望に応じて」という意味になるので、名詞の(A) requestが適切。ironing board「アイロン台」、available「利用できる」、guest「宿泊客」。
(B) to不定詞。前置詞の目的語にはならない。
(C) 過去形または過去分詞。
(D) 名詞だが、意味が通らない。

110 The finance department ------- reviews its quarterly statements carefully before they are released.

   (A) always
   (B) ahead
   (C) somewhat
   (D) almost

財務部は、四半期報告書が公表される前に、必ず慎重に見直します。

   (A) 常に
   (B) 前方へ
   (C) 幾分か
   (D) ほとんど

正解 A 選択肢は全て副詞の働きを持つ語。空所を除いた文の意味は「財務部は公表される前に四半期報告書を慎重に見直す」で、空所には、述語動詞reviewsを修飾する語が入る。(A) always「常に、必ず」が適切。finance「財務」、department「部、局」、review「～を見直す」、quarterly「四半期の、3カ月に一度の」、statement「計算書、報告書」、release「～を公表する」。
(B) 副詞として「(時間的に)前に、先に」という意味でも使われるが、空所の位置に置くのは不適切。
(C) (D) 意味の通る文にならない。

111 Though Bylertech's new video game is still being developed, some of its features have already been -------.

   (A) reveal
   (B) revealed
   (C) revealingly
   (D) to reveal

Bylertech社の新しいテレビゲームはまだ開発の途中ですが、その特徴の幾つかはすでに明らかにされています。

   (A) ～を明らかにする
   (B) 明らかにされた
   (C) あからさまに
   (D) ～を明らかにすること

正解 B 文頭からカンマまでは逆接を示す接続詞Though「～だが」に導かれる従属節で「Bylertech社の新しいテレビゲームはまだ開発の途中だが」という意味。空所は主節の述語動詞have beenに続いている。過去分詞の(B) revealedを入れると現在完了形の受動態になり、「その(＝新しいテレビゲームの)特徴のうちの幾つかはすでに明らかにされた」となって、意味が通る。video game「テレビゲーム」、develop「～を開発する」、feature「特徴」。
(A) 動詞の原形または現在形。名詞で「暴露」も表すが、意味が通らない。
(C) 副詞。
(D) to不定詞。意味の通る文にならない。

112 Ms. Takahashi's business trip will begin next Monday, ------- she leaves for Paris.

   (A) when
   (B) despite
   (C) such as
   (D) as well as

Takahashiさんの出張は次の月曜日からで、その日に彼女はパリに向かって出発します。

   (A) そしてそのとき
   (B) ～にもかかわらず
   (C) 例えば～のような
   (D) ～と同様に

正解 A 文頭からカンマまでの部分は「Takahashiさんの出張は次の月曜日に始まる」、空所の後ろはshe leaves for Paris「彼女はパリに向かって出発する」という意味で、いずれも〈主語＋動詞〉の形を含む節になっている。2つの節をつなぐ必要があるので、関係詞の働きを持つ(A) whenを入れると、カンマ以降が先行詞next Mondayに説明を加える関係副詞節となり、意味が通る。business trip「出張」、leave for ～「～に向かって出発する」。
(B) (C) 前置詞の働きを持つ。後ろに節は続かない。
(D) 接続詞の働きを持つこともあるが、意味の通る文にならない。

113 Because Mr. Lau has shown great ------- to his team, he was promoted to senior manager.

    (A) dedicate
    (B) dedicated
    (C) dedicating
    (D) dedication

Lauさんはチームに多大な献身を示したので、上級管理職に昇格しました。

    (A) ～を捧げる
    (B) 捧げられた
    (C) ～を捧げている
    (D) 献身

正解 D 選択肢は動詞dedicate「～を捧げる」と変化形や派生語。great ------- がhas shownの目的語になると考えられ、空所には形容詞greatに修飾される名詞が入る。(D) dedication「献身」が適切。promote「～を昇進させる」、senior manager「上級管理職」。
(A) 原形または現在形。
(B) 過去形または過去分詞。
(C) 現在分詞または動名詞。動名詞だとしても、「献身を示した」という意味にはならない。

114 Employees named to the innovations team should decide ------- themselves how to divide the work.

    (A) under
    (B) among
    (C) about
    (D) from

革新チームに指名された従業員は、どのように仕事を分担するかを自分たちで決める必要があります。

    (A) ～の下で
    (B) ～の間で
    (C) ～について
    (D) ～から

正解 B 選択肢は全て前置詞の働きを持つ語。主語は文頭からteamまでで、「革新チームに指名された従業員たち」。述語動詞はshould decide、その目的語はhow to divide the workで、「どのように仕事を分担するかを決める必要がある」という意味。空所に入る前置詞の目的語はthemselves「彼ら自身」であり、among themselvesで「彼らの間で、内部で」という意味になる(B) among「～の間で」が適切。name ～ to …「～を…に指名する」、innovations team「革新チーム」。

115 Leeds Accounting Group is seeking an administrative assistant ------- a variety of office tasks.

    (A) performs
    (B) performed
    (C) is performing
    (D) to perform

Leeds会計グループ社は、さまざまなオフィス業務を行う事務職員を探しています。

    (A) ～を行う
    (B) ～を行った
    (C) ～を行っている
    (D) ～を行うための

正解 D 動詞perform「～を行う」の適切な形を選ぶ。主語は Leeds Accounting Group、述語動詞はis seeking、目的語は an administrative assistantであり、ここまでで文として成り立つので空所以下は修飾語句と考えられる。空所の前の名詞句an administrative assistantを修飾できるto不定詞の(D) to performが適切。「さまざまなオフィス業務を行うための事務職員」という意味になる。accounting「会計」、seek「～を探す」、administrative assistant「役員補佐、事務職員」、a variety of ～「さまざまな～」、task「業務」。
(A) 三人称単数現在形。
(B) 過去形または過去分詞。
(C) 現在進行形。

116 At Thimbleweeds, the prices of carpets are fixed, so customers do not have to worry about ------- costs.

(A) recruitment
(B) added
(C) observed
(D) accommodation

Thimbleweeds社では、カーペットの価格は固定されているので、お客さまは追加の費用について心配する必要はありません。

(A) 新人募集
(B) 追加の
(C) 観察された
(D) 宿泊

正解 B 文頭からfixedまでは「Thimbleweeds社では、カーペットの価格は固定されている」、結果を示す接続詞soに続く節は「顧客は------- 費用について心配する必要はない」という意味。(B) added「追加の」を入れると、価格が固定されているため追加費用の心配は不要だという内容になり、意味が通る。fixed「固定した」、worry about ～「～について心配する」、cost「値段、費用」。
(A) (C) (D) 意味の通る文にならない。

117 Based on her ------- approach to land-use management, Ms. Yoon was appointed to the Fairview Development Committee.

(A) thinks
(B) thinker
(C) thoughtful
(D) thoughtfulness

土地活用管理への思慮深い取り組み方により、Yoonさんはフェアビュー開発委員に任命されました。

(A) 考える
(B) 思想家
(C) 思慮深い
(D) 思慮深さ

正解 C her ------- approach to land-use managementは前置詞onの目的語の名詞句と考えられる。よって、空所には名詞approach「取り組み方」を修飾する語が入る。形容詞の(C) thoughtful「思慮深い」が適切。文頭からカンマまでが「彼女の土地活用管理への思慮深い取り組み方に基づいて」となって、意味も通る。この部分は慣用的な分詞構文であり、Yoonさんが委員に任命された理由の説明になっている。based on ～「～に基づいて」、land-use「土地活用の」、management「管理」、appoint ～ to …「～を…に任命する」、committee「委員（会）」。
(A) 動詞の三人称単数現在形。
(B) (D) 名詞。後ろに名詞approachを続けて意味を成さない。

118 Westville Research employees have the leadership skills needed to ------- one or more assigned projects.

(A) disturb
(B) involve
(C) reduce
(D) oversee

Westville研究社の従業員は、1つあるいは複数の担当プロジェクトを監督するのに必要な統率力を持っています。

(A) ～を妨げる
(B) ～を巻き込む
(C) ～を減らす
(D) ～を監督する

正解 D 選択肢は全て他動詞の働きを持つ語。空所に続く名詞句one or more assigned projectsを目的語とし、the leadership skillsを修飾するneeded toに続く語として適切なものを選ぶ。the leadership以下は「1つあるいはそれ以上の割り当てられたプロジェクトを-------ために必要とされる統率力」という意味になるので、(D) oversee「～を監督する」が適切。leadership skill「統率力、指導力」、assign「～を割り当てる」。
(A) (B) (C) 意味の通る文にならない。

119 Almost all of Samsoline's new fitness centers became ------- within the first year of business.

(A) profit
(B) profited
(C) profitably
(D) profitable

Samsoline社の新しいフィットネスセンターのほとんど全店舗が、開業から1年以内に利益が出るようになりました。

(A) 利益
(B) 利益を上げた
(C) 有益に
(D) 利益の出る

正解 D 主語はAlmost all of Samsoline's new fitness centers。述語動詞becameに続く語を考える。becomeは補語（形容詞や名詞）を続けて「〜になる」という意味を表す。形容詞の(D) profitable「利益の出る」を入れると、利益が出るようになったとなり、意味が通る。almost「ほとんど」、within「〜以内に」、the first year of business「開業後の1年間、初年度」。
(A) 名詞。あるいは動詞の原形または現在形で「利益を上げる」。名詞は補語の役割も果たすが、ここでは意味が通らない。
(B) 動詞の過去形または過去分詞。過去分詞は形容詞的な役割も果たすが、ここでは意味が通らない。
(C) 副詞。

120 The ------- of sweet chocolate and salty toppings has made Kimmy's Coated Pretzels a sales success.

(A) maintenance
(B) resistance
(C) understanding
(D) combination

甘いチョコレートと塩味のトッピングの組み合わせで、Kimmy's Coated Pretzelsはヒット商品になりました。

(A) 整備
(B) 抵抗
(C) 理解
(D) 組み合わせ

正解 D 選択肢は全て名詞。The ------- of sweet chocolate and salty toppings「甘いチョコレートと塩味のトッピングの-------」がこの文の主語に当たる。(D) combination「組み合わせ」を入れると、combination of A and B「AとBの組み合わせ」という形で、ヒット商品の味を説明する内容となって意味が通る。a sales successは販売が成功した「ヒット商品」を表している。salty「塩気のある」、make 〜…「〜を…にする」、coated「コーティングされた」、pretzel「プレッツェル（塩味のビスケット）」。

121 Northland Spices ------- large amounts of paperwork when its new tracking software becomes operational.

(A) will eliminate
(B) eliminating
(C) to eliminate
(D) has eliminated

新しい追跡用ソフトウエアが稼働すれば、Northlandスパイス社は大量の事務作業をなくせるでしょう。

(A) 〜を取り除くだろう
(B) 〜を取り除いている
(C) 〜を取り除くための
(D) 〜を取り除いた

正解 A 動詞eliminate「〜を取り除く、〜を排除する」の適切な形を選ぶ。文頭からpaperworkまでが主節で、空所には述語動詞が入る。when以下は「新しい追跡用ソフトウエアが稼働すると」という「時」を表す副詞節で、現在形で未来のことを表している。よって、空所には未来形の(A) will eliminateが適切。large amounts of 〜「大量の〜」、tracking「追跡」、operational「機能している、使用できる」。
(B) 現在分詞、(C) to不定詞。いずれも述語動詞にならない。
(D) 現在完了形。従属節が未来を示しているため時制が合わない。

122 Springfield has completed renovations on the town hall to make it more ------- to all visitors.

(A) accessible
(B) eager
(C) tactful
(D) abrupt

スプリングフィールド市は、全ての来庁者にとってより利用しやすくするための市役所改修工事を完了しました。

(A) 利用しやすい
(B) 熱心な
(C) 機転の利く
(D) 唐突な

正解 A 選択肢は全て形容詞。文頭からtown hallまでの部分は、「スプリングフィールド市は市役所の改修工事を完了した」という意味。to make以下の部分は、「それ（＝市役所）を全ての来庁者にとってより-------にするための」という意味で、renovationsを修飾する。accessible to ～で「～にとって利用しやすい」の意味となる(A) accessibleを入れると、来訪者にとっての利用しやすさ向上のための改修工事をしたことになり、意味が通る。complete「～を完了する」、town hall「市役所」、make ～ …「～を…にする」。

123 Anberg Telecommunications sends customers monthly ------- of upcoming payment deadlines.

(A) reminded
(B) reminds
(C) reminders
(D) to remind

Anberg電気通信社は、次回の支払期限を知らせる月ごとの通知を顧客に送ります。

(A) ～を思い出させた
(B) ～を思い出させる
(C) 通知
(D) ～を思い出させること

正解 C 選択肢は動詞remind「～を思い出させる」の変化形や派生語。主語はAnberg Telecommunicationsで、述語動詞はsends。send ～ …「～に…を送る」の形になっており、customersが「～」に、monthly ------- of upcoming payment deadlinesが「…」に当たる。空所にはmonthlyとof upcoming payment deadlinesに修飾される語が入ると考えられるので、名詞の(C) reminders「（思い出させるための）通知」が適切。monthly「月ごとの、毎月の」、upcoming「近づいている、今度の」、payment「支払い」、deadline「期限」。
(A) 過去形または過去分詞。
(B) 三人称単数現在形。
(D) to不定詞。

124 The city has ------- increased the budget to better support community programs.

(A) substantially
(B) nearly
(C) accidentally
(D) tightly

市は、地域のプログラムをより良く支援するために、予算を大幅に増やしました。

(A) 大幅に
(B) ほとんど
(C) 偶然に
(D) きつく

正解 A 選択肢は全て副詞。述語動詞has increasedを適切に修飾するものを選ぶ。「市は、地域のプログラムをより良く支援するために、予算を-------増やした」という内容なので、空所に(A) substantially「大幅に」を入れると意味が通る。budget「予算」、support「～を支える、～を支援する」、community「地域（社会）」。

125 New patients should arrive early ------- that they have time to fill out the required paperwork.

(A) so
(B) because
(C) for
(D) even

新規患者の方は、必要な事務書類に記入する時間を取るために早くご来院ください。

(A) 〜するために
(B) 〜なので
(C) 〜のために
(D) 〜でさえ

正解 A 空所の前後がともに〈主語＋動詞〉の形を含む節であり、文頭からearlyまでは「新規の患者は早く到着すべきだ」、they以下は「彼ら（＝新規の患者）は必要とされる事務書類に記入するための時間がある」という意味。2つの節をつなぐ必要があるので、空所に (A) soを入れて、目的を表す接続詞の働きをするso that 〜「〜するために」の形にすると、記入の時間を取るために早く到着すべきだ、となって意味が通る。patient「患者」、fill out 〜「〜に記入する」、required「必要とされる」。

126 BD's Car Services may have to ------- its hiring policy in light of the worker shortage.

(A) filter
(B) locate
(C) reconsider
(D) see

BD's自動車サービス社は、労働者不足を考慮すると、雇用方針を再考しなければならないかもしれません。

(A) 〜をろ過する
(B) 〜の場所を探し当てる
(C) 〜を再考する
(D) 〜を見る

正解 C 選択肢は全て他動詞の原形で、空所に続くits hiring policy「同社の雇用方針」が空所の動詞の目的語となる。in light of the worker shortageは、「労働者不足を考慮すると」という意味。 (C) reconsider「〜を再考する」を入れると、BD's自動車サービス社は同社の雇用方針を考え直さなければならないかもしれないという内容になり、意味が通る。hiring「雇用、採用」、policy「方針」、in light of 〜「〜の観点から、〜を考えると」、shortage「不足」。

127 ------- volunteers to organize the retirement party for Ms. Chung will need to invite her family.

(A) Whom
(B) When
(C) Whose
(D) Whoever

誰であれ、Chungさんの退職記念パーティーの企画を引き受ける方は、彼女のご家族を招待する必要があるでしょう。

(A) 〜する人を
(B) 〜するとき
(C) 〜する人の
(D) 〜する人は誰でも

正解 D 選択肢は全て関係詞の働きを持つ語。主語は空所からMs. Chungまでの部分で、関係詞に導かれる名詞節になる。この名詞節の中ではvolunteers「〜を（進んで）引き受ける」が動詞の役割をしているが、それに対応する主語がないので、空所には主語になる語が入る。主語になり得るのは、先行詞を含む関係詞である複合関係代名詞なので、(D) Whoever「〜する人は誰でも」が適切。organize「〜（催し物など）を企画する」、retirement party「退職記念パーティー」、invite「〜を招待する」。
(A) 目的格の関係代名詞。
(B) 関係副詞。
(C) 所有格の関係代名詞。

128 The marine-biology building will be named after Dr. Mellisa Vasquez, who has conducted ------- research on dolphins.

(A) sociable
(B) groundbreaking
(C) amused
(D) cluttered

その海洋生物学の建物は、イルカについての革新的な研究を行ってきたMellisa Vasquez博士にちなんで名付けられる予定です。

(A) 社交的な
(B) 革新的な
(C) 楽しんでいる
(D) 散らかった

正解 B 選択肢は全て形容詞の働きを持つ語。空所に続く名詞句 research on dolphins「イルカの研究」を適切に修飾する語を選ぶ。(B) groundbreaking「革新的な」を入れると、「イルカについての革新的な研究」となり、意味が通る。なお、文頭からカンマまでは、「その海洋生物学の建物は、Mellisa Vasquez博士にちなんで名付けられる予定だ」という意味で、カンマから後ろは関係代名詞whoを用いてこの博士について説明を加えている。marine-biology「海洋生物学の」、name 〜 after …「…の名を取って〜を名付ける」、conduct「〜（研究など）を行う」。

129 To meet increased customer demand just before the holiday, salesclerks had to work ------- more hours than usual.

(A) signify
(B) signified
(C) significant
(D) significantly

休日直前の顧客の需要増加に対応するため、販売員たちは通常よりかなり長い時間働かなければなりませんでした。

(A) 〜を意味する
(B) 〜を意味した
(C) 重大な
(D) 著しく

正解 D 選択肢は動詞signify「〜を意味する」と変化形や派生語。空所に何も入れなくても文として成り立つので、空所には修飾語が入る。空所に続く形容詞moreを修飾する副詞の(D) significantly「著しく」が適切。work significantly more hours than usualで「通常よりかなり長い時間働く」という意味になる。meet「〜に対応する」、increased「増大した」、demand「需要」、salesclerk「販売員」、than usual「いつもより」。
(A) 原形または現在形。
(B) 過去形または過去分詞。
(C) 形容詞。

130 Highlake Toys sends a confirmation message to customers ------- they place an order online.

(A) during
(B) in particular
(C) along with
(D) as soon as

Highlake玩具社は、顧客がオンラインで注文をするとすぐに確認のメッセージを送ります。

(A) 〜の間に
(B) 特に
(C) 〜と一緒に
(D) 〜するとすぐに

正解 D 文頭から空所の前までは「Highlake玩具社は、顧客に確認のメッセージを送る」、空所の後のthey以下の部分は、「彼ら（=顧客）はオンラインで注文をする」という意味で、どちらも〈主語＋動詞〉の形を含む節。空所には2つの節をつなぐために接続詞が入る。接続詞の働きを持つ(D) as soon as「〜するとすぐに」を入れると意味も通る。
(A) 前置詞。
(B) 副詞の働きを持つ。
(C) 前置詞の働きを持つ。

PART 6

Questions 131-134 refer to the following article.

Construction of Research Facility to Begin

❶ KANSAS CITY (February 10)—Next month, construction will begin on a new research facility on Glenmore University's campus. The project ------- in collaboration with Lansing Pharmaceuticals.
131.
The facility will be a cutting-edge research center featuring state-of-the-art equipment.
-------, it will offer expanded opportunities for faculty and students in the university's
132.
world-renowned biomedical engineering programs.

❷ Glenmore University has long been an important part of Kansas City's -------. Once finished, the
133.
new research facility will bring hundreds of additional jobs to the community. -------.
134.

問題131-134は次の記事に関するものです。

研究施設の建設始まる

カンザスシティー（2月10日）——来月、Glenmore大学のキャンパスで新たな研究施設の建設が始まる予定だ。このプロジェクトにはLansing製薬社と共同で資金が提供されている。この施設は、最新機器を特色とする最先端の研究センターになるだろう。さらに同施設は、世界的に有名な同大学医用生体工学課程の教授陣や学生たちに、より幅広い機会を提供することになるだろう。

Glenmore大学は長い間カンザスシティー経済の重要な部分であり続けてきた。完成すれば、この新しい研究施設は地域に何百ものさらなる雇用をもたらすだろう。*このプロジェクトは3年後に完了する見込みである。

*問題134の挿入文の訳

Words & Phrases
construction 建設　facility 施設
〜 to begin　〜が始まる　★新聞・雑誌などの見出しでは、to不定詞が未来を表すのに使われる　❶ pharmaceuticals　製薬会社
cutting-edge 最先端の　feature 〜を目玉とする、〜を特徴とする　state-of-the-art 最新鋭の、最先端の
equipment 機器、設備　offer 〜を提供する　expanded 拡大された　opportunity 機会　faculty 学部の全教員
renowned 有名な、名高い　biomedical engineering 医用生体工学　❷ once （ひとたび）〜すれば
bring 〜 to … …に〜をもたらす　additional さらなる、追加の　community 地域社会、市町村

131 (A) to finance
(B) will finance
(C) is being financed
(D) to be financed

＊選択肢の訳は省略

> **正解 C** 動詞finance「～に資金を提供する」の適切な形を選ぶ。空所を含む文の主語はThe project「そのプロジェクト」であり、この文には述語動詞がないので空所に必要。in collaboration with Lansing Pharmaceuticals「Lansing製薬社と共同で」という副詞句が、空所の述語動詞を修飾すると考えられる。文脈より、このプロジェクトは資金を提供される側と考えられ、受動態の文にする必要がある。よって、現在進行形の受動態の(C) is being financedが適切。
> (A) to不定詞（能動態）、(D) to不定詞（受動態）。いずれも述語動詞にならない。
> (B) 未来形。述語動詞にはなるが、能動態では意味が通らない。

132 (A) Additionally
(B) Although
(C) For instance
(D) As long as

(A) さらに
(B) ～だが
(C) 例えば
(D) ～である限り

> **正解 A** 空所の直前の文は、「この施設は、最新機器を特色とする最先端の研究センターになるだろう」という意味。空所直後の部分は、「それは、世界的に有名な同大学医用生体工学課程の教授陣や学生たちに、より幅広い機会を提供することになるだろう」という意味で、いずれも新たに建設される研究施設を説明している。よって、副詞の(A) Additionally「さらに」を入れると自然な流れになる。
> (B) (D) 接続詞の働きを持つ。空所を含む文は複文（主節と従属節から成る文）になっていないので、ここに接続詞を入れることはできない。
> (C) 副詞の働きを持つが、空所を含む文は例示される内容ではないので不適切。

133 (A) protocol
(B) economy
(C) routine
(D) training

(A) 外交儀礼
(B) 経済
(C) 慣例
(D) 訓練

> **正解 B** 選択肢は全て名詞の働きを持つ語。空所を含む文は、「Glenmore大学は長い間カンザスシティーの-------の重要な部分であり続けてきた」という意味。直後の文で、「完成すれば、この新しい研究施設は地域に何百ものさらなる雇用をもたらすだろう」と、この新しい研究施設のもたらす経済効果について言及しているので、空所には(B) economy「経済」が適切。
> (A) (C) (D) いずれも文脈に合わない。

134 (A) Cooperation between universities and corporations has increased.
(B) Glenmore University offers 105 graduate programs.
(C) Lansing Pharmaceuticals was founded in 1956.
(D) The project is expected to be completed in three years.

(A) 大学と企業間の協働は増加してきた。

(B) Glenmore大学は105の大学院課程を提供している。

(C) Lansing製薬社は1956年に設立された。

(D) このプロジェクトは3年後に完了する見込みである。

> **正解 D** 空所の直前の文で、研究施設が完成すれば地域にさらなる雇用をもたらすだろうと述べられているので、空所に完成時期について述べている(D)を入れると、内容がつながって自然な流れになる。be expected to do「～する見込みである」、in three years「3年後に」。
> (A) Glenmore大学とLansing製薬社の協力について触れられているのは❶2行目なので、大学と企業間の協働について❷の最後で述べるのは不自然。cooperation「協力、協働」。
> (B) ここまで大学院に関する言及は特になく、唐突で文脈に合わない。graduate「大学院の」。
> (C) Lansing製薬社について❷では言及されていないため、空所で同社の説明を述べるのは不自然。found「～を設立する」。

TEST2 PART 6

Expressions

in collaboration with ～ 「～と共同で、～と協力して」（❶2行目）
This survey was conducted in collaboration with her foundation.
この調査は彼女の財団と協力して実施されました。

Questions 135-138 refer to the following review.

Village Brook Hotel and Conference Center: Guest Review

❶ I recently coordinated a conference at Village Brook and had a very positive experience. Though large, the hotel is well laid out and thus easy ------- . The hotel staff were all extremely
135.
knowledgeable and supportive. ------- . They made my job quite easy.
136.

❷ The conference center and hotel are connected. Therefore, the facilities were ------- for the
137.
attendees who stayed overnight.

❸ The hotel rooms themselves were a bit small, but they were comfortable and clean. Some attendees with street-facing rooms said traffic could be loud at night. So, if ------- is a concern,
138.
request rooms facing the courtyard instead of facing the street.

–S. Bak

問題 135-138 は次のレビューに関するものです。

Village Brook ホテルと会議場：利用者によるレビュー

私は最近、Village Brook で会議の調整役を務め、大変好ましい経験をしました。大きなホテルですが、うまく設計されているので、楽に行き来できます。ホテルのスタッフは皆、非常に知識が豊富で協力的でした。*彼らは、町のレストランで特別な夕食会を計画することまで手伝ってくれました。彼らのおかげで、私の仕事はとても楽になりました。

会議場とホテルはつながっています。それゆえ、この施設は宿泊した参加者たちにとって便利でした。

ホテルの客室自体はやや小さめでしたが、快適で清潔でした。通りに面した部屋に泊まった参加者の中には、夜は交通音がうるさい場合があると言う人もいました。ですから騒音が心配なら、通りに面した部屋でなく、中庭に面した部屋を要望してください。

——S. Bak

*問題 136 の挿入文の訳

Words & Phrases
review 批評、レビュー　conference center 会議場　guest 利用客
❶ coordinate 〜を調整する、〜をまとめる　positive 肯定的な、有益な　lay out 〜 〜を設計する、〜をレイアウトする
staff 職員　★集合的に用いられる。単数・複数のいずれの扱いもある　extremely 極度に、とても
knowledgeable 知識豊富な　supportive 協力的な　❷ connected 接続した、結合した　therefore それゆえ
facility 施設　attendee 参加者　stay overnight 一泊する　❸ a bit やや、少し　comfortable 快適な
street-facing 通りに面した　concern 心配事　face 〜に面する　courtyard 中庭　instead of 〜 〜の代わりに

135
(A) to navigate
(B) navigation
(C) navigator
(D) to have navigated

＊選択肢の訳は省略

正解 **A** 選択肢は動詞navigate「(正しい方向を把握しながら)〜を進む、〜をうまく通り抜ける」の変化形や派生語。カンマの後から空所までの部分は、「ホテルはうまく設計されているので、------- 簡単である」という意味で、主語は the hotel、述語動詞は is。空所は形容詞 easy に続くので、to不定詞の(A) to navigate を入れると、easy to navigate が「行き来するのが簡単な」となって、意味が通る。文の主語 the hotel は navigate の意味上の目的語に相当する。なお、文頭の Though large「大きいにもかかわらず」は、Though it(＝the hotel) is large の it is が省略されたもの。
(B) 名詞で「航行」、(C) 名詞で「航行者」。いずれも形容詞に続けることはできるが、意味が通らない。
(D) to不定詞の完了形。

136
(A) Village Brook consistently earns high customer ratings.
(B) We got a reduced rate on rooms because we booked as a group.
(C) They even helped me plan a special dinner at a restaurant in town.
(D) I was expecting the rooms to be larger.

(A) Village Brookは常に顧客の高い評価を得ています。
(B) 私たちは団体で予約したので、部屋代が割引料金になりました。
(C) 彼らは、町のレストランで特別な夕食会を計画することまで手伝ってくれました。
(D) 私は部屋がもっと広いだろうと思っていました。

正解 **C** 空所直前の文は、「ホテルのスタッフは皆、非常に知識が豊富で協力的だった」という意味。(C)を入れると、They が前文の The hotel staff を指すことになり、「知識が豊富で協力的だった」ことの具体例となる。また、直後の「彼らのおかげで、私の仕事はとても楽になった」という内容にも自然につながる。plan「〜を計画する」。
(A) consistently「絶えず、常に」、earn「〜を得る、〜を獲得する」、rating「評価」。
(B) reduced「減少した、引き下げられた」、rate「料金」、book「予約する」。
(D) expect 〜 to do「〜が…すると予期する」。

137
(A) optional
(B) convenient
(C) understandable
(D) important

(A) 任意の
(B) 便利な
(C) 理解できる
(D) 重要な

正解 **B** 選択肢は全て形容詞。空所を含む文は、「それゆえ、その施設は宿泊した参加者たちにとって ------- だった」という意味であり、文頭に Therefore「それゆえ」とあるので、直前の文を理由とした結果に当たると考えられる。直前の文で、「会議場とホテルはつながっている」と述べられているので、(B) convenient「便利な」を入れると、流れとして自然。
(A) (C) (D) いずれも、一泊した会議参加者の同施設に対する感想の表現として不適切。

138
(A) choice
(B) space
(C) usage
(D) noise

(A) 選択
(B) 空間
(C) 使用
(D) 騒音

正解 **D** 選択肢は全て名詞の働きを持つ語。空所を含む文は、「だからもし ------- が心配なら、通りに面した部屋でなく、中庭に面した部屋を要望してください」という意味であり、文頭に So「だから」とあるので、直前の文を受けた内容になると考えられる。直前の文では夜の交通騒音の可能性に言及されているので、(D) noise「騒音」が適切。
(A) (B) (C) いずれも、騒音の可能性について述べる直前の文とうまくつながらない。

Expressions

and thus 「それゆえ、〜なので」(❶ 2行目)

Jane didn't have enough time to prepare for the presentation and thus failed to appeal to the new clients.
Janeはプレゼンの準備に十分な時間がなかったので、新規顧客を引き付けることができませんでした。

Questions 139-142 refer to the following e-mail.

From: Kyung-Sook Gwan <ksookgwan@towen.ca>
To: Nancy Davis <ndavis75@mailcrate.com>
Date: 2 December
Subject: Cowriting opportunities

Dear Ms. Davis,

❶ Let me begin by introducing myself. I am Kyung-Sook Gwan, and I ------- Towen Ltd., a leading **139.** publisher based in Vancouver. I was referred to you by Dr. James Wilen, ------- said you were **140.** invaluable as a cowriter for the Brinwald Life Science Series.

❷ I would like to speak with you about several writing opportunities. Towen Ltd. is working with a number of ------- physicians. In fact, they are widely recognized experts in their fields. **141.** Nevertheless, they need assistance from experienced cowriters such as you with developing their manuscripts.

❸ I believe we have some opportunities you would enjoy. ------- . **142.**

Sincerely,

Kyung-Sook Gwan

問題 139-142 は次の E メールに関するものです。

送信者：Kyung-Sook Gwan <ksookgwan@towen.ca>
受信者：Nancy Davis <ndavis75@mailcrate.com>
日付：12月2日
件名：共同執筆の機会

Davis 様

自己紹介から始めさせてください。私は Kyung-Sook Gwan と申しまして、バンクーバーに拠点を置く大手出版社である Towen 社を代表しています。私は、James Wilen 博士からあなたのところに紹介されまして、博士はあなたが Brinwald 生命科学シリーズの共同執筆者として非常に貴重な人材であるとおっしゃいました。

数件の執筆の機会につきまして、あなたとお話ししたいと思っています。Towen 社は、多くの著名な医師の方々と仕事をしています。実際に、彼らはそれぞれの分野で広く認められている専門家です。しかしながら、彼らは原稿作成に際して、あなたのような経験豊富な共同執筆者の助力を必要としています。

私は、当社にはあなたにとって有意義であろう機会があると確信しています。*いつでもご都合の良いときに、私にご連絡ください。

敬具

Kyung-Sook Gwan

*問題 142 の挿入文の訳

Words & Phrases cowriting 共同執筆　opportunity 機会　❶ introduce *oneself* 自己紹介する Ltd. 有限責任会社、株式会社 ★Limited「有限責任の」の略。社名の後に付記する　leading 主要な、一流の　publisher 出版社 invaluable 計り知れないほど貴重な　cowriter 共同執筆者　life science 生命科学　❷ a number of ～ 多数の～ physician 医師、内科医　recognize ～を認知する、～を認める　expert 専門家　field 分野 nevertheless しかしながら、とは言うものの　assistance 助力　experienced 経験豊富な develop ～を開発する、～を作り出す　manuscript 原稿　❸ enjoy ～を享受する、～を満喫する

139
(A) represent
(B) represents
(C) representing
(D) representative

(A) 〜を代表する
(B) 〜を代表する
(C) 〜を代表している
(D) 代表者

正解 A 選択肢は動詞represent「〜を代表する」と変化形や派生語。空所を含む文の、I ------- Towen Ltd., a leading publisher based in Vancouverの部分は、「私はバンクーバーに拠点を置く大手出版社であるTowen社-------」という意味。この部分の主語はIで、空所には述語動詞が必要。現在形の(A) representが適切。目的語となるTowen Ltd.を、カンマ以降のa leading publisher based in Vancouverが同格の関係で補足説明している。
(B) 三人称単数現在形。主語がIなので不適切。
(C) 現在分詞または動名詞。単独で述語動詞にならない。
(D) 名詞。

140
(A) which
(B) what
(C) when
(D) who

(A) そしてそれは
(B) 〜するもの
(C) そしてそのとき
(D) そしてその人は

正解 D 選択肢は全て関係詞。空所を含む文は、冒頭からカンマまでが「私はJames Wilen博士からあなたのところに紹介された」という意味で、カンマ以降が「あなたはBrinwald生命科学シリーズの共同執筆者として非常に貴重な人材だと-------は言った」という意味。この文は空所以下が直前の語を説明する非制限用法の関係詞節になっていると判断できる。空所には動詞saidの主語に相当する語が入り、主語が示すのは直前で言及されているDr. James Wilenだと考えられるので、人を受ける主格の関係代名詞の(D) whoが適切。
(A) 人以外を受ける関係代名詞。
(B) 先行詞を含む関係代名詞。
(C) 時を表す関係副詞。

141
(A) extensive
(B) standard
(C) prominent
(D) thankful

(A) 広大な
(B) 標準的な
(C) 著名な
(D) 感謝している

正解 C 選択肢は全て形容詞の働きを持つ語。空所を含む文は、「Towen社は、多くの-------医師たちと仕事をしている」という意味で、空所にはphysicians「医師たち」を修飾する語が入る。続く文に、「実際に、彼ら（＝医師たち）はそれぞれの分野で広く認められている専門家だ」と述べられているので、(C) prominent「著名な」が適切。
(A) physiciansを修飾する形容詞として不適切。
(B) physiciansを修飾し得るが、続く文でIn fact「実際に」と強調して広く認められていると説明している内容と合わない。
(D) physiciansを前から修飾する形容詞として不適切。続く文の説明とも関連しない。

142
(A) Your book was published three weeks ago.
(B) We are pleased to offer you a full-time teaching position.
(C) I am very sorry for any issues this has caused.
(D) Please contact me whenever you are able.

(A) あなたの本は3週間前に出版されました。
(B) 私たちは、喜んであなたにフルタイムの教員の職をご提供いたします。
(C) これが引き起こしたどんな問題についても、私は非常に申し訳なく思います。
(D) いつでもご都合の良いときに、私にご連絡ください。

正解 D 空所はEメールの本文最後に当たる文。このEメールの送信者であるGwanさんは、❶で、受信者のDavisさんを貴重な人材として紹介された旨を説明し、❷で、医師たちと共同執筆する機会について話したいと書き、❸で、再度オファーを述べてEメールを締めくくっている。よって、空所に返答の連絡を依頼する(D)を入れると、流れとして自然。whenever you are ableは、後ろにto contact meが省略されていると考えられる。
(A) publish「〜を出版する」。
(B) be pleased to do「喜んで〜する」、offer 〜 …「〜に…を提供する」、teaching position「教員の職」。
(C) issue「問題点」、cause「〜を引き起こす」。

Expressions

refer 〜 to … 「〜を…に紹介する」（❶2行目）

I was referred to you by Ms. Carter, one of your clients.
私はあなたの顧客の一人であるCarterさんから、あなたのところに紹介されました。

Questions 143-146 refer to the following notice.

Cromley City Recycling Guidance

Recycling Center – 11 North Water Street　　　　　*Web site – www.cromleyrecycle.com*

❶ ------- . Residents who miss their recycling collection day are encouraged to drop off their
143.
recyclable items at the Cromley City Recycling Center. The center is open 24 hours a day,
seven days a week, and we have clearly marked bins ------- acceptable recycling materials. If you
144.
are uncertain about ------- your items can be recycled, visit our Web site and go to the "Recycling
145.
Inquiry" section.

❷ Computers and other types of electronic waste are accepted only during regular business hours,
from 8:00 A.M. to 4:00 P.M., when employees are on duty. The center is not ------- outside
146.
business hours, and residents are prohibited from leaving electronics without checking in first.

問題143-146は次のお知らせに関するものです。

クロムリー市リサイクルについてのご案内

リサイクルセンター ── ノースウォーター通り11番地　　　　　　　ウェブサイト ── www.cromleyrecycle.com

＊資源ごみは、隔週木曜日に市内の全戸から回収されます。資源ごみの収集日を逃してしまった住民の方々は、再生利用可能な品物をクロムリー市リサイクルセンターに届けることが推奨されています。当センターは、1日24時間、週7日開いており、分かりやすい印の付いた、受け入れ可能なリサイクル資材用の大型容器を用意しています。お手元の品目がリサイクル可能かどうかはっきりしない場合は、当センターのウェブサイトにアクセスし、「リサイクルについての質問」のセクションにお進みください。

コンピューターやその他の電子機器廃棄物は、午前8時から午後4時までの通常の営業時間中にのみ受け付けることができ、その時間帯は職員が勤務しています。当センターでは営業時間外には職員は配置されておらず、住民の方々が先に手続きをせずに電子機器を置いていくことは禁止されています。

＊問題143の挿入文の訳

Words & Phrases

guidance　案内、ガイダンス　❶ resident　住民　　miss　～を逃す　　collection　収集
be encouraged to *do*　～することが推奨されている　　drop off ～　～を届ける、～を(車から)降ろしていく
recyclable　再生利用できる　　item　品目、品物　　clearly　明確に　　mark　～に印を付ける　　bin　ふた付きの大箱、ごみ箱
acceptable　受け入れ可能な　　recycling material　リサイクル資材　　uncertain　確信がない、疑わしい　　inquiry　質問
❷ electronic waste　電子機器廃棄物　　accept　～を受け入れる、～を受け付ける　　business hours　営業時間
on duty　勤務している　　electronics　電子機器　　check in　預け入れ手続きをする

143
(A) The recycling department invites the public to attend all its board meetings.
(B) Recyclables are picked up every other Thursday from all properties in the city.
(C) Once sorted, recyclables are sent on to be used for manufacturing new items.
(D) Changes to the recycling regulations are approved by the sanitation department.

(A) リサイクル課では、一般の方々に、同課のあらゆる委員会に出席することをお勧めしています。
(B) 資源ごみは、隔週木曜日に市内の全戸から回収されます。
(C) 分別が済むと、資源ごみは新たな品物の製造に使われるために回送されます。
(D) リサイクルの規則に対する変更は、公衆衛生課によって承認されます。

正解 **B** お知らせのタイトルに「リサイクルについての案内」とあり、空所は本文の冒頭に当たる。空所の直後の文は、住民が資源ごみを収集日に出せなかった場合にすべきことの説明になっている。よって、資源ごみの収集日について説明した(B)が適切。recyclables「再生利用可能なもの、資源ごみ」、pick up ～「～を集める、～を収集する」、every other Thursday「隔週木曜日に」、property「地所、不動産」。
(A) 以降に委員会についての言及がないので、文脈に合わない。department「課、局」、invite ～ to *do*「～に…するように勧める」、the public「一般の人々」、board meeting「委員会」。
(C) 案内の冒頭文としては唐突であり、次の文にもつながらない。once「ひとたび～すると」、sort「～を分別する」、send on ～「～を回送する、～を転送する」、manufacture「～を製造する」。
(D) 以降に規則の変更についての言及がないので、文脈に合わない。regulations「規則」、approve「～を承認する」、sanitation「公衆衛生」。

144
(A) in
(B) up
(C) for
(D) than

正解 **C** 選択肢は全て前置詞の働きを持つ語。空所に続くacceptable recycling materialsは「受け入れ可能なリサイクル資材」という意味で、空所に入る前置詞の目的語になる。空所に(C) for「～のための、～用の」を入れると、for acceptable recycling materialsが直前の名詞bins「大型容器」を形容詞的に修飾することになり、意味が通る。

(A) ～の中の
(B) ～の上に
(C) ～のための
(D) ～よりも

145
(A) still
(B) another
(C) whether
(D) while

正解 **C** 空所直前のIf you are uncertain aboutは、「もしあなたが～について確信がないなら」という意味。空所を含めた ------- your items can be recycledの部分は、前置詞aboutの目的語になるが、〈主語＋動詞〉を含んでいるので、空所に接続詞を入れて名詞節にする必要がある。接続詞の(C) whether「～かどうか」を入れると、この部分が「あなたの品がリサイクル可能かどうか」という意味の名詞節になって、意味が通る。
(A) 副詞。
(B) 形容詞。
(D) 接続詞だが、「あなたの品がリサイクル可能である間に」という副詞節になってしまい、不適切。

(A) まだ
(B) もう1つの
(C) ～かどうか
(D) ～の間に

146
(A) staffed
(B) reflected
(C) capable
(D) dependable

正解 **A** 選択肢は全て形容詞の働きを持つ語。空所を含む文は「当センターは営業時間外は ------- ではなく、住民たちが先に手続きをせずに電子機器を置いていくことは禁止されている」という意味。直前の文で、コンピューターや電子機器は、職員が勤務している通常の営業時間にのみ受け付けると述べられていることから、(A) staffed「職員が配置された」を入れると、自然な流れになる。
(A) (B) (C) 前後の語句とのつながりが不自然で文脈に合わない。

(A) 職員が配置された
(B) 反映された
(C) 能力がある
(D) 頼りになる

Expressions

prohibit ～ from *doing* 「～が…することを禁止する」（❷3行目）

Staff members are prohibited from using mobile devices in this facility.
この施設内では、職員が携帯端末を使用することは禁止されています。

PART 7

Questions 147-148 refer to the following memo.

MEMO

From: Takori Apartment Management
To: All Residents
Re: Car park
Date: 15 October

❶ Sections 1 through 4 of the car park at the apartment complex will be closed for repair on a rotating basis in November. Please move your car to the guest parking area near the clubhouse during work on your section. Depending on what each section needs, there may be asphalt paving, seal coating, pothole repair, painting, or some combination of these four task types.

❷ Work will begin on section 1 in early November. We will work on the sections in numerical order, and we expect that each section will take one week to complete. We apologize for any inconvenience, but as you know, this work is essential.

Thank you.

問題147-148は次のメモに関するものです。

メモ

差出人：Takoriマンション管理部
宛先：居住者の皆さま
件名：駐車場
日付：10月15日

マンション建物の駐車場の区画1から4は、11月に修繕のために順次閉鎖されます。ご自分の区画の作業期間中は、お車をクラブハウス近くの来客用駐車場に移動してください。各区画が必要とすることに応じて、アスファルト塗装、シールコート処理、地面の穴の修理、ペンキ塗装、またはこれらの4種の作業を何らか組み合わせたものが行われる可能性があります。

作業は11月初めに区画1から開始いたします。番号順に全区画の作業を進めていき、各区画が1週間で完了すると見込んでいます。ご不便をお掛けして申し訳ございませんが、ご存じの通り、この作業は必要不可欠なものです。

よろしくお願いします。

147 What is the purpose of the memo?

    (A) To introduce residents to a new facility

    (B) To encourage residents to attend an event

    (C) To inform residents about a likely inconvenience

    (D) To explain a change in plans to residents

メモの目的は何ですか。

    (A) 新しい設備を居住者に披露すること

    (B) イベントに参加するよう居住者に勧めること

    (C) 起こりそうな不便について居住者に知らせること

    (D) 計画の変更を居住者に説明すること

| 正解 C | 差出人・宛先・件名より、これはマンションの管理部門が居住者に宛てた駐車場に関するメモだと分かる。❶ 1～2行目に、「マンション建物の駐車場の区画1から4は、11月に修繕のために順次閉鎖される」とあり、続く同 2～3 行目では、作業期間中は車を来客用駐車場に移動するよう依頼している。また、❷ 3～4 行目で、「不便を掛けて申し訳ないが、ご存じの通り、この作業は必要不可欠なものだ」と締めくくっている。以上より、メモの目的は修繕作業による不便を居住者に知らせることだと考えられるので、(C)が正解。inform ～ about … 「～に…について知らせる」、likely「起こり得る」。 |

(A) introduce ～ to … 「～を…(新しい物など)に触れさせる」、facility「設備」。
(B) encourage ～ to *do*「～に…するよう勧める」。
(D) 駐車場の修繕の計画について述べられているが、計画の変更は説明されていない。

148 According to the memo, about how long will it take for the entire project to be completed?

    (A) One week

    (B) Two weeks

    (C) Three weeks

    (D) Four weeks

メモによると、計画全体を完了させるのにおよそどのくらいの期間がかかる予定ですか。

    (A) 1週間

    (B) 2週間

    (C) 3週間

    (D) 4週間

| 正解 D | 計画全体とは、❶ 1～2 行目に書かれている、駐車場の区画 1 から 4 が順次修繕されること。❷ 1～3 行目に、We will work on the sections in numerical order, and we expect that each section will take one week to complete. とあり、1つの区画の完了に 1 週間かかることが分かる。よって、4 つの区画の修繕を完了するのに 4 週間かかると判断できるので、(D)が正解。entire「全体の」、project「計画、事業」。 |

Words & Phrases

management 管理　　resident 居住者、住民　　car park 駐車場 ★英国式の表現

❶ section 区画　　apartment complex （複数の棟がある)共同住宅・マンション　　repair 修理、修繕

on a rotating basis 交代制で　　clubhouse クラブハウス ★会員・居住者などが各種目的で利用する共有施設

paving 舗装(工事)

seal coating シールコート処理 ★アスファルト舗装のジョイント部に、耐久性向上、老朽化防止などを目的として行う処理

pothole 路面のくぼみ　　combination 組み合わせ　　❷ in numerical order 番号順に

expect that ～ ～だと思う、～だと推定する　　apologize for ～ ～を謝罪する　　inconvenience 不便、不自由

as you know ご存じのように　　essential 必要不可欠な、必須の

Expressions

depending on ～ 「～によって、～に応じて」(❶4行目)

  Depending on the number of items ordered, the price can go down.
  注文された品物の数によって、価格は下がる可能性があります。

Questions 149-150 refer to the following Web page.

https://www.oberlanderdestinations.com/employment

❶ Thank you for your interest in Oberlander Destinations, the world's fastest-growing resort chain. Before submitting your materials, please be sure you have done the following.

❷ 1. Completed all mandatory fields (marked with *)

2. Attached a résumé (and, optionally, a cover letter)

3. Accurately inputted your passport information (which will be encrypted for security)

4. Agreed to the Terms and Conditions

5. Checked the "Agree to Use of Electronic Signature" box and typed your full name

問題149-150は次のウェブページに関するものです。

https://www.oberlanderdestinations.com/employment

世界で最も急成長しているリゾートチェーン、Oberlander Destinations社にご興味をお持ちくださり、ありがとうございます。ご自分の資料を提出される前に、以下がお済みであることをご確認ください。

1. 全ての必須欄(*付き)に漏れなく記入した
2. 履歴書(と、任意でカバーレター)を添付した
3. パスポート情報(セキュリティーのために暗号化される)を正確に入力した
4. 諸条件に同意した
5. 「電子署名の使用に同意する」ボックスにチェックを入れて、氏名を入力した

Words & Phrases

❶ destination (観光などの)目的地　fastest-growing 最も急速に成長している
resort 行楽地、リゾート　chain チェーン(店)　material 資料　the following 次のこと
❷ complete ～に漏れなく記入する　mandatory 必須の　field 欄、フィールド
(be) marked with ～ ～が付けられて(いる)　attach ～を添付する　résumé 履歴書　optionally 任意に
cover letter カバーレター、添え状　★志望動機などを記入した応募書類で、履歴書と一緒に提出されることが多い
accurately 正確に　input ～を入力する　encrypt ～を暗号化する　agree to ～ ～に同意する
terms and conditions 諸条件　check ～に照合の印(✓)を付ける　electronic signature 電子署名
type ～を入力する、～をキーボードで打ち込む

149 Who most likely would view the Web page?

(A) A resort guest
(B) An online shopper
(C) A customs official
(D) A job seeker

誰がウェブページを見ると考えられますか。

(A) 行楽地の客
(B) オンラインの買い物客
(C) 税関職員
(D) 求職者

> **正解 D** ウェブページの冒頭の❶ 1〜2行目で、Oberlander Destinations社に興味を持ってもらったことに対するお礼が述べられ、同2〜3行目に、「資料を提出する前に、以下が済んでいることを確認してください」と書かれている。続く❷に列挙されている確認事項に、Attached a résuméとある。よって、このウェブページを見るのはOberlander Destinations社の就職口に応募したい人だと考えられるので、(D)が正解。ウェブページのURLにemployment「雇用」とあるのもヒントになる。view「〜を見る」。seeker「探す人、求める人」。
> (A) guest「客」。
> (B) shopper「買い物客」。
> (C) customs「税関」、official「職員」。

150 What is NOT a submission requirement?

(A) A résumé
(B) Passport data
(C) A cover letter
(D) An electronic signature

提出要件でないものは何ですか。

(A) 履歴書
(B) パスポートのデータ
(C) カバーレター
(D) 電子署名

> **正解 C** 提出資料の確認項目が記載された❷の2つ目に、Attached a résumé (and, optionally, a cover letter)とある。optionally「任意で」と書かれているので、カバーレターは必ずしも提出しなくてはならない資料ではないと分かる。よって、(C)が正解。submission「提出」、requirement「必要条件」。
> (A) ❷2つ目の項目、(B) 同3つ目の項目、(D) 同5つ目の項目より、いずれも提出が求められている。

Expressions

be sure (that) 〜 「必ず〜となるようにする、〜であることを確認する」（❶ 2〜3行目）

To prepare for a trip overseas, be sure that your passport and other travel documents are up to date.
海外旅行に備えて、パスポートと他の渡航文書が最新の状態であることを確認してください。

Questions 151-153 refer to the following article.

Elwidge Lavender Festival

❶ A major part of every Elwidge summer for over 100 years, the Elwidge Lavender Festival attracts thousands of visitors from the region and around the world. But how did it get started? — [1] —.

❷ In the early twentieth century, lavender was widely farmed in the areas surrounding Elwidge for use in perfumes and other toiletries. — [2] —. One year, after a dispute with an Elwidge soap maker, a group of area farmers found themselves with a surplus of lavender. To get rid of the flowers, the farmers set up stands in the center of town to sell them to the residents. — [3] —.

❸ Today, the lavender festival features vendors selling not only lavender flowers but an extraordinary assortment of handmade goods from around the region. — [4] —. Visitors young and old can also enjoy a funfair with a variety of carnival rides and activities along with dozens of food vendors selling a wide selection of foods.

問題151-153は次の記事に関するものです。

エルウィッジ・ラベンダー祭

100年以上にわたってエルウィッジの毎夏の重要な要素となっている、エルウィッジ・ラベンダー祭は、同地域や世界中から何千人もの観光客を引き付けている。しかしそれはどのようにして始まったのだろうか。

20世紀初頭、ラベンダーは、香水やその他の洗面用品用にエルウィッジ周辺の地域で広く栽培されていた。ある年、エルウィッジのせっけんメーカーとのもめ事の後、地域の農民グループがラベンダーが余っていることに気付いた。花を処分するために、農民たちは町の中心部にそれを住民に売るための売店を開いた。*こうして、ラベンダー祭は生み出された。

今日、ラベンダー祭は、地域中からの、ラベンダーの花だけでなく驚くほど多種多様な手作り商品も販売する売店を呼び物としている。来訪者は老いも若きも、幅広い品ぞろえの食べ物を販売する多数の屋台に加えて、さまざまな乗り物や催し物がある移動遊園地を楽しむこともできる。

*問題153の挿入文の訳

Words & Phrases
❶ major 主要な　attract ～を引き付ける　thousands of ～ 何千もの～　region 地域
get started 始める　❷ widely 広く　farm ～を栽培する　surround ～を囲む　perfume 香水
toiletries 洗面用品 ★歯磨き用品やせっけん類など　dispute 争い、口論　surplus 余剰
get rid of ～ ～を取り除く、～を処分する　stand 売店　resident 住民　❸ feature ～を呼び物とする
vendor 物売り　not only ～ but (also) … ～だけでなく…も　an assortment of ～ 各種の～
extraordinary 並外れた、驚くべき　handmade 手製の　goods 商品　funfair 移動遊園地
a variety of ～ さまざまな～　carnival ride 遊園地の乗り物　activities 娯楽活動　dozens of ～ 多数の～
selection 品ぞろえ

151 What is probably true about the lavender festival?

(A) It is best suited for older people.
(B) It is well-known in many countries.
(C) It is unpopular with locals.
(D) It is attractive to people who enjoy cold-weather activities.

ラベンダー祭についておそらく正しいことは何ですか。

(A) 年配者に最も適している。
(B) 多くの国でよく知られている。
(C) 地元の人に人気がない。
(D) 寒中の活動を楽しむ人々にとって魅力的である。

正解 B ❶ 1～4行目に、100年以上にわたって毎夏に行われているイベントとして、the Elwidge Lavender Festival attracts thousands of visitors from the region and around the worldとあるので、このイベントには世界中から観光客が訪れると分かる。よって、ラベンダー祭は多くの国でよく知られていると判断できるので、(B)が正解。
(A) ❸ 5行目にこのイベントを楽しむ来訪者について「老いも若きも」とあり、年配者に最も適しているという記述はない。be suited for ～「～に適している」。
(C) ❶ 1～4行目に同地域や世界中から観光客を引き付けているとあるので、地元の人も多く来場することが分かる。unpopular「人気がない」、locals「地元の人々」。
(D) ❶ 1～4行目より、ラベンダー祭は夏のイベントと分かる。attractive「魅力的な」、cold-weather「寒中の」。

---

152 What are NOT mentioned in the article as part of the lavender festival?

(A) Musical performances
(B) Products for sale
(C) Carnival rides
(D) Different kinds of foods

ラベンダー祭の一環として記事に述べられていないものは何ですか。

(A) 音楽の演奏
(B) 販売される製品
(C) 遊園地の乗り物
(D) さまざまな種類の食べ物

正解 A (B)については、❸ 1～4行目に、「今日、ラベンダー祭は、地域中からの、ラベンダーの花だけでなく驚くほど多種多様な手作り商品も販売する売店を呼び物としている」とある。(C)と(D)については、同5～9行目に、「来訪者は老いも若きも、幅広い品ぞろえの食べ物を販売する多数の屋台に加えて、さまざまな乗り物や催し物がある移動遊園地を楽しむこともできる」とある。音楽の演奏に関する言及はないので、(A)が正解。musical performance「音楽の演奏」。
(B) for sale「売りに出されて」。

---

153 In which of the positions marked [1], [2], [3], and [4] does the following sentence best belong?

"Thus, the lavender festival was created."

(A) [1]   (C) [3]
(B) [2]   (D) [4]

[1]、[2]、[3]、[4]と記載された箇所のうち、次の文が入るのに最もふさわしいのはどれですか。

「こうして、ラベンダー祭は生み出された」

正解 C 挿入文は冒頭にthus「このように」とあるので、ラベンダー祭が始まった経緯が述べられた後に続くと考えられる。❶はラベンダー祭についての紹介から始まり、同5行目で、その起源について問い掛け、次につなぐ形になっている。続く❷で、ラベンダーが地域で広く栽培されていたことや、農民が余ったラベンダーの販売を始めた経緯が書かれている。この❷の最後の(C) [3]に挿入文を入れると、この祭りが始まった経緯をまとめる形になり、今日のこの祭りの様子を記述した❸とも自然につながる。よって、(C)が正解。

Expressions

find *oneself* ～　「自分が～であるのに気付く」（❷6～7行目）

If you find yourself comfortable with the terms, please contact Jason Watts.
条項にご不満がなければ、Jason Wattsまでご連絡ください。

Questions 154-155 refer to the following text-message chain.

❶ Ravi Carelli (11:05 A.M.)
I think we need to do another test run of our marketing strategy presentation before we go to Sarsoni Luggage tomorrow. What do you think?

❷ Jeanine Ika (11:07 A.M.)
It is a little complicated in places, isn't it?

❸ Ravi Carelli (11:09 A.M.)
Exactly. We want to be as clear and smooth as possible in our delivery. How about this afternoon?

❹ Jeanine Ika (11:12 A.M.)
Is 3 P.M. a good time for you?

❺ Ravi Carelli (11:15 A.M.)
That works. I'll come to your office.

問題154-155は次のテキストメッセージのやりとりに関するものです。

Ravi Carelli（午前11時05分）
明日Sarsoni Luggage社に行く前に、私たちはマーケティング戦略のプレゼンテーションの予行演習をもう一度やる必要があると思います。どう思いますか。

Jeanine Ika（午前11時07分）
所々、少し複雑ですよね？

Ravi Carelli（午前11時09分）
その通りです。話す際はできるだけはっきりとよどみないようにしたいですね。今日の午後はどうですか。

Jeanine Ika（午前11時12分）
午後3時はご都合いいですか。

Ravi Carelli（午前11時15分）
それでいいです。あなたの執務室に伺います。

154 At 11:07 A.M., what does Ms. Ika most likely mean when she writes, "It is a little complicated in places, isn't it"?

(A) She does not understand some directions.
(B) She agrees with a suggestion.
(C) She worked very hard on a task.
(D) She believes some luggage is difficult to use.

午前 11 時 7 分に、"It is a little complicated in places, isn't it" という発言で、Ika さんは何を意味していると考えられますか。

(A) 幾つかの指示が分からない。
(B) 提案に賛成である。
(C) 仕事にとても熱心に取り組んだ。
(D) 幾つかの手荷物が扱いづらいと思っている。

正解 B Carelli さんが❶で、明日 Sarsoni Luggage 社に行く前にすべきこととして、「私たちはマーケティング戦略のプレゼンテーションの予行演習をもう一度やる必要があると思う」と発言した後、「どう思うか」と尋ねている。❷の 11 時 7 分の Ika さんの発言はそれに応答するもので、「それは所々、少し複雑だ」という意味。主語の It は直前で述べられているプレゼンテーションを指すと考えられる。その後、Carelli さんが❸で、Ika さんの発言に同意してプレゼンテーションの話し方について補足した後、2 人は会う時間を決めている。これらから Ika さんは、11 時 7 分の発言でプレゼンテーションが一部難しいと述べることによって、それをもう一度練習するという Carelli さんの提案に賛成であることを伝えていると判断できるので、(B) が正解。〜, isn't it? は付加疑問で、内容についての確認や同意を求める表現。agree with 〜「〜に賛成する」、suggestion「提案」。
(A) directions「指示」。
(C) work on 〜「〜に取り組む」、task「仕事」。

---

155 What is most likely true about Mr. Carelli?

(A) He is Ms. Ika's client.
(B) He is dissatisfied with Ms. Ika's work.
(C) He is an employee of Sarsoni Luggage.
(D) He is a colleague of Ms. Ika's.

Carelli さんについて正しいと考えられることは何ですか。

(A) Ika さんの顧客である。
(B) Ika さんの仕事に不満である。
(C) Sarsoni Luggage 社の従業員である。
(D) Ika さんの同僚である。

正解 D ❶の発言から、Carelli さんはマーケティング戦略のプレゼンテーションをするために Ika さんと一緒に明日 Sarsoni Luggage 社に行くことが分かる。また、その後のやりとりで、2 人は Ika さんの執務室でプレゼンテーションをもう一度練習する約束をしている。以上から、Carelli さんは Ika さんの同僚であると判断できるので、(D) が正解。colleague「同僚」。
(A) 2 人は一緒にプレゼンテーションの練習をしようとしているので、Carelli さんが Ika さんの client「顧客」であるとは考えられない。
(B) be dissatisfied with 〜「〜に不満である」。
(C) ❶より、Sarsoni Luggage 社は明日 2 人がプレゼンテーションのために訪れる取引先の会社と考えられる。

Words & Phrases
❶ test run 試運転　strategy 戦略　luggage 手荷物　❷ complicated 複雑な
❸ Exactly. まさにその通りです。　as 〜 as possible できるだけ〜　smooth 滑らかな　delivery 話し方、伝え方
❺ office 執務室、仕事部屋

Expressions

in places 「所々で」(❷)

We noticed that the paint was faded in places.
私たちはペンキが所々色あせているのに気付きました。

Questions 156-157 refer to the following review.

Please describe the employee's achievements and note any areas for improvement.

❶ Ms. Diamos is a valuable member of the accounting team I oversee. She transitioned to her current position as manager of accounts receivable only six months ago. Since that time, she has automated the billing process, drawing on her broad knowledge of accounting software. Additionally, she cleaned up the accounts-receivable database and developed a plan to recover overdue amounts.

❷ Ms. Diamos is always ready to help a colleague and quickly absorbs all the instruction I give her. In terms of development, I'd like to see her gain experience in preparing and presenting reports to top-level management.

問題156-157は次の評価に関するものです。

従業員の業績を記述し、改善すべき点を指摘してください。

Diamosさんは、私が監督する会計チームの貴重な一員です。彼女はほんの6カ月前に、売掛金勘定のマネジャーとしての現在の職に異動しました。その時以来、彼女は会計ソフトウエアの幅広い知識を活用して請求プロセスを自動化してきました。さらに、彼女は売掛金勘定のデータベースを整理して、未払金を回収する計画を策定しました。

Diamosさんはいつも進んで同僚を手助けし、私が与えるあらゆる指示を素早く理解します。成長という観点から見ると、彼女には経営陣に対して報告書を作成して発表する経験を積んでいってほしいと思います。

Words & Phrases　　review　評価　　describe　〜を記述する、〜を描写する　　achievement　業績
note　〜に言及する、〜を指摘する　　area　領域、分野　　improvement　改善　　❶ valuable　貴重な　　accounting　会計
oversee　〜を監督する　　transition to 〜　〜に移る　　accounts receivable　売掛金勘定　　automate　〜を自動化する
billing　請求書作成・発送　　draw on 〜　〜(知識・経験)を活用する　　broad　幅広い　　knowledge　知識
additionally　さらに　　clean up 〜　〜を整理する、〜を仕上げる　　develop　〜を開発する
recover　〜を取り戻す、〜を回収する　　overdue　支払期限の過ぎた、未払いの　　amount　額、量
❷ be ready to *do*　進んで〜する　　colleague　同僚　　absorb　〜を吸収する、〜を理解する　　instruction　指示
development　発展、成長　　gain　〜を得る、〜を手に入れる　　prepare　〜を準備する、〜を(報告書)を作成する
present　〜を発表する　　top-level　最高位の、トップレベルの　　management　管理者層、経営陣

156 Who most likely wrote the review?

(A) An administrative assistant
(B) A client
(C) A supervisor
(D) A technology-support staff member

誰が評価を書いたと考えられますか。

(A) 事務職員
(B) 顧客
(C) 上司
(D) 技術支援スタッフ

> **正解 C**　見出しに「従業員の業績を記述し、改善すべき点を指摘してください」とある。また、❶ 1 行目に、「Diamos さんは、私が監督する会計チームの貴重な一員だ」とあり、その後、Diamos さんに対する評価が述べられている。以上から、この評価は Diamos さんの上司が書いたものだと判断できるので、(C) が正解。supervisor「上司」。
> (A) administrative assistant「事務職員、役員補佐」。
> (D) technology-support「技術支援の」。

157 What part of Ms. Diamos' job does the review mention?

(A) Paying invoices
(B) Improving billing procedures
(C) Managing the technology team
(D) Keeping the office clean

評価は Diamos さんの仕事のどの部分について言及していますか。

(A) 請求書の支払いをすること
(B) 請求手続きを改善すること
(C) 技術チームを管理すること
(D) オフィスをきれいにしておくこと

> **正解 B**　❶ 3〜4 行目に、Diamos さんの業績として、she has automated the billing process, drawing on her broad knowledge of accounting software とあり、続く 4〜5 行目でも売掛金勘定のデータベース整理による未払金の回収計画策定を挙げている。これらの内容をまとめた (B) が正解。improve「〜を改善する」、procedure「手続き」。
> (A) invoice「請求書、送り状」については述べられていない。
> (C) ❶ 3〜4 行目で、Diamos さんは会計ソフトウエアの幅広い知識があると述べられているが、技術チームに関する言及はない。manage「〜を管理する」。
> (D) ❶ 4 行目に Diamos さんがデータベースを整理したとあるが、オフィスをきれいにしたとは書かれていない。

Expressions

in terms of 〜　「〜の点から(見て)、〜に関して」(❷ 2行目)

In terms of publicity, social media will play an important role in this business.
宣伝の観点から、ソーシャルメディアはこのビジネスで重要な役割を果たすでしょう。

Questions 158-160 refer to the following article.

News from Drakely Storage

❶ Let's admit it: the storage business has never been regarded as being particularly dynamic or innovative. Think about the storage facilities you've seen—they've probably been rows of dull, nondescript steel buildings. — [1] —. But recently, the industry has been undergoing some exciting changes. Here's a quick overview of a recent cutting-edge development in the world of self-storage.

❷ As storage companies open more new facilities, they are placing more focus on amenities to bring in tenants. Many new facilities provide attractive features such as staffed offices, keypad entry, and climate-controlled storage units. In urban areas, multistory facilities may exhibit visually appealing architectural features to blend in with their surroundings. — [2] —.

❸ Increasingly, the ground floor of storage properties is being used for offices and shops. An example of this can be seen in one of Drakely Storage's own facilities, located on Seventh Avenue in a thriving arts district in Vancouver, British Columbia. — [3] —. Haubert Ltd., the facility's newest tenant, has established a retail outlet on the storage facility's first floor. This fast-growing clothing company offers stylish clothing, which customers can see and try on in person at the outlet.

❹ This is only one example of new ideas in the modern self-storage industry. It seems likely that the industry will continue to make exciting advances in the coming years. — [4] —.

問題158-160は次の記事に関するものです。

Drakely倉庫社からのニュース

認めよう。倉庫ビジネスはこれまで、特に動的であるとか革新的であると見なされたことはなかった。あなたが見たことのある倉庫施設を思い浮かべてほしい——おそらく、単調で何の変哲もない鋼鉄製の建物の列であっただろう。しかし、最近、業界は幾つかの心躍るような変化を遂げてきた。ここで最近のレンタル倉庫業界における最先端の情勢をざっと概観してみよう。

倉庫会社は、より多くの新しい施設を開くにつれて、テナントを呼び込むためのアメニティーにより重点を置くようになっている。多くの新しい施設は、スタッフのいるオフィスやキー操作の入り口、温度と湿度が管理された保管区画といった魅力的な特徴を提供している。都市部では、高層の施設が、周囲と調和するような視覚的に魅力的な建築的特徴を示していることもある。*美しい外装デザインのため、これらの建物の幾つかは魅力的な歴史的建造物と間違えられてもおかしくない。

倉庫地所の地上階は、オフィスや店舗に使われることがますます増えている。その一例は、ブリティッシュコロンビア州バンクーバーの活気に満ちた芸術地区の7番街にある、Drakely倉庫社所有の施設の一つに見ることができる。同施設の最新のテナントであるHaubert社は、倉庫施設の1階に小売店を開設した。この急成長中の衣料品会社は流行の衣料品を販売しており、客はそれをこの小売店で直接自分で見て試着することができる。

これは現代のレンタル倉庫業界の新しいアイデアのほんの一例である。同業界は今後数年間、心躍るような進歩を続けるだろう。

*問題160の挿入文の訳

Words & Phrases

storage 倉庫、保管 ❶ admit ～を認める regard ～ as … ～を…と見なす
particularly 特に dynamic 動的な、活発な innovative 革新的な facility 施設、設備 row 列
dull 退屈な、単調な nondescript 特徴のない steel 鋼鉄製の undergo ～を経験する overview 概要
cutting-edge 最先端の development 出来事、新情勢 self-storage レンタル倉庫
❷ place focus on ～ ～に重点を置く amenities 快適にするもの、アメニティー bring in ～ ～を呼び込む
tenant テナント、賃借人 attractive 魅力的な feature 特徴 staffed スタッフのいる entry 入り口
climate-controlled 温度と湿度が管理された unit 区画 urban 都市の multistory 高層の exhibit ～を示す
visually 視覚的に、見た目に appealing 魅力的な architectural 建築の surroundings 周囲の環境
❸ increasingly ますます
ground floor 地上階 ★地面と同じ高さの階、1階。英国式で用いられることが多い property 地所
～ Avenue ～大通り、～街 thriving 繁栄している district 地区 establish ～を設立する、～を開設する
outlet 直売店 fast-growing 急成長の clothing 衣料品 stylish 流行の、おしゃれな try on ～ ～を試着する
in person 直接自分で ❹ It seems likely that ～ ～しそうである、～する可能性が高いと思われる
continue to do ～し続ける make an advance 発展する in the coming years 今後数年の間に

158 What is the purpose of the article?

- (A) To highlight the need for more storage facilities
- (B) To describe a trend in the storage industry
- (C) To compare storage facilities in different regions
- (D) To explain the process of renting a storage unit

記事の目的は何ですか。

- (A) より多くの倉庫施設の必要性を強調すること
- (B) 倉庫業界の動向を説明すること
- (C) 異なる地域の倉庫施設を比較すること
- (D) 倉庫の一区画を借りる手順を説明すること

正解 B ❶では、注目されてこなかった倉庫業界が最先端の発展をしており、記事ではその情勢を概観すると述べられている。❷では、倉庫会社の新しい施設で導入されているテナントを呼び込むための特色が述べられ、❸では、倉庫地所の1フロアがオフィスや店舗に使われている例が挙げられている。そして、❹では、レンタル倉庫業界は今後数年間進歩し続けるだろうと締めくくられている。よって、記事の目的は倉庫業界の動向を説明することだと考えられるので、(B)が正解。describe「～を説明する」、trend「傾向、動向」。
(A) ❷に新しく設けられる倉庫施設について言及があるが、より多くの倉庫施設が必要であるとの記述はない。highlight「～を強調する」、need「必要性」。
(C) ❸に具体的な倉庫施設への言及はあるが、異なる地域間で比較はしていない。compare「～を比較する」、region「地域」。
(D) 倉庫の一区画を借りる手順は述べられていない。rent「～を借りる」。

159 What does the article indicate about the Drakely Storage facility in Vancouver?

- (A) It houses the company's marketing department.
- (B) It was decorated by neighborhood artists.
- (C) It includes retail space for an apparel maker.
- (D) It currently has no vacant storage space.

記事はバンクーバーのDrakely倉庫社の施設について何を示していますか。

- (A) 同社のマーケティング部門が入っている。
- (B) 近隣の芸術家によって装飾された。
- (C) 衣料メーカーの小売りスペースを含んでいる。
- (D) 現在空いている倉庫スペースはない。

正解 C ❸1～6行目に、倉庫地所の1フロアがオフィスや店舗に使われることが増え、バンクーバーのDrakely倉庫社の施設もその例に当てはまるという記述がある。同7～9行目に、「その施設の最新のテナントであるHaubert社は、倉庫施設の1階に小売店を開設した」とあり、続く同9～12行目に、Haubert社について、「この急成長中の衣料品会社は流行の衣料品を販売しており、客はそれをこの小売店で直接自分で見て試着することができる」とある。以上から、Drakely倉庫社の施設には衣料メーカーであるHaubert社の小売りスペースがあると分かるので、(C)が正解。apparel「衣服」。
(A) Drakely倉庫社のmarketing department「マーケティング部門」への言及はない。house「～を備える」。
(B) Drakely倉庫社の施設の装飾への言及はない。decorate「～を装飾する」、neighborhood「近所(の)」。
(D) Drakely倉庫社の施設の空き状況への言及はない。currently「現在」、vacant「空いた」。

160 In which of the positions marked [1], [2], [3], and [4] does the following sentence best belong?

"With their fine exterior detail, some of these structures can even be mistaken for charming historic buildings."

- (A) [1]
- (B) [2]
- (C) [3]
- (D) [4]

[1]、[2]、[3]、[4]と記載された箇所のうち、次の文が入るのに最もふさわしいのはどれですか。

「美しい外装デザインのため、これらの建物の幾つかは魅力的な歴史的建造物と間違えられてもおかしくない」

正解 B 挿入文は建物の外観が歴史的建造物と間違えられるほど魅力的であることを述べるもの。挿入文中のthese structures「これらの建物」に注目する。❷6～9行目に、都市部の高層の倉庫施設が周囲と調和するような魅力的な外観をしていることが書かれている。この直後の(B) [2]に挿入文を入れると、these structuresが都市部の高層の施設を指すことになる。また、their fine exterior detail「美しい外装デザイン」がvisually appealing architectural features「視覚的に魅力的な建築的特徴」の追加説明となり、自然につながる。fine「美しい、素晴らしい」、exterior「外観(の)、外装(の)」、detail「細部、ディテール」、structure「建造物」、mistake ～ for …「～を…と間違える」、charming「魅力的な」、historic「歴史的な」。

Expressions

blend in with ～ 「～と調和する、～に溶け込む」（❷8～9行目）

Blend in with the culture and enjoy the beautiful views of Indonesia.
その文化に溶け込んで、インドネシアの美しい景色をお楽しみください。

Questions 161-164 refer to the following e-mail.

To:	Veronica Maybank <vmaybank@wbc.org.nz>
From:	Nicholas Teakel <nteakel@zipmail.co.nz>
Date:	11 October
Subject:	Book Club Talk

Dear Ms. Maybank,

❶ Thank you for inviting me to speak at a future meeting of the Wellington Book Club. I understand you meet on the first Friday of every month at Hilldale Hall at 8:00 P.M. and expect presentations to last about one hour, after which the floor will be open for questions and comments from members of the club.

❷ I would be honoured to address the club. My latest travel memoir has just been published, and I would be delighted to speak about it to your group. It is a detailed account of my travels to Kyoto and my meeting with one of Japan's foremost experts on cherry trees. My schedule is <u>clear</u> for the next two months. Please note that after that time I will go on a book tour.

❸ Please let me know as soon as possible what date you have in mind. I will bring a computer with presentation software, but it would be helpful if you could provide a screen so that I may include photographs of Kyoto and the trees.

Best regards,

Nicholas Teakel

問題161-164は次のEメールに関するものです。

受信者：Veronica Maybank <vmaybank@wbc.org.nz>
送信者：Nicholas Teakel <nteakel@zipmail.co.nz>
日付：10月11日
件名：読書クラブでの講演

Maybank様

Wellington読書クラブのこの先の会合での講演をご依頼くださり、ありがとうございます。皆さんが毎月第1金曜日に、Hilldale会館で午後8時に集まっていること、発表にはおよそ1時間を想定されていること、その後はクラブの会員からの質問や論評のための場となることを理解しました。

私がクラブの皆さんに向けて講演をすることができるなら光栄です。私の最新の旅行体験記がちょうど出版されたところで、皆さまの団体にそれについてお話しすることができれば大変うれしく思います。それは私の京都への旅と、桜の木の日本の第一人者との出会いに関する詳細な記述です。次の2カ月間、私の予定は空いています。その後、私は本の宣伝ツアーに出る予定であることにご留意ください。

どんな日取りをお考えか、できるだけ早くお知らせください。発表用ソフトウエアの入ったコンピューターを持参しますが、京都と木々の写真を含めることができるようにスクリーンを用意していただければ助かります。

敬具

Nicholas Teakel

Words & Phrases

❶ invite ~ to do ～に…するよう依頼する　　last 続く
floor 階、（ある目的のために設けられた）場所　　❷ address ～に向けて講演する　　memoir 体験記、回顧録
be delighted to do ～して大変うれしい　　account 報告、記述　　foremost 第一線の、随一の　　expert 専門家
note that ～ ～ということに注意する　　go on a tour ツアーに出る　　book tour 自著の宣伝のためのツアー
❸ as soon as possible できるだけ早く　　have ~ in mind ～を考えている、～を計画している

Expressions

be honoured to do 「～して光栄である」（❷1行目）　★honouredの米国表記はhonored

We would be honoured to introduce our new product to all of you.
皆さんに当社の新製品を紹介できるなら光栄です。

161 What most likely is Mr. Teakel's profession?

(A) Author
(B) Travel agent
(C) Computer technician
(D) Gardener

Teakelさんの職業は何だと考えられますか。

(A) 作家
(B) 旅行案内業者
(C) コンピューター技術者
(D) 庭師

> **正解 A** ヘッダーと署名より、TeakelさんはEメールの送信者と分かる。❷ 1～2行目でMy latest travel memoir has just been publishedと自著が出版されたことを述べ、続けて講演でそれについて話すつもりだと伝えている。また、
>
> 同4～5行目で、自著の宣伝ツアーに行くことにも言及している。よって、(A)が正解。profession「(専門的)職業」。author「作家」。(B) ❷ 2～3行目で旅に言及しているが、travel agent「旅行案内業者」である根拠にはならない。

162 What typically happens at the book club meetings at about 9:00 P.M.?

(A) Itineraries and schedules are distributed.
(B) Documentary films from Asia are shown.
(C) Tea and snacks are served.
(D) A speaker and audience members have a conversation.

通常、午後9時ごろに読書クラブの会合では何がありますか。

(A) 旅程と予定表が配布される。
(B) アジアからのドキュメンタリー映画が上映される。
(C) お茶と軽食が出される。
(D) 講演者と聴衆が会話をする。

> **正解 D** 読書クラブの会合について❶ 1～4行目に、「皆さんが毎月第1金曜日に、Hilldale会館で午後8時に集まっていること、発表にはおよそ1時間を想定していること、その後はクラブの会員からの質問や論評のための場となることを理解した」とある。つまり、午後8時から約1時間は発表の時間で、その後は会員からの質問などの時間となるので、午後9時ごろから
>
> は講演者と聴衆が話す時間と分かる。よって、(D)が正解。typically「通常」。audience「聴衆」、conversation「会話」。(A) itinerary「旅程」、distribute「～を配布する」。(B) documentary film「ドキュメンタリー映画」。(C) snack「軽食」、serve「～(飲食物など)を出す」。

163 The word "clear" in paragraph 2, line 4, is closest in meaning to

(A) open
(B) plain
(C) bright
(D) direct

第2段落・4行目にある "clear" に最も意味が近いのは

(A) 空いた
(B) 平易な
(C) 明るい
(D) 直接の

> **正解 A** ❷ 3～4行目の該当の語を含む文は、「次の2カ月間、私の予定は------である」という意味。続く同4～5行目で「その後、私は本の宣伝ツアーに出る予定であることに留意し
>
> てください」と述べているので、Teakelさんは2カ月後からツアーで忙しくなるがそれまでの日程であれば都合がつくと考えられる。よって、(A) open「(時間が)空いている、予定のない」が正解。

164 What does Mr. Teakel require Ms. Maybank's assistance with?

(A) Purchasing plane tickets
(B) Displaying photographs
(C) Repairing a computer
(D) Translating a lecture

Teakelさんは何に対してMaybankさんの助力を必要としていますか。

(A) 飛行機のチケットを購入すること
(B) 写真を表示すること
(C) コンピューターを修理すること
(D) 講演を翻訳すること

> **正解 B** ヘッダーと本文冒頭よりMaybankさんはEメールの受信者と分かる。Teakelさんは❸ 1～3行目で「発表用ソフトウエアの入ったコンピューターを持参するが、京都と木々の写真を含めることができるようにスクリーンを用意してもらえれば助かる」と述べている。よって、スクリーンの用意という助けを依頼しているのは写真を映すためと分かるので、(B)が正解。
>
> require「～を必要とする」、assistance「助力、援助」。display「～を(画面に)表示する」。(A) 飛行機のチケットへの言及はない。(C) コンピューターを持参すると述べているだけで、修理は話題にされていない。(D) translate「～を翻訳する」、lecture「講演、講義」。

Questions 165-168 refer to the following discussion-board chain.

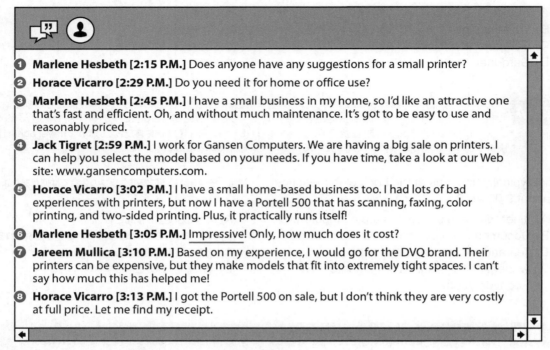

① **Marlene Hesbeth [2:15 P.M.]** Does anyone have any suggestions for a small printer?

② **Horace Vicarro [2:29 P.M.]** Do you need it for home or office use?

③ **Marlene Hesbeth [2:45 P.M.]** I have a small business in my home, so I'd like an attractive one that's fast and efficient. Oh, and without much maintenance. It's got to be easy to use and reasonably priced.

④ **Jack Tigret [2:59 P.M.]** I work for Gansen Computers. We are having a big sale on printers. I can help you select the model based on your needs. If you have time, take a look at our Web site: www.gansencomputers.com.

⑤ **Horace Vicarro [3:02 P.M.]** I have a small home-based business too. I had lots of bad experiences with printers, but now I have a Portell 500 that has scanning, faxing, color printing, and two-sided printing. Plus, it practically runs itself!

⑥ **Marlene Hesbeth [3:05 P.M.]** Impressive! Only, how much does it cost?

⑦ **Jareem Mullica [3:10 P.M.]** Based on my experience, I would go for the DVQ brand. Their printers can be expensive, but they make models that fit into extremely tight spaces. I can't say how much this has helped me!

⑧ **Horace Vicarro [3:13 P.M.]** I got the Portell 500 on sale, but I don't think they are very costly at full price. Let me find my receipt.

問題165-168は次のディスカッション掲示板のやりとりに関するものです。

Marlene Hesbeth（午後2時15分）	どなたか小型プリンターに関してお薦めはありますか。
Horace Vicarro（午後2時29分）	ご家庭用に必要なのですか、それともオフィスでの使用のためですか。
Marlene Hesbeth（午後2時45分）	私は自宅で小規模ビジネスをしているので、速くて効率のよい魅力的なものが欲しいのです。あ、それにあまりメンテナンスの要らないものですね。使いやすくて手頃な価格でなければなりません。
Jack Tigret（午後2時59分）	私はGansenコンピューター店に勤めています。当店はプリンターの大売り出しをしているところです。私は、あなたのニーズに基づいたモデルを選ぶお手伝いができますよ。お時間があれば、当店のウェブサイト、www.gansencomputers.comを見てみてください。
Horace Vicarro（午後3時02分）	私も小規模在宅ビジネスをしています。プリンターでは数々の嫌な経験をしましたが、今はPortell 500を持っており、スキャン、ファクス、カラー印刷、両面印刷ができます。その上、これはほとんど自動で動くのです。
Marlene Hesbeth（午後3時05分）	素晴らしい！　ですが、それは幾らしますか。
Jareem Mullica（午後3時10分）	私の経験に基づけば、DVQブランドが良いでしょうね。同社のプリンターは高いかもしれませんが、同社はとても狭いスペースに収まるモデルを作っています。これでどれほど助かっているか言い表せません。
Horace Vicarro（午後3時13分）	私はPortell 500を特価で手に入れましたが、定価でもあまり高額ではないと思います。レシートを探してみます。

Words & Phrases

discussion board　（インターネット上の）ディスカッション掲示板

❶ suggestion　提案、お薦めのもの　　❸ attractive　魅力的な　　efficient　効率のよい

have got to *do* = have to *do*　～しなければならない　　be reasonably priced　手頃な価格である

❹ help ～ *do*　～が…するのを助ける　　based on ～　～に基づいて　　❺ home-based　自宅で行う　　two-sided　両面の

plus　その上　　practically　事実上、～も同然　　run　～を動かす、～（プログラムなど）を実行する

❻ impressive　印象的な、素晴らしい　　❼ fit into ～　～にぴったり入る　　extremely　非常に　　tight　狭い

❽ at full price　定価で

Expressions

go for ～　「～を選ぶ、～を好む」（❼ 1行目）

That well-known pastry shop sells a wide variety of cakes, but I usually go for the cheesecake.

あの有名ケーキ店はさまざまな種類のケーキを売っていますが、私はたいていチーズケーキを選びます。

165 What is the main purpose of the discussion board?

(A) For consumers to sell their used electronics

(B) For the public to share questions and information

(C) For manufacturers to educate consumers about products

(D) For salespeople to advertise merchandise

ディスカッション掲示板の主な目的は何ですか。

(A) 消費者が中古の電子機器を売ること

(B) 一般の人々が質問や情報を共有すること

(C) 製造業者が消費者に製品について教えること

(D) 販売員が商品を宣伝すること

正解 B Hesbethさんが❶で「誰か小型プリンターに関してお薦めはあるか」と質問している。それに対して、Vicarroさんが❷で用途を尋ね、Hesbethさんは❸で、自宅でのビジネス用であると答えた後、希望するプリンターの特徴を説明している。その後、Tigretさんが❹で勤務先の店のセールについて述べたり、Vicarroさんが❺で多機能のPortell 500を、Mullicaさんが❼で狭い空間に収まるDVQブランドをそれぞれ薦めたりしている。これらから、この掲示板の主な目的は一般の人々が質問や情報を共有することだと考えられるので、(B)が正

解。the public「一般大衆」、share「〜を共有する」。
(A) consumer「消費者」、electronics「電子機器」。
(C) ❺でVicarroさんが特定のプリンターの機能を紹介しているが、Vicarroさんはユーザーであり、製造業者ではない。manufacturer「製造業者」、educate 〜 about …「〜に…について正しい知識を与える」。
(D) Gansenコンピューター店に勤務するTigretさんは❹で同店でのセールについて知らせているが、この掲示板の目的は商品の宣伝ではない。

166 What is indicated about Gansen Computers?

(A) It is offering a discount on printers.

(B) It is having a sale on desktop computers.

(C) It offers free printer-repair services.

(D) It specializes in corporate sales.

Gansenコンピューター店について何が示されていますか。

(A) プリンターの割引を提供している。

(B) デスクトップコンピューターのセールをしている。

(C) 無料のプリンター修理サービスを提供している。

(D) 企業向け販売を専門にしている。

正解 A Tigretさんが❹1行目で、I work for Gansen Computers. We are having a big sale on printers.と発言している。この内容をoffer「〜を提供する」、

discount「割引」を用いて表した(A)が正解。
(C) printer-repair「プリンター修理の」。
(D) specialize in 〜「〜を専門にする」、corporate「企業の」。

167 At 3:05 P.M., what does Ms. Hesbeth imply when she writes, "Impressive"?

(A) She likes a recommended Web site.

(B) She trusts Mr. Tigret's judgment.

(C) She admires Mr. Vicarro's home business.

(D) She likes the features of a product.

午後3時5分に、"Impressive"という発言で、Hesbethさんは何を示唆していますか。

(A) 薦められたウェブサイトを気に入っている。

(B) Tigretさんの判断を信用している。

(C) Vicarroさんの在宅ビジネスを称賛している。

(D) 製品の特徴を気に入っている。

正解 D Vicarroさんが❺2〜3行目で、自身が使用しているPortell 500という機種の特徴を紹介しているのに対し、Hesbethさんはその直後の午後3時5分に❻でImpressive!「素晴らしい!」と発言し、続けてその製品の価格を尋ねている。よって、この発言は紹介された製品の特徴を気に入って称賛したも

のだと考えられるので、(D)が正解。feature「特徴」。
(A) recommended「薦められた」。
(B) trust「〜を信用する」、judgment「判断」。
(C) admire「〜を称賛する」。

168 What can be concluded about Mr. Mullica?

(A) He is a friend of Ms. Hesbeth's.

(B) He lacks experience with printers.

(C) His work area has limited room for equipment.

(D) He once owned a Portell 500 printer.

Mullicaさんについて何が判断できますか。

(A) Hesbethさんの友人である。

(B) プリンターに関する経験が不足している。

(C) 彼の作業場は機材用の空間が限られている。

(D) かつてPortell 500プリンターを所有していた。

正解 C Mullicaさんは❼で、自身の経験に基づいてと前置きし、DVQブランドのプリンターについて「同社はとても狭いスペースに収まるモデルを作っている。これでどれだけ助かっているか言い表せない」と述べている。よって、Mullicaさんの作業場は機材を置く空間が限られていると判断できるので、(C)が正解。conclude「〜と推断する」。limited「限られた」、

room「空間、スペース」。
(B) プリンターについて自分の経験からアドバイスをしているので、経験が不足しているとは言えない。lack「〜が不足している」。
(D) Portell 500というプリンターに言及しているのはVicarroさん。own「〜を所有する」。

Questions 169-171 refer to the following article.

Avyjet 938 Launch

❶ MADRID (12 April)—Production on the long-awaited Avyjet 938 aircraft has come to a halt because of an <u>issue</u> with parts for the entertainment system.

❷ Avyjet, which is based in Spain, is having components for the entertainment system shipped from its partner factories in France and Germany. Unfortunately, those factories are waiting on materials needed to finish producing their respective parts.

❸ According to Avyjet's chief production officer, Guillermo Garcia, it may seem simple but it is not a quick fix. "The planes were designed to use components that were specifically manufactured by our partners in France and Germany," Mr. Garcia said to aviation journalists at a press conference.

❹ The Avyjet 938 has been promoted as being the most comfortable passenger aircraft ever made. Sandrikha Airlines has expressed interest in purchasing several planes from Avyjet to increase the size of its fleet and expand the number of routes it flies. Avyjet says it has several other large contracts it is currently negotiating.

問題169-171は次の記事に関するものです。

Avyjet 938の発売

マドリード（4月12日）——待望のAvyjet 938航空機の製造が、娯楽システムの部品に関わる問題のために中断された。

Avyjet社は、スペインに本拠があり、娯楽システムの部品をフランスとドイツの提携工場から出荷させている。あいにく、それらの工場はそれぞれの部品の製造を完了するために必要な材料を待っているところである。

Avyjet社の最高製造責任者、Guillermo Garciaによると、それは簡単に思えるかもしれないが、その場しのぎの解決策は通用しないという。「この飛行機はフランスとドイツの提携工場で特別に製造された部品を使用するように設計されました」とGarcia氏は記者会見で航空ジャーナリストらに語った。

Avyjet 938はこれまでに製造された中で最も快適な旅客機であると宣伝されてきた。Sandrikha航空社は、自社の保有航空機台数の増加と就航路線数の拡大のために、Avyjet社から数機の飛行機を購入することに関心を表明してきた。Avyjet社は他に現在協議中の大型契約が数件あると述べている。

Words & Phrases

launch 発売　❶ production 製造、生産　long-awaited 長く待ち望まれた　aircraft 航空機
issue 問題　part 部品　entertainment system 娯楽システム　★機内で映画や音楽などを鑑賞する設備
❷ be based in ~ ~に本拠がある　have ~ *done* ~を…してもらう　component 部品　ship ~を出荷する
partner （共同事業などの）仲間、共同出資者　unfortunately あいにく、不運にも　wait on ~ ~を待つ　material 材料
respective それぞれの　❸ chief 最高位の　officer 役員、幹部　quick fix 応急処置、手早い解決策
be designed to *do* ~するように設計されている　specifically 特に　aviation 航空　press conference 記者会見
❹ promote ~を宣伝する　comfortable 快適な　passenger 乗客、旅客　express ~を表明する
interest 関心、興味　fleet （ある会社が保有する）全航空機・船舶　expand ~を拡大する　route 経路、航路
contract 契約　negotiate ~（契約など）を取り決める

169 The word "issue" in paragraph 1, line 3, is closest in meaning to

(A) problem
(B) edition
(C) distribution
(D) result

第1段落・3行目にある "issue" に最も意味が近いのは

(A) 問題
(B) 版
(C) 流通
(D) 結果

> **正解 A** ❶の該当の語を含む文は、「待望のAvyjet 938航空機の製造が、娯楽システムの部品に関わる‑‑‑‑‑‑‑のために中断された」という意味。❷4〜6行目で、Avyjet社の提携工場が娯楽システムの部品の製造に必要な材料を待っている状態だとあり、❸3〜6行目では、この飛行機が提携工場で特別に製造された部品を使用するように設計されたことが述べられている。Avyjet 938航空機の製造は、特注の部品がないという問題のために中断していると分かるので、(A) problem「問題」が正解。

---

170 What does the article mention about Avyjet?

(A) It is considering some new routes.
(B) Its planes are designed to haul cargo.
(C) It obtains parts from multiple production sites.
(D) Its leadership structure recently changed.

記事はAvyjet社について何を述べていますか。

(A) 同社は新しい航路を検討している。
(B) 同社の飛行機は貨物を運ぶように設計されている。
(C) 同社は複数の製造拠点から部品を手に入れている。
(D) 同社の指導者層の構成が最近変わった。

> **正解 C** ❷1〜4行目で、Avyjet, which is based in Spain, is having components for the entertainment system shipped from its partner factories in France and Germany.と、Avyjet社がフランスとドイツの工場から部品を得ていることが述べられている。この内容をobtain「〜を手に入れる」、part「部品」、multiple production sites「複数の製造拠点」を用いて表した(C)が正解。
>
> (A) ❹3〜6行目より、新しい航路を検討しているのはSandrikha航空社。consider「〜を検討する」。
> (B) ❹2行目に、Avyjet 938についてはpassenger aircraft「旅客機」とあり、Avyjet社の飛行機が貨物運送用であるとの記述はない。haul「〜を(車などで)運ぶ、〜を運搬する」、cargo「貨物」。
> (D) leadership「指導者層」、structure「構造、組織」。

---

171 What is suggested about Sandrikha Airlines?

(A) It wants to grow its business.
(B) It flies mostly in European countries.
(C) It is considered the most comfortable airline.
(D) It is negotiating to have new entertainment systems installed.

Sandrikha航空社について何が分かりますか。

(A) 自社の事業の拡大を望んでいる。
(B) 主としてヨーロッパ諸国で航行している。
(C) 最も快適な航空会社と考えられている。
(D) 新しい娯楽システムを設置してもらうよう交渉している。

> **正解 A** ❹3〜6行目に、Sandrikha航空社について、「自社の保有航空機台数の増加と就航路線数の拡大のために、Avyjet社から数機の飛行機を購入することに関心を表明してきた」とある。従ってSandrikha航空社は自社の事業の拡大を目指していると判断できるので、(A)が正解。grow「〜を拡大する」。
>
> (B) mostly「主として、大部分は」。
> (C) ❹1〜3行目に、Avyjet 938は最も快適な旅客機として宣伝されてきたとあるが、Sandrikha航空社の快適性については述べられていない。
> (D) negotiate「交渉する」、install「〜を設置する」。

Expressions

come to a halt 「停止する、中断する」(❶2〜3行目)

All of our work came to a halt when the power went out.
停電したとき、私たちの仕事の全てが中断しました。

Questions 172-175 refer to the following job listing.

Job Opening at Genevierne Hospital

❶ **Position:** Licensed electrician

Anticipated Start Date: 14 January

Location: All fifteen structures on the hospital system complex and surrounding grounds

Reports to: The head of maintenance

❷ **Major Duties:**

1. Installs and maintains motors, coils, transformers, generators, pumps, substations, and all related control equipment.

2. Complies with all regulations, including general safety policies and procedures. Inspects and maintains equipment and tools to ensure their proper operation. Stays up-to-date on the techniques of electrical work.

3. Performs and documents preventive maintenance for electrical equipment and machinery.

4. Designs custom functional electric circuitry for electrical systems as needed.

❸ Application review begins 3 December.

❹ **To apply:** Send résumé and cover letter to Jonas Lewing, director of human resources, at jlewing@ghs.org.

問題172-175は次の求人情報に関するものです。

Genevierne病院の求人

職：有資格電気技師

開始予定日：1月14日

勤務地：病院システム複合施設および周辺の敷地内の15の建物の全て

直属の上長：保守管理部長

主な職務：

1. モーター、コイル、変圧器、発電機、ポンプ、変電所、および全ての関連制御装置の設置と保守。

2. 一般的な安全方針と手順を含む全ての規則の順守。適切な稼働を確実にするための装置および道具類の点検と保守。電気工事技術の最新情報の把握。

3. 電気装置および機械類の予防保全の実施と記録。

4. 必要に応じて、電気システム用の特注の機能的電気回路の設計。

応募審査は12月3日に開始する。

応募するには：人事部長Jonas Lewing宛てに、jlewing@ghs.orgまで履歴書とカバーレターを送付すること。

172 What is included in the job listing?

    (A) The name of the job's supervisor
    (B) The salary range
    (C) The date that the listing was posted
    (D) The name of the employer

何が求人情報に含まれていますか。

    (A) 仕事の監督者の名前
    (B) 給料の範囲
    (C) 求人情報が掲示された日付
    (D) 雇用主の名称

| 正解 D | 求人情報のタイトルにJob Opening at Genevierne Hospitalとあり、これが雇用主となる企業と判断できる。よって、(D)が正解。 |

(A) ❶のReports toの項目に役職名は書かれているが、名前は書かれていない。supervisor「監督者」。
(B) 給料に関する記載はない。salary「給料」、range「範囲」。
(C) 日付の記載があるのは❶の勤務開始予定日と❸の応募審査開始日。この求人情報が掲示された日付の記載はない。post「〜を掲示する」。

---

173 What does the listing indicate about the hospital?

    (A) It includes multiple buildings.
    (B) It is still under construction.
    (C) It has a new air-conditioning system.
    (D) It is operated by a nonprofit corporation.

求人情報は病院について何を示していますか。

    (A) 複数の建物を含む。
    (B) まだ建設中である。
    (C) 新しい空調システムがある。
    (D) 非営利法人によって運営されている。

| 正解 A | ❶のLocationの項目に、All fifteen structures on the hospital system complex and surrounding groundsとあるので、この病院には建物が複数あると分かる。よって、(A)が正解。include「〜を含む」、multiple「複数の」。 |

(B) 建設中とは述べられていない。under construction「建設中で」。
(C) 機械類に関連する用語が多く出てくるが、新しい空調システムへの言及はない。air-conditioning「空調の」。
(D) 運営者に関する記載はない。operate「〜を運営する」、nonprofit「非営利の」、corporation「法人」。

Words & Phrases
job listing 求人情報、求人案内　　opening （地位・職などの）空き、欠員　　❶ licensed 有資格の　　electrician 電気技師　　anticipate 〜を予想する　　structure 建物　　complex 複合施設　　surrounding 周辺の　　grounds 敷地、構内　　maintenance 保守管理、保守整備　　❷ major 主な　　duty 職務　　install 〜を設置する　　maintain 〜を保守・整備する　　transformer 変圧器　　generator 発電機　　substation 変電所　　related 関係する　　control 制御　　equipment 装置、機器　　comply with 〜 〜に従う　　regulations 規則　　including 〜を含めて　　general 一般的な　　procedure 手順　　inspect 〜を点検する　　tool 道具　　ensure 〜を確実にする　　proper 適切な　　operation 作動　　stay up-to-date on 〜 〜の最新情報を常に把握した状態でいる　　technique 技術　　electrical 電気の　　perform 〜を実施する　　document 〜を記録する　　preventive 予防の　　machinery 機械類　　design 〜を設計する　　custom 特注の、あつらえの　　functional 機能的な　　electric circuitry 電子回路　　as needed 必要に応じて　　❸ application 応募　　review 審査　　❹ apply 応募する　　director of human resources 人事部長

174 What is a stated requirement of the job?

  (A) To stay informed of practices in the field
  (B) To complete daily task lists by the end of each day
  (C) To file monthly electrical inspection reports
  (D) To perform landscaping work on hospital grounds

明記されている仕事の要件は何ですか。

  (A) その分野の実務の情報に常に通じていること
  (B) 一日の終わりまでに毎日の業務リストを終えること
  (C) 毎月の電気点検報告書を保管すること
  (D) 病院の敷地で造園作業を行うこと

> **正解 A** ❷のMajor Dutiesの項目の2つ目に、Stays up-to-date on the techniques of electrical work.とある。❶のPositionの項目より、募集しているのは電気技師なので、電気工事技術という専門技術について常に最新情報を把握していることが求められていると分かる。この内容を、stay informed of ～「～についての情報に常に通じている」、practices in the field「分野の実務」を用いて表している(A)が正解。stated「表明された、言明された」、requirement「要件」。practice「慣行、専門的な業務」、field「分野、領域」。
> (C) ❷の3つ目で電気装置の予防保全の実施と記録が求められているが、毎月の電気点検報告書に関する記載はない。file「～を整理保存する、～を提出する」、inspection「点検」。
> (D) landscaping「造園、景観設計」に関する記載はない。

175 According to the job listing, what will happen on December 3?

  (A) Applications will start to be accepted.
  (B) Human resources will begin evaluating job candidates.
  (C) The candidate selected for the position will be announced.
  (D) The successful candidate will start the job.

求人情報によると、12月3日に何が起こりますか。

  (A) 応募が受け付け開始になる。
  (B) 人事部が職の候補者の評価を始める。
  (C) その職に選ばれた候補者が発表される。
  (D) 採用された候補者が仕事を始める。

> **正解 B** 12月3日という日付に関しては、❸に、Application review begins 3 December.とある。なお、続く❹には、履歴書とカバーレターを人事部長に送付するよう書かれているので、候補者の審査は人事部が行うと判断できる。application reviewをevaluating job candidates「職の候補者を評価すること」と表現した(B)が正解。
> (A) 応募の受付開始日については記載がない。accept「～を受け付ける」。
> (C) 選ばれた候補者の発表日については記載がない。announce「～を公表する、～を発表する」。
> (D) ❶の2つ目より、勤務開始予定日は1月14日。successful「成功した、好結果の」。

Expressions

report to ～ 「～の監督下にある、～を上司とする」（❶ 5行目）

  Ms. Taylor reports directly to the president.
  Taylorさんは社長の直属です。

Questions 176-180 refer to the following reservation and e-mail.

1 予約

Lewisport Ferry Service

❶ **Customer:** Juanita Harris
Order date: September 5
Confirmation number: 3442
Round-trip reservation for October 14
Departing Lewisport at 8:30 A.M.
Departing Jonas Island at 4:30 P.M.

2 adult tickets	$24.00
1 vehicle	$31.00
Order total	$55.00

❷ **Departure:** To board the ferry, your vehicle must be in line 30 minutes in advance of the departure time. Failure to meet this requirement will result in the loss of your reservation.

Rescheduling: Reservations can be rescheduled by calling the ticket office at least one day before a scheduled departure.

Refunds: The Lewisport Ferry Service does not issue refunds.

Vehicle regulations: In accordance with government regulations, your vehicle's engine must be off while the ferry is under way.

Arrival time: The trip between Lewisport and Jonas Island takes about 45–60 minutes. Arrival times vary depending on weather conditions.

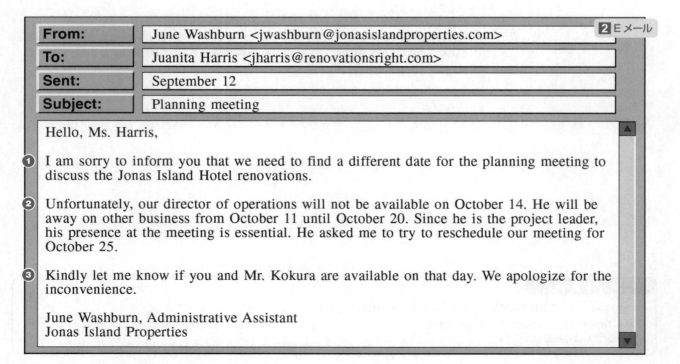

2 E メール

From:	June Washburn <jwashburn@jonasislandproperties.com>
To:	Juanita Harris <jharris@renovationsright.com>
Sent:	September 12
Subject:	Planning meeting

Hello, Ms. Harris,

❶ I am sorry to inform you that we need to find a different date for the planning meeting to discuss the Jonas Island Hotel renovations.

❷ Unfortunately, our director of operations will not be available on October 14. He will be away on other business from October 11 until October 20. Since he is the project leader, his presence at the meeting is essential. He asked me to try to reschedule our meeting for October 25.

❸ Kindly let me know if you and Mr. Kokura are available on that day. We apologize for the inconvenience.

June Washburn, Administrative Assistant
Jonas Island Properties

問題176-180は次の予約とEメールに関するものです。

Lewisport フェリーサービス社

顧客：Juanita Harris様
注文日：9月5日
確認番号：3442
10月14日の往復予約
午前8時30分　ルイスポート発
午後4時30分　ジョナスアイランド発
　　　大人チケット2枚　24ドル
　　　車1台　　　　　　31ドル
　　　注文合計　　　　　55ドル

出発：フェリーへのご乗船には、お客さまの車は出発時刻の30分前にお並びいただかなければなりません。この要件が満たされない場合、ご予約は失効となります。
予約の変更：ご予約は、ご出発予定の1日前までにチケットオフィスにお電話をいただくことで変更できます。
払い戻し：Lewisportフェリーサービス社は払い戻しを行いません。
車両規則：政府の規則により、フェリー航行中は、車のエンジンをお切りいただかなければなりません。
到着時刻：ルイスポートとジョナスアイランド間の移動はおよそ45〜60分です。到着時刻は天候状況により変わります。

送信者：June Washburn <jwashburn@jonasislandproperties.com>
受信者：Juanita Harris <jharris@renovationsright.com>
送信日：9月12日
件名：企画会議

Harris様

申し訳ありませんが、Jonas Island ホテルの改装をご相談する企画会議に別の日を設定する必要があることをお知らせします。

あいにく、当社の運営部長は10月14日に都合がつきません。彼は10月11日から10月20日まで、別件で不在となる予定です。彼がプロジェクトリーダーですので、会議への彼の出席は不可欠です。彼は10月25日への会議日程の変更を調整してほしいと私に依頼しました。

あなたとKokura様がその日にご都合がつくかお知らせください。ご不便をお掛けすることをおわび申し上げます。

役員補佐　June Washburn
Jonas Island 地所

176 What information is NOT included in the reservation?

(A) A confirmation number
(B) The refund policy
(C) Exact arrival times
(D) Rescheduling directions

予約に含まれていない情報は何ですか。

(A) 確認番号
(B) 払い戻し方針
(C) 正確な到着時刻
(D) 予約変更の仕方

> **正解 C** ❶予約を確認する。❶にHarrisさんの予約内容、❷に一般的な注意事項が記載されている。確認番号は❶の3つ目に、払い戻しの方針は❷の3つ目に、予約変更の方法については同2つ目に書かれている。到着時刻については、同5つ目に「到着時刻：ルイスポートとジョナスアイランド間の移動はおよそ45〜60分。到着時刻は天候状況により変わる」とあり、正確な到着時刻は書かれていない。よって、(C)が正解。exact「正確な」。
> (B) policy「方針」。
> (D) directions「指示、手引き」。

177 What government regulation is mentioned in the reservation?

(A) Automobiles must be turned off when the ferry is moving.
(B) Passengers must present photo identification.
(C) A confirmation number must be displayed in the automobile.
(D) Only one passenger is allowed per vehicle.

予約において、どんな政府の規則が述べられていますか。

(A) フェリーの航行中、自動車はエンジンを切っておかなければならない。
(B) 乗客は写真付きの身元証明書を提示しなければならない。
(C) 確認番号は車内に掲示しておかなければならない。
(D) 1車両につき1人の乗客のみ許可されている。

> **正解 A** ❶予約を確認する。❷の4つ目のVehicle regulationsに、In accordance with government regulations, your vehicle's engine must be off while the ferry is under way.とある。vehicleをautomobile「自動車」、while the ferry is under wayをwhen the ferry is movingと言い換えた(A)が正解。turn off 〜「〜(車のエンジンなど)を切る」。
> (B) identification「身元証明書」に関する記載はない。passenger「乗客」、present「〜を提示する」。
> (C) 確認番号は記されているが、車内掲示を求める記載はない。display「〜を掲示する」。
> (D) 乗客の人数制限に関する記載はない。また、❶で車1台と大人2人分のチケットが予約されている。allow「〜を許可する」、per「〜につき」。

178 What is the purpose of the e-mail?

(A) To propose a different location
(B) To postpone a scheduled meeting
(C) To welcome Ms. Harris to Jonas Island
(D) To share architectural plans for a project

Eメールの目的は何ですか。

(A) 別の場所を提案すること
(B) 予定された会議を延期すること
(C) Harrisさんをジョナスアイランドに歓迎すること
(D) プロジェクトの建築設計図を共有すること

> **正解 B** ❷Eメールを確認する。件名には、Planning meetingとある。❶1〜2行目には、Jonas Islandホテルの改装の相談について、「企画会議に別の日を設定する必要がある」と書かれている。❷では、運営部長が10月14日に都合がつかないため、会議を10月25日に変更したいと述べ、❸で、相手の都合を尋ねている。以上より、Eメールの目的は10月14日に予定されていた企画会議を延期することだと考えられる。よって、(B)が正解。postpone「〜を延期する」。
> (A) 変更に関する連絡だが、場所の変更は提案していない。propose「〜を提案する」。
> (C) Harrisさんを歓迎すること自体がEメールの目的ではない。welcome「〜を喜んで迎える」。
> (D) ホテルの改装への言及はあるが、architectural plan「建築設計図」に関する記述はない。share「〜を共有する」。

179 What can be concluded about Ms. Harris?

(A) She had expected Ms. Washburn to meet her at the ferry.
(B) She had planned to leave her car in Lewisport.
(C) She had expected to spend two days on Jonas Island.
(D) She had planned to travel together with Mr. Kokura.

Harrisさんについて、何が判断できますか。

(A) Washburnさんにフェリーで会うものと思っていた。
(B) 自分の車をルイスポートに置いていく計画だった。
(C) ジョナスアイランドで2日間過ごすつもりだった。
(D) Kokuraさんと一緒に移動する計画だった。

正解 D Harrisさんとは、**1**予約の顧客欄に名前がある人物であり、**2**Eメールの受信者。**2**は会議の日程変更を打診するEメールであり、同**3** 1行目に、会議の別の候補日について「あなたとKokuraさんがその日に都合がつくか知らせてください」とある。また、**1**の**1** 7行目に、「大人チケット2枚」とあることから、HarrisさんはKokuraさんと一緒にジョナスアイランドに行くことを計画していたと判断できる。よって、(D)が正解。
(A) Washburnさんは**2**の送信者。HarrisさんがフェリーでWashburnさんに会う予定だったという記述はない。expect ～ to do「～が…することを予期する」。
(B) **1**の**1** 8行目に「車1台31ドル」とあるので、車もフェリーに載せる予定だったと考えられる。
(C) **1**の**1** 4～6行目に、「10月14日の往復予約」とあり、ルイスポート発とジョナスアイランド発の2つの出発時刻が記載されているので、日帰りの予定だったと考えられる。expect to do「～するつもりである」。

180 What will Ms. Harris most likely do?

(A) Call the ferry ticket office by October 13
(B) Arrive at the ferry by 8:30 A.M. on October 14
(C) Rent a car for Mr. Kokura
(D) Find another location for the meeting

Harrisさんは何をすると考えられますか。

(A) 10月13日までにフェリーのチケットオフィスに電話する
(B) 10月14日、午前8時30分までにフェリーに到着する
(C) Kokuraさんのために車を借りる
(D) 会議のために別の場所を見つける

正解 A **1**予約の**1** 4行目から、Harrisさんは10月14日のフェリーの予約を済ませていることが分かるが、**2**Eメールで、10月14日に予定されていた会議を10月25日に変更できないか打診されている。**1**の**2** 2つ目のReschedulingに、「予約は、出発予定の1日前までにチケットオフィスに電話することで変更できる」とあるので、Harrisさんは出発予定日の10月14日の前日である10月13日までに、フェリーのチケットオフィスに電話すると考えられる。よって、(A)が正解。
(B) **2**より、10月14日に予定されていた会議は日程が変更されることが分かる。なお、当初の予定通りだとしても、**1**の**1** 5行目よりフェリーは午前8時30分に出発するが、同**2** 1～3行目に出発時刻の30分前には車で並んでいなければならないとある。
(C) **1**の**1** 8行目に、「車1台」とあるだけで、Kokuraさんのために車を借りるという記述はない。
(D) **2**では日にちの変更が打診されているだけであり、Harrisさんが別の場所を探す必要はない。

Words & Phrases

reservation 予約
1 予約　❶ confirmation 確認、承認　round-trip 往復の　depart ～を出発する　vehicle 乗り物、車
❷ departure 出発　board ～(旅客機・船)に乗り込む　in line 並んで　in advance of ～ ～より前に
failure to do ～の不履行、～しないこと　requirement 要件　loss 失うこと　refund 払い戻し(金)、返金
issue ～を発行する　regulations 規則、規制　in accordance with ～ ～に従って　government 政府、行政
under way (列車・船)運行中で　vary 変わる、変化する　depending on ～ ～によって、～次第で
condition 状況
2 Eメール　❶ inform ～ that … ～に…と知らせる　renovation 修復、改修　❷ operation 運営
presence 存在(すること)、出席　essential 必要不可欠な　❸ Kindly ～. どうぞ～してください。
apologize for ～ ～を謝罪する　inconvenience 不便さ　administrative assistant 役員補佐、事務職員
property 地所、不動産

Questions 181-185 refer to the following article and e-mail.

News Editor Promoted

① KEENE (December 1)—Jay Diaz, the current news editor for the Keene *Daily Arrival* newspaper, will soon become the executive editor. Mr. Diaz is a seasoned journalist who started at the *Daily Arrival* almost ten years ago. He has worked for local papers around the state, writing about local education issues for many years before moving into high school and college sports.

② Mr. Diaz takes over for Sandra Hoyer, who has held the position at the *Daily Arrival* for twenty years. She also wrote for various newspapers here in California as well as in her hometown of Miami, Florida, for a brief period. Ms. Hoyer is best known for her award-winning series on regional culinary traditions.

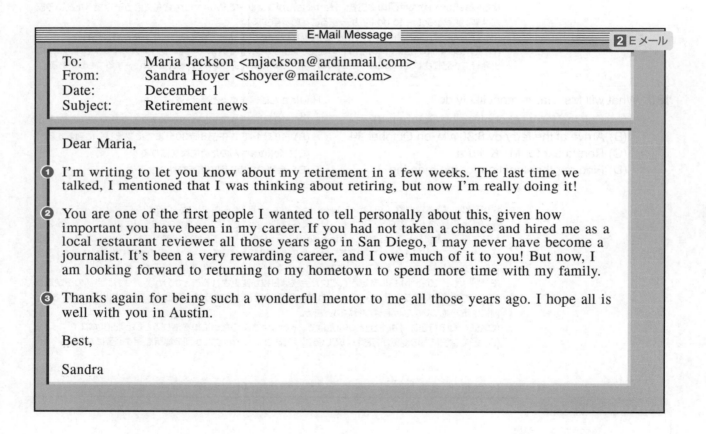

E-Mail Message

To:	Maria Jackson <mjackson@ardinmail.com>
From:	Sandra Hoyer <shoyer@mailcrate.com>
Date:	December 1
Subject:	Retirement news

Dear Maria,

① I'm writing to let you know about my retirement in a few weeks. The last time we talked, I mentioned that I was thinking about retiring, but now I'm really doing it!

② You are one of the first people I wanted to tell personally about this, given how important you have been in my career. If you had not taken a chance and hired me as a local restaurant reviewer all those years ago in San Diego, I may never have become a journalist. It's been a very rewarding career, and I owe much of it to you! But now, I am looking forward to returning to my hometown to spend more time with my family.

③ Thanks again for being such a wonderful mentor to me all those years ago. I hope all is well with you in Austin.

Best,

Sandra

問題181-185は次の記事とEメールに関するものです。

ニュース編集者が昇進する

キーン（12月1日）── 現在、キーンの新聞『デイリー・アライバル』のニュース編集者であるJay Diazは、間もなく編集長になる予定である。Diaz氏は、10年近く前に『デイリー・アライバル』で働き始めた経験豊かなジャーナリストである。彼は、州内のあちこちの地方紙で働き、高校・大学スポーツに移る前には長年地元の教育問題について執筆していた。

Diaz氏はSandra Hoyerの仕事を引き継ぐ。彼女は20年間『デイリー・アライバル』の同職にあった。彼女もまた、ここカリフォルニア州で、そして自身の故郷フロリダ州マイアミでも短期間、さまざまな新聞に記事を書いた。Hoyer氏は、地域の料理の伝統に関する受賞シリーズ記事で最もよく知られている。

受信者：Maria Jackson <mjackson@ardinmail.com>
送信者：Sandra Hoyer <shoyer@mailcrate.com>
日付：12月1日
件名：退職のお知らせ

Mariaさん

数週間後の退職についてお知らせするためにご連絡しています。この前私たちが話をしたとき、退職について考えていると言いましたが、実際にそうすることにしました！

私のキャリアにおいてあなたがいかに大切な人だったかを考えると、あなたは私がこれを最初に直接伝えたかった人々の一人です。もし何年も前のあの時、あなたがサンディエゴで私を地元レストランの評論執筆者として思い切って雇ってくれていなかったら、私はジャーナリストになっていなかったかもしれません。とてもやりがいのあるキャリアでしたし、これもひとえにあなたのおかげです！しかし今、私は故郷に戻ってより多くの時間を家族と共に過ごすことを楽しみにしています。

何年も前に私にとって非常に素晴らしい助言者でいてくれたことに、あらためて感謝します。オースティンのあなたにとって全てが順調でありますように。

ごきげんよう

Sandra

181 What does the article indicate about the *Daily Arrival*?

(A) It is currently hiring reporters.
(B) It has a new online edition.
(C) It is published in California.
(D) It is celebrating its twentieth anniversary.

記事は、『デイリー・アライバル』について何を示していますか。

(A) 現在、記者を雇用しようとしている。
(B) 新しいオンライン版がある。
(C) カリフォルニア州で発行されている。
(D) 20周年を祝っている。

> **正解 C** 　**1**記事を確認する。**❶**より、この記事はキーンという町で書かれたもので、『デイリー・アラ
> イバル』はキーンの地方新聞と分かる。**❷** 1〜3行目で、Hoyerさんが20年間『デイリー・ア
> ライバル』で編集長を務めてきたことが述べられ、続く同3〜4行目に「彼女はここカリフォルニア州でも
> さまざまな新聞に記事を書いた」とある。従ってキーンはカリフォルニア州内にあると判断できる。よって、
> 『デイリー・アライバル』はカリフォルニア州で発行されていると判断できるので、(C)が正解。
> (A) 記者の新規雇用については述べられていない。currently「現在」、reporter「記者」。
> (B) オンライン版に関する記述はない。edition「版」。
> (D) **1**の**❷**にHoyerさんが20年間編集長を務めたとあるだけで、『デイリー・アライバル』の創刊時期に
> ついては触れられていない。celebrate「〜を祝う」、anniversary「周年祭、記念日」。

182 What topic is Ms. Hoyer most known for writing about?

(A) Cooking
(B) Fashion
(C) Sports
(D) Education

Hoyerさんはどんな話題に関する執筆で最もよく知られています
か。

(A) 料理
(B) ファッション
(C) スポーツ
(D) 教育

> **正解 A** 　**1**記事の**❷** 6〜8行目に、Ms. Hoyer is best known for her award-winning series on
> regional culinary traditions. と紹介されている。よって、culinaryをcookingと言い換えた
> (A)が正解。
> (C) (D) **1**の**❶** 4〜10行目より、スポーツや教育について書いているのはDiazさん。

183 What is one purpose of the e-mail?

(A) To reveal a significant decision
(B) To suggest a restaurant for a celebration
(C) To offer someone a job
(D) To ask for a letter of recommendation

Eメールの一つの目的は何ですか。

(A) 重要な決断を明らかにすること
(B) 祝賀会のためのレストランを提案すること
(C) 誰かに仕事を提供すること
(D) 推薦状を求めること

> **正解 A** 　**2**Eメールを確認する。送信者はHoyerさんであり、**1**記事より、Hoyerさんは『デイリー・
> アライバル』の編集長の職をDiazさんに譲る予定だと分かる。**2**は件名がRetirement
> newsで、同**❶** 1〜2行目には、「数週間後の退職について知らせるために書いている」とあり、退職につい
> て考えていると以前話したことを実現しようとしているという内容が続いている。また、同**❷** 1行目には、
> 退職することを直接伝えたかった旨が書かれている。これらから、Hoyerさんは退職する決断をしたこと
> を知らせるためにEメールを書いたと考えられるので、それをreveal a significant decision「重要な決
> 断を明らかにする」と表した(A)が正解。
> (B) **2**の**❷** 2〜3行目にHoyerさんがかつてレストランの評論を書いたことが述べられているが、このE
> メールでレストランを提案してはいない。celebration「祝賀会、式典」。
> (C) offer 〜 …「〜に…を提供する」。
> (D) ask for 〜「〜を求める」、letter of recommendation「推薦状」。

184 According to the e-mail, what position did Ms. Jackson most likely hold?

(A) Travel agent
(B) Journalism professor
(C) Fashion designer
(D) Newspaper editor

Eメールによると、Jacksonさんは何の職に就いていたと考えられますか。

(A) 旅行業者
(B) ジャーナリズムの教授
(C) ファッションデザイナー
(D) 新聞の編集者

正解 D	❷Eメールを確認する。ヘッダーより、JacksonさんとはこのEメールの受信者と分かる。送信者であるHoyerさんは❷1～2行目で、Jacksonさんが自分のキャリアにおいてとても大切な存在であり、退職について最初に直接伝えたかった一人だと述べている。続く同2～4行目に、「もし何年も前のあの時、あなたがサンディエゴで私を地元レストランの評論執筆者として思い切って雇ってくれていなかったら、私はジャーナリストになっていなかったかもしれない」とある。HoyerさんはJacksonさんによって雇用されて新聞の編集者になったことから、Jacksonさんも同業であったと考えられるので、(D)が正解。

(A) agent「代理業者」。
(B) journalistという語はEメールに出てくるが、professor「教授」への言及はない。

185 Where will Ms. Hoyer most likely live once she retires?

(A) Keene
(B) Miami
(C) San Diego
(D) Austin

Hoyerさんはひとたび退職したらどこに住むと考えられますか。

(A) キーン
(B) マイアミ
(C) サンディエゴ
(D) オースティン

正解 B	Hoyerさんは、退職を知らせる❷Eメールの❷4～5行目で、I am looking forward to returning to my hometown to spend more time with my familyと、故郷に戻ることを伝えている。❶記事の❷5～6行目には、Hoyerさんについて、in her hometown of Miami, Floridaという記述がある。これらから、Hoyerさんは退職後、故郷のマイアミに住むと考えられるので、(B)が正解。

(A) ❶の❶1～4行目より、『デイリー・アライバル』が発行されている場所。
(C) ❷の❷2～4行目より、Hoyerさんがかつて地元レストランの評論執筆者として採用された場所。
(D) ❷の❸1～2行目より、Jacksonさんが現在住んでいると考えられる場所。

Words & Phrases

❶記事 editor 編集者　promote ～を昇進させる　❶ executive editor 編集長　seasoned ベテランの
journalist ジャーナリスト、報道記者　state 州　education 教育　issue 問題
❷ take over 引き継ぐ、交代する　hold ～(役職など)に就いている　various さまざまな
A as well as *B* *A*および*B*、*B*だけでなく*A*も　hometown 故郷　for a brief period 短い期間
award-winning 受賞した　series シリーズもの　regional 地域の　culinary 料理の　tradition 伝統

❷Eメール retirement 退職　❶ the last time ～ この前～したとき　★～には節が入る
mention that ～ ～ということに言及する　retire 退職する　❷ personally 自分自身で
given ～を考慮に入れると　career (専門的な)職業、経歴　take a chance (思い切って)やってみる
all those years ago 何年も前に、はるか昔に　rewarding やりがいのある
look forward to *doing* ～することを心待ちにする　❸ mentor 助言者、指導者

Expressions

owe ～ to … 「～については…のおかげである」(❷の❷4行目)

I owe what I am today to Professor Browning, who taught me a lot of things at university.
今日の私があるのはBrowning教授のおかげです。彼は大学で多くのことを私に教えてくれました。

Questions 186-190 refer to the following Web site, e-mail, and map.

■1 ウェブサイト

https://www.menloartscentre.ie/submissions

| Home | About | Events | **Submissions** |

1 The Menlo Arts Centre will once again hold its celebrated Spring Art Show. The show attracts many art lovers eager to appreciate new works and potentially take home a one-of-a-kind art piece. Both professional and amateur visual artists are invited to submit their work. A panel of area art experts will judge submissions. Accepted art will be displayed in the Willowbrook Gallery of the Menlo Arts Centre from 1 April to 15 April.

2 Artists can submit up to twelve pieces. The categories for submission are watercolour, oil painting, drawing, collage, graphic art, printmaking, sculpture, and photography. Applications are due by 5 January, and applicants will be notified by 15 February if any of their pieces have been accepted. Artists must live within 100 kilometres of Menlo, be over the age of 18, and not be related to a panel member.

3 If accepted, artists set the prices for their artwork and are responsible for framing and transporting their pieces.

■2 E メール

E-mail

To:	Leandra Hislop <lhislop@amail.ie>
From:	Hina Kaji <hkaji@menloartscentre.ie>
Subject:	Menlo Arts Centre submission results
Date:	15 February
Attachment:	📎 contract

Dear Ms. Hislop,

1 We are excited to let you know that the Menlo Arts Centre panel has reviewed your submission and would like to include all twelve of your pieces in the Spring Art Show. Yours were standout submissions among a record number of applications. The panel was impressed by the vivid images of life in Menlo in your series of photographs.

2 Please sign and return the attached contract if you would still like to participate. Once we have your contract, our show manager will reach out to you with further details.

Sincerely,

Hina Kaji, Spring Art Show Chair

■3 地図

SPRING ART SHOW
Willowbrook Gallery Map

| Collage 101 | Graphic Art and Printmaking 102 | Oil Painting 103 | |
| Drawing 107 | Photography 106 | Entrance / Sculpture 105 | Watercolour 104 |

問題186-190は次のウェブサイト、Eメール、地図に関するものです。

https://www.menloartscentre.ie/submissions

ホーム　　当センターについて　　イベント　　**出品**

メンロー芸術センターは名高い春季芸術展を再び開催いたします。この展覧会は、新しい作品を鑑賞するのに熱心で、場合によっては唯一無二の芸術作品をぜひとも自宅に持ち帰りたいと考えている多くの芸術愛好家たちを引き付けます。プロ、アマ共に、視覚芸術家の方はぜひ作品をご出品ください。地域の芸術専門家による審査員団が出品作品を審査します。承認された芸術作品は、4月1日から4月15日まで、メンロー芸術センターのWillowbrookギャラリーで展示される予定です。

芸術家は作品を最大12点まで出品することができます。出品部門は、水彩画、油彩画、素描、コラージュ、グラフィックアート、版画、彫刻、写真です。応募は1月5日を期限とし、作品のいずれかが承認された場合、2月15日までに応募者に通知されます。芸術家は、メンローから100キロメートル以内に在住であること、19歳以上であること、また審査員の関係者ではないことが要件です。

承認された場合、芸術家は自分の作品に値段を設定し、作品の額入れと輸送に責任を負っていただきます。

受信者：Leandra Hislop <lhislop@amail.ie>
送信者：Hina Kaji <hkaji@menloartscentre.ie>
件名：メンロー芸術センター　出品結果
日付：2月15日
添付ファイル：契約書

Hislop様

メンロー芸術センターの審査員団があなたの出品作品を審査し、12点全ての作品を春季芸術展に加えたく思っていることをお知らせでき、大変うれしく思います。あなたの作品は史上最多数の応募作品の中で際立ったものでした。審査員団は、あなたの一連の写真においてメンローの生活が鮮やかに写し出されていることに感銘を受けました。

今も参加をご希望であれば、添付の契約書に署名をしてご返送ください。私どもがあなたの契約書を受け取りましたら、芸術展の責任者がさらなる詳細についてご連絡を差し上げます。

敬具

春季芸術展委員長　Hina Kaji

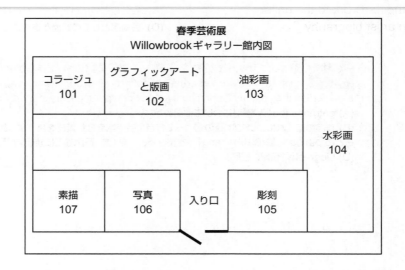

186 What is true about the Spring Art Show?

    (A) Its theme will be *Spring in Menlo*.

    (B) It will feature only professional artists.

    (C) It will take place over one week.

    (D) It will feature artwork for sale.

春季芸術展について正しいことは何ですか。

    (A) テーマは『メンローの春』である。

    (B) プロの芸術家だけを取り上げる。

    (C) 1週間にわたって開催される。

    (D) 販売される芸術作品を特色とする。

> **正解 D** 　1 ウェブサイトの ❶ 1 行目で春季芸術展の開催が伝えられ、ページ全体でこのイベントの詳細や出品の要件などについて説明されている。同 1～3 行目に「この展覧会は、新しい作品を鑑賞するのに熱心で、場合によっては唯一無二の芸術作品をぜひとも自宅に持ち帰りたいと考えている多くの芸術愛好家たちを引き付ける」とあり、同 ❸ 1 行目に、「芸術家は自分の作品に値段を設定する」とある。よって、春季芸術展では芸術作品が販売されると分かるので、(D) が正解。feature「～を特色とする」、for sale「販売用の」。
>
> (A) theme「テーマ」については言及がない。
>
> (B) 1 の ❶ 3～4 行目より、プロとアマチュア両方の芸術家が出品できる。
>
> (C) 1 の ❶ 5～6 行目より、春季芸術展の期間は 4 月 1 日から 4 月 15 日までの 2 週間と考えられる。over「～（特定の時期）の間、～にわたって」。

187 According to the Web site, what will happen on April 1?

    (A) Applications will be due for the Spring Art Show.

    (B) The judges will send letters to applicants.

    (C) The Spring Art Show will begin.

    (D) Winning artists will receive awards.

ウェブサイトによると、4 月 1 日に何が起こりますか。

    (A) 春季芸術展への応募が締め切りとなる。

    (B) 審査員が応募者に手紙を送る。

    (C) 春季芸術展が始まる。

    (D) 受賞した芸術家が賞品を受け取る。

> **正解 C** 　1 ウェブサイトを確認する。❶ 1～4 行目で春季芸術展について説明され、作品の出品が呼び掛けられている。続く同 5～6 行目に「承認された芸術作品は、4 月 1 日から 4 月 15 日まで、メンロー芸術センターの Willowbrook ギャラリーで展示される予定だ」とある。よって、4 月 1 日に春季芸術展が始まると考えられるので、(C) が正解。
>
> (A) 1 の ❷ 3 行目より、応募の締め切りは 1 月 5 日。
>
> (B) 1 の ❷ 3～4 行目より、承認された場合は 2 月 15 日までに応募者に通知される。judge「審査員」。
>
> (D) 賞については言及がない。winning「受賞した」、award「賞（品）」。

188 According to the Web site, what are accepted artists responsible for?

    (A) Paying an entrance fee

    (B) Hanging their artwork

    (C) Bringing their artwork to the gallery

    (D) Writing an artist biography

ウェブサイトによると、承認された芸術家は何に責任がありますか。

    (A) 入場料を支払うこと

    (B) 自分の芸術作品を展示すること

    (C) 自分の芸術作品をギャラリーに持ってくること

    (D) 芸術家としての経歴を書くこと

> **正解 C** 　1 ウェブサイトを確認する。❸ 1～2 行目に、出品した作品が承認された芸術家について、artists ...... are responsible for framing and transporting their pieces とある。transporting their pieces を bringing their artwork to the gallery と表した (C) が正解。
>
> (A) entrance fee「入場料」については記載がない。
>
> (B) 作品の額入れについては 1 の ❸ 1～2 行目に芸術家自身が責任を負うよう書かれているが、展示することについては記載がない。hang「～を掛ける、～を（壁・画廊などに）展示する」。
>
> (D) biography「伝記、経歴」。

189 What can be concluded about Ms. Hislop?

    (A) She grew up in the town of Menlo.
    (B) She submitted the maximum number of pieces.
    (C) She is well-known for her artwork.
    (D) She submitted work in multiple categories.

Hislopさんについて何が判断できますか。

    (A) メンローの町で育った。
    (B) 最大限の数の作品を出品した。
    (C) 自身の芸術作品で有名である。
    (D) 複数の部門に作品を出品した。

正解 B　Hislopさんとは、**2**Eメールの受信者。**2**の**1** 1～2行目に、「メンロー芸術センターの審査員団があなたの出品作品を審査し、12点全ての作品を春季芸術展に加えたく思っていることをお知らせでき、大変うれしく思う」とある。春季芸術展への出品について詳細を記述している**1**ウェブサイトの**2**1行目には、「芸術家は作品を最大12点まで出品することができる」とあるので、Hislopさんは出品可能な最大数である12点の芸術作品を出したと分かる。よって、(B)が正解。maximum「最大限の」。
(A) **1**の**2** 4～6行目の要件より、Hislopさんはメンローから100キロメートル以内に在住であること、**2**の**1** 3～4行目より、メンローでの生活を収めた写真を出品していることが分かるが、Hislopさんがメンローの町で育ったという記述はない。grow up「育つ」。
(C) **2**の**1** 3～4行目より、審査員団がHislopさんの作品に感銘を受けたことは分かるが、彼女が芸術作品で有名であるという記述はない。well-known「有名な」。
(D) **2**の**1**より、Hislopさんが写真部門に最大出品数である12点の作品を出品したことが分かるので、複数の部門には出品していないと判断できる。multiple「複数の」。

190 In what room will Ms. Hislop's work most likely be displayed?

    (A) 103
    (B) 104
    (C) 105
    (D) 106

Hislopさんの作品はどの部屋で展示されると考えられますか。

    (A) 103
    (B) 104
    (C) 105
    (D) 106

正解 D　**2**Eメールの**1** 1～2行目より、Hislopさんの作品が春季芸術展に承認されたことが分かり、続く同**1** 3～4行目には、審査員団が彼女の一連の写真に感銘を受けたとあるので、Hislopさんの作品は写真であると判断できる。春季芸術展の会場の館内図である**3**地図によると、写真の展示は106番の部屋。よって、(D)が正解。

Words & Phrases

1 ウェブサイト　submission 提出(物)　❶ celebrated 有名な、名高い　attract ～を引き付ける　lover 愛好家
(be) eager to *do* ぜひ～したいと思う　appreciate ～を正しく理解する、～を鑑賞する
potentially 可能性として　one-of-a-kind 唯一の、他にはない　piece 作品　professional プロの
amateur アマチュアの　visual artist 視覚芸術家　★visual arts「視覚芸術」は絵画・彫刻などの造形美術を指す
panel 審査員団　expert 専門家　judge ～を審査する　accept ～を受け入れる、～を承認する
gallery 画廊、ギャラリー　❷ up to ～ 最大～まで　category 部門
watercolour 水彩画　★米国表記はwatercolor　oil painting 油彩画
drawing 素描、スケッチ　★鉛筆・ペンなどを使用した単色の線画　collage コラージュ　printmaking 版画
sculpture 彫刻　photography 写真(術)　due (提出物などが)期限が来て　notify ～に通知する
be related to ～ ～と関係がある　❸ artwork 芸術作品　be responsible for ～ ～に対して責任がある
frame ～を額に入れる　transport ～を運ぶ

2 Eメール　result 結果　attachment 付属物、(Eメールの)添付ファイル　contract 契約書　❶ review ～を審査する
standout 際立った　a record number of ～ 記録的な数の～、史上最多の～
be impressed by ～ ～に感銘を受けている　vivid 鮮明な　image 画像
a series of ～ ひと続きの～、一連の～　❷ sign ～に署名する　attached 添付の　participate 参加する
once いったん～すれば　reach out to ～ ～とコミュニケーションを取る　chair 議長、会長

3 地図　entrance 入り口

Questions 191-195 refer to the following receipt, Web page, and e-mail.

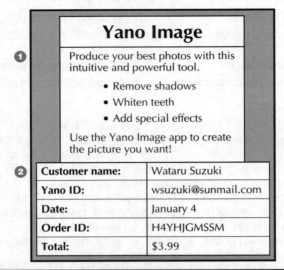

Yano Image

Produce your best photos with this intuitive and powerful tool.

- Remove shadows
- Whiten teeth
- Add special effects

Use the Yano Image app to create the picture you want!

Customer name:	Wataru Suzuki
Yano ID:	wsuzuki@sunmail.com
Date:	January 4
Order ID:	H4YHJGMSSM
Total:	$3.99

https://www.yano.com

Yano Image	Yano Music	**Customer Service**	Account Sign In

Request a Refund for Yano Apps Purchases

All purchases from Yano Image and Yano Music are eligible for a full refund when requests are made within 24 hours of purchase. You may request a refund online by following these steps.

1. Sign in to your Yano account at yano.com.

2. Go to the drop-down menu titled "What Is the Issue?" and select "Refunds."

3. Choose the app or subscription for which you desire a refund.

4. Describe the reason you are requesting a refund.

Refund requests take up to 48 hours to process. Please note that once your refund request is processed, you will lose access to the app or subscription immediately.

To:	Wataru Suzuki <wsuzuki@sunmail.com>
From:	Customer Support <customersupport@yano.com>
Date:	January 6
Subject:	Refund request
Attachment:	Yano document R34

Dear Mr. Suzuki,

This e-mail confirms receipt of your refund request. The purchase price has been credited to your account. You may view the details in the "Claims Status" section of your Yano account.

I appreciate your continued support as a loyal customer. Remember that your account has a full list of your current app subscriptions along with renewal dates.

To help us serve you better, please take a few minutes to complete the attached survey to let us know your opinion about the Yano Image app.

Best regards,

Vincent Pham, Customer Service Manager

問題191-195は次のレシート、ウェブページ、Eメールに関するものです。

Yano画像
使いやすく高性能なこのツールを使って最高の写真を作ってください。
・影を取り除く
・歯を白くする
・特殊効果を加える
お望みの写真を作るにはYano画像アプリをお使いください!

お客さま氏名:	Wataru Suzuki
Yano ID:	wsuzuki@sunmail.com
日付:	1月4日
注文ID:	H4YHJGMSSM
合計:	3.99ドル

---

https://www.yano.com

Yano画像　　Yano音楽　　**顧客サービス**　　アカウントサインイン

Yanoアプリ購入品の返金請求

Yano画像とYano音楽からの全ての購入品は、購入後24時間以内に返金請求された場合、全額返金可能です。次の手順に従って、オンラインで返金請求をしていただけます。

1. yano.comでご自身のYanoアカウントにサインインしてください。
2. 「問題は何ですか」というタイトルのプルダウンメニューに進み、「返金」を選択してください。
3. 返金を希望するアプリや定期契約物を選択してください。
4. 返金を請求する理由を述べてください。

返金請求は処理に最大48時間かかります。ひとたび返金請求が処理されると、即座にそのアプリや定期契約物をご利用できなくなりますのでご注意ください。

受信者:Wataru Suzuki <wsuzuki@sunmail.com>
送信者:顧客サポート <customersupport@yano.com>
日付:1月6日
件名:返金のご請求
添付ファイル:Yano文書R34

Suzuki様

このEメールはお客さまのご返金請求の受領を確認するものです。ご購入金額がお客さまのアカウントに入金されました。Yanoアカウントの「ご請求の状態」のセクションで詳細をご覧になれます。

お得意さまとしての継続的なご愛顧に感謝いたします。お客さまのアカウントには、更新日と併せて現在のアプリの定期契約物の全リストがあることをお忘れなく。

当社がお客さまにより良いサービスをご提供できるよう、数分のお時間を取って添付のアンケートにご記入いただき、Yano画像アプリに関するご意見をお聞かせください。

よろしくお願いいたします。

顧客サービス責任者　Vincent Pham

191 According to the receipt, what can Yano Image do?

    (A) Recommend beauty products
    (B) Edit photographs
    (C) Create photo albums
    (D) Identify fashion trends

レシートによると、Yano画像は何をすることができますか。

    (A) 美容製品を薦める
    (B) 写真を編集する
    (C) フォトアルバムを作る
    (D) ファッション動向を特定する

> **正解 B** ❶レシートを確認する。❶1～2行目に、「使いやすく高性能なこのツールを使って最高の写真を作ってください」とある。また、同3～5行目に「影を取り除く」、「歯を白くする」、「特殊効果を加える」とできることが具体的に書かれており、同6～7行目には「望みの写真を作るにはYano画像アプリを使ってください」とあることから、Yano画像は写真を編集できるアプリだと分かる。よって、(B)が正解。edit「～を編集する、～に修正を加える」。
> (A) recommend「～を薦める」、beauty「美容」。
> (C) album「アルバム」への言及はない。
> (D) identify「～を特定する」、trend「傾向、動向」。

---

192 What does the Web page indicate about refund requests?

    (A) They require a customer signature.
    (B) They are processed within 48 hours.
    (C) They can be made by calling the customer service department.
    (D) They require a manager's approval.

ウェブページは、返金請求について何を示していますか。

    (A) 顧客の署名を必要とする。
    (B) 48時間以内に処理される。
    (C) 顧客サービス部に電話することによって行うことができる。
    (D) 責任者の承認を必要とする。

> **正解 B** ❷ウェブページを確認する。❶に「Yanoアプリ購入品の返金請求」とあり、❷以降に返金に関する説明が書かれている。❹1行目に、Refund requests take up to 48 hours to process.とある。この内容をwithin「～以内」を用いて表した(B)が正解。
> (A) signature「署名」に関する記載はない。require「～を必要とする」。
> (C) ❷の❷2～3行目から、オンラインで返金請求ができると分かる。電話による返金請求については言及されていない。department「部署」。
> (D) approval「承認」。

---

193 What is most likely true about Mr. Suzuki regarding his request?

    (A) He will be refunded $3.99.
    (B) He should expect another e-mail in two days.
    (C) He needs to open a new customer account.
    (D) He must fill out a survey to finalize the process.

請求に関連し、Suzukiさんについて正しいことは何だと考えられますか。

    (A) 3.99ドル返金される。
    (B) 2日後にもう1通のEメールが来るのを待つべきである。
    (C) 新しい顧客アカウントを開く必要がある。
    (D) 手続きを終わらせるためにアンケートに記入しなければならない。

> **正解 A** Suzukiさんとは、❶レシートと❸Eメールを受け取った人物。❸の件名に「返金請求」とあり、同❶1行目で返金請求が受領されたことが述べられ、続けて「購入金額はあなたのアカウントに入金された」と書かれている。❶の❷5行目から、Suzukiさんはアプリの購入に3.99ドル支払っていることが分かるので、それが返金されると考えられる。よって、(A)が正解。refund ～ … 「～に…(料金)を払い戻す」。
> (B) ❷の❹に、返金請求の処理に最大2日かかるとあるだけで、2日後に次のEメールが送られるという記述はない。
> (D) ❸の❸1～2行目から、アンケートはYano画像アプリに関するもので、サービス向上を目的としたもの。同❶1～2行目から、返金の処理はすでに完了していることが分かり、手続き完了のためにアンケートへの記入が必要なわけではない。process「処理、手続き」。

194 What can be concluded about Mr. Suzuki?

    (A) He recently signed in to his Yano store account.

    (B) He used the Yano Image app for one week.

    (C) He did not intend to purchase the Yano Image app.

    (D) He wants to make a purchase at Yano Books.

Suzukiさんについて何が判断できますか。

    (A) 最近Yano社のストアアカウントにサインインした。

    (B) 1週間Yano画像アプリを使った。

    (C) Yano画像アプリを購入するつもりはなかった。

    (D) Yano書籍で買い物をしたいと思っている。

> **正解 A**　**3**Eメールの**❶** 1～2行目で、Suzukiさんからの返金請求が受領されて購入金額がアカウントに入金されたことが述べられている。返金請求については、手順が書かれた**2**ウェブページの**❸** 1つ目に、「yano.comであなたのYanoアカウントにサインインしてください」とある。Suzukiさんは、返金請求のためにこの手順に従いYanoアカウントにサインインしたと判断できるので、(A)が正解。
> (B) **2**の**❷** 1～2行目より、購入後24時間以内に請求しないと返金されないことが分かる。**3**よりSuzukiさんは返金を受けているので、彼は24時間を超えてアプリを使用していないと判断できる。
> (C) 意図せず購入したという記述はない。intend to *do*「～するつもりである」。
> (D) Yano書籍に関する記述はない。make a purchase「買い物をする」。

195 What is indicated about Mr. Suzuki in the e-mail?

    (A) He is having trouble opening an account.

    (B) He wants to renew a membership.

    (C) He is a Yano employee.

    (D) He has purchased products from Yano before.

Eメールで、Suzukiさんについて何が示されていますか。

    (A) アカウントを開くのに苦労している。

    (B) 会員資格を更新したいと思っている。

    (C) Yano社の従業員である。

    (D) 以前Yano社から商品を購入したことがある。

> **正解 D**　**3**Eメールを確認する。ヘッダーから、これはYano社の顧客サポートからSuzukiさんに送られたEメールと分かる。**❷** 1行目に、「お得意さまとしての継続的な愛顧に感謝する」とあり、続けて「あなたのアカウントには、更新日と併せて現在のアプリの定期契約物の全リストがあることを覚えておいて」とある。このことから、Suzukiさんは以前にもYano社の商品を購入したことがあると考えられるので、(D)が正解。
> (A) have trouble *doing*「～するのに苦労する」。
> (B) renew「～を更新する」、membership「会員資格」。

Words & Phrases

1 レシート　**❶** produce　～を作る　　intuitive　直観的な、(感覚的に操作できて)使いやすい　　remove　～を取り除く
shadow　影、暗い部分　　whiten　～を白くする　　effect　効果　　app　アプリ　★applicationの略
create　～を作る

2 ウェブページ　sign in　サインイン(する)　　**❶** refund　払い戻し、返金　　**❷** full　完全な、満額の　　follow　～に従う
❸ drop-down menu　プルダウンメニュー　★クリックなどの操作によって複数のメニュー項目を表示させるもの
title ～ …　～に…という表題を付ける　　issue　問題　　subscription　定期購読、サブスクリプション　★アプリや
サービスなどを一定期間利用するために一定の金額を支払う契約形態　　desire　～を強く望む
describe　～を述べる　　**❹** process　～を処理する　　note that ～　～ということに注意する
access　アクセス、利用する権利　　immediately　即座に

3 Eメール　**❶** confirm　～を確認する　　receipt　受領　　credit ～ to …　～(金額)を…に入金する　　view　～を見る
claim　請求　　status　状態　　**❷** appreciate　～に感謝する　　continued　継続的な
loyal customer　得意客　　remember that ～　～ということを覚えておく　　along with ～　～と一緒に
renewal　更新　　**❸** serve　～に応対する、～の役に立つ　　attached　添付の　　survey　アンケート
opinion　意見

Expressions

be eligible for ～　「～の資格がある」(**2**の**❷** 1～2行目)

Only those 60 years old or older are eligible for the discount.
60歳以上の方のみ、割引を受ける資格があります。

Questions 196-200 refer to the following article and e-mails.

1 記事

Biography About Chef Tops Nonfiction Bestseller List

1 TORONTO (January 8)—*Rochelau's Savory Dreams*, Brandon Dawsly's new biography of pioneering chef Christiane Rochelau, has just reached the top spot in this week's nonfiction bestseller list.

2 Dawsly, whose previous biographies of football stars and celebrities have also made the list, has confirmed his status as a titan in the genre.

3 Delmina Trevisano, editor in chief at Fisley Books, which published the Rochelau biography, had high praise for the book.

4 "Rochelau was a pioneering figure in Canadian cuisine," said Trevisano, "and Dawsly beautifully captures both the trials and successes in her life."

5 Trevisano is reportedly in talks with Greenlight Group about a possible cinematic adaptation of *Rochelau's Savory Dreams*. If it materializes, the film would be the latest in a series of documentaries about innovative chefs.

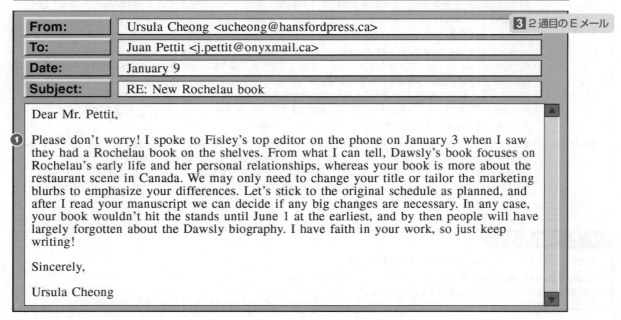

E-mail

2 1通目のEメール

From:	Juan Pettit <j.pettit@onyxmail.ca>
To:	Ursula Cheong <ucheong@hansfordpress.ca>
Date:	January 9
Subject:	New Rochelau book

Dear Ms. Cheong,

1 Did you see yesterday's article about the most recent bestsellers? I had heard rumors someone else was writing about Rochelau, but I didn't know a book was already in print. Now I'm worried that my own book will be irrelevant. I was preparing to submit the full manuscript to you by January 31 as agreed upon, but perhaps I should rewrite some portions, focusing less on Rochelau and more on other chefs.

2 If you agree with this plan, I could have the revised manuscript to you by March 31. I trust your wisdom as my editor, so let me know what you think.

Sincerely,

Juan Pettit

3 2通目のEメール

From:	Ursula Cheong <ucheong@hansfordpress.ca>
To:	Juan Pettit <j.pettit@onyxmail.ca>
Date:	January 9
Subject:	RE: New Rochelau book

Dear Mr. Pettit,

1 Please don't worry! I spoke to Fisley's top editor on the phone on January 3 when I saw they had a Rochelau book on the shelves. From what I can tell, Dawsly's book focuses on Rochelau's early life and her personal relationships, whereas your book is more about the restaurant scene in Canada. We may only need to change your title or tailor the marketing blurbs to emphasize your differences. Let's stick to the original schedule as planned, and after I read your manuscript we can decide if any big changes are necessary. In any case, your book wouldn't hit the stands until June 1 at the earliest, and by then people will have largely forgotten about the Dawsly biography. I have faith in your work, so just keep writing!

Sincerely,

Ursula Cheong

問題196-200は次の記事と2通のEメールに関するものです。

シェフについての伝記が
ノンフィクションのベストセラーリストの首位に

トロント（1月8日）——先駆的シェフChristiane Rochelauに関するBrandon Dawsly著の新しい伝記、『Rochelauの美味なる夢』が今週のノンフィクションのベストセラーリストで首位になった。

Dawsly氏は、旧著の人気フットボール選手や有名人の伝記もリストに載っており、このジャンルにおける巨匠としての地位を確かなものにした。

このRochelauの伝記を出版したFisleyブックス社の編集長Delmina Trevisanoは、この本を絶賛した。

「Rochelauはカナダ料理界における先駆的な人物でした」とTrevisano氏は述べた。「そして、Dawslyは彼女の人生の試練と成功の両方を見事に捉えています」。

Trevisano氏は、『Rochelauの美味なる夢』の映画化の可能性についてGreenlightグループ社と話し合っていると伝えられている。もしそれが実現すれば、その映画は革新的なシェフを取り上げたドキュメンタリー作品シリーズの中で最新のものとなるだろう。

送信者：Juan Pettit <j.pettit@onyxmail.ca>
受信者：Ursula Cheong <ucheong@hansfordpress.ca>
日付：1月9日
件名：新しいRochelauの本

Cheong様

最新のベストセラーに関する昨日の記事をご覧になりましたか。他の誰かがRochelauについて書いているといううわさを耳にしていましたが、本がすでに出版されていたとは知りませんでした。今、私自身の本は見当違いのものになるのではないかと心配しています。合意した通り1月31日までに完全原稿をあなたに提出するよう準備していましたが、ことによると私はRochelauの比重を下げて他のシェフにより重点を置き、幾つかの部分を書き直すべきかもしれません。

この案に同意していただけるなら、私は3月31日までに修正した原稿をお手元にお届けできそうです。担当編集者としてのあなたの見識を信頼していますので、お考えをお知らせください。

敬具

Juan Pettit

送信者：Ursula Cheong <ucheong@hansfordpress.ca>
受信者：Juan Pettit <j.pettit@onyxmail.ca>
日付：1月9日
件名：RE：新しいRochelauの本

Pettit様

どうかご心配なさらないでください！　Rochelauの本が棚に並んでいるのを見て、私はFisley社の編集長と1月3日に電話で話しました。私が知る限り、Dawsly氏の本はRochelauの若い頃と彼女の人間関係に重点を置いているのに対して、あなたの本はむしろカナダのレストラン業界に焦点を当てた内容です。私たちは、あなたの本のタイトルを変える、あるいは販促用宣伝文を調整して違いを強調すればいいくらいかもしれません。計画通りに当初の日程で行きましょう。そして、私があなたの原稿を読んでから、私たちは何らかの大きな変更が必要かどうか決めてもいいでしょう。いずれにしても、あなたの本はどんなに早くても6月1日まで発売されることはないですし、その時までに人々はDawsly氏の伝記についてほぼ忘れてしまっているでしょう。私はあなたの作品を信頼していますので、このまま書き続けてください！

敬具

Ursula Cheong

196 What is indicated in the article about Mr. Dawsly? 記事ではDawslyさんについて何が示されていますか。

- (A) His book has been the top seller for five weeks.
- (B) He has written multiple best-selling books.
- (C) He often plays football with celebrities.
- (D) He has lived in Canada for most of his life.

- (A) 彼の本は5週間にわたってベストセラーになっている。
- (B) 複数のベストセラー本を書いた。
- (C) しばしば有名人とフットボールをする。
- (D) 人生の大半をカナダで暮らしてきた。

正解 B ❶記事を確認する。❶で、Dawslyさんの書いた新しい伝記が今週のノンフィクションのベストセラーリストで首位になったことが述べられている。続く❷1〜3行目に、Dawsly, whose previous biographies of football stars and celebrities have also made the listとあり、このthe listはnonfiction bestseller listを指すと考えられる。リストに載った伝記はprevious biographiesと複数形なので、Dawslyさんは最新の著書だけでなく、過去の複数の著書もベストセラーになっていることが分かる。よって、(B)が正解。multiple「複数の」、best-selling「ベストセラーの」。
(A) ベストセラーリストに載っている期間については書かれていない。seller「売れる製品」。
(C) ❶の❷1〜2行目に、人気フットボール選手や有名人の伝記を書いたとあるだけ。
(D) ❶の❹1〜2行目でカナダと関連付ける記述があるのは料理人のRochelauさんについてであり、Dawslyさんがカナダで暮らしてきたとの記載はない。

197 According to the article, what kind of company is Greenlight Group? 記事によると、Greenlightグループ社はどんな種類の会社ですか。

- (A) An automobile manufacturer
- (B) A restaurant chain
- (C) A book publisher
- (D) A film studio

- (A) 自動車メーカー
- (B) レストランチェーン
- (C) 出版社
- (D) 映画会社

正解 D ❶記事を確認する。❺1〜3行目に、「Trevisano氏は、『Rochelauの美味なる夢』の映画化の可能性についてGreenlightグループ社と話し合っていると伝えられている」とあり、続く同3〜6行目には映画化が実現した場合のことが記されている。Trevisanoさんとは、❸より、この本を出版した出版社の編集長と分かるので、映画化について話し合っているGreenlightグループ社は映画会社だと判断できる。よって、(D)が正解。studio「映画会社、スタジオ」。
(A) automobile「自動車」、manufacturer「メーカー、製造会社」。

198 According to the first e-mail, why is Mr. Pettit concerned? 1通目のEメールによると、Pettitさんはなぜ心配していますか。

- (A) Another writer has published a book similar to his.
- (B) He heard rumors that his editor was switching firms.
- (C) He was not able to finish his book manuscript on time.
- (D) His recent book dropped off the bestseller list.

- (A) 別の著述家が彼のものと似た本を出版した。
- (B) 彼は自分の担当編集者が会社を変えるといううわさを聞いた。
- (C) 彼は期限通りに本の原稿を終えられなかった。
- (D) 彼の最近の著書がベストセラーリストから落ちた。

正解 A ❷1通目のEメールを確認する。❶3行目で、Pettitさんは自分の本が見当違いのものになることを心配している。その理由として同1〜3行目に、「他の誰かがRochelauについて書いているといううわさを耳にしていたが、本がすでに出版されていたとは知らなかった」とある。続く同4〜5行目には、Rochelauよりも他のシェフに重点を置いて書き直すべきかもしれないとあることから、PettitさんもRochelauについての本を執筆中であると分かる。よって、(A)が正解。similar「似ている」。
(B) switch「〜を変える」、firm「会社」。
(C) ❷の❶3〜4行目で述べられている合意した原稿の期限は、1月31日という未来の日付。on time「時間通りに」。
(D) drop off 〜「〜から落ちる」。

199 Who did Ms. Cheong most likely speak to?

    (A) Brandon Dawsly
    (B) Christiane Rochelau
    (C) Delmina Trevisano
    (D) Juan Pettit

Cheongさんは、誰と話したと考えられますか。

    (A) Brandon Dawsly
    (B) Christiane Rochelau
    (C) Delmina Trevisano
    (D) Juan Pettit

> **正解 C** Cheongさんは、**2**1通目のEメールの受信者であり、**3**2通目のEメールの送信者。**3**の❶1〜2行目で、CheongさんはFisley社の編集長と電話で話したと書いている。Fisley社の編集長については、**1**記事の❸1〜3行目に、「このRochelauの伝記を出版したFisleyブックス社の編集長Delmina Trevisanoは、この本を絶賛した」とある。つまり、Cheongさんが電話で話した相手はTrevisanoさんと判断できるので、(C)が正解。

---

200 By when should Mr. Pettit send a manuscript?

    (A) January 9
    (B) January 31
    (C) March 31
    (D) June 1

Pettitさんはいつまでに原稿を送るべきですか。

    (A) 1月9日
    (B) 1月31日
    (C) 3月31日
    (D) 6月1日

> **正解 B** **2**1通目のEメールでのPettitさんからの相談に対し、Cheongさんは**3**2通目のEメールの❶1〜5行目で、Pettitさんの本はDawslyさんの本とは重点的に扱っている内容が異なるため心配は不要だと述べ、続く同5行目で、計画通りに当初の日程で原稿の準備を進めるよう提案し、Eメールの最後で、このまま書き続けるよう伝えている。**2**の❶3〜4行目に、「合意した通り1月31日までに完全原稿をあなたに提出するよう準備していた」とあるので、これが当初の日程と考えられる。これらから、Pettitさんは1月31日までにCheongさんに原稿を送るべきだと判断できるので、(B)が正解。
> (A) **2**・**3**のEメールの送信日。
> (C) **2**の❷より、Pettitさんが提案している原稿を書き直した場合の提出予定日。
> (D) **3**の❶6〜8行目より、Pettitさんの本の最短での発売予定日として触れられている日付。

Words & Phrases

1 記事　　biography 伝記　　top 〜のトップとなる　　❶ savory 風味のよい、おいしそうな　　pioneering 先駆的な
top spot 首位　　❷ previous 以前の　　celebrity 有名人　　make the list リストに載る
confirm 〜を固める、〜を確定する　　status 立場、社会的評価　　titan 巨匠　　genre ジャンル
❸ editor in chief 編集長　　praise 称賛　　❹ figure 人物、著名人　　cuisine 料理
capture 〜を捉える、〜を表現する　　trial 試練　　❺ reportedly 伝えられるところによると　　talks 会談、交渉
possible 可能性のある、候補の　　cinematic 映画の　　adaptation （本などからの）改作作品
materialize 実現する　　the latest 最新のもの　　a series of 〜 一連の〜　　innovative 革新的な

2 Eメール　　❶ rumor うわさ　　in print 出版されて　　be worried that 〜 〜ということを心配している
irrelevant 不適切な、見当違いの　　full 完全な　　manuscript 原稿　　as agreed upon 同意した通りに
rewrite 〜を書き直す　　portion 部分　　focus on 〜 〜を重点的に取り扱う　　❷ agree with 〜 〜に同意する
revised 修正された　　trust 〜を信頼する　　wisdom 賢明さ、見識

3 Eメール　　❶ shelves shelf「棚」の複数形　　from what I can tell 私が言える範囲では、私が知る限り
personal relationship 人間関係　　whereas 〜であるのに対して　　the 〜 scene 〜界、〜事情
tailor 〜 to do …するように〜を合わせる　　blurb （新刊本・新製品の）宣伝文　　emphasize 〜を強調する
as planned 計画通りに　　necessary 必要な　　in any case いずれにしても
hit the stands （新聞・雑誌などが）発売される　　at the earliest 早くとも　　have faith in 〜 〜を信頼している
keep doing 〜し続ける

Expressions

stick to 〜 「〜にこだわる、〜を忠実に守る」（**3**の❶5〜6行目）

If I don't stick to the rules as a teacher, students are not going to either.
教師として私が規則に従わなければ、生徒たちも従おうとはしないでしょう。

CD トラック・特典音声ファイル 一覧表

● CD1

Test	Track No.	Contents
サンプル問題	1	タイトル
	2	Listening Test Directions/ Part 1 Directions
	3	Q1
	4	Part 2 Directions
	5	Q2, Q3
	6	Part 3 Directions
	7	Q4-6
	8	Q7-9
	9	Part 4 Directions
	10	Q10-12
TEST 1	11	Test 1
	12	Listening Test Directions/ Part 1 Directions
	13	Q1
	14	Q2
	15	Q3
	16	Q4
	17	Q5
	18	Q6
	19	Part 2 Directions
	20	Q7
	21	Q8
	22	Q9
	23	Q10
	24	Q11
	25	Q12
	26	Q13
	27	Q14
	28	Q15
	29	Q16
	30	Q17
	31	Q18
	32	Q19
	33	Q20
	34	Q21
	35	Q22
	36	Q23
	37	Q24
	38	Q25
	39	Q26
	40	Q27
	41	Q28
	42	Q29
	43	Q30
	44	Q31
	45	Part 3 Directions

Test	Track No.	Contents
TEST 1	46	Part 3 Q32-34 会話
	47	Q32-34 問題
	48	Q35-37 会話
	49	Q35-37 問題
	50	Q38-40 会話
	51	Q38-40 問題
	52	Q41-43 会話
	53	Q41-43 問題
	54	Q44-46 会話
	55	Q44-46 問題
	56	Q47-49 会話
	57	Q47-49 問題
	58	Q50-52 会話
	59	Q50-52 問題
	60	Q53-55 会話
	61	Q53-55 問題
	62	Q56-58 会話
	63	Q56-58 問題
	64	Q59-61 会話
	65	Q59-61 問題
	66	Q62-64 会話
	67	Q62-64 問題
	68	Q65-67 会話
	69	Q65-67 問題
	70	Q68-70 会話
	71	Q68-70 問題
	72	Part 4 Directions
	73	Q71-73 トーク
	74	Q71-73 問題
	75	Q74-76 トーク
	76	Q74-76 問題
	77	Q77-79 トーク
	78	Q77-79 問題
	79	Q80-82 トーク
	80	Q80-82 問題
	81	Q83-85 トーク
	82	Q83-85 問題
	83	Q86-88 トーク
	84	Q86-88 問題
	85	Q89-91 トーク
	86	Q89-91 問題
	87	Q92-94 トーク
	88	Q92-94 問題
	89	Q95-97 トーク
	90	Q95-97 問題
	91	Q98-100 トーク
	92	Q98-100 問題

● CD2

Test	Track No.	Contents
TEST 2	1	Test 2
	2	Listening Test Directions/ Part 1 Directions
	3	Q1
	4	Q2
	5	Q3
	6	Q4
	7	Q5
	8	Q6
	9	Part 2 Directions
	10	Q7
	11	Q8
	12	Q9
	13	Q10
	14	Q11
	15	Q12
	16	Q13
	17	Q14
	18	Q15
	19	Q16
	20	Q17
	21	Q18
	22	Q19
	23	Q20
	24	Q21
	25	Q22
	26	Q23
	27	Q24
	28	Q25
	29	Q26
	30	Q27
	31	Q28
	32	Q29
	33	Q30
	34	Q31
	35	Part 3 Directions
	36	Q32-34 会話
	37	Q32-34 問題
	38	Q35-37 会話
	39	Q35-37 問題
	40	Q38-40 会話
	41	Q38-40 問題
	42	Q41-43 会話
	43	Q41-43 問題
	44	Q44-46 会話
	45	Q44-46 問題
	46	Q47-49 会話

次ページの「音声を使った学習例の紹介」を参考に、問題に解答した後の学習用教材としてもご活用ください。

音声ダウンロードの手順▶本誌 p.3　　音声を使った学習例▶別冊 p.200

Test	Track No.	Contents
TEST 2	47	Part 3 Q47-49 問題
	48	Q50-52 会話
	49	Q50-52 問題
	50	Q53-55 会話
	51	Q53-55 問題
	52	Q56-58 会話
	53	Q56-58 問題
	54	Q59-61 会話
	55	Q59-61 問題
	56	Q62-64 会話
	57	Q62-64 問題
	58	Q65-67 会話
	59	Q65-67 問題
	60	Q68-70 会話
	61	Q68-70 問題
	62	Part 4 Directions
	63	Q71-73 トーク
	64	Q71-73 問題
	65	Q74-76 トーク
	66	Q74-76 問題
	67	Q77-79 トーク
	68	Q77-79 問題
	69	Q80-82 トーク
	70	Q80-82 問題
	71	Q83-85 トーク
	72	Q83-85 問題
	73	Q86-88 トーク
	74	Q86-88 問題
	75	Q89-91 トーク
	76	Q89-91 問題
	77	Q92-94 トーク
	78	Q92-94 問題
	79	Q95-97 トーク
	80	Q95-97 問題
	81	Q98-100 トーク
	82	Q98-100 問題

● 特典（ダウンロード）

Test	File No.	Contents
TEST 1	01	Part 5 Q101 問題
	02	Q102 問題
	03	Q103 問題
	04	Q104 問題
	05	Q105 問題
	06	Q106 問題
	07	Q107 問題
	08	Q108 問題

Test	File No.	Contents
TEST 1	09	Part 5 Q109 問題
	10	Q110 問題
	11	Q111 問題
	12	Q112 問題
	13	Q113 問題
	14	Q114 問題
	15	Q115 問題
	16	Q116 問題
	17	Q117 問題
	18	Q118 問題
	19	Q119 問題
	20	Q120 問題
	21	Q121 問題
	22	Q122 問題
	23	Q123 問題
	24	Q124 問題
	25	Q125 問題
	26	Q126 問題
	27	Q127 問題
	28	Q128 問題
	29	Q129 問題
	30	Q130 問題
	31	Part 6 Q131-134 問題
	32	Q135-138 問題
	33	Q139-142 問題
	34	Q143-146 問題
	35	Part 7 Q147-148 文書
	36	Q149-150 文書
	37	Q151-152 文書
	38	Q153-155 文書
	39	Q156-157 文書
	40	Q158-160 文書
	41	Q161-163 文書
	42	Q164-167 文書
	43	Q168-171 文書
	44	Q172-175 文書
	45-46	Q176-180 文書
	47-48	Q181-185 文書
	49-51	Q186-190 文書
	52-54	Q191-195 文書
	55-57	Q196-200 文書
TEST 2	58	Part 5 Q101 問題
	59	Q102 問題
	60	Q103 問題
	61	Q104 問題
	62	Q105 問題
	63	Q106 問題
	64	Q107 問題

Test	File No.	Contents
TEST 2	65	Part 5 Q108 問題
	66	Q109 問題
	67	Q110 問題
	68	Q111 問題
	69	Q112 問題
	70	Q113 問題
	71	Q114 問題
	72	Q115 問題
	73	Q116 問題
	74	Q117 問題
	75	Q118 問題
	76	Q119 問題
	77	Q120 問題
	78	Q121 問題
	79	Q122 問題
	80	Q123 問題
	81	Q124 問題
	82	Q125 問題
	83	Q126 問題
	84	Q127 問題
	85	Q128 問題
	86	Q129 問題
	87	Q130 問題
	88	Part 6 Q131-134 問題
	89	Q135-138 問題
	90	Q139-142 問題
	91	Q143-146 問題
	92	Part 7 Q147-148 文書
	93	Q149-150 文書
	94	Q151-153 文書
	95	Q154-155 文書
	96	Q156-157 文書
	97	Q158-160 文書
	98	Q161-164 文書
	99	Q165-168 文書
	100	Q169-171 文書
	101	Q172-175 文書
	102-103	Q176-180 文書
	104-105	Q181-185 文書
	106-108	Q186-190 文書
	109-111	Q191-195 文書
	112-114	Q196-200 文書

＊CDに収録の問題音声は全て、TOEIC®公式スピーカーによるものです。

＊特典音声は、CDとは別に収録したもので、標準的な北米発音を採用しています。

スマホや PC を使ってさらにひと学習！

音声を使った学習例の紹介

『公式 TOEIC® Listening & Reading 問題集 10』は、付属 CD の音声の他、特典として TEST 1、2 のリーディングセクションの読み上げ音声（設問と選択肢を除く）を、スマートフォンや PC にダウンロードしてお聞きいただけます。以下に音声を使った公式問題集の学習法の一例をご紹介しますので、学習の参考になさってください。

準備するもの：別冊「解答・解説」（本書）、音声をダウンロードしたスマートフォンまたは PC

＊ Part 1 〜 4 の音声は付属 CD でも聞くことができます。Part 5 〜 7 の特典音声を含む全ての音声の利用は、abceed への会員登録（無料）とダウンロードが必要です。本誌 p. 3 の「音声ダウンロードの手順」に従ってサイトにアクセスし、『公式 TOEIC® Listening & Reading 問題集 10』をダウンロードしてください。リーディングの特典音声のスピードが速くて聞き取りが難しいと感じる方は、abceed のアプリなどのスピード調整機能を利用しましょう。初めのうちは 0.8 〜 0.9 倍などで聞いてもいいでしょう。

Part 1、2

1. 「解答・解説」で正解の英文の意味内容を正しく理解する。
2. 音声を聞き、発音やイントネーションをまねて音読する（リピーティング）。最初はスクリプトを見ながら行い、慣れてきたらスクリプトを見ずに行う。

> Part 1 では写真を見ながら正解の描写文だけを、Part 2 では質問と正解の応答を、音読してみましょう。自分が発話しているつもりで音読すると、表現が定着しやすくなります。

Part 3、4

1. 「解答・解説」でスクリプトの英文と訳を確認。知らない語の意味や英文の内容を把握する。
2. スクリプトを見ながら会話やトークを聞く。発話と同じスピードで英文を目で追い、即座に意味を理解できるようになるまで繰り返す。
3. スクリプトを見ずに会話やトークを聞く。聞き取りづらい箇所や意味が理解できない箇所をスクリプトで確認し、再び音声だけで理解できるか挑戦する。

> Part 3 ではスピーカー同士の関係や会話の目的、Part 4 では場面やトークの趣旨をまず把握し、徐々に理解できる範囲を増やしていくつもりで、細部の情報まで聞き取るようにしましょう。

Part 5、6

1. 「解答・解説」で英文と訳を確認。知らない語の意味や英文の内容を把握する。
2. 本誌の TEST 1、2 の該当ページ(p.42-48 と p.84-90)のコピーを取り、音声を聞いて空所の語や文を書き取る。知っている語彙や文法の知識も用いて空所を埋め、書き取ったものと実際の英文を比較する。最後に、もう一度音声を聞く。

> 聞き取れない箇所は、飛ばしたりカタカナで書いたりしても構いません。音声だけに頼らず、語彙力や文法の知識を用いて挑戦してみましょう。Part 5 は短い文なので、ディクテーションをするのもよいでしょう。

Part 6、7

1. 「解答・解説」で英文と訳を確認。知らない語の意味や英文の内容を把握する。その際、読み方に迷った箇所に印を付けておく。
2. 音声を聞きながら英文を目で追い（初めはスピードを遅めにしても可）、英語の語順のまま理解できるようになることを目指す。分からなかった箇所は適宜、訳を確認する。
3. 1. で印を付けた、読み方に迷った箇所の言い方を確認する。
   例：数字や記号の言い方（日付、住所、飛行機の便名、価格、URL）など。

> 1. は構文や語彙の学習、2. は速読の学習です。2. では意味のまとまりを意識しながら英文を読み進めていくようにすると、取り組みやすいでしょう。3. は、実際の会話の際にも役立つので積極的に覚えるとよいでしょう。